ELLEN

Bread

WITH LOVE FROM
JEAN AND TED

SATURDAY
16/7/2005

To Pat Hayes, 1942-2004. Lovely man, great friend, and important contributor to TGWU education for more than thirty years

British Library Cataloguing in Publication Data.
A catalogue record for this book is available from the British Library

Published in partnership with London Metropolitan University and the North West Institute of Further & Higher Education, Derry.

Typeset by e-type, Liverpool
Printed in Great Britain by Cambridge University Press

ISBN 1 905007 07 8

Bread on the Waters

A History of TGWU education 1922-2000

John Fisher

Lawrence & Wishart
LONDON 2005

Contents

Acknowledgements

Many people have contributed to this book, not least all those tutors, students and TGWU committee members who wrote their reports and course evaluations over the years, and placed this great and complex story on the record. I would particularly like to thank Martin Norris, TGWU member of staff, who assisted with the technicalities of putting a mass of scattered evidence into a digital format.

Also of particular help in either bringing the book together or correcting it were Irene Dykes, Joyce Ajimotokan, Carol Hillaby, TGWU staff, and Mike Hayes, formerly of London Metropolitan University.

Many other people took part in interviews, or contributed their experience and knowledge by checking parts of the book that concerned them directly. These include Tony Corfield and Frank Cosgrove, former Directors of Studies, Tony Woodley, General Secretary, Jack Jones and Ron Todd, retired General Secretaries, the late Jack Lucas, former Regional Organiser, Barry Camfield and Ray Collins, Assistant General Secretaries, Joe Irvin, Head of Policy, Margaret Prosser, retired Deputy General Secretary, Bob Purkiss, retired National Equalities Secretary, Jane McKay, former GEC member, Chris Russell, Regional Organiser, Jim Mowatt, National Chemicals Secretary, Pete Batten, Liam McBrinn and Gordon Pointer, retired Regional Education Organisers, the late Patrick Hayes, formerly of London Metropolitan University, Les Ford and Gareth Richards, Senior Tutors, Harry Lees, retired Regional Organiser, Adrian Weir, Senior Researcher, Keith Jones, Bob Sissons, Ann McCall and Mick Bond, Regional Education and Development Organisers, Lesley Sutherland, former Regional Education Organiser, Diana Holland, National Organiser, and Sid Forty, retired Administrative Officer.

Cover picture: dockers banner, courtesy TGWU.

Preface by Jack Jones

An outstanding feature of trade union development has been the growth of education and information services. All enthusiastic members want to know as much as possible about the aims and efforts of their union.

Over the years since the formation of the TGWU, and with the background to the many unions which have come together in the Union as we know it today, the need for a strong and effective educational aspect has been increasingly recognised.

This is very much the case for the members who hold office in the union, from shop floor ones to those in most senior posts.

Learning by doing active work in supporting fellow workers when called upon is a vital part of development, but the role of the specialist educational and information services is most essential. This service strengthens our efforts to effectively represent our needs and aspirations in the industrial field, and to successfully represent our fellow workers and ourselves. Such a service is thus worthy of study. And the specialist development of the educational activities in the T&G is worthy of study in itself. This work has grown and has become an essential part of the effective representation of members' needs.

I truly believe this book will help with a better understanding of union activity and meeting members' needs and I commend it accordingly. Knowledge leads to influence. It is part of the march forward of a successful trade union – one that is of the members, and fights always in the interests of trade unionism: 'One for all and all for one'.

Keep right on!

Foreword by Brian Roper

London Metropolitan University is proud of its commitment to social inclusion, social justice and widening participation in education. It is thus natural that in working with partners to achieve these aims it forms alliances with other bodies working for similar objectives.

Trade Unions are, of course, such bodies. Working for the emancipation of labour, they are natural allies of this University. Hence, this University currently provides programmes about trade unions and for trade unionists at all levels, acts as a consultant to trades unions and labour movements and has a major research focus upon the realities of contemporary working lives.

There is no more important facet of this than our partnership with the Transport and General Workers Union. Since 1996 we have had a formal partnership to provide courses, at both further and higher levels. This partnership has stimulated developments at both undergraduate and postgraduate levels in the University. These courses cover such areas as Health and Safety and Environmental Influences on representation, as well as more fundamental aspects of the union representative's role. Our partnership is fulfilling our joint aim of not only understanding the world but also of changing it.

We are proud to partner the T&G in this important endeavour, and to be partners in the publication of this book.

Foreword by the North West Institute of Further and Higher Education

The TGWU (ATGWU) has played a core role in the expansion of progressive developments within the Irish trade union movement for many years and has being instrumental in advancing progressive strategies through trade union education.

With the deteriorating community and political situation in Northern Ireland, the ATGWU education department 1979-1985 was able to develop an essential progressive education approach in addressing key issues. In particular it was the motivating force in securing wide-spread ICTU support for anti-sectarian policies and active direction in workplaces and communities. Throughout the period 1985-2003, under the stewardship of Liam McBrinn, the regional programme was expanded throughout the region and new partnerships developed.

The valuable and distinctive learning partnership between the ATGWU and the North West Institute of Further and Higher Education (NWIFHE), established in 1999, has brought major and positive developments to the Region 3 membership. The introduction of information computer technology (ICT) suites in many of the union offices offered training for workplace representatives, union learning reps, members, staff and officers. This has encouraged the union's programme to expand energetically, giving working men and women throughout Ireland an opportunity to improve and develop their own skills and knowledge.

The Institute is proud of its partnership with ATGWU in supporting these developments.

Seamus Murphy (Director)
Ciaran Brolly (Head of Continuing Education Department)
NWIFHE, Derry, Northern Ireland.

Introduction

This book tells the story of the education programme in the Transport and General Workers Union (TGWU) from the years of its foundation in 1922 up to the end of the twentieth century.[1] Neither of those dates, of course, is the true beginning or end of the story, on the one hand because an enormous amount of mostly informal education and cultural transference went on before 1922 in the amalgamating unions, and on the other hand because TGWU education is currently thriving and no doubt will continue to do so into this new century and as long as the union itself survives.[2] Apart from being an interesting and under-reported story, the outburst of energy and activity associated with the education programme raises a number of important questions about the past and future role of trade unions and of the process of education, particularly the education of adults. The great majority of the participants in the TGWU education programme were manual workers with little or no formal education. It is unlikely that they would come into an educational process if it had not been for their membership of the union.

With the exception of the short-lived Army Bureau of Current Affairs (ABCA) programme during the Second World War,[3] trade union education (if we include the work of the Worker's Educational Association (WEA) and Labour Colleges) was the most important mass adult education programme carried out specifically for working-class people during the last century. The TGWU had, and has, the largest of these programmes amongst affiliates to the TUC, and for the greater part of the century had a larger one than that of the TUC itself.

This study is based on original sources, statutory union reports, and interviews with participants. I have tried not to link the story of the education programme to any specific quantitative analysis, nor tried to test any particular specific hypothesis. The difficulty of taking this approach was made clear by Arthur Deakin, TGWU General Secretary in the 1950s and 1960s.

> Money spent on education is always bread cast upon the waters. We can't make a tidy balance sheet, as we can with other union benefits. What we CAN do is show confidence in our members, and have faith

> in their ability to make good use of the facilities offered them. I have no doubt about the value of the investment.[4]

The story in the main is one of the formal education programme funded primarily by the union, with some contributions from outside agencies and organisations, mainly the state, employers and educational providers such as the WEA and Labour Colleges. It cannot be emphasised enough that the informal system of trade union education – conversations in the workplace between the experienced and the novice, hard lessons learned through the failure or success of a particular episode of industrial action or similar event, involvement in the local trades council or political party organisation, attendance at conferences, visits overseas, significant books read, and so on – played just as important a part in the development of the individual trade unionist, and of the union and the movement, as the formal system. Thus there is no claim that this particular chronicle fully charts the intellectual development of the union through the years, as the many millions of these encounters have never been recorded and cannot be reported in any systematic way.

The TGWU is only one union within the trade union movement, representing about one-seventh of all trade union members. Its education programme, though of more significance within the organisation than that of most unions, is part of a wider tradition of trade union education, and needs definition, especially for those who have not encountered it before, or who are unclear as to its purpose. Such attempts are rare, and as Holford points out: 'no theory of trade union education has emerged. It is truly remarkable that no book-length study has been published ... apart from official and semi-official reports'.[5] One of these reports was written in 1959 for the WEA by Hugh Clegg and Rex Adams – two senior academics engaged by the WEA to review its work. It presents a reasonably comprehensive survey of trade union education in the late 1950s, but is more concerned with practical advice for the improvement of trade union education programmes than their definitions. However, its main conclusion was that 'the central purpose of trade union education must be to provide education suited to the needs and the abilities of active or potentially active trade unionists'.[6] No one would dispute this, but it cannot be held to be a comprehensive definition.

Within the TGWU, the debate on the purpose of trade union education has always been held in terms of policy and financial choices within an accepted understanding that education is a 'good thing'. The internal policy objectives of encouraging the membership to learn more about the workings of the union, or strengthening the activities of shop stewards, or promoting equality for women or other groups within the organisation, or external ones such as promoting the war effort and a progressive peace, learning about work study or

HRM, or developing knowledge and skills in health and safety, have set the objectives, and the educators were generally left to get on with designing and delivering programmes which met these needs most effectively. In the 1980s, Doug Miller and John Stirling reported that the union had defined its requirements in the North-East Region as 'to study the broader economic and political issues and at the same time keep the knowledge within the framework of the union and build on shop stewards' training'.[7] This is about as close as the union would come to defining the objects of its programme. In the TGWU the view has been that so long as there is no intention to remove political content and emasculate the overall purpose of union activity, then it is legitimate to use all education methods, and that active learning has a very important part to play.

Bevin and Deakin believed that understanding the union's constitution would protect the union by encouraging the involvement of more members at the expense of 'agitators' led from outside, accepting that this was likely to increase membership involvement in the constitution; Frank Cousins and Jack Jones supported the summer schools and regional education as a way of strengthening the then 'unofficial' shop stewards, and more recently the new forces of women and ethnic minorities have strengthened their position deliberately through the education programme. Education, then, can be an internal force for liberation and development within trade unions, and the TGWU programme has not been an exception to this. It would not be true to say that the key figures in the programme over the years were in any way agitators wanting to undermine the union, but neither were they bureaucrats wedded to the *status quo*. All of them experienced and understood in their time the liberating force of the educational encounter in a union setting.

Breathing life into an organisation like the TGWU through its education programme has affected the lives of millions of working people and their families over the years, and has also had a major impact on the state and the body politic. Of course, it is the Labour Movement itself, rather than its constituent parts, the TUC and less so the TGWU, which really impacted on society in the twentieth century, but the whole is made up of its parts, and the TGWU and its education programme made an important contribution.

Chapter one looks at the establishment of the union; the response of the TGWU to the debate on the nature of independent working-class education; and how the defeat of the 1926 General Strike influenced this debate. It also looks at the establishment of the union's first education scheme and the experiences of TGWU students in adult classes provided by external educational bodies. The book will also consider the development of women's organisation in the union and the influence of education on this. Chapter two reviews the change in the political and economic climate in the 1930s and the role of Ernest Bevin in responding to this with the establishment of the union's own education programme, through its correspondence course.

Chapter three examines TGWU education through the war years, and the development of day-schools and local innovations linking education with shop-floor organisation. Chapter four explores the post-war years, and the great expansion of education under Arthur Deakin, including the establishment of national summer schools for Branch Officials and shop stewards. Chapter five reviews TGWU education in the regions in the years after the war, and the influence of day-release and joint education work with employers.

Chapter six covers the era of Jack Jones in the 1960s and 1970s, which heralded an expansion of the programme and introduced Regional Education Officers and a national education centre at Eastbourne. Chapter seven considers the difficult years under Mrs Thatcher, and the response of the education programme to this. Chapter eight goes into the education programme in the 1990s, which began with a financial crisis in the union and the effects of this in shaping the programme. The final chapter looks at education in the regions in the 1980s and 1990s.

NOTES

1. The abbreviation TGWU will be used throughout, rather than the more modern T&G. The reason is that TGWU was more commonly used. However, T&G will be used in quotations. Note also that in references to TGWU records, minutes and so on, the acronym TGWU will be omitted at the start, to avoid tedious repetition. So 'TGWU: Minutes of the GEC' becomes 'Minutes of the GEC'.
2. See, for example, C. Griggs, *The TUC and the Struggle for Education 1868-1925*, Lewes: Falmer 1983. This looks at nineteenth-century examples of trade union education.
3. The Army Bureau of Current Affairs (ABCA) was introduced as a programme of using education methods to instil war aims, but was taken over by progressive tutors and students alike, and in the first half of the war at least, was turned into a debating society looking at social policies for the post-war world and criticising what had gone on pre-war. It was said to have played a role in the Labour victory of 1945. See S. P. Mackenzie, *Politics and Military Morale*, Oxford: Clarendon Press 1992; P. Addison, *The Road to 1945*, London: Quartet 1975.
4. *The Record*, September 1950, p92, emphasis in the original.
5. J. Holford, *Union Education in Britain: A TUC Activity*, University of Nottingham 1994, p250.
6. H. A. Clegg and Rex Adams, *Trade Union Education*, London: WEA 1959, p9.
7. D. Miller, and J. Stirling, 'Evaluating Trade Union Education', *The Industrial Tutor*, Vol. 5, No. 5, Spring 1992: 22.

Chapter 1

The First Steps 1922–1937

This chapter looks at the establishment of the first education scheme in the union, and the part played by the TGWU in the 'great debate' on the principles of independent working-class education, which took place in the 1920s. It considers the key personalities involved in the union's education provision, and the experiences of TGWU students taking part in adult education at the time. It also looks at the involvement of the union's women members in the education programme.

'Three cheers for the new union!' With these words, Ernest Bevin closed the Leamington Conference on 29 September 1921, the founding conference of the Transport and General Workers Union. Minutes earlier, Harry Gosling, of the Lightermen's Union, and soon to be the only President of the TGWU, had inspired the delegates by saying that they had to get to the point 'where one card represents trade unionism in the whole country, and then when you have got one card representing all of this nation, that is only another step, because you have to get one card representing labour all over the world'.[1] This conference marked the culmination of years of effort by Bevin and his colleagues to bring together the 14 separate unions who were to form the TGWU. These unions mainly organised manual workers in docks, waterways, and road transport, but they also included a significant group of white-collar employees, mainly represented by the National Union of Docks, Wharves and Shipping Staffs and the National Union of Ships' Clerks. No less than five of the fourteen amalgamating unions already had significant white-collar membership, and these unions had already been heavily involved in the debates surrounding independent working-class education following the Ruskin College strike of 1909, the formation of the WEA and WETUC, and the Labour College Movement.[2]

Some of the manual unions also had a strong commitment to education. For example, the objects of the Dock, Wharf, Riverside and General Workers Union, of which Bevin was the Assistant General Secretary, included 'The training of officers and members upon industrial history and kindred subjects'.[3] Bevin himself had taken part in adult education in Bristol, and had been a member of the committee which produced the '1919 Report' on adult education. Others of his closest associates during the process of amalgamation had also a keen interest in working-class education. These included John Twomey, General Secretary of the Swansea-based National Amalgamated Labourers' Union (NALU), Alf Short and Arthur Creech-Jones of the National Union of Docks, Wharves and Shipping Staffs, and Harold Clay of the United Vehicle Workers.

The ballot paper on which the amalgamation vote was taken in December 1920 included as one of the objectives of the new union the 'promotion and support of Parliamentary action through the Labour Party, and Labour representation in Parliament, on Local Authorities etc; educational work, research, publicity etc'.[4] At the Leamington Conference, a specific commitment was made to implement this pledge. The proposed set of rules sent out to all the organisations who were to attend the conference included one which stated that one of the objects of the new union was 'the provision of grants and endowments, including scholarships, to members and to the colleges or institutions having among their objects the education of trade unionists'.[5] This rule remains today unchanged as Rule 2(e) iii in the current TGWU rule book. The United Vehicle Workers inserted an amendment calling for the establishment of a scholarship scheme at a Labour College, but it was decided that the issue was to be dealt with only when the new union was firmly established.

The new General Executive Council of the TGWU held its first meeting from 2 to 5 August 1922, in company with the Provisional Executive who had carried through the final process of amalgamation following the Leamington Conference. Both Alf Short, by now an MP, and John Twomey were trustees of the new union. Harold Clay had become the Area Secretary in Area 9 (Leeds) and Creech-Jones quickly followed Alf Short as National Secretary for ACTS, the new union's white-collar section. Thus some of the men with a commitment to education were involved in influential positions from the outset. Ernest Bevin's first report as General Secretary included his view of the importance of 'education', although this was meant in a general sense, rather than as part of a specific union education scheme. During this first meeting of the GEC, a message was received from the Central Labour College asking whether it was the intention of the union to send students to the college, pointing out that the new academic year began in September. It was resolved that 'the question of sending students to the Labour College be deferred pending the drawing up of the education scheme in accordance with the instructions of the Leamington Conference'.[6] This first Executive also took a decision which would be repaid many times over in the future, by agreeing to support the maintenance at Ruskin College of John Price of Newport, South Wales, formerly of the NALU. Price was to return to the union fifteen years later to play a central role in the development of its education programme.[7]

Pressure built up to implement the decision to establish an education scheme, whilst Bevin was, as always, conscious of the financial implications. At the November 1922 meeting of the GEC, the Council considered a resolution from the National Trade Group Committee of ACTS, which recommended the GEC to call representatives of all the trade groups together 'with a view to arriving at a comprehensive scheme of education for the whole of the membership'. It was resolved to defer the consideration of this matter until the new year when the balance sheet of the union was to be issued.[8]

In July 1923 the TGWU held its first Annual Delegate Conference, in Central Hall, Westminster.[9] At this conference, it was agreed that future conferences would be biennial. A delegate from Area 1 ACTS (once again, the shipping clerks) moved a resolution which 'recommends the NEC to consider a scheme for the provision of educational facilities in economics and social science for the members, and to co-operate with the Educational Committee of the TUC to this end'.[10] Creech-Jones had already been given responsibility as the union's spokesman on education matters, and was to carry out that role on behalf of the union at the 1923 TUC Congress in the debate on the structure of trade union education. At the TGWU conference he argued that the purpose of the resolution was not to confine education to one particular principle, but to provide a comprehensive scheme for the whole of the membership of the union in order that any member might make use of any of the various labour education bodies in existence. He reported that the TUC General Council had given consideration to the whole problem, and had appointed a committee of inquiry with a view to introducing a comprehensive scheme embracing the various Labour Movement education providers. The resolution was carried unanimously.[11]

At the next meeting of the GEC, in August, the General Secretary was instructed to prepare a report on education, and in November 1923 this was submitted, setting out a scheme to implement the conference decision. However, the GEC delayed their full support for the proposals on the grounds that 'before arriving at a definite decision the Council should have before them full details as to the financial position of the union, owing to the fact that the introduction of an education scheme would entail expenditure of a considerable sum of money'.[12] They resolved that consideration of the report be deferred to the next meeting of the Council.

In April 1923, Alf Short MP relinquished the position of National Secretary of ACTS, and the National Trade Group Committee recommended Creech-Jones as National Secretary. The union's Finance and General Purposes Committee (F&GP) accepted this recommendation and appointed Creech-Jones.[13] He worked on the design of an education scheme, but the GEC, clearly nervous of committing the union to any significant expenditure, deferred discussion of the matter. It was eventually tabled on 17 May 1924, and, 'after considerable discussion' it was resolved that 'consideration of the whole question of education be deferred until the termination of the existing Ruskin College scholarship; in the meantime, the position of this Council in relation to the matter be frankly placed before the branches for consideration, in conjunction with the circular on the proposal to introduce a levy, or, alternatively, an increased contribution'.[14] The 'Ruskin College scholarship' is a reference to John Price.

Whilst being supportive of the principle of an education scheme, Bevin was clearly not going to allow it to threaten the insecure financial position of the new union.

THE FIRST TGWU EDUCATION SCHEME

At the meeting of the union's F&GP on 17 October 1924, Creech-Jones submitted a report setting out an education scheme for the union. It was adopted by the Committee but 'in view of the present financial obligations of the union, the maximum amount to be expended in connection with the scheme shall not exceed a figure of £250 per annum [£7,000 at today's values] whilst the contributions are at their present level'.[15] This proposal was endorsed by the full GEC on 10 November 1924. In preparation for this meeting, Bevin made clear his satisfaction with the limited commitment being made by the union:

> You will see that the F&GP have approved a scheme ... and wisely, in my opinion, definitely limited the yearly amount to be expended in connection with the scheme.[16]

With an annual limit of £250, it was not likely that the union's 'education scheme' would amount to much, and indeed 'scheme' is too grandiose a word for what amounted to the minimum of support for a small number of individuals taking part in programmes organised by other educational bodies. The union offered scholarships to cover board, lodging and tuition for one week at a school chosen by the member. This meant in practice that although support was given on the basis of individual awards, there was no general support for involvement in classes. Apart from the few who received scholarships, travel expenses were not paid, nor were class fees able to be remitted. The scholarship of John Price at Ruskin College was not repeated for other students, and although a payment of five guineas (£5.25 – £150 at today's values) was made to the WEA and the NCLC each year, this was not a true affiliation based on membership, as those organisations and their supporters in the union would have wished. The facilities offered under the union's education scheme were designed to enable members to take part in non-vocational educational activities, and the union followed the principle of trying to spread the education grant so as to offer facilities to the greatest possible number of members:

> In allocating expenditure we are guided by applications received and the interest shown from year to year, and we also have regard to the range of facilities provided by the various educational organisations. We do not attempt to support indiscriminately all the activities of these organisations, but we endeavour, so far as the grant will allow, to provide the facilities which are most in demand amongst our members and to keep the educational activities going all the year round.[17]

The bulk of the expenditure was devoted to the awarding of scholarships for correspondence courses, day schools, weekend schools and summer schools. Small grants were also made to students attending residential institutions. All applications for scholarships and grants were to be submitted through the area secretaries,[18] who were to make recommendations. In the case of correspondence courses scholarships were to be awarded on these recommendations alone, until the number available was exhausted. When granting scholarships to the various schools, however, the union was to take into consideration the member's record of work for the union and the Labour Movement, and previous participation in classes and correspondence courses. The emphasis was on individual participation, and there was no attempt to establish any collective provision at this stage. In practice, the scheme amounted to the willingness of the union to advertise the educational facilities offered by the various bodies, and, apart from those who successfully applied to their area committees for support, no real assistance was forthcoming from the union. On the other hand, much of the activity at local level in the Labour Colleges and the Workers' Education Trade Union Committee (WETUC) was free, and based on self-help and financial support from these organisations in their commitment to working-class adult education. The WEA also received financial support from the government Board of Education, a constant source of criticism from the Labour Colleges. In the context of the time, one essential feature of the TGWU scheme was that it tried to avoid a commitment to any particular provider, whether the WEA/WETUC, NCLC, the Central Labour College or Ruskin College. To understand the significance of this, we need now to look at the background developments in working-class and trade union adult education.

THE GREAT DIVIDE IN TRADE UNION EDUCATION

The conflicts within trade union education have been well documented elsewhere, and it is not my intention to cover these in detail beyond their interaction with developments in the TGWU.[19]

The Labour Colleges based their approach on what they claimed was *independent* working-class education, although in reality many of their tutors were middle-class, if left-wing, intellectuals, teachers and MPs, such as Maurice Dobb, Raymond Postgate and Arthur Woodburn MP. The key to its 'independence' was that it received no financial support from the state. By 1921, the Labour Colleges had joined with district organisations from around the country to form the National Council of Labour Colleges (NCLC), which began life in March 1922 under the secretaryship of J. P.M. Millar (who held it until the end of the NCLC in 1964).

At first the WEA saw its role as that of making up for the defects of an inadequate initial education, providing opportunities for individuals who never had and never would have had the opportunity to enter Higher Education, and tried to use sympathetic lecturers from the universities as its tutors. It accused the NCLC of confusing education with propaganda, and of teaching its students *what* to think rather than *how* to think. The NCLC, on the other hand, questioned the independence of an organisation which took money from a capitalist state, and referred to the WEA as 'a sheep in wolf's clothing', leading its students along a collaborationist path. By 1923, the NCLC had gained nine affiliations from national trade unions, and by 1926 from 28 unions, including the TGWU, although as has been noted, the union was never fully affiliated.[20] In order to focus its work on the trade unions, the WEA established the WETUC in 1919, as a rival to the Labour Colleges. The WETUC also had trade union support amongst the steelworkers, post office workers and later the TGWU. One of the attractions of the WETUC was that, so long as it was controlled by the WEA, and not entirely by trade unions, it qualified for state funding, and thus was less of a drain on scarce union funds.[21]

In June 1923 the WEA wrote to the TGWU asking for affiliation and for a nominee to its General Council and Executive Committee. The GEC resolved that the affiliation be renewed, and that Creech-Jones be nominated to the WEA Executive Committee.[22] The TGWU tried to maintain what it claimed was an 'even-handed' approach to all the external education providers. In 1924 the union referred to the 'non-political WEA and class-conscious Labour Colleges',[23] and the 1925 GEC statement on education included a reference to the philosophical debate on the two 'schools' of trade union education:

> As is well known, there are two well-defined schools of thought on the subject of education of the workers, but we do not propose to enter upon a discussion of this subject. In order that the members who will take advantage of our scheme may understand the viewpoint of the two schools of thought, and choose the method which they consider the best, we are also publishing an exposition of the two ideas by Mr G.D.H. Cole and Mr J.P. Millar to state to our members the point of

> view of the schools of thought they represent in working-class education ... we trust that intending students will study both sides of the question before making their choice.[24]

The Record published this 'debate' in early 1925. Millar stressed that the NCLC represented independent working-class adult education, with the implication that the WEA, by being subsidised, was in the pocket of the government and the ruling class:

> One group of workers' educational organisations stands for the extension of university education to the workers, which in my view is employing class education, while another – the NCLC – stands for *independent* working-class education ... It was because the trade union students at Ruskin College in 1909 realised that the university type of education provided was biased and that the working class would have to provide education, not only under its own control, but of an *entirely different character*, that they founded the first of the Labour Colleges.[25]

Cole, on the other hand, entitled his piece 'Thinking for Yourself', implicitly characterising the NCLC as a propagandist rather than an educational organisation. He argued that WETUC

> ... does not start out by saying to the trade unionist: 'This is how you ought to do it; this is what you ought to believe'. It comes and asks the trade unionist what he wants to and, when he has stated his need, does its best to make him – not believe any particular set of doctrines – but think for himself, and make up his own mind ... Very many who have passed through the WETUC are now doing finer and better work for the Labour Movement by reason of what they have learned. They are not mere parrots repeating a lesson; but men and women who can adapt themselves to the difficult work of political and industrial organisation, because they have learned to think for themselves, and to give clear and forcible expression to what they think.[26]

For his part, Millar was never in doubt that the TGWU leaders favoured the WEA:

> Grudgingly, during its formative years, the NCLC negotiated six limited schemes with unions which were about to enter into an agreement with WETUC. For example, Britain's largest union, the TGWU, offered £50 each to the WETUC and the NCLC for educational facilities. The NCLC accepted, simply to avoid leaving the field entirely clear to the WETUC and in the hope of increasing the shabby payment later. This union's national officials, until Jack Jones' time, were WEA in outlook.[27]

Corfield notes that 'curiously enough there was no discernible NCLC lobby in the union at all. Although there were several debates on educational policy at the union's conferences in the early 1920s, nobody spoke up for the NCLC. It was hardly surprising therefore, that the TGWU decided in 1924 to throw in its lot with WETUC'.[28]

The conflict between the two organisations and their supporters came to a head at the 1924 TUC Congress. The TGWU leaders were faced with a clear demand for what would be an expensive programme of education, but their priority was to protect the financial base of the new union. Therefore, they avoided taking sides in the conflict, and tried instead to have the TUC take over the financial responsibility for trade union education, in co-operation with all the educational bodies. The composite on workers' education was put forward in the name of the TGWU. It instructed the General Council to take a more active part in the furtherance of adult working-class education and to adopt schemes in co-operation with the WEA, WETUC, Ruskin, NCLC and the Central Labour College and any other body, so long as the TUC had an element of control over it. An attempt was made to limit involvement to the NCLC, but it was withdrawn. Creech-Jones was part of the TGWU delegation, and moved the resolution. He wanted to extend educational facilities to the rank and file of the trade union movement:

> Our trade unions themselves have equally supported the two sides of the Movement. What we want is really the co-ordination of the existing facilities. We want to finance the policy which has been pursued by the General Council, and we want these educational facilities to be brought under the control of the Working-Class Movement.

It is difficult to imagine that Creech-Jones, an experienced man in the field of adult education, really believed that a Congress resolution could overcome the quite fundamental divisions in the trade union education movement, which we can see with hindsight were never to be healed, and his call for the bodies to co-ordinate all their existing facilities was unrealistic even at the time. On the other hand, there had been agreement at the 1921 Congress for the TUC to take over Ruskin and the CLC, but this had foundered on financial grounds. It seems likely that Creech-Jones and Bevin were influenced by their commitment to the survival and growth of the TGWU. If they could convince the TUC to set up and finance an education scheme, then a major difficulty for the TGWU would be overcome. Bevin's later record would show that, compared to the survival of the union, divisions of principle amongst trade union educators would count for little.

ATTITUDES TO EDUCATION: ERNEST BEVIN

Bevin, of course, was central to the progress of the education scheme in the union, and to every other aspect of the TGWU's early development. There is no question that he was, and considered himself to be, a firm advocate of the value of education. He had particular views as to what the term actually meant, but of course he was not alone in that. Bevin was suspicious of intellectuals as a breed, believed in self-help, and had no doubts that people from 'humble' backgrounds had the right and the ability to fulfil themselves and to take on important roles to create a better society. He himself was, of course, the most obvious example of the validity of that belief. Bevin was always concerned about the future, and always saw trade union education as particularly important for the 'next' generation, whether he was speaking in 1919 or 1939.

Along with key figures in adult education such as Robert Mansbridge, Sir Henry Jones, R.H. Tawney, and Basil Yeaxlee, Bevin was a member of the committee which produced the '1919 Report', long thought to be a landmark in the development of adult education in the UK, particularly in its philosophical and theoretical justification. The report is eloquent in its understanding of the motives for what is now called 'lifelong learning':

> The motive is also partly social. Indeed, so far as the workers are concerned, it is, we think, this social purpose which principally inspires the desire for education. They demand opportunities for education in the hope that the power which it brings will enable them to understand and help in the solution of the common problems of human society. In many cases, therefore, their efforts to obtain education are specifically directed towards rendering themselves better fitted for the responsibilities of membership of political, social and industrial organisations.[29]

As has already been noted, despite his general commitment to education, Bevin's priority was always the survival and growth of the new organisation, particularly the maintenance of a sound financial base, and union education, along with other services, had to take second place to this objective.

ARTHUR CREECH-JONES AND HAROLD CLAY

Whilst recognising the primacy of Bevin's influence over the education policy of the union, it is certainly worth remembering that there were others who played a key role in the early years. The two most important were Creech-Jones, and Harold Clay, National Secretary for Passenger Transport. These two officials were formally responsible for the union's education scheme from February 1926 until the arrival of John Price in 1937.

Before the amalgamation, Creech-Jones had been instrumental in encouraging his union to affiliate to the WEA. He was also one of the earliest supporters of the WETUC, representing his union at its founding conference in 1920. Harold Clay was a Leeds tramworker and member of the United Vehicle Workers. This union was already affiliated to the WEA and provided scholarships for its members to attend Ruskin College. He was personally involved in the WEA and was, at this stage, treasurer of its Yorkshire district. Both these men had educational ideas of their own, and were both lifelong champions of the WEA approach to education. Tony Corfield points out that 'these two influential officers in the TGWU felt a deep personal debt to the WEA. They both owed much of their own intellectual development to their experience as tutorial class students'.[30] Clay was elected Vice-President of the WEA as early as 1929 and President of the WEA in 1945, and also played a role in setting up the union's correspondence course in the 1930s and in the early TGWU day-schools.

Harold Clay's view of education also reflected his connection with the WEA. In 1938, for example, Clay presided at the Annual Conference of the WEA in place of R.H. Tawney, who was absent owing to illness. He took the opportunity to present his view of adult education: 'Education is not merely a matter of absorbing information, it is a process by which men transcend the limitations of their individual personalities and become partners in a world of interests which they can share with their fellows.'[31] Clay took part as a tutor in the first TUC Ruskin College summer schools, which began in 1929. Unlike the WETUC and NCLC schools, the TUC schools were orientated towards industrial relations, social insurance and trade union administration. At the 1936 school, Clay introduced what was then an innovation:

> A novel idea was tried by Brother Harold Clay, National Secretary of the Passenger Road Transport Group, at the TUC summer school, held at the Ruskin College, Oxford, from July 4 to 11. He was the tutor to the class studying industrial relations and industrial negotiations ... he formed the class into a Joint Industrial Council, who argued out a wages claim. Half of the students took the employer's side and the other half the workers' side. The idea proved both interesting and instructive.[32]

Throughout the 1920s and 1930s, both Creech-Jones and Clay tried to persuade Bevin that the amounts of money allocated to education were inadequate. For example, in their jointly-presented 1929 Finance Report they proposed that following the amalgamation with the Workers' Union, the allocation of £250 per year had become even more inadequate than before, and the Executive was asked to consider increasing the education grant at least to £1000 per year (£30,000 at today's values). They also regularly attached extracts of letters of appreciation from students. They were to keep up this pressure and influence Bevin's thinking in the next decade, with some success. Thus the union leadership already had individuals who were able to combine a deep commitment to adult education and to the Labour Movement and in particular to the TGWU. They were in a position and had the power to use education to help the development of the union and move ahead very quickly. Unfortunately, events were to create circumstances in which a real leap forward was to be delayed for more than a decade.

THE 1925 DECISION

The debate around the control of trade union education did not go unnoticed in the union, and 1925 was to be the year of the first Biennial Delegate Conference, when there would be a need to report to the membership on the progress in setting up an education scheme, following the decision at the November 1924 Executive; they would also need to deal with the demands from some sections for a closer link with the NCLC and a possible break with the WEA. The new year began with a statement on education from the General Executive Council and an article in the January edition of *The Record,* entitled 'An Education Scheme for the Union'. It referred back to the last delegate conference, where the GEC was requested to prepare a scheme for the provision of educational facilities 'for the study of history and economic and social problems'. Perhaps anticipating criticism of the limited scope of the proposals, *The Record* stated that the GEC had now adopted a scheme:

> Which is capable of expansion in the districts if the members are sufficiently responsive. It is not proposed to institute residential scholarships at the labour colleges, but to make educational facilities available to the whole of the membership ... We believe very much in solid educational work, and one of the best methods for the trade union in equipping its members for their industrial and political work is encouragement of schemes of educational development. Later on, scholarships will be offered for weekend schools and summer schools. At the moment our immediate concern is to get short-course classes going on economics and industrial history or some other subject eagerly desired by the members.[33]

In the meantime it was proposed to give scholarships for correspondence courses with Ruskin College to six members in different parts of the country for a period of six months. Branches were asked to nominate a member to the area secretary for the consideration of the area committee, who would recommend to London. At the first GEC meeting of 1925, in February, Creech-Jones gave a report on developments in establishing the scheme,[34] and Bevin made his view clear in his report to the GEC:

> The education scheme, as sanctioned by you, has been generally circulated, and in most of the districts the officers have personally visited the branches in relation to same, and have done a great deal to stimulate interest. The greatest handicap the trade unions have in extending schemes of this character – which are beneficial to the membership – is their limited funds.[35]

In preparation for the forthcoming Biennial Delegate Conference, the GEC and Executive Officers issued a statement in May 1925 outlining the details of the scheme. This statement referred back to the decision taken at the 1923 Annual Delegate Conference, and noted that the union was already affiliated to the WEA, and, at that time, was supporting a scholarship at Ruskin College. The first issue raised in the statement was their concern for the cost of a comprehensive scheme:

> While we agree that educational work is of the utmost importance, we have to state that we could not see our way clear to launch an extensive scheme on the present contribution.

The GEC explained that the scheme placed control of policy and expenditure in the hands of the union, but also provided for co-operation with the TUC, other unions and the WETUC, in order that the organising expenses could be offset, particularly through Government and Local Authority grants.

In addition to this very restricted provision, the GEC also confirmed the earlier decision that 'in view of the present financial obligations of the union, the maximum amount to be expended in connection with the scheme shall not exceed a figure of £250 per annum, whilst the contributions to the union remain at their present level'.[36]

At the 1925 BDC, a number of resolutions on education were withdrawn following the statement from the GEC. It was resolved 'that the education policy, as outlined in the Report of the GEC, be approved'; however, there was an implied criticism of the restrictiveness of the scheme in the same agreed resolution, which asked 'that the decision of the EC regarding the education policy be reconsidered, with a view to initiating a more liberal policy and to continue to co-operate with working-class educational bodies now participating in the union's education scheme'.[37]

By the end of 1925, therefore, the basic principles which were to last until 1939 were established, with a tiny budget of £250 per year, no residential scholarships, and a reliance on the WETUC and to a lesser extent the NCLC to fund the courses. The main hope at this time was that the decision taken at the 1925 TUC Congress to establish an education scheme with a college at Easton Lodge would provide the comprehensive programme which was required but which the union would not provide. These hopes, however, were to disappear in the aftermath of the General Strike in the coming May.

1926 AND THE GENERAL STRIKE

The scheme agreed at the 1925 TUC Congress provided for representation of the TUC on the governing bodies of all the main educational organisations, and allowed the General Council to develop its own initiatives in the field of education. At the 1925 TUC Congress it was also suggested that the two colleges, Ruskin and the Central Labour College, should be taken over and transferred to the same site. Later that year Lady Warwick offered her home, Easton Lodge, to the TUC as the venue for a residential college. The gift of Easton Lodge was discussed at the TGWU GEC in February 1926, and it was noted that the TUC 'had accepted the generous offer of Easton Lodge as a free and unconditional gift, to be used as an education centre for trade unionists. It was stated that the TUC required £50,000 to place the college on a sound financial footing'.[38] The Council resolved to defer the appeal to its next meeting.

The handing-over ceremony was publicised in the March edition of *The Record*, with Lady Warwick being described in glowing terms:

> The gift was made by one who has spent 30 years of her life in the Labour and Socialist movement; and it was accepted in the same spirit on behalf of the trade unions for the purpose of establishing a trade union centre for the educational activities of the Working Class Movement under the General Council's control.

It was made clear that at this point Easton Lodge was intended to become the centre of TGWU education activities, as 'existing educational institutions do not supply exactly what we need for the men and women who have to carry on the work of the Labour Movement today, most of whom have to leave school at an early age long before their education can be considered complete'.[39]

The Record commented that the TUC was planning for a great extension of education work on both its national and international side, and that preparations were being made for housing some 200 students in a hostel in the form of a quadrangle. It also made reference to the estimated £50,000 cost of the venture (£1.5 million at today's values).

Bevin also gave his personal support to the Easton Lodge development:

> We visualise the development of a workers' university forming a real centre of education with tremendous potentialities for both the National and International Movements ... The education which we shall endeavour to provide at Easton Lodge, when our plans for creating there a residential college are matured, will, I am sure, be worthy of this fine aspiration and justify our utmost endeavour.[40]

These comments were published in the September 1926 edition of *The Record*, but had been drafted before the TUC Congress, where the TGWU led the rejection of the scheme to take over Easton Lodge, mainly on financial grounds. They may even have been written before the General Strike itself, but it seems that this original support was undermined by the events of the summer.

The General Strike had a devastating effect on the finances of the TGWU. Bevin had reported to the GEC in 1925 that he was 'justly proud – the income for the year 1924 was £472,960, an increase of £81,633 over the 1923 income of £391,327'.[41] For his final report for 1925 he noted that 'the financial statement shows a surplus of nearly £28,000 [£800,000 at today's value] on the quarter, which is most gratifying'.[42] Following the General Strike the membership of the union dropped by a tenth and the support payments made to members drained the finances to an alarming degree. Bevin set out the position in his report to the next BDC:

> During the 5 years of the union's existence the expenditure in the payment of dispute and victimisation benefit has totalled a sum of £778,377 ... we now have an outstanding liability of £227,000 ... the position is that the National Strike has wiped out our reserves.[43]

During the July-September 1926 quarter, £52,662 was paid out in dispute and victimisation benefits.[44] TGWU officials often had to get members to agree to accept a commuted one-off payment of £2 (£56 at today's values). The financial position was such that the GEC considered a compulsory levy of £1 per branch, but decided instead on a voluntary levy and a loan of £20,173 16s 11d via the International Transport Workers Federation (ITF). This loan came from railway workers and transport workers in Switzerland, Germany, Poland, Sweden, Holland, Czechoslovakia (including Sudeten Germans) and Austria. By December 1926 the loan had increased to £27,667 8s 4d. It was to be repaid in instalments: 25 per cent by October 30, 1927, 25 per cent by October 30, 1928, and the remainder by October 30, 1929.[45] The GEC also decided to borrow £163,000 from the Co-op Bank, on the securities of the union.[46]

Bevin gave the financial recovery of the organisation his absolute priority. The damaging effect of the General Strike on the finances of the trade unions, and thence on trade union education, dominated the debate at the 1926 TUC Congress, when, in Tony Corfield's words, 'the movement for educational unity came dismally and humiliatingly to a halt'.[47] The TUC General Council proposed that the Easton Lodge project, which would require the sum of £50,000, should be supported. But, after a long debate, this recommendation was rejected, partly as a result of NCLC pressure, but also because of the unwillingness to produce the money. On a card vote it was defeated by 2,441,000 to 1,481,000. The reference back was proposed by the TGWU.

No doubt anticipating a reaction within the union, the leadership used the October edition of *The Record* to explain their actions:

> Our members will recollect that at the TUC this union moved the reference back of the General Council's scheme to make Easton Lodge into a Labour College ... The main reason for our opposition to the proposal of the GC to impose a levy on the affiliated unions of a penny per member per year for a period of 3 years was financial. We felt that in view of the immediate condition of our union funds it was wiser for us not to enter into additional financial commitments at the present time, particularly as such commitments would involve us in expenditure not only now, but for many years to come.[48]

In direct contrast to the earlier praise which Bevin had lavished on the Easton Lodge idea, *The Record* article now sought to question the educational value of the abandoned project:

> There was also a feeling in our minds that the GC had not fully set out in their report the purpose for which Easton Lodge would be used. It was not sufficient to say that it would be a residential college. The questions in the minds of our delegates were: What sort of college? What purpose would it serve? How would it be financed? How would this residential work be related to the rest of the educational work of the trade unions? Would the energies of the Movement go in the maintenance of residential work to the neglect of class work and other educational developments in which not a selected few but the whole of the membership would share? What was the place of Easton Lodge in the scheme of workers' education?[49]

Despite these rather disingenuous comments, it is clear that the abandonment of the TUC scheme was a reaction to the financial crisis following the strike. Another casualty of the financial crisis was the Central Labour College. The money from the college's main supporters, the South Wales Miners and the NUR, could not be maintained, and appeals from both unions to the TUC made in 1927 and 1928 fell on deaf ears. The unions were not in a position to take over or continue with these payments, and in 1929 the college closed.

In the TGWU, a recovery was in progress by the end of the decade. The balance of the loan was paid by the end of the year. Also, the prospect of a merger with the Workers' Union was a justifiable source of optimism for the future financial stability of the organisation. The crisis of 1929-31, and the consequent depression, however, were to remove the opportunity for a campaign to return to the ambitious education plans of the 1920s.

Leaders and members settled down to take what advantage they could of a reduced provision, and in the TGWU itself, a skeletal education scheme. The organisation had survived its first decade, and begun to build the disparate formerly-independent organisations into a unit, and it had survived the crushing blow of the defeat of the General Strike. The union had never flinched from supporting the idea of trade union education and encouraging its members to take part in it. What it had not been willing or able to do was to deliver the financial and organisational support necessary to build an education programme commensurate with its size. That was to begin to happen in the next decade.

THE EDUCATION PROGRAMME IN PRACTICE, 1922-1939

In practical terms, the philosophical differences between the two main providing organisations mattered less at the local level, and many of the student debates on WETUC or NCLC courses would have been very similar. In the early 1930s Jack Jones was Secretary of the Liverpool Labour College, but in his view:

> The difference between Labour College classes and WETUC ones was that the WETUC had more university and professional people as tutors. For the rest of it they were almost the same ... We weren't concerned to talk about music and history and art and all that sort of thing. We wanted to talk about industrial law, the structure of trade unionism and what Socialism meant, international affairs, international labour politics, international economic matters ... So in that sense these classes attracted good trade unionists who wanted to see just beyond their own individual job.[50]

At the local level, activists like Jack Jones would attend both Labour College and WETUC classes, and organisers like Jack Hamilton of the NCLC in Lancashire built up credibility amongst all unions in the area:

> It wasn't just the Liverpool Labour College classes that were alive, it was also the similar classes run by WETUC. They also organised schools at the weekend, and I used to go along with some of my fellow dockers to take part ... the Steel Workers' Union and the TGWU weren't affiliated to the NCLC. That didn't prevent local branches affiliating to the local Labour College and we did.[51]

Creech-Jones used *The Record* to advise members how to become involved, and formally maintained the 'even-handedness' towards the providers:

> If there is a group of 20 or 30 members of this union who desire a class on any particular subject, either through the NCLC or the WEA or WETUC, will they please inform either the district secretary of these bodies or the (TGWU) area secretary, who will get in touch with the various organisations which can provide the facilities the members ask

> for. Members are asked to pay the small class fees themselves, but these do not amount to more than about 2/6 (12.5p) per term.[52]

In practice, of course, to expect that a group of 20 or 30 would be able to identify the need for a class and make contact with the machinery on their own behalf was unrealistic in most circumstances; and in reality it was WETUC organisers and local Labour College secretaries who made the running, more often than not attracting individual TGWU members along with participants from other unions. This meant that at the local level the picture was uneven, depending on circumstances.

The 1925 NCLC summer schools included as lecturers A.A. Purcell, George Hicks MP and A.J. Cook of the Miners' Federation, and Communists such as Maurice Dobb and Mark Starr, along with Plebs League stalwarts Raymond Postgate and J.F. Horrabin. The subjects covered International Trade Union Organisation, Economic Geography, History, and Economics. These schools were also intended for students who had attended NCLC classes and who wished to train as tutors. Among the subjects covered were teaching methods and The Psychology of Teaching.[53] These types of courses were regularly advertised in *The Record*.

The 1927 NCLC summer school was held at Kiplin Hall, Yorks, and the TGWU reporter noted that 'W. Citrine, Secretary of the TUC, was very instructive on trade unions and general strikes'. Ellen Wilkinson MP was there: 'A most impressive scene was when, on the conclusion of the week's business, the delegates from Russia, Germany, France and America joined with representatives from all parts of Great Britain and Ireland to sing the *Internationale*.'[54] The 1928 NCLC summer school was held at Newdigate Holiday Camp. 'May 5th, being the birthday of Karl Marx, the first lecture was on Marxist economics. In the evening Comrade T. Ashcroft gave a play recital, *The Hairy Ape*, a real proletarian play and one that appeals to all members of the Working Class Movement.[55] The second lecture by Comrade Ashcroft was on "Control in Industry"'.[56]

Notwithstanding Jack Jones's experience in his local area, WETUC schools were normally somewhat different. As early as 1923 TGWU members attended a London Division WEA week-end school, at 'Shornells'.[57] This was a typical example from the period. There were 45 present, and ACTS members were invited. The school was conducted by G.D.H. Cole, and began at 4pm on Saturday, with a lecture on 'Problems of the WETUC', followed by discussion, supper and a social gathering. Sunday began with a ramble, after which, at 11am, Cole lectured on 'Workers' Control in the Postal and Railway Services'. After lunch, there was a discussion on study circles. Lectures were held outside. The reporter commented that 'Our members would do well to follow the lead of the two unions (UPW and Railway Clerks Association) who took part and urge our organisation to provide facilities on similar lines'.[58]

Lecturers for the 1925 WETUC programme included G.D.H. Cole, Hugh Dalton, Harold Laski, and Barbara Wootton. Another school was held at Shornells on 3 and 4 October 1925. Twelve members attended from Area 1 of the TGWU, but the school was attended by 50 students from six unions. A report of this school was sent to *The Record* by a local official and future Area Secretary, Charles Brandon, described as 'Education Officer, Area No. 1 TGWU'. He was able to characterise the school as typical of the WEA education of the day:

> Commencing at 11am on the Sunday the lecture proper 'Social Power and the Way to It' was handled in a deliberately provocative way by the lecturer – Mr R.S. Lambert – whose capacity for making students think is little short of miraculous. So successful was his cunningly-devised method of presentation that almost every student present contributed to the keen discussion that raged throughout the Sabbath, until the tea-gong put an end to a very valuable and interesting week-end. Even during tea the students kept up the discussion and, after good-byes had been said, little groups homeward-bound on trams and buses continued to compare notes to the edification, one must hope, of their fellow-travellers.[59]

The tutor on this course, R.S. Lambert, was a staff tutor on the London University Joint Committee and the editor of the WEA journal, *The Highway*. *The Record* gave it a recommendation and described Lambert as one 'who understands thoroughly the problems which face students in classes and the movement as a whole'.[60] Lambert was a pioneer of educational broadcasting, who later became the editor of *The Listener.* Another WETUC school was held in Durham from 31 July to August 2nd 1926, with 55 students in attendance. The key discussion point was 'Should the trade union movement remain a hostile force opposed to the employers?', and some flavour of the debate can be gathered from the report in *The Record*:

> It was shown that these questions were bound up with the question of leadership, and the question arose whether the old type of trade union leader, drawn from the ranks of his own union, was sufficient to meet the future development of the Movement, and whether trained economists and statisticians were not wanted to act as advisers to union leaders. The advisability and possibility of beginning to train young union members for this purpose was also discussed, and it was shown that these questions depended greatly on the objective the Movement had before it.[61]

It is unlikely that an NCLC summer school would have approached this question in quite the same way! Occasionally a TGWU, TUC or other union official was the tutor. For example, in July 1927, a WETUC weekend school in Pontypool had Harold Clay as the tutor. There were 60 students on the course, including 15 women. Twenty-five came from the TGWU.[62] Sometimes, even the few days' attendance associated with a summer school seemed to have an instantaneous transforming effect on a TGWU member, as with this student, Bro. C. Weales of Birmingham, who attended a school at Ruskin College in the summer of 1926:

> I had a very good time and benefited very much. The arrangements were admirable, and everything went off swimmingly. The tutors were excellent fellows, and the students were chummy.[63]

No wonder the NCLC was concerned about academic education as an instigator of class collaboration!

LOCAL INITIATIVES

The ceding by the union of its educational provision to the WEA and NCLC meant that while these two bodies tried to attach TGWU students to their regional and national systems of delivery, the organisation from within the union was patchy, and left to particular groups and enthusiastic individuals at local level. One of the first of these was the Bristol and District Social and Educational Council, which had been set up with Bevin's support in the days of the DWRGLU, and had been adopted by Area 3 of the TGWU. In 1924 the GEC wrote off a £100 debt which the council had outstanding from the DWRGWU 'in view of the valuable propaganda work performed by the Bristol Social and Educational Council'.[64] The rarity of having one's debts written off by Bevin's union shows the extent of his indulgence.

The council acted as a local WEA and had close links with that organisation and with Bristol University, whose lecturers gave their services free. It consisted of delegates from branches up to a maximum of eight, with local permanent officials as *ex officio*. The key official in the early days was TGWU district official Bro. Burgess, who was also a councillor in the city. Programmes were of a general educational nature. In 1923, for example, the Bristol Educational Council Sunday lectures in the Dockers' Hall, Bedminster, included such subjects as Municipal Trading, Our Responsibility to One Another, Co-operative Politics and Work on the Board of Guardians. As an additional attraction, 'Musical items will be rendered by Miss Jones'.[65] The Council also sponsored inter-branch sports competitions.

Although by the late 1920s the Council's courses were suffering from competition from the WEA – and it had to cancel its programme in 1929[66] – it survived the 1930s and gained new life during the War, when the subjects offered also became more immediately focused on union issues. Arthur Deakin, Ellen McCullough, John Price and Harold Clay all attended its seminars as speakers, and Ellen McCullough operated as its Acting Secretary.

Creech-Jones's associates from the Shipping Clerks were in the forefront of support for education in the early days. One of these in particular was W.B. Dixon, a shipping clerk employed by the PLA and a trustee of the National Union of Docks, Wharves and Shipping Staffs. Dixon, who also had two short spells on the GEC, was an enthusiastic attendee of WETUC schools in the London area, and used *The Record* to promote education. He gave a report on a WETUC school in October 1924, which summed up the type of education then available to TGWU members. The school was again held at Shornells, with 45 in attendance, from organisations including the Postal Workers, Railway Clerks, the Iron and Steel Trades and Draughtsmens' Union:

> The students assembled at 4pm on Saturday. The tutor [once again, R.S. Lambert] gave an interesting discourse on 'Social Theories of Today', and traced the changes which have taken place in our ideas of the place which the state should hold in the social structure and the inevitable change which is still going on and permeating society ... An excellent programme of music, songs etc. was then arranged and continued until we reluctantly retired some time after midnight ... After breakfast came a ramble in the neighbourhood until school assembled at 11am. Then followed another excellent discourse on 'Do the Financiers Control Industry?', after which dinner was served and the afternoon was spent in discussion. The serving of tea brought to an end a most enjoyable time.[67]

In the London area, as noted earlier, the principal enthusiast was Charles Brandon, who apart from attending courses himself tried to encourage the union to allocate more resources to education. For example, in 1928 he pointed out that the union had offered three scholarships for a school in Sydenham and in fact had 17 applications. He also argued that 'I feel certain that it would be by no means difficult to run a weekend school for our own members in London alone if the facilities were obtainable'.[68] Brandon became involved with Clay on the executive of WETUC, and retained his WEA involvement even when becoming Area 1 Secretary in June 1940.

North Wales was another active area, with the local officers R.T. Jones and J. Williams organising a comprehensive programme in co-operation with the local WETUC. Subjects included economics, Welsh literature, Welsh history, music, biology and social and industrial history.[69] Other full-time officials encouraging education at this time were Ivor Thomas of Newport, Richards of Plymouth, and Timmis of Hanley (Power Group), Fitzgerald in Yorkshire, and Kyle in Belfast. In the early 1930s, Arthur Deakin, the future General Secretary, also received a mention for his involvement in education when he was active in North Wales.[70]

During 1925, scholarships were given to TGWU members to attend 17 weekend schools arranged by the WETUC and 14 schools arranged by the NCLC. Fifteen TGWU members received scholarships to university summer schools, and TGWU members attended summer schools organised by the NCLC in Rothesay, London, Birmingham and Belfast. These scholarships covered board, lodging and tuition for one week at a school chosen by the member.[71] Considering that the WEA held 30 weekend schools during 1925 with over 1000 students, the involvement of 30 or 40 TGWU members was of no great significance, and the Executive tried to encourage more participation: 'We would like to see branches clamouring for more classes, and meeting regularly as study circles to hammer out the many difficult problems which confront them in their trade union and industrial experience'.[72]

In 1926, WETUC held 30 weekend schools with 1097 students; 59 TGWU members attended 16 of these schools. WETUC summer schools were attended by 157 students, including 19 TGWU members.[73] In 1926, four TGWU students attended the NCLC summer school, and 36 attended day or weekend schools arranged by the NCLC.[74] For most of the 1930s, course attendance reflected the limited and tightly-controlled financial regime. Statistics for course attendance were not kept in a systematic way, with categories being constantly re-defined. For example, in the late 1920s the total number of WEA or NCLC TGWU students was reported, whereas later on the categories were broken down into particular types of course. The figures for 1930-38 are as follows:

Year	TUC summer schools	University summer schools	Ruskin correspondence courses	NCLC correspondence courses	NCLC summer schools
1930	5	26	19	18	1
1931	7	35	31	46	6
1932	12	43	46	50	8
1933	4	44	44	34	11
1934	11*	50	25	50	19
1935	7	53	50	52	11
1936	12	45	50	52	13
1937	N/A	60**	43	36	N/A
1938	N/A	57	50	50	21

* Held in Dorchester as part of the Tolpuddle Martyrs Centenary

** Figures are for combined University/NCLC Summer school attendance

(Source: TGWU Annual Education Reports 1930-39)

As well as attendance at these schools, three TGWU students attended the residential course at Ruskin in 1929 and 1931, and in 1932 there were two TGWU students at Ruskin, one at the LSE and one at Fircroft. One attended Coleg Harlech in 1929 and 1932, and two in 1931. However, it should be remembered that these were not fully-funded students. The union only made a small supporting grant. In 1930, the NCLC claimed 518 TGWU students.[75]

TGWU members also attended the annual TUC summer school, inaugurated in 1929 and normally held at Ruskin College. Harold Clay and other TUC and trade union officials were regular tutors on these courses, which were innovative both in their focus on practical administrative and industrial issues, and their use of active learning methods such as role-play and case studies. For example, at the 1933 school Walter Citrine 'did not lecture; he just permitted himself to be a trade union "Aunt Sally" and for well over an hour he allowed us to bombard him with questions from every angle of the Trade Union Movement. This was a new feature of the school, and proved very popular'. W. Milne-Bailey of the TUC Research Department also took an innovative approach:

> After the classes, Mr Milne-Bailey's class staged an 'Industrial Court' in which an actual case, once argued before an American Industrial Court, was considered.[76]

The union usually offered eight scholarships to the school, and the 1931 timetable is typical:

- July 10 and 17 – Opening address by Mr Ernest Bevin
- July 12 and 19 – Lectures by Prof. Harold Laski
- July 13 and 20 – Lectures by Mr Arthur Hayday, MP (Chair of the TUC)
- July 14 and 21 – Open session for questions on the work and policy of the TUC to be answered by Sir Walter Citrine
- July 15 and 22 – Lectures by Sir Arthur Pugh
- July 16 and 23 – Lectures by Mr H. Vincent Tewson.

The programme also included classes on issues such as a Survey of Industrial Relations and Negotiations (first week, George Woodcock; second week, Harold Clay); Factory Legislation; Workmen's Compensation and Trade Union Accountancy and Administration. By the mid-thirties speakers such as Harold Laski included sessions on Hitler and Fascism. In 1929, five TGWU members attended this school and seven members attended in 1930.[77] The TUC also introduced a correspondence course in 1936 at 6d a copy, but it was overtaken by the TGWU's own course, as will be discussed later.

CORRESPONDENCE AND LONGER COURSES

At this time, the main correspondence courses were offered by Ruskin College and the NCLC. Members of the WETUC were steered towards Ruskin by being able to register at reduced rates. Given that the great leap forward for TGWU education in 1937-39 was to be built around the introduction of a correspondence course, it was ironic that from the early days this statement was regularly included as a preamble to GEC education reports:

> It is not the policy of the union to encourage study by the correspondence course method as members invariably derive greater benefit from studying in classes in association with others.[78]

The Ruskin courses included mainly academic subjects such as elementary economics, history, literature, law and politics, whilst the NCLC courses were slightly more targeted, covering such subjects as English grammar and essay writing, Public Speaking and Voice Production, Labour Movement history, Revolutionary Periods in History, economic geography (a favourite of Horrabin's) and Esperanto. Courses lasted for either six months or a year, with the union being willing to award a 'scholarship' of £1 1s (£1.05p or £30 at today's values) – sufficient for the six months' course with Ruskin College or a twelve-lesson course with the NCLC. Two such awards were made available per year for each area of the union. However, as *The Record* blithely pointed out, 'that does not prevent a student from taking a twelve-months course and paying the extra £1 1s'.[79]

The take-up of these courses was very small in the early days. For example, in 1925 thirteen members enrolled on the Ruskin course, and in 1926 seven were given correspondence course scholarships with the NCLC. In 1928 fourteen members received correspondence courses with Ruskin College and seven with the NCLC.[80]

Longer residential courses were also offered by Ruskin College and by some Oxford and Cambridge colleges. From 1925 until the late 1930s there were no Ruskin students directly supported by the union, although there were TGWU members who were supported by the TUC or by other means. In 1926, for example, there were three TGWU members at Ruskin College, one with support from the TUC, and two with local authority support.[81] In 1928 grants were made to TGWU members, Sis. Stangroome and Bro. Batstone, to attend Ruskin College, and a small grant for books was also made to Bro. Bradfield studying a course at LSE.[82] After John Price, these were the first TGWU members to undertake the residential course at Ruskin College. For 1929, two grants were made to Ruskin students, and one for a student at Coleg Harlech.[83]

These grants, it should be noted, were only for assistance in purchasing books and food, and were not scholarships in the normal sense, as covering accommodation or fees. On the other hand, in 1930 the TUC scholarship for Ruskin College was £150 (£4200 at today's values), a reasonable sum in those days. It was estimated at the time that £175 was the sum necessary to cover the full cost of a Ruskin student, and the TGWU grant was to cover the cost of the whole or part of the £25 deficit.[84] The number was maintained at the same level throughout the 1930s, reaching a maximum of seven members of the union during the college year 1937-38.[85]

Oxford and Cambridge also offered scholarships to adult students, funded by a government grant. In April 1927, *The Record* described the procedure:

> It is estimated that the cost of three terms' residence in Cambridge is £225 for a man and £175 for a woman [£6300 and £4900 respectively at today's value]. The bursaries (from the Board of Extra-Mural Studies) will cover these expenses. Holders of the bursaries join one of the colleges, and if possible obtain rooms in college. They are free to choose their subjects of study and receive advice as to the lectures and classes which it would be best for them to attend; there is a special library where such students can read and meet together. Otherwise they live the life of the ordinary undergraduate, taking part in games, debates, concerts and similar social activities in the normal way.[86]

Candidates had to give evidence of previous systematic study which would fit them for university work, and those selected were mostly men and women from university tutorial classes and university extension courses, from educational settlements and the Central Labour College, these experiences being used in what would now be called 'access' studies. By 1928, Cambridge had a number of trade unionists under this scheme, including members of the Miners' Federation, London Compositors, Railway Clerks, AEU and Foundry Workers. There was a catch, however: 'Only in exceptional circumstances will permission be given to take a degree'.[87] There is no evidence of a TGWU member being supported by the union under this scheme, even though the union promoted it. One member of the Cambridge Extra-Mural Board was from the TGWU, and it is likely that some individual students were members of the union.

INTERNATIONAL PERSPECTIVES

In the 1930s, a new feature was the introduction of the analysis of Fascism and a growing interest in the international situation generally. In 1936, a WETUC weekend school at Blackpool was attended by 40 union representatives. The lecturer dealt with the Italo-Abyssinian problem, and the issues of pacifism and the policy of continuing sanctions were discussed. The report to *The Record* was sent in by Jack Jones, one of the participants, about to leave Liverpool to fight in Spain.[88] The NCLC also included these subjects in its schools in the

1930s. For example, the 1933 summer school included as its main subjects the Menace of Hitlerism and Fascism, Workers' Control in Industry, and a debate on Capitalism versus Socialism.[89]

A peculiar feature of the interest in internationalism in this period was the promotion of the manufactured international language, Esperanto. In 1925 the TUC Congress carried a resolution instructing the General Council to adopt Esperanto as its official international language, and to insist on its being included in the curriculum of all educational bodies connected with the TUC. The supporters of the resolution urged that it was easy to learn and could be acquired in the space of three months.[90] In March 1927, Area 1 Committee decided to affiliate to the British Esperanto Association on a basis of 40 members, and the 1929 BDC agreed that Esperanto should be the official language of the union in international relationships. Esperanto was included as an NCLC correspondence course, taught by Mark Starr, and *The Record* promoted the study of the language on a regular basis. The largest group of TGWU Esperantists was centred on the Manchester and Sheffield tramworkers. Manchester tramworkers corresponded with Leningrad tramworkers in Esperanto,[91] and practical examples such as this from 1929 were regularly included in *The Record*:

> *Letter from a Brussels tramworker:*
>
> Bro. J. Lea, a Manchester tramworker, is a keen Esperantist and frequently corresponds with tramworkers abroad, who speak the language. The following is a letter he recently received from a Brussels tramworker. The letter described a visit of a Stockholm tramworker to Brussels.
>
> 'The engineer's explanations were translated into Esperanto by a fellow Esperantist employed by Brussels tramway ... Nillsson spoke to a well-attended meeting in the tramwaymens' union hall ... Esperantists at the meeting understood perfectly our visitor's speech, and the secretary of the Esperantist group translated for the others'.[92]

In the pre-war period, however, apart from Esperanto, the union tried to promote other ways of encouraging its members to learn foreign languages without being able to attend long courses or foreign visits, such as this example from 1927, French made Easy:

> The University of London, after four years intensive research work by the Phonetic Department, has finally approved a new system ... The university staff have made a survey of the whole French vocabulary, and have reduced it, for the purpose of their course, to exactly 1,000 words ...we can eliminate entirely the use of the Preterite – and students will

> thus be relieved of a tense that has been a bugbear to past generations. In the same way they will be spared the Second Person Singular; and the use of the whole Subjective Mood has been retarded except in the case of certain colloquial phrases ... By means of a few curves and straight lines a student can now see at a glance the intonation that constitutes the subtlety of a spoken sentence.[93]

Not surprisingly, there is no evidence of a mass take-up in the union, or indeed of the survival of this particular system.

WOMEN'S EDUCATION IN THE TGWU BETWEEN THE WARS

From the earliest days, *The Record* had its 'Women's Page', through which women members were encouraged to involve themselves in TGWU and other union education. Despite the predominance of men in its membership,[94] the union tried to keep a high profile amongst women. Mary Quaile and Mary Carlin had been appointed as women's officers from 1922, when the TGWU was formed, and their importance was increased when Julia Varley, Florence Hancock, and Ellen McCullough were all taken on to the TGWU staff after the merger with the Workers' Union in 1929.

In the early years, it was Mary Carlin who was most associated with the promotion of education amongst TGWU women. As soon as the 1925 TGWU education scheme was agreed, the 'Women's Page' advertised union education:

> We wish to draw the attention of our women members to the education scheme which was announced in *The Record* last month ... Classes can be formed in almost any subject of social interest to suit the convenience of our members, and if the women wish to have a short course class entirely for themselves as a preliminary arrangement this can be done. Individual women, can, of course, join any of the classes which are being arranged, and particulars of these can be obtained from the women organisers. We hope later, occasionally, to offer scholarships to our women members to attend weekend schools.[95]

Occasionally, Mary Carlin made a personal appeal through the pages of *The Record*, as here in 1927:

> The Women's Committee of the WEA are making strenuous efforts to encourage the women in the industrial world to take up lectures and study classes ... we would like our members to try the experiment of going on a short course. I feel that it will create an appetite, and once they have started they will, like Oliver Twist, ask for more.[96]

A number of initiatives were attempted in the 1920s and 1930s to increase the involvement of women. In 1925 the London Women's

Education Committee was established by the London District WEA, the Southern Co-op Education Association, the Women's Advisory Committee of the London Labour Party and 16 trade unions having women members in London, including the TGWU. The purpose of the committee was to bring more women into educational activities by helping to meet their specific needs and difficulties, particularly by speaking to branches, arranging courses of lectures, conferences and weekend schools, and also hoping to develop course leaders from amongst women participants. In the three years between 1925 and 1928 the committee organised 200 lectures. Twenty-four courses were arranged during the winter of 1927-8, including History of the Working-Class Movement, Problems of Industry, Problems of Local Government, and other typical WEA sessions.

From 1925 Ruskin College advertised a scholarship to the value of £135 (£100 for fees, and £35 for expenses; a total of £3780 at today's values) for women aged 20-35 in trade unions, Labour Party or Co-op. In August 1926 it was reported to the GEC that Middlesex County Council had awarded a scholarship to Ruskin for two years to Sis. Stangroome of the Area 1 Bovril branch of the union. Creech-Jones secured extra funding from the TUC to the tune of half the cost of the scholarship.[97] In these early days, the union gave such members a great deal of attention, with Sis. Stangroome being given the congratulations of the GEC, and more than one feature in *The Record*, being personally promoted by Mary Carlin:

> I have received a letter from Miss O. Stamgroome, (sic)[98] who is at present taking a scholarship course at Ruskin College. Miss Stamgroome says 'I like Ruskin College very much, and I believe I am getting along with my studies quite well. I shall be glad, though, to get back to London and start work again. I miss my committees – the Organising Committee and the Women's Education Committee ... I am keeping up my membership of the union, as I wish to keep in touch with my old work friends'.

Mary Carlin added:

> I am sure all our women members will be encouraged by this news of Miss Stamgroome, to endeavour, like her, to take advantage of the classes run by the WEA and NCLC. We want people in the movement with the best possible mental equipment, so as to meet the other side on equal terms.[99]

During the 1920s and 1930s, whilst the union did not have an organised education programme for women, individual female TGWU members could take advantage of special scholarships to particular colleges. For example, in 1933 *The Record* advertised two weekend schools for women in the year, organised by the TUC; one in Lancashire and one at Dudley Training College.[100]

There were also opportunities for individual women to travel abroad for education. For example, in 1927 the TUC offered a scholarship for a woman to go to the Socialist Peoples' College, in Germany, for a three-month study visit. In 1939 a TGWU member, Sis. M. Durkin from Barnsley Passenger 9/9 branch, was awarded a scholarship to the Bryn Mawr summer school, USA.[101] The Bryn Mawr summer schools for women workers existed from 1921 to 1938, in Philadelphia. The school welcomed as applicants women between the ages of 18 and 34 who had an elementary school education and two years of industrial experience. The term 'worker' referred to someone working with 'the tools of her trade', not in a supervisory capacity. Specifically excluded were teachers, clerical workers and saleswomen. The school attracted about 100 women annually.

> The Bryn Mawr summer school for women workers can been seen as a prime example of a suffrage inspired, social feminist institution ... The school's founders aimed to create a community of industrial women, representing a cross-section of occupations, regions, religions, and races, with a balance maintained between union and non-unionised workers.[102]

The union gave £30 to Sis. Durkin, and £5 was given to Sis. Sandland, who won a WEA scholarship to the International People's College at Elsinore in Denmark.

Although these were once-in-a-lifetime opportunities for individual women, there was no systematic education provision for women in the union on a collective basis until much later.

CONCLUSION

Although the union always gave support to the principle of working-class education, and regularly advertised and applauded courses for trade unionists offered by both the WEA and the NCLC, its practical support for its members taking part in these activities was woefully inadequate for the size of the organisation and for its strategic role in the new mass-production and transport industries. That TGWU participants in these formal education programmes could be measured in the tens, and an annual national budget measured in the hundreds of pounds is an indictment of the formal system. The result of this was the emergence of an 'unofficial' education system at local level which paralleled the 'Rank and File' movement within the union structure. At local level, TGWU members were still educated through the system of the traditions of the movement being passed down through the activists, and the Communist Party network played a key role in this process, as it did in the 'Rank and File' movement, whether or not it was formally carried into the Labour College network. In the 1920s, the WEA and the NCLC claimed thousands of students each year. If those figures were remotely accurate, then many of these must have been TGWU members who, with a mixture of local involvement with educational and political bodies, and self-help, were provided with a far more comprehensive programme than that which was formally supported and registered with the union.

In their different ways, however, both the WEA and the NCLC created a sense of dissatisfaction amongst their trade union students. The WEA gave a glimpse of the sedentary, academic life and the world of ideas and learning which could never truly be reached by the vast majority of their students, who could only become 'barrack-room' intellectuals. The NCLC, despite criticism from Tom Bell and the CP, left its students with a revolutionary, transformational perspective, in which the union's limitation to 'a fair day's pay for a fair day's work' was implicitly or even explicitly criticised.

It was almost the case that the more educated a member was, the more alienated he (or rarely she) would be from the union's structure and purpose. The almost exclusive emphasis on political and strategic issues, as Bevin recognised from his own perspective, left an enormous gap in the union's education provision in the areas of the practical issues of the union's own history and structure, and on the day-to-day issues of industrial relations, collective bargaining (including practical skills) and the state regulation of terms and conditions. It was to fill this gap, as well as to counter the influence of the Left, that the leadership supported a radical extension to the education programme at the end of the 1930s, which changed its character and orientation for the rest of the century.

The development of the programme was also influenced by the changing economic and political situation which developed through the 1930s. As new industries grew in importance and the TGWU's place in these became central, new demands were placed on the organisation, and these included the demands for more education, including understanding the new industries and the union's role in them, and a greater understanding of the union's own structure and its democracy.

NOTES

1. Quoted in K. Coates and T. Topham, *The Making of the Transport and General Workers Union, Vol1. Part 11*, London: Blackwell 1991, p833. The two volumes of this book provide an excellent and detailed guide to the events which led to the amalgamation of the TGWU in 1922.
2. Ibid., p827.
3. *Statement from DWRGWU to Amalgamation Committee*, 30 June 1920, TGWU Archives.
4. *Proposed Amalgamation Scheme and Ballot Paper for Transport and General Workers*, signed by Bevin and Gosling on behalf of the Amalgamation Committee, 1921, TGWU Archives.
5. Proposed rule 2(d) iii. Agenda of the Leamington Conference, September 1921, p3. Modern Records Centre, University of Warwick MSS.126/TG/61195/TEMP.34

6. GEC, 5 August 1922, Minute No 88, p14.
7. See below.
8. Finance and General Purposes Committee, Vol. 1, 1922-23, Minute No 238, p16.
9. It had to be transferred from Hull at the last minute because of trouble in the docks and the wish of the officials to be on hand for negotiations.
10. Report of TGWU 1923 Annual Delegate Conference, Minute No 45, p23.
11. Ibid.
12. GEC, Vol. 1, 1922-23, Minute No 866, p14.
13. Ibid., Minute No 275, p12.
14. GEC, Vol. 2, 1923-24, Minute No 351, p23.
15. GEC, Vol. 2, 1923-24, Minute No 477, p18.
16. Ibid., General Secretary's Report, November 1924, p48.
17. Description of the TGWU scheme provided by John Price at the first meeting of the Education Committee, 3 May 1939.
18. The TGWU is currently divided into regions. Until 1950, these were referred to as areas. Over the years, the number has reduced from 13 to 11 to 8. I will refer to 'areas' up to 1950, then 'regions'.
19. B. Simon, *The Search For Enlightenment*, London: NIACE 1992; J. Holford, *Union Education In Britain*, University of Nottingham, 1994; W.W. Craik, *Central Labour College*, London: Lawrence and Wishart 1964; J. Atkins, *Neither Crumbs Nor Condescension: The Central Labour College 1909*-1915, Aberdeen: Aberdeen People's Press/WEA 1981; J.P.M. Millar, *The Labour College Movement*, London: NCLC 1979; A.J. Corfield, *Epoch in Workers' Education*, London: WEA 1969; R. Fieldhouse et al, *A History of Modern British Adult Education*, Leicester: NIACE 1996; C. Griggs, *The TUC and the Struggle for Education 1868-1925*, Brighton: Falmer 1983; G. Goldman, *Dons and Workers: Oxford and Adult Education Since 1850*, Oxford: Clarendon 1995.
20. See below.
21. Simon, op. cit., p39.
22. GEC, Vol. 1, 1922-23, Minute No 335, p5.
23. *The Record,* November 1924, p96.
24. *The Record,* January 1925, p121.
25. Ibid., p124 (emphasis in the original).
26. Ibid., p125.
27. Millar, op. cit., p42.
28. Corfield, *Epoch in Workers' Education*, op. cit., p22.
29. *Interim Report of the Committee on Adult Education Industrial and Social Conditions in Relation to Adult Education*, London: HMSO, 1918, p3.
30. Corfield, op. cit., p57.
31. *The Record*, November 1938, p87.
32. *The Record*, September 1936, p31.
33. *The Record*, January 1925, p124.
34. GEC, 18 February 1925, Minute No 129, p21.
35. General Secretary's Report, February 1925, p46.
36. TGWU Report, 1925, pp67-68.
37. Minutes of 1925 BDC, p29.
38. GEC, 16 February 1926, Minute No 225, p50.
39. *The Record,* March 1926, p189.

40. *The Record*, September 1926, p44.
41. GS Report to GEC, February 1925, p44.
42. GS Report to GEC, November 1925, p39.
43. GEC Report to 1927 BDC, p158.
44. £1.7 million at today's values.
45. F&GP, 4 November 1926, Minute No 905, p245.
46. Minutes of GEC, 24 August 1926, Minute No 739, p182.
47. Corfield, op. cit., p53.
48. *TGWU Record*, October 1926, p83.
49. Ibid.
50. J. Jones, 'A Liverpool Socialist Education', *History Workshop Journal*, Issue 18, Autumn 1984, p98.
51. Ibid., p97. See also E. & R. Frow, 'The Spark of Independent Working-Class Education' in Simon, *The Search for Enlightenment*, op. cit., pp71-104.
52. *The Record*, September 1925, p41. Signed 'ACJ'. 12.5p is equal to £3.50p at today's values.
53. *The Record*, April 1925, p206.
54. *The Record*, October 1927, p84.
55. The play was written by Eugene O'Neill, and was a common feature at NCLC events.
56. *The Record*, May 1928, p297.
57. 'Shornells' was owned by the Royal Arsenal Co-operative Society and situated on Bostall Heath, Plumstead, South-East London, overlooking the Thames. It was built in 1882 as a private house, but during the First World War, the house was used as a hospital for wounded officers, and purchased by the RACS in 1920. It was used as an education centre by the Co-ops, the WEA and sometimes by the union for special meetings up to the 1970s, and demolished following a fire in 1988. There is now a hospice on the site. I am grateful to Mr R. Roffey of RACS for this information.
58. *The Record*, October 1923, p3.
59. *The Record*, October 1925, p59.
60. Ibid.
61. *The Record*, October 1926, p82.
62. *The Record*, July 1927, p363.
63. *The Record*, September 1926, p50.
64. Minutes of the GEC, 11 November 1924, Minute No 721, p9.
65. *The Record*, October 1923, p2.
66. GEC Annual Report, 1929.
67. *The Record*, January 1925, p125.
68. Letter, 12.4.1928, Annual Report on the Union's Educational Scheme, 1928.
69. Annual Report on the Union's Educational Scheme, 1928.
70. Ibid., 1931 Report, p2.
71. *The Record*, May-July 1926, p246.
72. Ibid.
73. *The Record*, April 1927, p269.
74. GEC Report, 1927, p41.
75. Annual Report on the Union's Educational Scheme, 1929, p2.
76. N.G. Pinnock, *The Record*, August 1933.
77. Annual Reports on the Union Education Scheme, 1930 and 1931.
78. GEC Report, 1928, p39.

79. *The Record*, December 1925, p117.
80. Annual Report on the Union Education Scheme, 1928, p1.
81. GEC Report, 1927, p41.
82. Annual Report on the Union Education Scheme, 1929, p1.
83. Annual Report on the Union Education Scheme, 1930, p1.
84. *The Record*, January 1930, p178.
85. *The Record*, October 1937, p63.
86. *The Record*, April 1927, p269.
87. *The Record*, March 1927, p233.
88. *The Record*, June 1936.
89. *The Record*, August 1933.
90. *The Record*, September 1925, p38.
91. *The Record*, November 1928, p119.
92. *The Record*, October 1929, p83.
93. *The Record*, August 1927, p13.
94. Women's membership in the TGWU has never significantly exceeded 20 per cent of the total.
95. *The Record*, February 1925, p166.
96. *The Record*, January 1927, p188.
97. GEC, 25 August 1926, Minute No 771, p188. Also *The Record*, September 1927, p42.
98. The union seemed unsure about the spelling of Miss Stangroome's name (if that is correct). It was spelt Stangroome, Stamgroome and Stangroom in *The Record* and by the minute secretary to the GEC.
99. *The Record*, March 1927, p246.
100. *The Record*, June 1933, p334.
101. *The Record*, March 1939, p217.
102. Joyce L. Kornbluh and Mary Frederickson (eds), *Sisterhood and Solidarity: Workers Education for Women, 1940 to 1984*, Philadelphia: Temple University Press 1984, p115.

Chapter 2

The Great Leap Forward 1937–1939

This chapter looks at the decisions taken by the union in the late 1930s to introduce its own education scheme, separate from the WEA or the NCLC. These decisions included the employment of the first Head of Education, John Price, the establishment of the GEC Education Committee, and the launch of a completely new correspondence course, Your Union, Its Work and Problems. *These developments were just reaching completion as war broke out in the autumn of 1939. They amounted to a significant increase in the specialisation of the programme, and also prepared the ground for the introduction of a collectivist perspective through the wartime day schools.*

THE CALL FOR CHANGE IN THE 1930S

The later part of the 1930s saw a quantum leap in the union's education provision, and established a pattern of course structure, internal control and administration whose essential elements are still in existence. This fundamental change came about for a number of reasons, some of which were internal to the organisation and others the product of external industrial, economic and political circumstances and their impact on the union's leadership, particularly on Bevin.

After the crises of the General Strike and the break-up of the Labour Party in 1931, it was not until the mid-1930s that Bevin once again began to promote 'education' as a central objective for the union. By this time, his primary themes were the need to combat Fascism on the one hand and Communism on the other, particularly the influence of 'Rank and File' movements within the union, such as the group within the London bus workers.[1] He was also acutely aware that the generation which had established the union was passing away, and that a new generation with different values based on industries such as cars, chemicals and aircraft manufacture, was coming to the fore. Bevin saw 'education' as an important element in meeting these new challenges. However, in the early 1930s he had still not yet come to the conclusion that a systematic union-controlled education scheme could play an important role in harnessing and leading new developments. In 1933 he addressed the GEC:

> We must not be daunted. If we can do something ... to relieve the weight of unemployment, this will act as a check and give the trade unions an opportunity to make another forward move in the improvement of the standard of life of the workers. Our present method of publicity must be changed. We have got to get back to the leaflet and the house-to-house visitation, and, with your approval, I propose to draft a series of leaflets in simple terms explaining trade unionism to the new generation. This will involve some expenditure of money, but I think it will be worthwhile if we can have the co-operation of the local officers and committees in its distribution. I know it is casting bread upon the water, but if persisted in, I am sure it will lead to a great development of membership.[2]

After the rise of Hitler, Bevin saw the essential appeal of Fascism as providing easy solutions to the uneducated mind: 'In this country unless we are alive to it, the very fact that it is new may appeal to unthinking people. If the Fascist movement does succeed in obtaining a hold, and the employers see the workers turning towards it, they will begin to find money for it, as they did in Italy and Germany; even if the industrialists do not, the bankers certainly will.'

It was always easy for Bevin to move from criticising Fascism to criticising 'disruptive' (in other words, Left/Communist) elements within the union, and he habitually saw education aimed as much against these as against Fascism: 'The paramount thing to remember and to get over to the members is that the trade unions represent the only effective organisations the workers possess, and that if they are to be developed, they must be strengthened by the consciousness of the lay members themselves'.[3]

However, as the economy and the size and activity of the union picked up in the mid-1930s, he became very optimistic and saw the new TGWU education scheme as both following and facilitating the link between the union and the new generation. At the end of 1935, he began to sense the possibility of an upturn in the economy and in the position of the union, and he began to see both the opportunity and the challenge to the union represented in these new developments:

> I feel sure that lying just ahead of us is a fairly big demand for an upward movement in wages and conditions, because it must be remembered that the post-war generation is at the point of finding its position in industry. They do not know anything about the pre-war [i.e. the First World War] position; to them, it is just another historical period. All the desires, effects of the higher standard of education, ideals, etc., will begin to seek an outlet in the near future. The union must be ready to organise and find expression for this new generation. We must keep our minds attuned, ready to turn each new phase to good account.[4]

However, it was not only external pressures which forced Bevin to rethink his approach to the union's education scheme. Apart from organising TGWU students to take part in education programmes, Creech-Jones, Clay and enthusiastic local officials kept up a constant pressure to encourage Bevin and the GEC to allocate more money to education.

This pressure was kept up by Harold Clay when he took over sole responsibility for education following Creech-Jones's resignation in 1930. In his report to the GEC for that year he argued forcefully for more money:

> The Executive have been asked to increase the grant with a view to meeting the increasing demand for educational facilities; £350 per annum for a union of the size of ours is a very inadequate allowance. We often have it brought to our notice how much more is being done by other organisations in regard to education. It is hardly necessary to emphasise the importance to the union of an educated rank-and-file membership. Money spent on educational work should be regarded as an investment which would yield an unfailing return'.[5]

By the early 1930s, Clay was asking for at least £1,000 per year, a fourfold increase in expenditure, from £7,000 to £30,000 at today's values. He was supported by a resolution from the National Committee of the ACTS Trade Group, the General Workers Group, the Passenger Services Group, and also by resolutions from both Area 1 and Area 2 Committees asking for more money to be allocated to education and criticising the earlier decision in the light of the size of the union.[6] Indeed, in 1932 both Area 1 and Area 4 Committees made a grant to supplement their education expenditure.[7] Nevertheless, the GEC only raised the grant to £350.[8] In 1931 the GEC increased the educational grant to £500 and set a further £100 to be spent on special forms of education (£15,000 and £1,750 respectively at today's value). Clay then argued that the two amounts should be consolidated. In the report to the GEC for 1934 he argued that:

> We have been concerned with using the limited sum of money available for education purposes to the best possible advantage. In view of the increasing demands which have been made upon the fund it has been extremely difficult to keep within the amount allocated by the Executive, in fact, this year we have spent considerably more than that amount, the difference having been made up mainly by grants from areas and scholarships received from outside sources, so the total expenditure for that year was £649 18s 2d. (£649.91p).[9]

As a result, in March 1935 the General Executive Council decided to increase the grant for union education to £600 (£17,000 at today's values). The GEC also empowered the General Secretary to arrange annual visits of selected officers and staff to Geneva for education in addition to the ordinary education scheme. This in fact represented the start of a new era, as Bevin had renewed his contact with the ILO and the European trade union movement, and in particular with John Price, who was soon to become the first Head of Education and Research. John Price was able to secure this substantial increase on the grounds that the range of education offered by the union had increased enormously, so that by 1939 the education grant had been increased to £1,250 per year (£37,500 at today's values).

The pressure to increase expenditure on education came to a head at the 1935 BDC. A resolution from the 1/230 branch (Central London Taxicabs, a stronghold of the CP) instructed the GEC 'to prepare a full national education scheme, in conjunction with the NCLC, for all members to be entitled to educational facilities including free correspondence courses'.[10] Another resolution standing in the name of the 1/669 branch (Mattesson Meats, E London) called for the remission of tutorial class fees. Although the former was lost and the latter withdrawn following a GEC statement, the debate brought to the surface the resentment in the union at the paucity of financial support for education, and, given his central role in the debate, is likely to have convinced Bevin that he must take positive action or lose control of it. This would have been a greater problem if the union were to become exclusively attached to the NCLC, which in Bevin's eyes was almost synonymous with the Communist Party and hence with the 'Rank and File' movement within his own union. During the debate, an NCLC supporter put it very well:

> We should participate in the full scheme of the NCLC because the education you get at these schools is a wonderful education because it is definitely prejudiced to class bias and that is what we, the working class, want. This NCLC school is purely a school which gives working-class education.[11]

The defeat of the resolution calling for full affiliation to the NCLC was a close-run thing. Bevin argued that the amount being called for would result in a payment of £5,000 – £6,000 (£150,000 to £180,000 at today's values) to the NCLC, which was more than the union's affiliation to the TUC.[12] He pointed out that the union was not actually affiliated to either the NCLC or WETUC in the true sense:

> We are not affiliated at all. What we did was that we voted a certain amount for education and we only deal with the demand of participating members, that is members who take the course – we divide that money between the WEA, WETUC and the NCLC in about equal proportions. It really depends to a very large extent on the form of requests that we get ... we pay for the participating members only. The

affiliation proposal is the whole of the membership whether they participate or not, and that is what the Executive is opposed to.[13]

Despite the fact that these resolutions were defeated, it is clear that the debate here and the pressure to pay more for education persuaded Bevin that if they were going to be spending more, they should spend it on the union's own scheme rather than make a full affiliation to the NCLC and the WETUC.

By 1937, in response to both the upturn in the fortunes of the economy and the union, and the persistence of Communist influence in the TGWU, Bevin was beginning to focus his thoughts on the establishment of a structured education programme. Early in that year, he wrote a seminal piece of work in *The Record*, which made the connection between the need to hold on to the 'centre' in the union, and the importance of the union's education programme. Grandly entitled *The Future of Our Union*, it brought together his thoughts on the current political and industrial situation and the importance of union education, and set the scene for the appointment of John Price and the launch of the union's own education scheme at the forthcoming 1937 BDC. The article was presaged by a short piece which extolled the virtues of the traditional branch meeting as a source of union education:

> Remember that those who occupy positions in the Greater Labour Movement to-day would not be doing so had they not taken advantage of the education opportunities offered by the branch – the clash of wit, and the arguments, sometimes intense, sometimes noisy. The consideration of the various problems, industrial, political and international, which came up before the union, was ventilated at the branch meetings. Opinions were formed and outlook was developed. The knowledge so gained was discussed at the workshop during the meal hour, at the club, or in other places, and again opinion was formed.[14]

However, the main article actually focused on the union's intention to introduce a more formal and targeted education programme:

> If the fullest advantage is taken of the educational facilities offered by the union, another great opportunity presents itself for service ... The Executive Council are very interested in the cause of education and are now considering the possibility of extending the union's educational work – not to conflict with the institutions I have mentioned, but to give greater facilities to our members so that they may understand the problems the union has to face ... And it would be well if more of these classes and correspondence courses were taken up by the members. If democracy is to thrive, trade unionists particularly must equip themselves, because they never know in what capacity they may be called upon to serve.[15]

Bevin's respect for education, but his simultaneous mistrust of intellectuals, whether from the universities or the political wing of the Labour Movement, set the scene for an education scheme directly controlled by the union. Personally, Bevin enjoyed debating with intellectuals, as his correspondence shows[16] – indeed, by any standard, both he and John Price *were* intellectuals – but he would not countenance their having any control over the affairs of the union, unless, as in Price's case, they were strictly under his authority as staff members. According to Jack Jones, 'Bevin was persuaded by Harold Clay to support adult education. Bevin's attitude to the WEA and NCLC at the time of setting up the correspondence course was "a plague on both of their houses; let's do it ourselves"'.[17]

ENTER JOHN PRICE

A number of innovations were set in place to achieve the goal of a new education system for the union. Included in these were the appointment of John Price as the first specialist Research and Education Officer, the re-organisation of the Research and Education Department, the setting up of an Education Sub-Committee of the GEC, and the establishment of a correspondence course and union-only schools as a further development from this. The first step was to persuade John Price to leave the office of the Labour and Socialist International in Brussels and take on his new role in the union. There is no direct evidence that John Price was influencing Bevin in his thoughts at this time, but the fact that by 1937 Bevin had invited Price to take up his post suggests it may be likely that Price was influencing Bevin's thinking on this issue, so far as anyone could influence so strong a personality as Bevin.

Tony Topham outlined the background to John Price's appointment in his appreciative article:

> In 1937 John Price was, in modern parlance, 'head-hunted' by the General Secretary of the TGWU. Having known him first as a Ruskin student then as a college organiser he had continued to meet him at the LSI. John Twomey (the General Secretary of Price's father's and his own union, the NALU) was an intimate of Bevin and had already spoken of his worth. A former docker with an education which he had placed at the service of the Movement was a rare prize.[18]

John Price was born in 1901 in Newport, Monmouth, where his father was also a docker. He won a scholarship to Newport High School, a most unusual achievement for a docker's son at that time, and after leaving school he tried various jobs before joining his father in the docks. His father was very much involved in the National Amalgamated Labourers' Union, centred on South Wales, whose President was Robert Williams, who played a leading role in the formation of the TGWU in 1922. After the amalgamation, John Twomey became TGWU National Organiser for General Workers.

Topham takes up the story:

> NALU had instituted a union scholarship to Ruskin College, and one day in 1920 John Price received a letter 'out of the blue' from John Twomey informing him that his name had been submitted for entry to Ruskin under its terms. His father had spoken to Twomey about his scholarly-minded son, and ensured the success of the application. In the following year, when NALU joined the new amalgamation, John Price became the first of the TGWU's scholars.[28]

At its very first GEC meeting, in August 1922, the new union agreed to enable him to complete the two-year Ruskin course. The scholarship covered the £100 per year college fees, and added a grant of £35 per year to cover travelling, books and personal expenses during terms and holidays (a total of 4,000 at today's value). This was a significant vote of confidence in John Price, for the new union was in serious financial straits, and because of the 1925 scheme, no further residential scholarships would be awarded until 1937. 'John Price became, as he wryly recalled, "something of a prize exhibit – a Ruskin Scholar"'.[20]

He was awarded the University's Diploma in Economic and Political Science with distinction at the age of 21. He then became an organising secretary at Ruskin College, concentrating on promoting and administering the college's correspondence courses, combining that duty with continued service as secretary of his dockers' branch in Newport. After four years he was made redundant by the financially hard-pressed college, but he soon obtained a post as co-ordinator of the Brussels staff of the LSI, serving there from 1927 to 1937. This is where he learned French and German to interpreter level and acquired a good working knowledge of Spanish, Italian, Dutch and Swedish.

Although John Price was in his late 30s when he was appointed, and his mid-40s when he left the union, he was always thought of as 'one of Bevin's young men', as Francis Williams refers to him.[21] This is partly because of his gentle style, but also because in the context of the time, his ideas were so advanced. He believed in education materials which were targeted on the union role which the student was expected to carry out, and was instrumental in developing union-only day-schools taught by officers and staff of the union, rather than by academics from WETUC or the NCLC. His whole approach was that the knowledge and the teaching skills to provide a successful education programme already existed within the union, something which was music to Bevin's ears, and which has remained with the union ever since. Although an anti-Communist, Price was fair-minded and had a strong trade union-oriented internationalist perspective.[22] Price's first major task was to produce an education scheme which was controlled by the union and which would take the organisation forward.

He opted for a programme which had at its core a correspondence course, to be called *The Union, Its Work and Problems*, to be supplemented with union-only day and weekend schools in the districts. The choice of the correspondence course was surprising, for as we have already noted, throughout the inter-war years up to Price's appointment, the union had discouraged this type of study. Paradoxically, as late as 1943, four years after the introduction of its own scheme as the centrepiece of the education programme, the union was still recommending that wherever possible members should study in classes rather than through the correspondence method.[23] John Price was the only person who in the early years was given the chance by the union to promote correspondence courses. In 1928, whilst employed at Ruskin College, he was allowed a piece in *The Record* advocating the correspondence course method:

> No one believes that a correspondence course is a satisfactory alternative to a course in residence at a college. Nor does anyone maintain that the average student can learn as quickly by a correspondence course as he can in a class where he meets his tutor face to face. At the same time there can be no doubt that correspondence courses can and do play a valuable part in working-class education. The correspondence course is just the thing for workers who cannot or will not attend classes or enter a college. Most workers find it impossible to enter a college. Some, because they must do night work, shift work, or Sunday work, cannot even attend a class. Others, who could attend a class, will not do so because of shyness, or because they are impatient to get on quicker than the others, or because they are afraid they will hold up the class by learning too slowly ... it can be useful for the one who would spoil a class by being too argumentative.[24]

Price's – and Bevin's – vision was to move the correspondence course away from the format of being a basic introduction to an academic subject, into being a guide-book for the history, structure, activities and policies of the union, so that any new or existing member had an induction into what the union was about and how it operated. Bevin was prepared to meet the cost of what would be a free course, and to win the strategic argument with the GEC and the BDC, although, as has been seen already, there was already strong support for the extension of education. In early 1937, Bevin reported that the financial position was better than ever and that a £1 million surplus should be possible within the near future.[25] At the GEC meeting in March 1937 it was agreed that the F&GP be directed to examine the educational facilities under the union's scheme. Bevin laid the groundwork at this meeting by raising with the Council the growing demand for education within the union.[26] At the June 1937 GEC meeting Bevin outlined the proposals for merging the Political, Education and Research departments together. He also informed the Council that he had engaged John Price 'in a clerical capacity' to take charge of the merged department under his direction.[27]

Having prepared the groundwork for the introduction of the new scheme, he then went to the BDC to win support for his ideas and to head off any further attempt to bring the union closer to the NCLC. There were a number of resolutions on education submitted to the conference, with a particular focus on making the union increase its financial support for students attending WETUC and NCLC classes. The Standing Orders Committee submitted a report recommending that a statement was to be made to the conference with regard to the GEC policy on union education. Bevin then put his case. He stated that Council recognised the need for extending the union's educational facilities, particularly with reference to the internal work of the union, its constitution, machinery and methods of negotiation, national and international industrial affairs. 'It was not the purpose of the Council to interfere with the existing scheme in its relation to the WEA and the NCLC. On the other hand the Council took the view that the educational facilities offered by the union could be wisely extended in the manner indicated by the introduction of internal classes, lectures and correspondence courses, on a systemised basis'.[28] Subject to the approval of conference, it was the intention of the GEC to proceed with the formulation of such a scheme in order that 'yet another beneficial service, at a comparatively small cost, might be made available to members of the union desiring to improve their knowledge'.[29]

After listening to Bevin's announcement, the conference agreed that most of the resolutions calling for an expansion of education should be withdrawn. In place of these, it was resolved to approve the extension of the educational facilities of the union on the lines indicated by the General Secretary. Bevin had only one battle left to win. A resolution asked the union to pay for travelling expenses to WEA classes, and this had not been withdrawn, as the new scheme would not rule out the attendance of TGWU members at WEA or NCLC classes. The resolution asked for 'all reasonable expenses incurred by members attending classes in connection with the scheme, and lost time expenses and railway fares for members attending schools for which they have been awarded union scholarships'.[30]

Bevin himself replied, 'If we pay board and lodgings for a residential student and all tuition fees, I think really it is a fair contribution for a man in order to improve his knowledge which in turn is bound to help him in his career'. However, he went further and used the occasion to argue for the expansion of internal union control over education:

> You are being asked to make a present of that to a body over which you have no control at all. To that extent the resolution marks the departure

> of the policy that this union has adopted from the beginning of its educational work. We have taken the view over a long period of years that as the demand for educational facilities has increased so our grant would increase but the control over payment would rest with the union and not with an outside body ... Moreover a good number of classes are not classes at all. They are occasional meetings and occasional lectures and in some cases they are public meetings drawn together by active people in the Labour Movement. Surely we are not asked to made a contribution for that particular kind of work ... The fundamental thing is this, when we pay money for educational work the union must be in a position that it reserves the right to control how much money should be spent ... In view of our past policy when we have linked up the educational working-class movements in this country, if we make one provision for one side, we have got to make a like provision for another. That immediately commits us to an expenditure of roughly £11,000 to £12,000 [£350,000 at today's values]. The union itself is embarking on an educational scheme which is fairly costly and with these facts before you I have no doubt whatever that the resolution will not be carried.[31]

The resolution was duly defeated and the conference moved on, having made the momentous decision to shift the emphasis of TGWU education towards internal control over finance and development. This emphasis has never since been reversed.

BUILDING THE NEW SCHEME

Six weeks after the BDC, in August 1937, John Price gave his first report to the GEC. At this meeting, he outlined the general direction of the new scheme, and its objective 'to provide special facilities to the members with particular reference to the internal affairs of the union as affecting constitutional and organisational matters, and methods of negotiation'.[32]

Throughout the winter of 1937-38 and the following summer, the members of the Department, in particular John Price and Ellen McCullough, worked with a number of national secretaries in drafting the correspondence course. The link with Bevin was provided by Alf Chandler, the GEC Minutes Secretary and in effect the first Administrative Officer of the union, and Ivy Saunders, Bevin's Secretary, who played an active part in developing the course. Bevin himself kept a close eye on progress, and Topham relates that when Ellen McCullough was typing the drafts, she would become aware of Bevin's large presence, as he looked over her shoulder to observe progress.[33] A memo from Alf Chandler to John Price from early 1939 gives a good illustration of how Bevin edited the content as it progressed:

> The General Secretary indicated the changes which he would like in Part 5 of the syllabus, and it was agreed ... that the section on Workers' Control be omitted.[34]

Bevin was highly enthusiastic about the scheme, but hugely underestimated the time it would take to produce the final version. As early as December 1937 he was extolling its virtues:

> It is not complete yet, and I propose to have another meeting with the officers during the third week in January next, when I hope the scheme will be put in final form for submission to the Council. I feel that wise expenditure on the educational side ought to result in bringing in active and enthusiastic workers, especially among the younger generation if they are handled right, because, however powerful we are we cannot have officers for everything. We must encourage initiative on the part of the active members in the branches to be used on right lines with a very good understanding of the union.[35]

In fact, it began to be recognised that because of the size of the task, the scheme would take much longer to prepare. In March 1938, Bevin had to tell the GEC that he hoped the drafts would be available for its next meeting, but by May he again had to report that they were not yet ready:

> It involves a considerable volume of effort and we feel it is better to take a little more time in order to get the basis right. When it is completed the result will be that we shall have, in concise form, a very complete textbook of the union.[36]

In August 1938 Bevin had to propose a new timetable to the GEC:

> A syllabus of the new union educational scheme is practically complete and copies will be circulated to you at an early date. You will appreciate that it will not now be possible to introduce the scheme during the coming winter period, and the General Secretary, therefore, proposes with your concurrence to launch the scheme on the occasion of the 1939 Biennial Delegate Conference. Delegates will be present at the conference from all parts of the country and the occasion will be used to secure co-operation in publicising the scheme.[37]

At this meeting, the GEC formally agreed that the new scheme would be introduced at the 1939 BDC.[38]

The first draft was completed in November, and during the winter of 1938-39 the various sections were made into final drafts and submitted to the GEC for approval. At the GEC meeting in March 1939, Bevin set out the timetable for the launch of the new scheme. The syllabus was to be issued to all branches, officers and committees in March or April, accompanied by a publicity campaign to reach its climax at the BDC in July. This publicity campaign was to be continued after the conference with branches being provided with application postcards. The first season was set to begin in

September/October and to continue through the 1939-1940 winter period, and publicity was to be resumed during the summer of 1940 in preparation for the second season in the winter of 1940-1941.

During the first season the scheme was to be confined to correspondence courses with an occasional day or weekend school. Bevin also proposed that the GEC should agree to grant two full scholarships to Ruskin College covering fees and personal allowances, to be open to students who had taken the correspondence course. He also proposed that when awarding scholarships to weekend and summer schools organised by the TUC, ILO, WETUC, and NCLC, preference was to be given to members who had taken the course whilst, at the same time, paying regard to an applicant's work for the union, Labour Movement, and previous educational activities. He also proposed that at the end of the first season there should be a review of its operation with a view to possible extension to study groups. The leaders of the study groups should be chosen from amongst the members who had taken the correspondence course during the first season, and prepared for their role with weekend training schools. Bevin completed his blueprint with a personal endorsement of the new scheme: 'I have worked out the administration of the scheme very carefully. It will be economical, but, in any event, I take the view that the union will be amply repaid if, as a result of the scheme, it can create enthusiastic organisers and intelligent men and women to carry on its work'.[39]

This was an ambitious and forward-looking programme building on from an introductory correspondence course through short-course programmes and study circles led by TGWU activists who had risen through the ranks of the union and the education programme. It was unfortunate that its launch took place almost simultaneously with the outbreak of war, at the end of which both Bevin and John Price would have departed the union. Nevertheless, as we shall see, the launch did take place and the scheme was a success, although its detailed and comprehensive plan could not be carried through on the original pattern.

THE CORRESPONDENCE COURSE

The Union, Its Work and Problems comprised 6 pamphlets:

1. The background to the union; 'a survey of the conditions which led to the formation of the union; events and achievements; and the union today'.
2. Structure of the union; rights, duties and responsibility of membership.
3. The union at work; functions: organising and negotiating; services; information and research; political activities; provision of benefits; legal advice and assistance; health services; publicity; finance and administration.
4. Problems of organisation; improving conditions of employment.

5. Voluntary negotiating machinery; statutory wage-fixing bodies.
6. Women and young persons; industrial legislation; industrial health; safety at work; statutory control of industry.[40]

The book set out its purpose at the beginning:

> These pamphlets have been written for the members because we want them to understand their own organisation to the full. There are now many thousands of them who do not remember the original amalgamation and do not realise what problems had to be solved and what pitfalls avoided in the light of early trade union history. We want them to know these things, so that they may appreciate what has been done and be in a position to explain the union to others.
>
> There is another point. Industry is rapidly developing and constantly changing. New problems are continually arising, new situations have to be met. Our officers have a far more difficult task than they had in the days before the War. Our members have far greater responsibility towards their organisation ... In these days we need an increasing number of members who not only believe in trade unionism but who also know and understand the facts and problems of modern industry, and the changing situations which the union has to face.[41]

Much of the course was practical and related to the structure and industrial relations activities of the union. It covered the origins of the union, and the way it was divided into area and trade group sections. It also looked at the then existing system of industrial relations in the principal industries covered by the TGWU. It also had sections on the basics of workmen's compensation, and on the various regulations covering the employment of women and young persons, and so on. Whilst the orientation was generally practical, pages 15 and 16 of Part 2 of the book included a philosophical section looking at the relationship between the individual and the organisation and even included references to Plato and Aristotle, Socialism and Communism. The point was to persuade the individual of his or her responsibilities towards the wider functioning of the organisation, something in which Bevin was extremely interested.

The book was intended to be read, studied and digested, and there were very few concessions made to pictures or interactive methods. As Topham comments: 'There were no presentational devices in the text to make it more digestible; no charts, no diagrams, cartoons, no role-playing exercises, none of the modern pedagogy of adult education. Only text, and more text'.[42] The booklets were provided to each student free of charge, once a month, accompanied by a bibliography. Students received in addition a set of notes on how to study the course, together with hints on writing. For each month there were also special leaflets containing notes on the work for the month and guidance for those who wished to undertake additional reading. The written work sent in by the students was 'marked' at Central Office and returned with comments and suggestions.[43] The course was designed to last for six months.

Certification was dealt with on an extremely rigorous basis. Arrangements were made for the award of certificates to students who completed the course and who also submitted an additional essay set by the Education Department. Once the scheme was underway, a student could complete as non-certificated (the great majority), or achieve 'Satisfactory' and 'With Distinction' certificates, on the decision of the Education Committee. In the award of certificates regard was had both to the quality of the additional essay and to the candidate's record of work throughout the course. The certificates were printed and were signed by the General Secretary,[44] the Chairman of the GEC, and the Secretary of the Education Committee (John Price). Topham comments on the process: 'Initially these were sent directly to the student, but John Price soon realised that the incentive of the "piece of paper" would be enhanced by more public acknowledgement and he then sent the certificate to the branch secretary for a presentation ceremony at a branch meeting'.[45] The Education Committee considered all awards of certificates very strictly, and often refused to award. When a certificate of distinction was introduced, the committee was even more strict, only awarding very rarely, and having no compunction in telling students that they had not achieved the standard.

Soon after the introduction of the new scheme, the question arose that future candidates for official positions in the union should be required to produce certificates awarded to them under the scheme as evidence of their suitability for employment. This issue came up before the GEC, who were of the opinion that it would be inadvisable to accept such evidence on the grounds that the certificates would only testify that the holders had satisfactorily completed the course 'and it would not follow that they possessed all the other qualifications required for an official appointment'.[46] It was, however, accepted from the start that members who had taken the course would be given preference in the award of scholarships and grants for correspondence courses, weekend and summer schools and courses at residential colleges.

LAUNCHING THE SCHEME

In the winter and spring of 1938-39, and in particular in the run-up to the BDC, the union set about promoting the new scheme. Whilst opening the new TGWU office in Oxford in July 1938, Bevin referred to the decision of the union to expand education for its members. He said he was anxious that the rank-and-file should have the fullest possible knowledge of the structure and administration of the union. Such a knowledge was necessary for the leadership of the future:

> We must have a union of men and women who are not only critics but who are constructive and have a wide knowledge and understanding of the problems to be dealt with.[47]

He announced to the GEC in May 1939:

> I regard this publication as one of the best things we have done in the union, and I would ask, therefore, that you make it a special feature in your report to the area committees, and also in any addresses given to branches.[48]

In typical lofty style, Bevin also managed to link the introduction of the new scheme, the threat of war, and the progressive nature of the Labour Movement in one sweeping paragraph:

> I hope that the education scheme now being established will enable more members to become propagandists. We have nothing to apologise for. Never in the history of the world has any movement either rendered such service, given such detailed attention or contributed greater effort to the social progress of the people than we are doing day by day. And it must also be remembered that we are carrying this work on when the powers that be throughout the world seem to have made a dead set against social progress by diverting the energies of humanity into the arms of war and conflict, and yet somehow I have a feeling that rising up against them there is an indefinable moral power which, in the end, will overthrow reaction.[49]

Also in May 1939, *The Record* featured the correspondence course in a leading article which had Bevin's fingerprints firmly on it:

> In preparing a course and offering it free of charge to members the union has rendered a service of inestimable value. It has brought within the reach of all members the means of acquiring that wider knowledge of the union that is vitally necessary if those whose destiny it is to wage the struggle of their own day and generation are to do so intelligently and in an organised manner ... It is essential if orderly progress is to be maintained they should be supported by a membership not only well-informed and intelligent but with a full sense of their duties as trade unionists ... The course offers them an opportunity of equipping themselves with a sound knowledge of the union, its history, structure, machinery, services, problems and the part it plays in the wages and conditions in the various industries it covers ...
>
> They will become educated trade unionists proud of their class and jealous of the great democratic traditions of labour organisations. They will take a keener interest in what goes on around them, and will be able to appreciate the significance to themselves of economic changes and

> events. They will be better equipped to understand the present, forecast the future and determine policy. They will go forward strengthened by the confidence and courage that enlightenment brings, deeply conscious the while of their own responsibilities and duties in the age-long struggle of their class for the right to live.[50]

The climax of the launch of the new scheme was the BDC, in the first week of July 1939. There were other resolutions on the agenda dealing with education, in particular once again the call for full affiliation to the NCLC and the paying of expenses and costs to TGWU students attending courses. All of these resolutions were lost, and the real focus of the conference was on the new correspondence course, support for which was carried unanimously. Bevin himself opened the debate. He first of all followed his familiar theme of change in industry and its effect on the character of the union:

> We have got to create in a union like this a great bulwark of understanding in order that at all times we will have key men [sic] who understand our principles, our policy and responsibility and duties in order to guide the rest of our fellows. Then we think there ought to be a greater knowledge of the union at work.[51]

After complimenting John Price, Ellen McCullough and Alf Chandler, Bevin then introduced John Price as the seconder, to make his only appearance before a BDC to describe the details of the new scheme. John Price duly outlined a brief history, claiming that as far as he knew, the scheme was unique. He also made the point that one of the reasons the scheme was narrowly focused on the union was that he did not want to cut across the existing provision of the WEA and NCLC, whilst at the same time linking the union to the wider community. He reminded the delegates that the correspondence course was only a first step, and that the plan was to extend it into union-only classes. He made it clear that this was an activity to be encouraged, and that 'there is no objection whatever to members taking the course, meeting together, discussing their work and then going home to prepare their work themselves, but we are not in a position at the moment to provide facilities for group leaders and class tutors'.[52]

In the following debate, the Chairman could see that there was such overwhelming support that he had to ask explicitly for any speakers against.

The debate was summed up, in typical style, by Bevin:

> There is another thing in this book that I would say to you – you do not want to be hewers of wood and drawers of water all the time. We must train men to take their place on governing authorities as they are created

> for the purpose of management, and in this series there will be a development. We will be able to train a wider number for serving on bodies as the state develops, to take their place in actual management, and that is very vital, because it is not any good calling for workers' control unless you train your men to control when you have got the power.[53]

The proposal was carried unanimously, and the GEC was requested to arrange for the scheme to be introduced 'forthwith'. The initial order for the course books was for 10,000 sets, and during the summer of 1939 application cards were sent out to branch secretaries, shop stewards and officers. A letter was also sent from the General Secretary to each officer and member of staff individually, and a further letter was sent to area secretaries asking them to handle officer and staff applications as well as those from lay members. As war approached, the applications began to flood into Central Office.

THE EDUCATION COMMITTEE

As an administrative adjunct to the new education scheme, Bevin wanted to establish an Education Committee of the GEC to oversee the new developments, make recommendations as to the certification or otherwise of students, and to generally be a focus for issues of budget and education content. The GEC agreed to this in February 1939, and that GEC members G. Edwards, F.T. Hobbs and H.J. Smith, together with the Council Chairman, should constitute the committee. The establishment of the new committee was to be timed with the launch of the new scheme.[54]

The first meeting of the TGWU Education Committee was held at 3:00pm on 3 May, 1939, with three Executive members including the Chair, John Price as Secretary and Alf Chandler, the Minutes Secretary, in attendance.[55] The Committee listened to a report from John Price on the education programme. He outlined the facilities offered by the union under the old scheme, setting out the principles for delivering 'non-vocational educational activities' and the means by which the union's education expenditure was spread as thinly as possible amongst the members and the external education providers. The Committee then received a progress report on the arrangements for the new scheme, and statistical information on the number of places awarded to WEA and NCLC courses. It also received reports on TGWU students at Ruskin College and from the students attending the ILO summer school in 1938. Thus the constitution and working practice of the TGWU Education Committee was established at the outset, and in essence remains the same today.[56]

In the 1930s, with life once more beginning to stir in the body politic, with industrial change transforming the nature of work and the economy, and with the rise of Fascism and Communism presenting a fundamental threat to his most cherished political structures and beliefs, Bevin saw that he would need to use education to strengthen what he thought of as the centre-ground inside the union and in the wider society. In the space of three years, the union had laid the foundation for a transformation of its education provision, from a drifting, almost reluctant programme dependent on outside agencies, to an innovative, dynamic system with new vision and purpose, which was to become much more integrated into the union's central objectives. It had also moved away from a scheme entirely focused on the individual, into one which at least created the potential for collective education provision, and increased yet again the specialisation of the programme. With the establishment of the Education and Research Department and the creation of the GEC Education Committee, it had created a supervisory and administrative system which maintained close control, but also provided a forum where new ideas could be discussed and laid before the full GEC. The outbreak of war threatened to stifle the new system at birth, but, as we shall see, the massive release of wartime energy also provided the conditions for one of the most heroic periods of TGWU education.

NOTES

1. See K. Fuller, *Radical Aristocrats*, London: Lawrence and Wishart 1985.
2. General Secretary's Quarterly Report, 23 May 1933, p144.
3. Ibid.
4. General Secretary's Report, August 1935, p225.
5. Annual Report on the Union's Educational Scheme, 1930, p2.
6. Minutes of the GEC, 26 May 1930, Minute No 369, p96.
7. Annual Report on the Union's Educational Scheme, 1932, p1.
8. Minutes of the GEC, 18 February 1930, Minute No 140.
9. Annual Report on the Union's Educational Scheme, 1934, p1, £649 is £20,000 at today's values.
10. 1935 BDC, Minute No 21, p14.
11. BDC Verbatim Report, 2 July 1935, p169.
12. In reality, had the union entered negotiations with the NCLC or WEA on a full affiliation, negotiations would no doubt have resulted in a substantially smaller sum.
13. Ibid., p172.
14. *The Record*, February 1937, p182.
15. 'The Future of Our Union', *The Record*, February 1937, p183.
16. As collected in the Modern Records Centre, University of Warwick.
17. Interview with Jack Jones, 27 May 1998.
18. T. Topham, 'Education Policy in the Transport and General Workers Union, 1922 to 1944: A Tribute to John Price', *The Industrial Tutor*, Volume 5, No 5, Spring 1992, pp51-52.
19. Ibid.
20. Ibid.
21. F. Williams, *Ernest Bevin*, op. cit., p 217.
22. When the Fascists seized power in Austria in 1934 he spent five weeks there organising relief work and legal aid. At the start of the Spanish Civil

War in 1936 he was a member of a delegation from the L.S.I, which went to Spain to form the Spanish Committee of the International Solidarity Fund. During his ILO years, Price had a major dispute with the American General Secretary of the ILO for producing a report on Soviet trade unions which was balanced and which emphasised the virtues as well as the vices of Soviet trade unions, much to the anger of the 'Cold Warriors'.
23. *The Record,* October 1943, p86.
24. *The Record,* March 1928, p235.
25. General Secretary's Report, March 1937, p88.
26. Minutes of the GEC, Minute No 159, 3 March 1937, p53.
27. Ibid., Minute No 414, 2 June 1937, p148.
28. BDC 1937, Minute No 72, p 36 'Education'.
29. Ibid.
30. Ibid.
31. Ibid.
32. Minutes of the GEC, Minute No 717, 18 August 1937, p263.
33. Topham 1992, op. cit., p54.
34. 'Note of Interview between the General Secretary, Assistant GS and John Price on the education scheme', 7 March 1939, Bevin Papers, Modern Records Centre, University of Warwick.
35. General Secretary's Report, December 1937, p387.
36. General Secretary's Report, 27 May 1938, p200
37. General Secretary's Report, August 1938, p302.
38. Minutes of the GEC, 16 August 1938, p278.
39. General Secretary's Report, March 1939, p125.
40. *The Union, Its Work and Problems*, TGWU, 1939.
41. Ibid., pp1-2. At the front of the book the union listed the contributors as: Bevin, Arthur Deakin, Stanley Hurst, (Financial Secretary), P Akroyd, (National Officer, ACTS), Alf Chandler, Harold Clay, Jack Corrin, (National Secretary Commercial Services), Andrew Dalgleish, (National Secretary, Metal and Chemicals), Jack Gill, (Editor of *The Record)*, Tom Hodgson, (National Officer, Flour Milling), D. Melford, (National Secretary, Docks), Bill P., (Manager, National Health Insurance Department), Leslie Pearmaine, (National Secretary, General Workers), Tom Pugh, (National Officer, Building), John Price, and Frank Stillwell, (Secretary of the Legal Department). It was indicated that the book was compiled by Price, Chandler, and Miss Ivy Saunders, (Secretary to Bevin).
42. Topham, 1992, op. cit., p55.
43. It is worth noting that the course was 'marked' as in schools at that time, with grades and comments. At one time, several staff were employed full time on marking the scripts.
44. In practice, they were actually signed by the Acting GS, Arthur Deakin, once Bevin had joined the government.
45. Topham, 1992, op. cit., p55.
46. Minutes of the GEC, 28 May 1940, Minute No 514, p 152.
47. *The Record*, July 1938, p313.
48. General Secretary's Report, 15 May 1939, p234.
49. Ibid., p235.
50. Leading Article 'Our Point of View', *The Record*, May 1939, p274.
51. Ibid.

52. Ibid.
53. Ibid., p175.
54. Minutes of the GEC, Minute No 231, 28 February 1939.
55. In August, the full GEC endorsed the addition of Price, Chandler and Miss Saunders to the Committee 'in order to combine the administration of the Education Scheme on the Executive side', Minutes of the GEC, 15 August 1939, Minute No 870, p316.
56. In 2000 the Education and International Committees were merged to become the GEC Education and International Committee.

Chapter 3

TGWU Education in Wartime 1939-1945

This chapter looks at the influence of the war years on TGWU education – and also at the influence of the union on the war itself. Bevin, of course, became the dominant figure on the Home Front, and promoted his own ideas and those of individuals, such as John Price, who shared them. Price's book Labour in the War *was very influential in the debate over war aims, and Price himself moved away from the union towards the ILO in this period. Despite the war situation, the Home Study course flourished, and the provision of union-only day schools rose to a peak in 1945. The unionisation of women was also strengthened in the war years, and a new generation of local leaders, typified by Jack Jones in Coventry, began to use trade union education in new ways linked to workplace organisation and the increasingly important role being played by shop stewards.*

The August 1939 meeting of the Education Committee, held only four weeks before the outbreak of war, noted that 1,907 applications had been received for the correspondence course thus far.[1] When war was declared on 3 September, enrolments were still being registered in large numbers. As late as November 1939, *The Record* commented that there had been a 'magnificent response' to the home study scheme. Nevertheless, in September, in response to the war situation, the GEC took the decision to suspend the new course with 'a review in the light of the circumstances prevailing, with a view to deciding the date of re-introduction'.[2] However, as the 'Phoney War' progressed, and neither invasion nor mass air attack materialised, the decision to suspend was reversed. In November, Bevin announced to the GEC that the scheme would be resumed 'and the indications are that the majority of the members who enrolled will continue the course, the main exceptions being those who have been called up for service'.[3] By this time there were 2,277 applications for the course and 1,607 enrolments. The largest by far were from Area 1 (London) and Area 6 (Northwest), and from Passenger and General Workers.[4]

It was during the winter and summer of 1940, when the war really got underway, that its effects began to be felt. A large number of the original applicants had to withdraw and many others who enrolled later were obliged to drop out because of National Service, overtime, or increased work for the union. Later, when the air raids began, study became more difficult still. The pressure began to show early in 1940, and by February of that year, of the 1,875 students who originally enrolled approximately 1,045 had withdrawn or were more than three months late with their written work. Of these, 114 were compelled to withdraw because of the claims of National Service, and 212 for other reasons. The remaining 719 did not reply to letters from the union asking about their situation.[5]

In March 1940, a resolution was sent to the GEC from the 1/617 Dover branch requesting the suspension of the correspondence course on the grounds that it was the wrong time to commit the expenditure involved and that many members who had previously decided to take the course now found they were unable to do so. However, the GEC also received many letters of appreciation from members who had completed the course, and the union was also aware that approximately 1,000 members were at present taking the course. On this basis, the GEC resolved that to act on the request made in the branch resolution would be 'rendering a disservice to the membership'.[6] In spite of all these difficulties, over 200 members went through the course by the end of December 1940. Under the scheme for the award of certificates to members who completed an additional paper, 31 certificates were awarded up to December 1940. Also in 1940, 99 members of staff and 44 officers enrolled on the correspondence course. However, 91 staff members withdrew for reasons connected with National Service and 12 officers withdrew owing to pressure of union work.

The Education Committee continued to insist on a high standard of work, and it was not until March 1941 that the first certificate 'With Distinction' was awarded, to Brother G.E. Thomas of 4/172 branch (Islwyn Borough Council bus transport). As this was the first such award, it was agreed by the GEC 'that in addition to the certificate, the member should be presented with a suitable book bearing the signatures of the Chairman of the Council and the Acting General Secretary'.[7] In order to appreciate the stringent approach of the Committee, it is worth noting that at their March 1941 meeting the Committee awarded 'Satisfactory' certificates to two members who had completed the course, but six other applications were rejected, as also were two second applications from members who had previously competed for certificates without success. There were also three applications from members who had already received the ordinary certificate and who wished to be considered for the certificate 'With Distinction'. In none of these cases did the Committee feel it was able to make the higher award. By the middle of 1941, 34 'Satisfactory' and one 'Distinction' certificates were awarded. The first member of the union's staff to receive a certificate 'With Distinction' – and the youngest so far – was Miss Doreen Searle of 1/494 branch (East Anglia) in October 1940, and the GEC 'noted with satisfaction the award of a certificate to this member of the staff'.[8]

Throughout 1941, about 250 students took the course, and in November the union agreed that it would accept the cost of correspondence courses for servicemen and women who had been 'good members of the union prior to entering the armed forces'.[9] By April 1942, the union had received 3,314 applications, 2,598 enrolment forms and received 3,348 essays. A notable completion in 1942 was Brother R.J. (Ray) Padley of 1/128 (Central Office) branch who became Deputy Head of Research in later years.[10] In 1943, there was an increase in the number of enrolments for the course, which passed the 400 mark. Over 4,000 essays had been assessed, and 400 students had completed. At their meeting on 10 February the Education Committee issued the sixth certificate 'With Distinction'.[11] By October 1944, there were 337 students engaged on the course, 532 had completed since the start, and by December 1944, 83 'Satisfactory" certificates were awarded while 8 members had obtained an award 'With Distinction'. Six thousand essays had been received.[12] During that year E.G. (Ernie) Allen of branch 2/121 completed the course and later became Regional Secretary of Region 2. The first quarter of 1945 brought a large increase in the enrolment for all types of courses. The enrolments for Ruskin College and the NCLC were the highest ever reached in a single quarter; 361 essays were received during the quarter, the largest figure since its inception.[13] By August 1945, 600 students had completed the course.[14]

Given the particularly difficult circumstances of its birth, the correspondence course maintained itself reasonably well during the war years, and established itself as a central feature of TGWU education throughout the years to come. At this particular time, however, the union was caught between the need to deliver the course, which had been heavily promoted and which was, after all, the centrepiece of the new education scheme, and the vital and immediate need to respond to the war situation. There is no doubt that an evaluation of the course from this distance in time would judge it to have been an excellent idea and a successful initiative by Bevin and John Price. In modern terms, it was bookish and lacking in stimulating and interactive learning devices, and in essence amounted to a book about the union which the student had to read, digest and then regurgitate in question and answer and essay form. However, when one considers the later editions of this course, including the current one, the format is not substantially different. Indeed, for the individual learning-based correspondence course, it is difficult to escape from this model. The really radical innovations came with the development of dedicated TGWU courses using active learning methods and linked to the core objectives of the union, especially the development of shop stewards and safety representatives. These were to be introduced in later years, but in the TGWU it was the correspondence course which opened the door for the union one-day and weekend school, and without this course, these may not have developed, or developed at a later date or in a different way.

THE UNION AND THE WAR

Everything changed for Bevin and John Price in the summer of 1940, when Bevin joined Churchill's War Cabinet, never to return to the union. On 13 May, Bevin discussed with the GEC the invitation for him to join the government, and received their full endorsement.[15] He was also determined to find a use for John Price in the war effort, and set him to work in making contact with trade union victims of the Nazi regime throughout Europe, work which was to lay the foundation of his subsequent resumption of international work at the ILO. Bevin also encouraged Price to develop a positive role for the trade unions in the struggle against Fascism, at a time when many Communists were torn between their natural hatred of Fascism and supporting the Soviet alliance with Germany. John Price began work immediately on a book, *Labour in the War*, which was published by Penguin in November 1940, with an introduction by Bevin. This book achieved wide circulation and is still referred to in the histories of the time.

Price sought to place the trade unions at centre stage in the struggle to defend democracy:

> The unions, in common with many other organisations, represent the idea of the value of human personality as against the totalitarian theory that the individual exists for the state. On this question the long tradition of the unions in the struggle for decent conditions of labour, for improved standards of living and for a higher degree of education and culture; their benevolent activities; their Socialist philosophy; and the idealism which has inspired them in their efforts, leave no room for doubt.[16]

Not only did he firmly place the unions in the vanguard of the struggle, but he went far beyond a defensive nationalist position, setting out ideas which were extremely advanced for 1940, so early in the war:

> One thing is clear, organised labour is not fighting to restore things as they were before the war. There is a widespread feeling in the country that many of the changes introduced during the war have got to stay. After the war organised labour will expect to see the country's industry and system of government adapted for the purpose of promoting the well being of the people. They will remember that this was a war for

> democracy and liberty against dictatorship and repression. But democracy implies something more than the enjoyment of political rights; there must be industrial and social democracy before a state can be truly democratic. And liberty does not mean only physical liberty – such as freedom of movement, freedom of organisation, freedom of assembly. Nor does it end with liberty of the mind – freedom of thought, freedom of conscience, freedom of expression. It presupposes equality of opportunity, without which true liberty is unattainable.[17]

He also gave a hint of his future interest, and his essentially internationalist perspective, with the comment that 'when peace returns, there will need to be more co-operation and understanding between nations',[18] and set out a perspective in which the future United Nations and ILO fitted perfectly. This book was no apology for the British Establishment, but one which sought to turn the energy released by the war situation into a progressive agenda, and to make demands on the ruling class for progressive change which transcended limited war aims. In this regard, John Price's work mirrors that of Tom Wintringham, who not only trained Local Defence Volunteers in guerrilla warfare at Osterley Park, but also developed a theoretical perspective on why the Left should unambiguously support the war.[19] As Topham comments,

> John Price's book reflects that mood, and advances those demands, not in a spirit of flag-waving patriotism, but as an expression of working-class aspiration to take a large grip on power – power to combat Fascism, the enemy of trade unionism. He makes a root-and-branch attack on appeasement and the Chamberlain government, and contrasts its pusillanimous conduct in the first eight months of the war, with trade union commitment to victory ... credit should be accorded to at least the largest trade union in expressing, quite publicly, a radical version of 'contract', which embodied from the start the concept of redistribution – not only of income and wealth, but of power.[20]

The book achieved a wide circulation in the country and abroad, but within the union Price sought to promote these ideas through special articles in *The Record* in the summer of 1941. The articles were entitled 'Wartime Opportunities' and 'The Wider Aims of Trade Unionism'. The first, in March, tried to make TGWU members see that the war gave them new opportunities to realise their long-term aims: 'We have said that the workers' trade unions are entitled to a recognised place in the social system. We have tried to show that, both in war and peace, the unions have positive and constructive functions to perform, not only for their own immediate members but also for the community. Now is our opportunity to show that these contentions have been justified'.[21] The article went on to advertise the union's education programme as a key way of preparing to exercise this new-found influence and responsibility. Older union members were targeted, as well as the young or inexperienced. 'It is precisely the active members, dealing with problems and making decisions day by day, who would benefit by the additional power and capacity that come from wide reading and disciplined thoughts. Common sense is not enough'.[22]

As well as promoting these ideas in books, speeches and articles, John Price also secured agreement to launch a special correspondence course, called *The Union and The War*. This idea was first raised at the Education Committee in July 1940, in response to a report that registrations on the regular course had declined to 481.[23] In August 1940, Price reported to the GEC that there had been a decline in the number of students enrolling for the regular correspondence course and suggested that they consider the possibility of introducing a supplementary correspondence course relating to the work of the trade unions in wartime with particular reference to the activities of the TGWU.[24] The original intention was to cover the trade union movement as a whole, but this was rejected on the grounds that it would cut across the work of the WEA and NCLC.

The draft syllabus had been approved in principle by the Education Committee and was adopted by the GEC. This supplementary correspondence course was in two sections, each based on a period of three month's study. Part 1 of the first section examined the position built up by the trade union movement before the outbreak of the war, with special reference to the period since 1914. The rationale for this, according to John Price, was that 'it is easier to understand the position of the union during the present war if we bear in mind the general lines of trade union development before the war and the decisions that were taken during the last year or two before the war broke out'.[25] Part 2 described how war affected trade union work and indicated the problems with which the union was confronted when war seemed to be imminent. Part 3 outlined the trade union attitude towards the war and discussed the policy which the Movement was pursuing. The second section of the course examined the effects of war on such questions as working conditions, wages and the cost of living. The next part of this section looked at the wartime Acts of Parliament, orders and regulations affecting industry and labour, while the final part was concerned with the principal boards and the councils and committees established to deal with wartime industrial and social problems.

It can be deduced even from this brief description that there was not much chance of the course taking off, as the main attraction of the normal course was to provide activists and members with an understanding of the union and some support for carrying out their union roles. This course was more concerned with political and organisational issues in the war, and leaving aside those who would have preferred to read Price's book *Labour in the War*, there was no real pay-off for the prospective student. Indeed, the course never succeeded in attracting a significant number of students. It was introduced on 17 October 1940, with a fanfare from *The Record,* which described it as being 'a document of great historical value'.[26] In the first 11 weeks, 43 applications were received and 39 students registered. However, there were only 37 students working on the course by the end of January 1941. By April 1942, there were only 28 students and only 3 enrolments were received during the quarter. At its meeting in February 1942 the Education Committee expressed its satisfaction with progress in relation to the general course, but 'noted with regret the limited interest being displayed in the supplementary course *The Union and the War*'.[27] By mid-1944 only 13 students had completed the first section and 21 had completed both sections. By November 1944 the union had to face the facts, and at the Education Committee meeting in that month there was a discussion about how the union might end the course.[28] It was also discovered that almost all those who were following the course had already completed the regular correspondence course.[29] At the end of 1944 *The Record* advised the membership that no new entrants were required for the course, and it was quietly terminated.

Evaluating *The Union and the War* with the benefit of hindsight, we can see that a separate course was unnecessary, and that union members were gaining strength through their involvement in Joint Production Committees and from the rise in membership full employment, a supportive government in which Bevin played the key role, and the spirit of confidence and militancy which grew in wartime and reached a climax in the election of 1945.[30] However, in the days of 1940, even with the lifting of an immediate threat of invasion, not only was the nation's survival threatened, but there was a real fear that Fascism had won the battle of ideas and for non-Communists – like Bevin, Deakin and John Price – there was a desperate need for a set of progressive war aims. In the armed forces, the need to identify such war aims was the main reason for the military establishment's agreement to the *ABCA* scheme of mass political education, which made its contribution to the radicalisation of the army.[31] In adult education generally, concern was being expressed, for example by Michael Stuart:

> Looking across Europe, we saw one dictator after another using the schools to promote belief in tyranny, militarism, racialism, blood and iron. Were the democracies to be held back by a dread of indoctrination from doing anything to promote a belief in their own values?[32]

John Price's book and *The Union and the War* were part of the TGWU's contribution to meeting this need in the early war years. The course did not succeed because, as Price himself saw at the time, the main demand for TGWU activists was to build their knowledge of their own organisation and increase their involvement, skills and confidence that way. With typical insight and honesty, he informed the Education Committee as early as 1942 that the experience of the WEA and NCLC with such schemes was very similar, and 'it could only be assumed, therefore, that a great majority of the workers who are educationally interested were more concerned in securing a knowledge of the development of the Movement and its basic problems in the industrial and political world'.[33] Whilst the mainstream correspondence course flourished, *The Union and the War* did not as expected last for the duration of the war, and made little impact on TGWU education at any time and certainly not beyond 1941.

STUDY GROUPS AND DAY-SCHOOLS

It had always been Bevin's intention to accompany the correspondence course with informal study groups (or 'study circles' as they would now be called), and with union day-schools. No real thought had been given to linking these into a system of education as we would understand it, nor to the syllabus or purpose of the day-schools. Much of this was unknown territory, as the benchmark was the type of weekend school run by the WEA or NCLC. There were three types of local TGWU schools in the early years. One was used by innovators like Jack Jones, District Officer in Coventry since August 1939, and Tom Wylie, his equivalent in Birmingham, as a basis for the local organisation and development of shop stewards in their districts; the next was usually based around a single branch and linked to the correspondence course, (the 'study group'); and the third was the series of nationally-sponsored day schools, which were organised by John Price and would nowadays be more likely to be referred to as a 'road show', with Price and senior officials appearing in the localities as if on a lecture-tour, as often as not with the area secretary in the chair. These schools developed because they were always intended to be a part of the revived union education programme which had the correspondence course as its core. In the turbulent war years, these schools were able to mirror the growth of membership and the upsurge of energy created under wartime conditions. The instant success of these schools was naturally welcomed by Price, Bevin, and Deakin, but their first responses indicate also a relief that the experiment or 'risk' (the word actually used) had paid off.

The first of the union's own day-schools was held on Saturday, 20 January 1940, at the Ambassadors Hotel, Upper Woburn Place, London.[34] The school was opened by Arthur Deakin, Assistant General Secretary, and the lecturers were John Price, who spoke on Trade Unions and Legislation, and Harold Clay, whose subject was Industrial Relations and Negotiations. A large number of students applied for the event, and it was decided to limit the number to 50 and to hold another school at the same hotel on 11 February for those who were unable to attend the first school. The students came from all sections of the union and included a few women workers.

The reporter (probably W.G. Glazebrook) was thrilled with the occasion: 'If anyone had prophesied in those far-off days that some day a union will arise that will hold a school for the education of its members in a London hotel we should have probably replied that, cheerful optimists as we were, such a prophesy was a poor joke'.[35] John Price's session looked at the political action of trade unions in the days before the Labour Party and direct representation in Parliament, and explained how the political work of the unions was carried on within the Party. 'In conclusion he stressed the fact that but for the watchfulness of the unions, much of the legislation they had initiated would be a dead letter. They and their members had to act as an unofficial inspectorate in order to hold what had been won'. The reporter commented that: 'Brother Price handled a difficult subject with masterly ease, and although his lecture took more than an hour to deliver, he was followed throughout with keen interest. At the end he answered a large number of questions'.[36] Harold Clay's lecture traced the industrial relationship between employer and worker from the days of individual bargaining to collective bargaining, and also dealt with the techniques of negotiation. Clay also spoke for over an hour.

This first day-school was welcomed with rapture in the pages of *The Record*, and was given a leading article to itself. The success of the school was said to prove beyond all doubt that an urgent need had been satisfied, and *The Record* argued that in the trade union movement as a whole such events 'will give new hope and courage to those who sometimes express doubts about the willingness of the workers to learn more about the Trade Union Movement and to fight for its preservation'.

The next school took place on Saturday, 30 March 1940, at the Grand Hotel, Hanley. On this occasion collaboration between the union and the WETUC created a 'TGWU school within a [WEA] school'. Seventy Stoke-on-Trent TGWU members attended, and the rest were drawn from miners, potters, railway clerks, printers, iron workers and other trade unionists. In August 1940 a school was held in Wrexham. The lecturers were again Harold Clay and John Price, and by this time Price had changed the focus of the schools to concentrate on Trade Unionism and the War. During the summer of 1940, Jack Jones had requested a school to be held in Coventry, as part of his strategy of developing a shop stewards' organisation in the city. However, because of the massive Luftwaffe air raid on 14 November, the day-school had to be postponed, and eventually took place on 21 June 1941. The school was attended by 50 members of the union in the Coventry District, with the area secretary in the chair and Harold Clay (by now the Acting Assistant General Secretary) and Andrew Dalgleish (Metal and Engineering National Secretary) as tutors. The link with Jack Jones's organising drive can be seen in the invitation to Dalgleish to act as a tutor, and during the questions it was pointed out by a woman delegate that over 1,000 women engineering workers in Coventry had joined the union in the six weeks leading up to the school.[37]

Union day-schools continued on an 'as and when' basis throughout 1941 and 1942. Thirty-five people attended a school in Stockton on 14 June 1941, and a one-day school was held in Bath on 3 October, with John Price and Jack Donovan, National Docks Group Secretary; 35 people attended. The first school in Scotland was held in Glasgow on 24 October 1942, with Arthur Deakin and Harry 'H.J.' Edwards, Chairman of the GEC, with the area secretary presiding over 57 students. A Birmingham school was held on 28 November where Harold Clay lectured to 50 students, chaired by the area secretary.[38] From August to October 1943, venues included Maidstone, Bangor, Sidcup, Gillingham, Nottingham, Tonbridge and London. At the Nottingham school on 26 September, John Price was the lecturer and the subjects were 'The Rights of Trade Union Membership' and 'Should Workers Control Industry?' The first school to take place in London after the Blitz of 1940 was held on 10 April 1943 at the Shaftesbury Hotel. Harold Clay and John Price were the lecturers and 102 students attended, but more than this number had to be refused.[39] Because of the demand, a further school had to be arranged for Saturday, 29 May with the same speakers, and 50 students turned up for this overspill school.[40] John Price returned to his birthplace at Newport, Monmouthshire, in December 1942 to give a lecture (presumably for the WEA), and as a result, a TGWU school, the first in Area 4, was held on 13 March 1943 with over 70 students in attendance. Arthur Deakin joined Price as co-tutor. John Price lectured on 'Today and Tomorrow', whilst Deakin talked on the subject of 'The Union Faces the War'.[41] The first ever Brighton school was held in the Royal Pavilion on 8 August 1943 with 'Jock' Tiffin (an Area 1 officer and future General Secretary) and John Price as the speakers; 200 people attended.[42]

By 1944, the success of the day-schools was obvious, and Deakin himself gave his personal support to their continuation:

> I am glad to note the gradual extension of the facilities for one-day schools. The desire for these schools is undoubtedly growing, and I am of the opinion that considerable value is accruing in consequence of the efforts we are making. The understanding of the work and problems of the union is increasing amongst those who are participating in this type of study.[43]

Deakin was a supporter of union education, and took part in these schools when he could.

As day-schools became an accepted part of union activity, experiments were attempted, often adopting the more modern approach of linking the school with real organising objectives. For example, on 2 December 1944, John Price and Ellen McCullough lectured at a one-day school organised at Edenbridge, Kent. This was a pioneer school, the bulk of the branches represented being those who had only begun to function since the outbreak of war. Many of the students came from rural areas and very few of them had had an opportunity of taking part in union education before. On 3 December an experimental one-day school for shop stewards in the building industry was held at the Bonnington Hotel, London.[44] By 1944, as victory was in sight, the focus of the schools changed again, mainly to include a discussion on the shape of the post-war world. Harold Clay conducted a one-day school in Bristol on 24 February, on the subject 'Trade Unionism and Working Class Standards in the War and After'. Another school was held in Maidstone on 11 February with the title 'Post-War Industry'.

The provision of day-schools reached a peak in 1945. By March of that year, 22 schools had been organised, including the first weekend school, which was held that year on 8 and 9 September, at Hardcastle Craggs near Halifax. The lecturers were a trade group secretary, a district officer, and Ellen McCullough. She was very enthusiastic about the week-end format in that on a weekend school students had the opportunity of informal discussions as well as formal lectures.[45]

Other experiments were attempted; Area 1 organised a school in Cambridge on a weekend in June 1945, with two schools together, one for building trade workers and the second for members of the agricultural section. Another school was held for agricultural workers at Belford, Northumberland on 12 May: 'It was, however, so successful that the members have asked for another when the harvest is over'.[46] Twenty members attended this school, and union officers acted as tutors. A school held in Middlesbrough in April had the area secretary and Ellen McCullough in charge of 50 students with the Chairman of the GEC, Harry Edwards, a Middlesbrough docker, in the chair. The first one-day school to be held in Area 2 took place in Portsmouth on 7 July 1945, led by the area secretary along with Ellen McCullough.[47] Jack Jones organised another school in Coventry, dealing particularly with problems connected with the Motor and Engineering Industry. The Passenger Group organised a special school on bus schedules. A school in Manchester was organised in June with Alf Chandler and the area organiser, and was led by E. Higgins, Secretary of the Chemical Group.

Towards the end of the war, the value of these schools was apparent to all. A month after the end of the war in Europe, Arthur Deakin formally recognised the transformed situation which the wartime education programme had brought the union. This wartime outburst of activity had completely transformed the nature of the union's education provision in only a few short years. From being the preserve of academics (no matter how well-intentioned), and political proselytes, and therefore easily seen as not central to its purpose, the union's education provision was moving ever closer to merging with its mainstream activities, and thereby achieving for itself a much more permanent and respected place, not least in the minds of those senior officers who acted as tutors, who could see for themselves both the hunger of the members for knowledge and involvement, and the positive results of their own endeavours in the education field. The day-schools were central to this change, as they provided a supportive environment where the members and the officials could interact. Looked at from this point of view, the main value of the correspondence course was to provide the mechanism for the organisation of the day-schools. Beyond the boundaries of the union's education programme, the day-schools and the correspondence courses were also the TGWU's contribution to the battle of ideas during the war, and the day-schools in particular made a significant contribution to the debate on war aims and the nature of the post-war settlement.

The study groups associated with the correspondence course were less significant, and had a different purpose, being essentially a part of the more formal education process, organised through the branch. By 1942, study groups had been formed in the 1/316, (SE London buses) 9/12 (Leeds City Transport) and 1/811 (Road Transport) branches. Two other groups were running, one in Area 8 and another one in Area 1 based around 'The Union and the War'.[48] These groups were given a boost in 1942 when the union produced a shortened, popular version of the correspondence course called 'Introducing the TGWU'. This provided a brief explanation of the union's background, organisation and purpose, and was another excellent John Price innovation. This had emerged from ideas raised by him in an attachment to the Education Committee on 5 February 1941, entitled *Some Ideas on Publicity*, which represented the most advanced thinking so far in the development of the TGWU education programme. In this paper, Price argued that the wartime shortage of paper and the difficulty of holding branch meetings meant that these were not the best ways of publicising education activities. He therefore looked at other means of publicising the courses and developing the programme, such as extending the role of full-time officers, who could be asked to recommend courses; membership cards could advertise courses; the rulebook could have an announcement on the back cover which at that time was blank, and so on. He also went on to suggest a new generation of explanatory publicity materials:

> Another method which is more elaborate but of permanent value would be the issue to new members of a short pamphlet and handbook giving, amongst other things, a brief statement of the principles and objectives

> of trade unions, an outline of the structure and working of this union, and an invitation to become better-acquainted with these through the medium of the education scheme.[49]

These ideas were welcomed by the Committee and by Arthur Deakin, and the first step was taken with the publication of a diagram of the union's structure in *The Record* of November 1941, which was very well received. It was recommended that readers cut out the page and a leaflet was produced and sent out to the branches. In June 1942, the GEC accepted *Introducing the TGWU*. The booklet, described in *The Record* as 'something new in trade union literature',[50] had a first edition of 20,000 copies and another 20,000 were printed almost immediately. There were 541 applications from branch officials for supplies, which resulted in a distribution of 18,891 copies and 425 individual applications for single copies. By the end of the war, over 43,000 of the booklets had been distributed. A special leaflet, *One in a Million,* was prepared for the BDC held on 16 October 1942; other leaflets were: *What is the TGWU?* and *Yes, but Why Should I Join?*

These materials were themselves used as the basis for 'study groups'. In Coventry, in 1942, 5/336 (City Council branch), and then other branches under Jack Jones's guidance, ran a series of lectures using the booklet as a basis.[51] Bro. Melton, the district officer for Halifax, also ran a discussion group based around the booklet. Compared with the demonstrative success of the day-schools, however, the study groups made no lasting impact on the union's education programme as a whole.

It is also worth noting that the involvement of TGWU students with the external educational bodies WETUC and NCLC continued throughout the war. TGWU students attended day classes, summer schools and university short courses as before, although the numbers attending summer schools were nowhere near those attending the union's own one-day schools, which were almost always held on a Saturday.

TGWU students attending external summer-schools, 1938-1944

Places	TUC	WETUC	NCLC
1938	7	41	9
1939	18	50	8
1940	10	20	2
1941	9	15	5
1942	16	16	12
1943	19	23	12
1944	18	59	11

Source: Acting Education Secretary's Report, 16 October 1944

Relationships with the external educational providers continued as before, with all the main participants in this story so far, Deakin, Clay, Creech-Jones, Ellen McCullough and John Price all sitting on the controlling councils of the WEA, WETUC and NCLC. For example, in the war years the WEA Central Executive Committee had Harold Clay as President, Creech-Jones as Vice-President, John Price until 31 October 1943, and Ellen McCullough from 1 November 1943. The WETUC had Harold Clay as Treasurer, Arthur Tiffin (AGS from 1948 and General Secretary in 1955), John Price (until 31 October 1943) and Ellen McCullough (from 1 November 1943). The NCLC Executive had John Price (until 31 October 1943) and Ellen McCullough (from 1 November 1943). Creech-Jones represented the union on the governing council of Ruskin College.

The union's educational expenditure appears to have been extremely small, but much of the central activity, especially the correspondence course and the day-schools, was hidden in the general cost of administration and salaries. The visible expenditure was calculated in terms of student grants, and in wartime these were inevitably reduced, so that it was not until the end of the war that the full amount of the grant was actually spent. The total amount expended in 1939 (to the nearest £[52]) was £1,293, with an unexpended balance of £643, and in 1940 only about one third of the grant of £1,250 was spent, leaving a cumulative balance of £1,504 unexpended. In 1945, £1,502 was spent during the year. This was an increase of £290 over the figure for 1944.[53] This was the first time since the outbreak of war that the grant had been almost used up with the balance being less than £40. The Education Committee decided, 'in view of the growing interest in the union's educational facilities', to recommend that the education grant should be increased to £2,000 for the year beginning in 1945.[54]

LOCAL INITIATIVES

Within the framework of a generally-expanding programme of day-schools, particular officers made a special commitment and attempted a systematic link between union organisation and union education. Foremost among these in this period were Jack Jones in Coventry, Tom Wylie in Birmingham, Harry White in Maidstone, and the officers associated with the Bristol Educational and Social Council. In Area 8, staff member Miss Grieve was commended by the GEC for her organising work in education, and referred to as the 'Area Education Agent'.[55]

The question of developing a systematic link between the Centre and the areas for organising and administering the education provision was first raised by John Price in his paper *Some Ideas on Publicity* in February 1941, and remained unresolved throughout the war and beyond. However, he also raised questions of strategy in this paper. He identified that the key to the future development would be the link between local organisation and the area structure of the union. He anticipated the need to focus the link between the education provision and local union development through a local education organiser:

> To all of these plans, the key lies in the areas. It is of little use to try, from the Centre, to impose tasks on a very loaded area machine, unless there exists both a wish to help and a reasonable opportunity to do so. To secure this it might be possible to have in each area some one person who would act as a link between this office and the area machinery, and who would (under the general direction of the area secretary) work out the details. It is not suggested, of course, that this should be a full-time job at present. Nor does it seem necessary for the person appointed to be an officer. In many areas there must be clerks who have the ability and the inclination to do this work, who may have had WEA or similar experience and who would, perhaps, welcome the chance to undertake duties of a non-routine character.[56]

Price's ideas were carried forward by the Education Committee, who reported to the GEC that their idea was for someone who would become 'virtually the education officer within the area'.[57] In response, Deakin undertook 'to discuss the development of an effective link between the Department and the areas at the next area secretaries' conference in order to create the right spirit'.[58] Arising from a discussion at this conference, held on 28 September 1941, arrangements were made for the necessary link between the areas and the Centre, with either an officer or senior member of the staff being appointed to act as the contact for education matters.[59] In some areas this was the area secretary himself, and the area secretaries resisted the creation of a specialised, dedicated official through this mechanism. In 1942 the Education Committee referred to the fact that 'correspondence has taken place with the area education correspondents regarding the possibility of one day schools'.[60] The title 'area education correspondents' was a compromise position following the refusal of the area secretaries to accept dedicated education officers. These correspondents would as often as not have been clerical assistants working for the area secretaries. Whilst supportive of the principle of union education, most area secretaries were reluctant to attach officer status to those organising education provision, fearing it would weaken their authority. Throughout the union's history, there have been area/regional secretaries who have adopted a suspicious and even hostile attitude towards education officers, as later chapters will show.[61]

During the first years of the war, the main drive at local level came from committed local district officials, who wanted to use education as a means of building the industrial base of the union. Foremost among these was Jack Jones. After he had been appointed Coventry District

Organiser in August 1939, he used his earlier experiences with education in Liverpool as a guide, and set about building the local organisation, using education in an instrumental and collective manner:

> We developed teach-ins and educational courses with maximum participation as a means of organising the motor industry, and a large part of the rest of Coventry's industry. We found that by involving the members as a whole, not only did we get strength, but we got an informed approach to industrial problems too. It was an important part of our success in keeping up war production through Coventry's terrible blitz. Moreover, it meant that groups of workers were always throwing up new lay negotiators out of their own ranks, men of considerable ability and intelligence who could perhaps never have been drawn out by the formal, individual methods of education, however well organised academically ... Real strength of trade union organisation lies in the stimulation of its active members that comes from contact and day-to-day collective activity with their mates.[62]

Jones used the union office as a local education centre to build out from the sparse TGWU organisation. He would use the 'Branch Nights', where union subscriptions were collected in pub rooms, to make contact with the shop stewards and to persuade them to accept some training. 'In those days the union office opened five-and-a-half days and on Saturday morning I used this for education sessions. At lunchtime we went to the pub and then to football'.[63] Sunday morning was also used for education and the sessions were led by Jack Jones himself and his other officers, George Massey and Harry Urwin. He also organised evening classes and invited people like factory inspectors and other officials to speak to the shop stewards. At that time the AEU was the leading union in Coventry, with the works convenor always being a skilled tool-room worker; therefore, education was very important in building the organisation of the TGWU where the membership was mainly amongst the unskilled workers. The main problem was that people did not know their industrial agreements, or how to negotiate, even though they now had the right to negotiate. Jack Jones would directly involve shop stewards in the negotiating process, normally led by himself, as part of building their education.[64]

By 1944 the education and organising system was well underway, meriting a special report in *The Record*. The report noted that three series of lectures and discussions were held during 1942 and 1943 and in the main they were enthusiastically supported.

> The first series was conducted entirely by Brother J.L. Jones (District Organiser) and included such subjects as *The History of the Trade Union Movement in the Engineering Industry, Trade Agreements and Working Conditions in the Engineering Industry, The Factory Acts,*

> *Workmen's Compensation* and the *Rules and Constitution of the TGWU*.[65]

As part of the educational work, a meeting was arranged for leading members and shop stewards to discuss post-war problems, with the address being given by Arthur Deakin. Regular one-day schools were held, and a trade union library was set up in the district office. As Jack Jones commented in later years: 'The union office became a workshop for the exchange of information and training of shop stewards'.[66] Jack Jones was to extend these ideas when he became Regional Secretary after the war.

Another midlands innovator was Tom Wylie, who had been appointed as an officer in the Birmingham District in 1941. He had already been involved with Fircroft College and the WEA when he was appointed, and was at the time the Vice-Chairman of the West Midlands District WEA, and also a member of the Divisional Committee of WETUC. Wylie used his position in the union to establish a comprehensive district education programme, although not with such a clear integration between education and industrial organisation as in Coventry. He would circulate all branches with news of local education events, and tried to establish linked programmes. For example, in co-operation with King's Norton District WEA, he taught a course on 'Trade Unions and Their Social Policy' between October to December, 1943, and between October and December 1944, a course on 'Full Employment'. All the students were shop stewards in the King's Norton area. He also organised regular day-schools, for example on 18 December 1943 in Worcester, on 'The Union and its Work'. On the 11 November 1944, in Birmingham, John Price lectured to 55 students on 'Labour is Not a Commodity' and 'Education For Democrats'. A winter class was held from December 1943 to March 1944 with 40 to 50 students discussing 'Shop Stewards and Their Problems'. The union's Education Committee appreciated the work of Area 5, and particularly the work of Tom Wylie, and in May 1945 they sent him a letter of commendation.[67] Wylie left the union in the mid-1950s, to move into education full-time at Birmingham Technical College.

As Area 1 Secretary, Charles Brandon was in a position to encourage education in the latter part of the war. He had been associated with the movement for independent working-class education in 1919, and kept his involvement with the WEA. He was a member of its Central Executive Committee, Finance and General Purposes Committee, a member of the Central EC of WETUC and Vice-Chairman of the London WEA. He was at one time a member of the University of London Extramural Board and served as Vice-Chairman. He was able to encourage local officers such as Harry White of Maidstone who arranged a series of schools in his district, the first being held on 6 October 1944. In the same month *The Record* published an article on education written by White called 'Use Your Loaf', arguing the case for involvement in education in modern terms:

> The power and influence of the Trade Union Movement depends upon the knowledge and intelligence of its members ... A good negotiator is not born; the ability to negotiate is acquired by training and study – by men and women who 'use their loaf'.[68]

Meanwhile, in Area 2, the Bristol Educational and Social Council continued its activities, and staged something of a revival during the war. In 1943 it arranged a six-lecture course using *The Union, its Work and Problems* as a syllabus. The lectures were given by area and national officials, including Arthur Deakin. The exercise was repeated in 1944, when the series was given the title *The Union Faces the Future*. The lecturers were Florence Hancock, Jack Donovan, Harry Nicholas, (future Deputy General Secretary), Bro. Burgess (the local official), John Price and Ellen McCullough. Deakin suggested that a library should be established in Bristol, and recommended that the GEC make a grant towards the cost.[69] Deakin himself contributed a number of books to the library, and arrangements were made to pass over books which were duplicated within the Central Office Education Department.

At the end of 1945 Deakin and the GEC tried to recommend the Bristol model, pointing to 'the valuable work being carried out in the field of Adult Education by the Bristol Educational and Social Council', and expressing the view that this example might be followed with advantage throughout the areas. This is perhaps a sign that John Price had now departed, for, worthy as the Bristol Council's work was, it was essentially an old-fashioned 'Liberal Adult Education' model, whereas the true innovation, recognised by Price but perhaps not by others, was the kind of work being organised by Jack Jones in Coventry.

TGWU WOMEN'S EDUCATION IN WARTIME

In 1939, the GEC decided to initiate a campaign for the organisation of women workers, including the transfer of Florence Hancock from Area 3 to Central Office.[70] Florence Hancock had joined the Workers' Union in 1913, and in 1917 she was appointed District Officer for Wiltshire and held that position until the amalgamation with the TGWU when she was appointed Women's Officer for Area 3. In November 1942 the GEC authorised the appointment of a National Women's Officer for service with the Metal, Engineering and Chemical Group and the General Workers Group and appointed Florence Hancock to the position.[71] Women in the union began to flex their muscles, and before the end of 1944, women convenors had been elected at GEC in Coventry, Rolls-Royce, Hillington, and at G & J Weir's in Glasgow.[72] Individual women like 29-year-old Mrs Sillett, featured in *The Record* in 1942, stood out:

> She had trained as a mechanic, and when she went into a garage on war-work she organised everyone there into the TGWU. She then organised several local building sites into a new branch of the union, of which she became the first branch secretary. As the local TGWU official remarked, not only was she an accomplished recruiter, but she had the advantage of being less likely to be called up for military service'.[73]

Innovators like Jack Jones took advantage of the reluctance of craft unions like to AEU to accept women into membership:

> In the early years of the war the TGWU in Coventry faced no opposition from other unions in the recruitment of female workers; other unions regarded their entry into the factories as temporary and AEU officials would be heard to say 'they'll be chucked out at the end of the war!'[74]

The rise in women's membership and involvement also influenced trade union education. The TUC began to hold women's schools, which some TGWU women members attended. By 1943 the union was looking at developing day schools for TGWU women, and in May Deakin reported to the Education Committee on the considerable development in the membership of the union amongst women and expressed the view that 'a useful purpose would be served by utilising the services of a National Women (sic) Officer from time to time in lecturing to one-day schools confined to women members'.[75] As a result, schools for women members only were organised in the summer of 1943. The first of these was held in Yeovil (Florence Hancock's old union base) on 17 July, with herself and John Price as the lecturers. Another was held in Birmingham on 24 July; this time, she joined Harold Clay as co-speaker.[76] At the Yeovil school there were 33 students employed in Engineering, Aircraft, Land Army, Laundries, Textile and Transport.[77] Another school was held in London in October.

In June 1943, the GEC agreed to call a special national delegate conference representative of the whole of the women membership. It was agreed that the conference should be held in London on 7 and 8 October 1943, and that there should be one delegate for each 1,000 women members within each area, making provision for a conference of approximately 300 delegates. This was the TGWU women members' first national delegate conference. Branches were invited to send in resolutions of a general character with special reference to women's problems.[78] One resolution carried by the conference was a request for the extension of schools for women under the union's education scheme.

All-women schools continued into 1944, and a meeting of women shop stewards and officers in the aircraft industry branches in

Rochester was held on 15 January 1944, addressed by Ellen McCullough.[79] There was a school in Yeovil on 24 June, and one at Liverpool on 22 July, and at the request of the area committee this was an all-women school.[80] Florence Hancock delivered a lecture on wartime legislation affecting women workers, and after it led a discussion on the subject. She also spoke of her experiences at the ILO.[81]

THE DEPARTURE OF JOHN PRICE

Bevin's decision to leave the union for government office had two major consequences for the TGWU education programme; the advent of Arthur Deakin, and the departure of John Price. Although he is looked on unkindly by posterity, being seen as a 'Cold Warrior' and contrasted unflatteringly with his successors Frank Cousins and Jack Jones, Deakin was a supporter of education, and knew enough about it to preside over the expansion and innovation of the war years. This is recognised by his biographer Vic Allen: 'In one important respect Arthur Deakin displayed administrative leadership ability. He encouraged and gave practical support to the provision of educational services in the union'.[82] With regard to the growth of the education programme during the war, Allen comments that 'the idea belonged to Bevin, not Deakin, but the fulfilment of the idea was Deakin's achievement'.[83]

Deakin had had an early interest in educational activities. He had been a prominent member of the Local Education Authority in Flintshire when he was an assistant district secretary. His appreciation of the union's own education provision was motivated, he said, by the poor quality of candidates for official jobs in the union whom he had interviewed for many years. Given his reputation, it is surprising to note the generous tone of these 1943 comments on the programme of day-schools:

> In my view the one-day schools which have been held have had the effect of creating a better outlook and standard amongst our members. I personally was particularly impressed with the zeal and desire of our womenfolk who have attended these schools to equip themselves for service with the union. It was really exhilarating to find this attitude of mind developing.[84]

A few months later, in 1944, he addressed a personal letter to every branch secretary, permanent official and member of the clerical staff, describing the education facilities, and made sure that 'arrangements are being made to ensure that all newly-elected or appointed officers and newly-appointed clerks shall be similarly informed'.[85]

The nature of the personal relationship between Deakin and John Price is unknown, although Deakin, as Assistant General Secretary, had worked with Price in 1937-39 to develop the correspondence course, and no doubt he was impressed with the work. He also placed no barriers in the way of John Price and the education programme when he became Acting General Secretary. Price, however, had a particularly close personal link with Bevin, and as soon as Bevin entered the government he began making use of Price in the war effort and as part of his plan to establish a post-war settlement on the twin foundations of the United Nations (underpinned by the US) and the tripartite International Labour Organisation, the ILO. Bevin saw John Price as 'his man' in the trade union aspect of this strategy. Since his first visit to the ILO in the late 1920s, Bevin had always been a strong supporter of the institution, which he considered as the instrument to promote the advance of commonly-accepted labour standards. During the 1930s, he gave encouragement to visits of TGWU officers and lay members to Geneva, and, according to Francis Williams, for Bevin the ILO 'was creative work which gave both his energy and his imagination a great deal to wrestle with, and there is little doubt that if war had been avoided – or for that matter Labour had not been returned to office after the war – he would dearly have liked the opportunity to become Director of the ILO'.[86]

In the midst of the war, it was not clear whether or not Bevin was to have the opportunity to direct the organisation in the future, but to have Price in place at the ILO would suit Bevin one way or the other. As Topham has pointed out, 'Bevin turned to John Price in 1943, quite clearly because he saw [the ILO] as central to the global post-war settlement, the equivalent on Labour's side to what would evolve, on the finance side, as the Bretton Woods Agreement. He wanted his man in place for that day'.[87]

Even as the Germans were attacking in the West and the Chamberlain government was crumbling, John Price was taking part in a Royal Institute of International Affairs study on the International Labour Movement. He was also invited to become part of a World Order Study Group set up at Chatham House, which became known as the 'Steering Committee on International Order'.[88] By July 1940, only two months after Bevin had joined the government, Price was reporting to the GEC his involvement with the International Transportworkers' Federation (ITF) and his work with the International Department at the Ministry of Economic Warfare, at that time the headquarters of the Special Operations Executive (SOE). This department, headed by Hugh Dalton, had the job of stimulating resistance in Europe, and Attlee argued that this was a task best accomplished 'from the Left'.[89] As the Nazis extended their control over more and more territory, international trade union bodies such as the ITF moved to London. In agreement with Bevin and Deakin, Price established relations with the BBC and the Ministry of Information, where he helped to arrange broadcasts specifically addressed to workers in Germany and the occupied countries, for example taking part in a special broadcast to French and German workers sent out by the BBC on May Day 1941. He became part of a small committee set up in Transport House which included representatives from the TUC and the Labour Party. Bevin also established an International Department at the Ministry of Labour under T.T. Scott who was formerly at the International Labour Office in Geneva. Price became part of this organisation, with its obvious link to the ILO.[90]

By the Autumn of 1940, Price was broadcasting to occupied Europe and the Commonwealth and promoting the ILO. Some of his comments were published in *The Record*:

> One of the things we wanted to secure from this war was social justice, the result we hoped to achieve after the last war. We built up the League of Nations and the ILO to help us get a just system of society, and although we were a long way off yet, we still have the machinery. The ILO was one of the few good things that had come out of the last war, and it had been planned while the war was still on.[91]

The TUC was providing material for these broadcasts, which were at that time being delivered twice a week. In September 1940, Price was asked by Hugh Dalton if he could act as a link between the minister and the trade union representatives from Germany and the occupied countries. With the support of Deakin, it was agreed that he should give half his time to this work, which he began to do from October.[92] One of his jobs was to maintain contact with exiled labour representatives from the occupied countries, and there was a clandestine element to some of his activities. The neutral countries were used as a meeting-place, and he visited Sweden and Finland during the summer of 1941, and Iceland in 1943, following which, for security reasons, he gave a verbal report to the GEC for which no minutes were taken.[93]

In 1941 the Labour Party established a committee to inquire into post-war reconstruction, and John Price was appointed to a sub-committee established to draw up proposals on international relationships.[94] He also attended the session of the Joint Maritime Commission of the ILO held in London from 26 to 30 June 1942 in the capacity of advisor.[95] Throughout 1942 he attended meetings of the council and various committees of the Royal Institute of International Affairs, and also presided at some of its mid-day meetings. The RIIA set up a committee to enquire into the problems of Anglo-French relations in the post-war period, and Price was invited to take part in this work.[96] He also represented the ITF on a joint council set up with the Miners' International and the IMF.[97]

In early 1943 the Director of the ILO came to London from Montreal for consultations, and Price met with him and some of the officials at the London office.[98] One of the issues discussed was the preparation of study materials and of other literature to encourage the study of ILO problems in the Labour Movement.

In July 1943, Deakin reported to the GEC that John Price had been approached by the ILO as to the possibility of obtaining leave of absence from the union for a period of two years. Deakin supported the suggestion and it was agreed by the GEC on the grounds that he should be entitled to return to the employment of the union at the expiration of the appointment.[99] It was agreed that there should be a grant of 12 months leave of absence, from 1 November 1943. The option of a further 12 months was granted, if necessary, in order to complete the special work undertaken on behalf of the ILO, and the condition was accepted that he could revert to his position as Secretary of the Department. Arrangements were made for Ellen McCullough, then Senior Clerk in the Department, to act as Secretary during Price's temporary absence. The last appearance of John Price before the Executive was 16 September 1943.[100] At the end of 1943, he went to the ILO headquarters in Montreal, then returned to London. The GEC meeting in October 1944 agreed to his request for a further 12 months leave,[101] and on 6 March 1945, Price tendered his resignation to the GEC by virtue of the fact that he had accepted the appointment of position of chief of the new Industrial Relations section of the ILO. The view of the GEC was that 'whilst the union would regret the loss of his services, it was clear that the appointment with the ILO would enable him to render a valuable service, not only to this union but to the wider movement, and the opportunity of continuing close contact and co-operation with the union'.[102]

His resignation was accepted 'with regret' with effect from 14 February 1945. In his article on Price, Topham comments that 'it was a very considerable wrench for John Price to agree to the move to the ILO'.[103] He also reported that Bill Simpson, former General Secretary of the British Foundry Workers Union and later Director of Industrial Relations at the ILO, observed that: 'It was a devil of a job to get you to join the ILO ... With such an attractive and promising career in the UK, it is no wonder that you were reluctant to give it all up'. John Price stated that it was 'under pressure from Ernest Bevin that I moved to the ILO'.[104] With respect to the opinions of those, such as Price himself, who ought to know, it would appear from this distance that Price took to the ILO 'like a duck to water', and that he was completely embroiled in international work in the immediate period before his departure. He was also very close to Bevin, and must have been privy to – or at least guessed – Bevin's intention not to return to the union but to seek high political office nationally or internationally. John Price continued to work for the ILO in Geneva, and retired at the age of 60 in 1961. He then returned to the UK and assisted the Merchant Navy Officers' Association and the Organisation of Retired UN Civil Servants. He died in 1995.

The first Education Committee attended by Ellen McCullough as Acting Secretary was held on 17 November 1943, and she attended the

GEC for the first time at its December meeting. Ellen McCullough had been a clerk in the Workers' Union since 1925 when she was 16, and her father had been involved with that union. She helped to form the Hendon branch of the WEA, and was active in the Labour Party in North London. In 1933 she had won the Mary McArthur scholarship for working women, for the University of London Diploma in Public Administration and Sociology. She also attended the first ILO/WEA summer school in Geneva in 1934, writing a report from a student's point of view.[105] She cut her teeth in the union's education programme whilst developing the correspondence course, and Jack Jones characterised her as having little direct experience of industry but a commitment to workers' education.[106] With some interruptions, she was to remain in charge of TGWU education throughout the 1940s, 1950s and 1960s, never breaking her links with the WEA.

As the war drew to a close, the union had undergone the same fundamental changes as society as a whole. The war brought death, loss and destruction, but it also transformed attitudes and placed a new generation at the centre of affairs. The TGWU had lost its General Secretary and its newly-appointed Head of Education, but on the other hand it had become used to working closely with government and being consulted on important national and international matters. It had introduced an innovative form of union education under its own control, broken away from the liberal adult education system of the external providers, and in some localities had begun to use education as a key organising tool. To maintain and then extend such an education programme in the conditions of total war is a truly remarkable feat. This programme contributed no small amount to the 'battle of ideas' throughout the war, and held firmly to progressive war aims. Even more remarkably, the programme was comfortable in the debate about future security and the establishment of the UN and the ILO. The union had tapped into the great release of energy which the war had produced, and by 1945 the number of TGWU students on the correspondence course, the day-schools and WETUC and NCLC courses was the highest ever. The union itself was also growing, moving towards 1.5 million in the late 1940s. There were also new issues such as equal pay for women, time and motion study and the recognition of shop stewards coming onto the agenda. If 'reconstruction' was in the air, for the union education programme, the real task was to consolidate the gains and to keep the new link between education, union organisation and development.

NOTES

1. Of the 1,907 applications for the correspondence course, 589 were from Area 1, 234 from Area 6 and 224 from Area 7. By Trade Group 403 were from Passenger, 198 from General Workers, 127 from Metal Chemical and Oil Engineering, and 126 from ACTS.

2. TGWU: *Organisation and Administration of the Union under War Conditions*, appendix to the GEC Minutes, Minute No 982, 25 September 1939, p371.
3. General Secretary's Report, November 1939, p434.
4. GEC Meeting, 17 October 1939. This is not exactly proportionate to membership. Region 1 and the Passenger Group were the largest in the union, but Region 6 and General Workers, though important, were not.
5. Education Committee meeting, 7 February 1940.
6. Minutes of the GEC, Minute No 232, 5 March 1940, p66.
7. Memo from A.J. Chandler, Minute Secretary, to J. Price, 25 March 1941.
8. Memo from A.J. Chandler to John Price, 22 November 1940.
9. Report of the Education Committee Meeting, 12 November 1941, Minute No 122.
10. Meeting of the Education Committee, 7 August 1942.
11. Report of the Political, Research and Education Department, 18 February 1943.
12. Trade Group and Departmental Review for 1944, p126.
13. Meeting of the Education Committee, 7 February 1945.
14. Report of the Education Committee, 25 August 1945.
15. Ibid., Minute No 396, 13 May 1940, p122.
16. J. Price, *Labour in the War*, Penguin Books, 1940, p23.
17. Ibid., p173.
18. Ibid., p174.
19. See D. Fernbach, 'Tom Wintringham and Socialist Defence Strategy', *History Workshop Journal*, Issue 14, Autumn 1982, pp63-91. Also T. Wintringham, *New Ways of War*, 1940, in which he made the following comments: 'Men must be persuaded, made to understand, given the enthusiasm that will change their discipline from an acceptance of orders to an eager use of all their powers in pursuit of a common aim. They must be made to feel that their own contribution has value and is accepted, that the war is their war. This can only be done on a political basis', p50. See also H. Purcell 'The Last English Revolutionary: Tom Wintringham 1898-1949', Stroud: Sutton 2004.
20. Topham, 1992, op. cit., pp58-59.
21. 'Wartime Opportunities' by John Price, *The Record*, March 1941, p162.
22. Ibid.
23. Minutes of the Education Committee, 10 July 1940, Minute No 62, p3.
24. Minutes of the GEC, Minute No 890, 23 August 1940, p252.
25. 'Union and the War' by John Price, *The Record*, October 1940, p67.
26. *The Record*, December 1941, p126.
27. Education Committee Meeting, 18 February 1942, Minute No 125.
28. Education Committee Meeting, 8 November 1944.
29. Acting Secretary's Report, 29 January 1945.
30. See P. Addison, *The Road to 1945*, London: Quartet Books, 1977.
31. See Mackenzie, 1992, op. cit.; A. Calder, *The People's War*, London: Pimlico, 1969.
32. M. Stewart, *Life and Labour: An Autobiography*, London, 1980. Quoted in Mackenzie, 1992, op. cit., p60.
33. Education Committee Meeting, 18 February 1942, Minute No 125.
34. Still a hotel, owned by the Co-op and now next door to the headquarters of the General Federation of Trade Unions (GFTU).

35. Ibid.
36. Ibid.
37. *The Record,* July 1941, p29.
38. *The Record*, December 1942, p115.
39. Education Committee: Report of the Secretary dated 28April 1943.
40. Report of the Secretary dated 15 August 1943.
41. Ibid.
42. Report of the Secretary dated 15 August 1943.
43. Acting General Secretary's Report, June 1944, p139.
44. Acting Education Secretary's Report, 29 January 1945.
45. Minutes of the Education Committee meeting, 19 November 1945.
46. Report of the Education Committee, 25 August 1945.
47. Education Secretary's Report, 7 May 1945.
48. Education Secretary's Report dated 30 July 1942.
49. Attachment to the Minutes of the Education Committee, 5 February 1941.
50. *The Record,* March 1943, p175.
51. Report of the Secretary dated 22 October 1942.
52. The actual figures were £1,293 11s 8d, £1,504 6s 11d, £643 1s 1d, £640 14s, £1,211 10s 4d, £570 16s 4d, £1,502 4s 10d , and £290 14s 6d.
53. Source: Annual Reports on the Union's Education Scheme, 1939-1945.
54. Annual Report on the Union's Educational Scheme, 1 February 1945.
55. *The Record*, August 1944, p48.
56. Ibid.
57. Minutes of the GEC, Minute No 319, 13 March 1941, p89.
58 Acting General Secretary's Report, June 1941, p199.
59. Report of the Education Committee Meeting, 12 November 1941.
60. Report of the Secretary of the Department dated 28 April 1942.
61. See in particular chapters 8, 9 and 10.
62. J. Jones, 'A Liverpool Socialist Education', op. cit., p101.
63. Interview with Jack Jones, 27 May 1998.
64. Ibid.
65. 'Trade union education in Coventry', *The Record*, August 1944, p48.
66. J. Jones, *Union Man*, op. cit., p93.
67. Meeting of the Education Committee, 7 February 1945.
68. *The Record,* October 1944, p78.
69. Acting General Secretary's Report, March 1944, p65.
70. Minutes of the GEC, Minute No 705, 23 June 1939, p261.
71. Minutes of the GEC, 18 November 1942.
72. Croucher, op. cit., p276.
73. Ibid., p275.
74. Jack Jones, *Union Man*, op. cit., p105.
75. Meeting of the Education Committee, 12 May 1943, Minute No 186.
76. Report of the Education Secretary dated 15 August 1943. The TUC had arranged a day school for women on 18 July 1943 in London. The STUC organised a school for women trade unionists in Edinburgh on 26 and 27 June 1943.
77. *The Record,* September 1943, p58.
78. Ibid.
79. Acting Education Secretary's Report, 31 January 1944.
80. A Resolution was received from Area 12 Committee urging upon the

Council the desirability of granting facilities for one-day schools for the women membership within the area during the current year. It was resolved that this be approved and referred to the Acting Secretary (i.e. Ellen McCullough) for action. Minutes of the GEC, 1 March 1944, Minute No 230.

81. Acting Education Secretary's Report, 25 June 1944.
82. V. Allen, *Trade Union Leadership*, op. cit., pp243-244.
83. Ibid., p244.
84. Acting General Secretary's Report, December 1943, p257.
85. Report of the Political, Research and Education Department, 12 February 1944.
86. F. Williams, *Ernest Bevin*, op. cit., p203. An officer who attended the ILO Summer school in 1939 in Geneva was G.A. Brown of Area 1. This was the George Brown who became Deputy Leader of the Labour Party, Education Committee meeting, 17 October 1939.
87. Topham, 1992, op. cit., p60.
88. Report of Political, Research, Education and International Department, 14 May 1940.
89. See Addison, 1977, op. cit., p113.
90. Minutes of the GEC, Minute No 892, 23 August 1940, meeting of Education Committee, 10 July 1940.
91. 'Brother John Price broadcasts to New Zealand', *The Record*, November 1940, p192.
92. Minutes of the Political, Research Education and International Department, 30 October 1940, p4.
93. 'Your verbal statement covering your recent visit to Iceland was adopted by the Council', Memo from A. Chandler to J. Price, 27 September 1943.
94. Minutes of the Political, Research, Education and International Department, 18 November 1941.
95. GEC, 19 August 1942, Minute No 759.
96. Report of the Political, Research and Education Department, 18 February 1943.
97. Report of the Political, Research and Education Department, 17 May 1943.
98. Ibid.
99. F&GP, 15 July 1943, Minute No 545, p139.
100. F&GP, 21 October 1943, Minute No 804, p202.
101. F&GP, 5 October 1944, Minute No 886, p215.
102. GEC Minutes, 6 March 1945, Minute No 193, p43.
103. Topham, 1992, op. cit., p60.
104. Ibid.
105. This report is in the Modern Records Centre, University of Warwick.
106. Interview with Jack Jones, 27 May 1998.

Chapter 4

Expansion and Innovation 1946–1959

This chapter will look at the principal developments in the national education programme within the regions in the immediate post-war years. As education expanded and diversified, the regions gradually became more important, and area/regional diversity became reflected in the education programme. At the national level, this period saw the introduction of several innovations and improvements in the programme, overseen by an indulgent (so far as education was concerned) General Secretary, Arthur Deakin. At the start, the education programme was built around the correspondence course on the union's structure, but gradually it turned towards the newly-emergent shop stewards and the union's role in the workplace. This new focus was institutionalised through the establishment of a programme of summer schools at the Royal Agricultural College, Cirencester, provided in partnership with the WEA, whose influence on the TGWU programme grew under Ellen McCullough, but only on the union's terms. This time also saw the appointment of Tony Corfield, who brought new focused learning methods with him and established the key style of TGWU education.

In 1945, along with the rest of British society, the TGWU had to begin the process of demobilisation, and entered the period of post-war recovery and reconstruction. Some of the union schools in the latter part of the war had contemplated the structure of the post-war world, but they were inevitably bound up with wartime thinking, focusing on issues like international security and the promotion of democracy, which featured less in the real post-war debates, particularly once the Cold War had begun. Throughout the immediate post-war period, the main focus was on nurturing the new generations of shop stewards, and building expertise in industrial relations, collective bargaining, and in the education methods used to achieve these goals. It is significant that Arthur Deakin comes out of this particular part of the story as a genuine champion of TGWU education, at the same time as he was enthusiastically embracing the crusade against Communism and driving through the infamous 1949 BDC resolution banning Communists from holding office in the union. Deakin was quite comfortable with an education programme which, like Bevin before him, he saw as essentially focused on the industrial role of the union, and which he believed produced educated members who would more readily reject 'extremism' of whatever kind.

This was the period of Deakin and Frank Cousins in the leadership of the union, but Ellen McCullough was the one who led or influenced the union's education programme throughout the whole period, though not – as we shall see – always formally in office. Tony Corfield was also a key figure throughout most of this period, and under McCullough's protection he was able to introduce innovative and focused ideas throughout the education programme. The period ends on the verge of yet another generation rising to extend the education programme systematically into the regions, to take advantage of the new practice of day-release and exploit the growing involvement of companies in a joint training culture.

POST-WAR RECONSTRUCTION

The immediate post-war period began quietly enough, and, with a majority Labour government in office for the first time, with some optimism. Twenty-two members of the union's official list stood for election in 1945, and 20 were elected. TGWU members in Parliament included Bevin, Arthur Greenwood as Lord Privy Seal, John Wilmott and Ben Smith in the Ministry of Supply, Walter Edwards as Lord of the Admiralty, Creech-Jones at the Colonial Office, Parker at the Dominion Office, Key and Oliver at the Minister of Health, Arthur Woodburn in Supply and many others on the back benches. This was the first time in its history that the union had had such political influence, and one of Bevin's main reasons for supporting union education, namely that if workers were to extend their influence over the state, they would need to match the employers and the ruling class in their knowledge and ability, was brought more sharply into focus.

Ellen McCullough was promoting *Trade Union Talks*, produced by the WETUC and intended to be an introduction to trade unionism for 'new members and those who have been out of touch with the union'.[1] Ruskin College was reopened in 1945 and also in that year a special course in Trade Union Studies was established at the London School of Economics (LSE), taking one year for day students and three years for evening students. The TUC also announced that the first of its short training courses would begin in April 1947 and proposed to offer scholarships. Two international schools were held for the first time. The Anglo-Scandinavian school took place in Oslo, while the Anglo-French school was organised by the WETUC at Hillcroft College.

By early 1946, nine members of the TGWU were resident at Ruskin College, three of them on scholarships wholly financed by the union. Eight members were following a full-time course at the LSE, six of them wholly financed by the union. In addition, one member was training at Barnet House in Oxford, and the union awarded four scholarships for the part-time course at the LSE.[2] The LSE had introduced its evening course in Trade Union Studies at a fee of £31 10s (£31.50p) per student. The decision of the union was to adopt this course so long as applicants could also be officers and members of the staff employed in the union's London offices. The Education Committee agreed to award four scholarships, three for lay members and one for officers and staff in the London Area including Central Office. One of those awarded a scholarship was Bob Dyke, 1/128 branch, employed in the Central Office Finance Department, who later became Executive Finance Secretary of the union during the later 1950s and 1960s. For the full-time course at the LSE, the union awarded six full-time scholarships to commence on 9 October 1946. There were fourteen applicants including E.G. Allen, 2/121, and E.C. Sheehan, 1/325. Both Ernie Allen and Ted Sheehan were accepted for one of the LSE scholarships, and both later became regional secretaries, of Regions 2 and 1 respectively, and both were enthusiasts for union education.

The March 1946 GEC agreed to increase the Education Grant to £3,750,[3] and the union began discussions with Ruskin College for the award of a Ben Tillett Memorial Scholarship to provide funding for a second year of study for TGWU students. Ben Tillett had died in January 1943 aged 82, and the scholarship was the outcome of a resolution passed by Area 1 Engineering Group, which had asked that a fitting memorial should be raised in appreciation of his services. This was supported by the Area 1 Committee and they felt the most suitable memorial would be the establishment of a scholarship. Arthur Deakin had been in touch with Lionel Elvin, Principal of Ruskin College, and they agreed that the scholarship for £400 would be awarded to a second year student.[4] The first student to be awarded the scholarship was Bro. T.W. Clarke of Potter's Bar, in August 1946.

Other relationships were being re-established. The Executive reaffirmed its May 1939 decision accepting the principle of awarding a scholarship at Coleg Harlech, the award to begin in the college year 1947.[5] The union had a curious relationship with academics and full-time educators at this time. On the one hand, the General Secretary made the effort to include in his report to the GEC that 'at the moment 18 members of the union are receiving full-time tuition of university standard',[6] and the GEC made special recognition of the success of members such as Bro. R. Jefferies who won a scholarship from Ruskin College to a two-year honours degree university course in Modern History at Exeter University[7] (Reg Jeffries, a Bristol lorry driver, later became General Secretary of the WEA). The union required that it be the normal practice for bursary interviews with the Education Committee to include the Principal of Ruskin College, something that was not maintained in later years.

On the other hand, attempts at closer personal links between Labour Movement teachers and the union were rebuffed. For example, an application for membership of the union from the Principal of Ruskin College was refused by the GEC on the grounds that the applicant was not employed in an industry or trade for which the union normally catered.[8] When the University of Sheffield appealed for union subscription to a fund which had been established for the purpose of facilitating expansion of the activities of the university in the field of trade union education, this was also refused. It was recognised by the GEC that although trade unionists in the district supported this, the union could not set a precedent by supporting one particular university in a locality.[9]

In the areas, the union's education programme continued at the relatively high level reached at the end of the war, but in a very uneven way, and without much direction. Up to the end of 1946, 5,125 students enrolled for the correspondence course, and the number of students admitted to summer schools in 1946 was the highest ever recorded, at 100. Ellen McCullough was keen to support residential weekend schools and she began the process of organising the first ones for TGWU members only, which would begin in 1947. The areas carrying out most education at the end of the war were 3 (South-west), 5 (Midlands) and 8 (Northern). Other areas began considering the establishment of special committees for education work. General schools were held at Leicester in March and courses were still running at Maidstone and Halifax and in Area 8, schools were being organised at Workington, Darlington and Belford, Northumberland. In all, 22 day-schools were organised by the union during 1945. In the Midlands, seven Birmingham members who had taken advantage of TGWU education facilities were elected to the Birmingham City Council on 1 November 1945. Tom Wylie was running a comprehensive programme of education centred around Birmingham Technical College, and also at Wolverhampton Tech. and at Birmingham University. The Bristol Educational and Social Council was still organising lectures on Sunday afternoons.[10]

Discussion on the organisation and direction of post-war trade union education had already taken place in the movement and in the union from 1944 onwards. In May of that year, the Education Committee received a detailed paper written by Ellen McCullough entitled *Memorandum on the Question of Post-War Policy in Relation to Workers' Education*. She had submitted this to the WETUC on behalf of the TGWU. In this memorandum she sought to draw the distinction between what could be provided by the WEA and what could be provided by the unions themselves. She started by pointing out that the 'developments in the technique of trade union administration and industrial relations and the quantity and complexity of legislation meant that there was an ever-widening field in which trade union officials and active trade unionists need to be really well-informed'.[11] She noted that many of these subjects could be studied at university, but the orientation of universities was not particularly suitable for active trade unionists or officials, who did not normally have the time for such detailed study. She also made the point that the active trade unionist is more likely to want to study such issues 'from the particular to the general':

> Many trade unionists find it more stimulating to approach the study of a subject from a personal angle, than to work, so to speak, from the general to the particular. For example, such a student, beginning with the account of the growth of his own union, will go on to study trade union development and thence to social and industrial issues. He might have been unwilling to begin by studying the background from which his union sprang. The same general argument could be applied to the study of economics, political science, or government, and, of course, subjects like social insurance, industrial legislation etc.[12]

She argued that the unions should cover these issues and that the WEA role should be to cover others such as the principles on which trade unions based their objects and the way unions grew up, their rights and duties, their relationship with the wider movement and matters such as trade union administration, principles of negotiation and so on. McCullough then covered the question of how this knowledge was to be conveyed to people who were not particularly used to study; she examined the different types of schools such as one-day or week-end schools, 1, 2 or 3-year courses, programmes of lectures, summer schools and correspondence courses. She concluded that there was a need for a new approach:

> In post-war years, plans may be made for all-the-year-round residential courses, including one to four weeks initial and refresher courses for officials ... it is, of course, essential that all these courses should be planned in the closest co-operation with the trade unions. In addition, wherever possible, experienced trade union officials should take part in the actual work of teaching. It is not suggested that they should be asked to deliver courses of lectures or conduct tutorials. Few have either the time or training for this. What is intended is that they should be asked to co-operate by delivering talks and taking part in discussions at certain stages. For instance, a course of lectures, or a class, on the machinery of collective bargaining would be greatly assisted by the attendance at one of its sessions of a man (sic) with wide first-hand experience of the way in which JICs and statutory bodies work. Similarly, an official specialising in compensation cases could provide a valuable stimulus to a group studying industrial law. Day and weekend schools could have a similarly 'mixed' programme.[13]

In the post-war period, Ellen McCullough was able to turn many of these ideas into reality, when union-only residential schools were established at initial and follow-on level, and some TGWU officials became regular participants on regional and sometimes national courses. The WEA and university extra-mural departments became involved in a new way; not as the organising body, as WETUC and the NCLC had been, but as specialist contributors alongside the union's own tutors and officials.

DEVELOPING SHOP STEWARDS' EDUCATION

Whilst in the immediate post-war period there was a focus on the re-establishment of TGWU students at Ruskin College, the LSE and on similar programmes, the bread and butter of TGWU education was still the correspondence course and the short courses provided on a day basis in the local district. The correspondence course continued at a steady level, with 764 students completing the course by May 1946, rising to 909 one year later.[14] At this time, Ellen McCullough was keen to develop the provision of weekend, rather than one-day schools. Her view at this time was that 'a residential school providing for three sessions, and an opportunity for private discussions with individual students, is of far greater value than several one-day schools, where there can only be two sessions, after which the lecturer and students are officially obliged to separate quickly in order to catch trains or buses'.[15] By 1947 her encouragement had begun to bear fruit. In April, a weekend school was organised by the Bristol Educational and Social Council. The first residential union weekend school in the London Area was held at the Clarion Youth Hostel, Hoddesdon, on 21 and 22 June 1947. The students were the London Oil Trades Group, and at their request, a special syllabus was worked out relevant to their industry. Frank Cousins and Ellen McCullough were the lecturers. A weekend school for union members only was held at Tong Hall, near Bradford, on 3 and 4 May 1947, with Florence Hancock and A.J. Heale (Area Secretary) as the tutors. One-day schools also continued in a number of localities, with Ellen McCullough and sometimes Harry Nicholas, later to become Deputy General Secretary, as tutors.

There may have been more purely educational value in the weekend school, but a problem which had been carried over from John Price's time was that the pattern of day and weekend schools lacked any real industrial focus, nor were they part of a strategic development of the increasingly important component within the union – the shop steward. Shop stewards had increased their number and their influence immediately before and during the war, encouraged by younger and more innovative officials, and if TGWU education was to remain a central part of the union's organising activity, then it would need to come to terms with this reality. The union would also need to extend the earlier focus of the correspondence course and day schools, which were primarily about understanding the structure and function of the union as an organisation, and with general political and economic issues, and introduce courses relevant to the shop steward's agenda.

As early as 1945, some of the areas had recognised this. For example, in September 1945 a resolution was sent to the GEC from the Area 13 (North Wales and the Wirral) calling for extra education facilities to be made available to branch secretaries and shop stewards in order to place them 'in a position of equality when meeting the fully-trained personnel deputed by managements to deal with questions arising in relation to wages and conditions of employment'.[16] Area 13 kept up the pressure and in 1947 sent a further remit recommending the inauguration of a training scheme for the specific purpose of selecting and training suitable members and shop stewards as 'industrial leaders' at workshop and factory level.[17] Some of the union's industrial groups made similar demands: for example, in December 1947 the General Workers Group submitted a remit to the GEC:

> Having regard to the introduction of modern techniques in industry such as rate-fixing, and to the increasing use of the time and motion study method in particular, the General Workers Trade Group National Committee requests the GEC to give serious consideration to the education on these matters of lay members and permanent officers directly concerned in the industries affected, in order that they will be at no disadvantage when negotiating with the employers' highly-trained labour officers'.[18]

The General Workers Group was also keen to make representations to WETUC and NCLC to ask them to include the theory of Time and Motion Study in their syllabuses. That the union itself, rather than external bodies, would have to take responsibility for this type of subject was emphasised by Deakin, who took the view that this was outside the legitimate scope of the bodies referred to, whose primary function was one of liberal education. These new demands were a response to the American management techniques which accompanied the growth of the new mass-production industries. Along with the reorganisation of work, typified by the 1949 Standard Motors Agreement negotiated by Jack Jones, there was a growth in 'Scientific Management', which placed new demands on union representatives. Tom Wylie had taken due note of this in the Midlands, and in March and April 1947 he was given a large feature article in *The Record* called 'Incentives, the Worker, and Production'. This looked at issues like Time and Motion Study and strongly advocated education and training for shop stewards to match the expertise of Time and Motion specialists.[19] A second article in September was entitled 'Training for Management', and focused even more directly on the new demands on trade union education:

> Every educational and training scheme within the Trade Union Movement has confined itself to the social sciences such as economics, sociology, psychology, politics, industrial history and legislation, and has left such subjects as pure and applied science, mathematics, mechanics, draughtsmanship and industrial administration in general universities and technical colleges. This has produced men skilled in the human problems of industry, and not so highly skilled in questions of general factory organisation and business administration.[20]

He outlined a programme of special courses to be organised with Birmingham Technical College, looking at the responsibility of workers' representatives in the changing economy, the growth and structure of modern industry, organisation of the manufacturing company, organisation of the workshop, the importance of the Factories Acts, planning and control of work, methods of work measurement, job evaluation, control of factory costs, and job management.[21] Wylie did not only write about this issue, but organised a comprehensive education programme in the Birmingham area. For example, in June 1949 in the Area 5 office there was a school on the purpose of motion study, the tutor being G.P. Wade of the Department of Industrial Administration, Birmingham Technical College. This course was one of a series of four for shop stewards to help them to understand the changes taking place in industry. Other lectures were provided on time study and its application, methods of job evaluation and engineering agreements.[22]

This more systematic and industry-oriented approach to union education was given a boost from two other directions. In the first place, some of the newly-nationalised industries began trade union or joint union-management training around industrial relations issues. In February 1949, the Road Transport Executive, which included Harold Clay, approved a document proposing staff training and education. Also, the Dock Labour Board had started to organise schools and conferences; the first one being for Hull dockers, held at the Adelphi Hotel, Scarborough, on 7 and 8 May 1949. Jack Donovan, the union's Docks National Secretary, was one of the speakers at this school.[23] Secondly; targeted shop stewards' training had been strongly promoted by the Training Within Industry (TWI) initiative. This system had been introduced from America during the war by Bevin, as part of the drive to increase productivity through joint production techniques. It was primarily aimed at supervisors and foremen to assist them in 'instructing others, handling workers and improving methods'.[24] By mid-1945, the Ministry of Labour claimed to have trained over 10,000 supervisors, and the scheme was extended to residential courses at universities for what would now be called personnel or human resource managers. After the war, TWI was extended to shop stewards at a limited number of technical colleges, primarily Leicester,

Nottingham and Birmingham. TWI included many of the education methods which we would now recognise as fundamental in trade union education: targeted objectives and measured outcomes, role-play and other active learning techniques, team-teaching, interactive course materials and other 'props' such as slide-rules. It also included training in leadership and in improving working methods, and the 'job safety' programme, which focused on accident prevention. In particular, it included the military 'drill' approach to handling industrial relations problems:

1. Get the facts
2. Weigh and decide
3. Take action, and
4. Check results.[25]

This method was to be central to the TGWU approach to shop stewards' education throughout this period and beyond.

Some of the students who attended TWI sessions at the Ministry were TGWU officials such as Fred Horne, Area 1 Metal and Engineering Trade Group Secretary, and an enthusiast for this type of education. The Ministry of Labour's Training Department was willing to arrange courses at the convenience of the union, and officers could attend in rotation. Having attended the initial course, the officers were then expected to continue by training other groups on their own. Fred Horne began the two-day courses on TWI lines and on the first day had 60 students from the Engineering Group.[26] Jack Lucas remembers that Fred Horne tried out courses based on the TWI scheme in 1949 with hand-picked stewards and extended it to all full-time officers within the group. Fred Horne did the administration for the courses and younger officers like Lucas taught the courses – receiving half-a-crown (12.5p) allowance for a weekend school.[27] Other places where TWI was tried out at this time were Area 4 (Wales), Area 5, particularly Coventry and Birmingham, and Area 8, mainly Newcastle, Stockton, and Middlesbrough, led by Bro. Hills, the Area Secretary. In Area 12 (Liverpool), five officers of the General Workers Group undertook tutor-training as part of the scheme.

THE 1949 BDC AND THE FIRST SUMMER SCHOOLS

These new developments were reflected in a debate on education in the union which came to a head at the 1949 BDC. There had been some criticism at the 1947 BDC on the basis that although the union was growing, it was still spending only a small amount – less than a halfpenny per member – on education. This criticism was repeated at the 1949 BDC, but Ellen McCullough and Deakin, in response to the new opportunities, had prepared a comprehensive statement on the future of education within the union. Ellen McCullough was challenged about expenditure and on the fact that out of a total membership of 1,323,000 only 1,500 members had taken part in education. However, she and the General Secretary were able to win over the conference with their comprehensive proposals. Arthur Deakin took the whole block of resolutions which ranged from asking generally for more money to be spent, and for summer schools, loss of earnings for union students, asking for full-time education officers and tutors in each area and asking the union to fully affiliate to the NCLC. He asked for all these to be remitted to the GEC on the grounds that the union was about to make a substantial increase in educational provision and that these resolutions would be taken into account when the union decided to expand its education programme:

> I am prepared to make very solid recommendations by way of substantially increasing the amounts we are prepared to spend for educational facilities for the benefit of our members ... We provide a type of educational service incomparable in the history and experience of the Trade Union Movement, and I hope this conference will at once agree that the whole question becomes the subject of further examination and revise the extent of this scheme at the earliest possible moment.[28]

Deakin particularly promised systematic training of branch officers and shop stewards and the setting up of an advisory service on technical and managerial training. This statement was accepted by acclamation by the conference.

At its August 1949 meeting, the Education Committee began the process of translating the BDC commitment into a detailed programme, and by November, proposals were put to the Committee setting out the plans for the extension of the union education scheme. The proposals were accepted on the basis of an overall allocation of £25,000 (£500,000 at today's values) per annum to meet the cost of the new scheme. £25,000 represented 6d (2.5p) per head of one million members, and an enormous increase in expenditure.[29] The details of the new scheme, agreed at this meeting, were presented to the full GEC in December 1949. The special appendix on the future scheme for TGWU education accepted by the GEC began by identifying the union's interests in the field of adult education as threefold:

1. General education of a liberal kind, including the use of language, economics, history, philosophy, psychology and sociology.
2. Education and training for specifically trade union purposes, including the education of branch officers and workshop representatives, etc.
3. Education in connection with the industries in which our members are engaged, including technical training and training for management. In connection with the first of these we do not regard ourselves

> as the *providing* body. The work is best carried out in co-operation with the WEA, WETUC, and the NCLC and the colleges etc.[30]

The document proposed that the second area, training of branch officers, was the most important of all and the responsibility of the union. The third group, technical training and training for management, was the job of the universities and the technical colleges and of institutions like TWI and the British Institute of Management. In the first group were included correspondence courses, day and weekend schools on union problems, and external day and weekend schools, summer schools, TUC training courses, and full-time scholarships to the colleges.

Bearing these principles in mind, the following proposals were made, which were to shape the union's education programme for a generation. First of all, every area was encouraged to consider the extent to which the TWI service could be adapted to their use. Officers trained by TWI were encouraged to hold two-day courses for shop stewards in their own localities and trades. The union was to meet the full cost of these courses by paying the members attending them as if they were on union business, including payment for 'loss of time'. The union would also provide further training for two full weeks at one of the technical colleges offering TWI to those completing the first level of courses. Initially, twelve places were reserved for TGWU members as an experiment. The two weeks full-time course covered human relations in industry, industrial management, English, costing, incentive schemes, industrial law, works councils and joint industrial councils. Most significantly, the union was to introduce summer schools, organised by the WEA for the union, for branch chairmen (sic), branch secretaries and for 'other branch officers' (meaning shop stewards).[31] Initially, the union considered approaching the British Institute of Management for help with syllabus planning, and hoped to borrow the outline of a handbook for shop stewards, which had been approved by the TUC. However, in reality this was produced by the union itself, along with appropriate course materials. The programme of publicity for the new scheme was to include a press conference addressed by the General Secretary, branch circulars and personal letters from him to permanent officials, notices in *The Record* and the issue of leaflets and posters. The pamphlet produced in July 1950, *A Guide to the Union's Educational Facilities,* included a quote from Francis Bacon on the cover: 'Reading maketh a full man, conference a ready man and writing an exact man'.

THE NEW RESIDENTIAL SCHOOLS

Although the public launch of the new scheme was postponed because of the 1950 general election, the newly-focused commitment of the union had an immediate effect in increasing the provision of education. First of all, it encouraged the continuing involvement with shop steward training via TWI, and second, and most important, it led to the first experiments in residential summer schools, a format that was to become a mainstay of TGWU education. By 1950, the union had begun to participate in TWI training for shop stewards at a number of venues. Eight students attended the first three-week shop stewards' course at Leicester College of Technology in March 1950. One of these was J. Brandie who came from Portsmouth, and was soon to make his mark as an official, organising courses in Region 2. Students attending these special schools and courses were paid allowances as if they were engaged on union business. A special weekend school was offered to those who attended the shop stewards' training course and the first of these was held in London in May 1950, with the WEA providing the lecturers. The syllabus included sessions on the development of the shop steward in modern trade unionism, and the place of the shop steward in negotiating machinery, workshop organisation, and joint consultation.[32]

The aim of the three and four-week courses was to create an awareness of the problems involved in management and in the relationships which arose in the workplace. Arrangements were made for members to stay together in hotels since it was recognised that a valuable feature of residential courses was the out-of-session discussions. This in itself would have been a novelty for trade unionists at the time. Guest lecturers from industry and government agencies met the students, and the courses included visits to local factories and workplaces. In the summer of 1951 Nottingham Technical College joined the scheme. By this time, however, some problems were beginning to emerge. First of all, there was a great demand for the courses from companies for their managers and supervisors. It proved impossible to gain admission for TGWU students to the summer 1951 courses at Birmingham Technical College. Although involvement in the programmes continued into 1953, there was a cooling-off and a shift towards the union providing its own programmes on TWI lines. The main difficulties were discussed at the Education Committee in May 1953:

> While undoubtedly these courses have advantages, they are not totally suitable for our members, mainly because the general administration of technical schools is not suited to adults who have been trained to do a responsible trade union job. While it is not part of our intention to indoctrinate our members, there remains the difficulty that the teaching of economics or history is difficult for people who have no great interest in the Working-Class Movement, who are apt to regard these subjects as being just items in a syllabus.[33]

This represented a rather convoluted way of recognising that there was in practice a difference between a TWI-based course for supervisors, and one for shop stewards, and that the main difference was not methodological or in the areas of industrial relations covered by these courses, but was essentially ideological. The wartime pattern of joint production committees, into which TWI fitted very well, had broken down by the early 1950s, and there was a need to reinforce the independence of trade unions and in particular the role of the shop steward.

By the end of 1952, 80 TGWU students had been through these courses, and the last recorded involvement of TGWU students is a course at Nottingham Technical College in late 1952 for Regions 6, 7 and 8.[34]

Shorter schools on TWI lines, whether residential or not, proved to be a much better prospect. Taking advantage of the new policy, the Education Department lost no time in organising residential schools for shop stewards. A successful school took place at Dalston Hall, near Carlisle, in June 1950. All the arrangements were planned and carried out within the Northern Region. A southern school, organised with Fred Horne, was held at the Co-operative Youth Centre, Bexhill-on-Sea, for a week in late June 1950. Preference to this school was given to branch chairmen (sic) and secretaries as there was only room for 51 students. The WEA provided the academic staff, and lectures were also given by the General Secretary and Financial Secretary, the Secretary of the Legal Department and one of the area secretaries. Harold Clay also lectured on Labour Problems in Nationalised Industries. The format of the summer school was one borrowed directly from the WEA, which had begun special schools for trade union students at Beatrice Webb House, Dorking, in 1948 and 1949.[35] However, the real innovation was to move the school away from the open philosophical discussions typical of the pre-war WEA and the incorporation of the 'drill' approach of TWI. Fred Horne and a new generation of adult education tutors made sure that these new methods were central to the approach adopted at these schools. The new initiative proved very popular with the membership, and there were some 170 applicants for 51 places.

A thorough evaluation of the lessons of the first, experimental, school took place throughout the winter of 1950-51, and in June 1951 the programme was repeated in an expanded version over two weeks with a more elaborate format and 73 students, the majority of whom were branch officers from the southern half of the country. Although the syllabus covered two weeks, each week was a separate school and each student attended for one week only, establishing a pattern lasting almost forty years. The Director of Studies for this school was W.E. Styler, from the WEA, and tutors included leaders in the new generation: Tony Corfield, Bill Pritchard and V.L. (Vic) Allen. Lectures were delivered by Arthur Deakin, Ellen McCullough, Frank Stillwell, Harry Nicholas, Frank Cousins and Bill Glazebrook. The system of study adopted was to divide students into four seminar groups, each group comprising around ten students. Seminars met for two hours each morning, from 9.15 to 11.15, followed by a period of reading and private study from 11.30 to 12.05. The seminars had titles including: 'The Problem of Defence Expenditure and Working Class Standards', tutor T.D. Jones, 'The Growth of the Idea of Workers' Control in Industry', tutor Tony Corfield, 'Collective Bargaining in Theory and Practice', tutor Bill Pritchard, and 'Recent Productivity Reports', tutor Vic Allen. The main full school lectures were given by officers such as the General Secretary. There were also visitors to the school from Malaya, Norway and the USA.[36]

A northern school, organised through the WEA, was also held in September 1951 at Dalston Hall, with 79 students in attendance over two weeks. The Director of Studies was Mr B. Abrahart, with the Region 8 Regional Secretary as the resident union officer. Tutors included H.A. Turner from the TUC, and other lectures were given by Arthur Tiffin, Frank Cousins, Frank Stillwell, Ellen McCullough and Harold Clay.

In the winter of 1951-52, the TWI approach was extended to local courses. A special intensive training course for shop stewards from Region 1 Metal, Engineering and Chemical Group was held in October 1951. This was a large school of 40 students under the direction of Fred Horne, accompanied by other officers including Jack Lucas and Ted Sheehan, Regional Organiser. The course involved role-play, with two groups playing the part of employers and engaging in collective bargaining, and case-study techniques were also used. The school also included a two-hour 'Twenty Questions' contest on trade union subjects devised by the officers in which student teams competed against each other, and then an 'Any Questions' hour at which students could fire questions at their officers. Following the casework and the quiz, Fred Horne delivered a lecture on trade union history, illustrated by a filmstrip prepared by G.D.H. Cole. On the third day, the students had to provide answers to detailed problems that they had been set and had to defend their reports against criticism. It was clear from the report that this was tremendously innovative in terms of course materials, active learning methods, role-play and the relationship between the officers and the students. Ellen McCullough was very enthusiastic, as was an American observer from the UAW who attended the course throughout.[37]

A similar two-day school on TWI lines was organised by the Region 1 General Workers Group in October 1951. This was for newly-appointed shop stewards who had little experience of their role and of study. The tutors were officers; Len Neal, soon to feature in our story in his own right, and P. Lagden, both of whom had been trained in TWI methods. Again, in October 1951, a shop stewards' weekend school was organised by the WEA in London. This school was intended for students who had already completed a correspondence course, had attended a union school on TWI lines and had been selected for full-time study at one of the technical colleges. 'The intention was to give those students a final opportunity to consider the historical development of the shop steward and his (sic) function in relation to the union as a whole'.[38]

In the summer of 1952, the experiment with a northern and a southern summer school was repeated, with the northern school being held first, in June, and the southern school in July.

BEATRICE WEBB AND CIRENCESTER

All this activity had to lead somewhere, and began to consolidate the union's focus on the shop steward as the key constituency for its educational effort. During 1952, the *TGWU Shop Stewards' Handbook* was prepared for circulation throughout the union, and was launched in early 1953. The new handbook was workplace-based, and linked into the new focus of the education programme. In order to consolidate the new approach, the education grant for 1953 was increased to £30,000 (£550,000 at today's values) and throughout 1952 Ellen McCullough negotiated with the WEA to provide a large-scale programme of residential courses on a continuing long-term basis, which would also replace the long shop stewards' courses at the Technical Colleges. In this she was enthusiastically supported by Deakin, who justified the increased expenditure to the GEC in wide-ranging terms:

> Arrangements have been tentatively made with the WEA to conduct a series of weekly schools and a special curriculum, bringing in approximately 300 students for the first year and progressively increasing from that figure. This means that we shall not use the special courses at the technical schools to the extent that we have done in the past, this conclusion being based upon our experience of the value of this particular type of education. Altogether, the need for greater educational facilities is urgent. The need for more and better education for definite social purposes is more pressing than ever. We must do all we can to contribute our quota to the development of that intellectual powerhouse which will enable us to generate the greatest possible amount of light amongst the masses of the people.[39]

There was also clearly a need to employ at least one new member of staff who was committed to the new focus on shop stewards and conversant with the new active-learning and TWI-based teaching methods. Ellen McCullough's choice was Tony Corfield, at that time employed by the Civil Service. Corfield was born in Charlton, South London, and his mother was a Socialist who regularly attended classes and discussion groups at Shornells. He went to Oxford in 1938 and his tutor there had an association with Ruskin College. He was called up into the Army in 1940 and was a soldier until 1947, where he was involved in training for the Parachute Regiment as a weapons training officer. He kept in touch with his Ruskin tutor and after the war went back to Ruskin College for a one-year diploma. He also received an MA from Oxford, and joined the WEA in 1948. He then joined a government department writing the official wartime history and was a civil servant for five years, researching the role of the Ministry of Labour, led, of course, by Bevin. He visited the TGWU for information and as a result, he began his involvement with the education programme.

The key to understanding Corfield's approach is the word *drill.* Building from his Army experiences, he was unashamedly committed to a structured and systematic approach to education, with predetermined methods and outcomes, which he felt was most suitable for TGWU students, rather than the traditional WEA 'liberal' approach. TWI suited him perfectly:

> My main contribution to trade union education was to realise that it was based on method and the achievement of practical ends ... I brought the practical stuff in ... I learned a lot from the Army, particularly from the German Army method of education and training.

The important thing was logic, order and measured outcomes.

> What is your job, what is your purpose? Trade union education should be very close to drill.[40]

Much later, in 1968, in an article on the revised *Shop Stewards' Handbook,* he described how he had been influenced by the German Army approach to training:

> The *Stewards' Handbook* which had just arrived from the printers reminded me of an experience I had during the later years of the war when I attended a course at the School of Infantry. I remember being rather amused to discover that we were being taught German military tactics. We were taught these not just to know how the enemy managed things: we were expected to apply them in the British Army. After some consideration this arrangement ceased to appear odd. German tactics are much better than anything we had produced on our own. Why should we not take a leaf or two out of their book?[41]

Tony Corfield defended his position at length in the 1964 edition of the *Trade Union Branch Officers' Manual* written by himself and Ellen McCullough for a wider audience than the TGWU. This included a foreword attributed to Frank Cousins, but clearly penned by Tony Corfield:

> It is assumed that training in a systematic way still is frequently regarded as unnecessary. It is assumed that such people can pick up what they need as they go along. Unfortunately, the journey often proves both long and painful. No doubt experience is still the best teacher, even if it is also the hardest; it can be powerfully supplemented by education and training ... The emphasis of the training worked out within the TGWU has been upon system. Indeed some functions are taught literally as drills. The essential phases of each job are analysed and if possible enumerated. A surprising number of the functions of a voluntary officer can be effectively reduced in this way.[42]

This approach became the norm within the union, from the early 1950s up to the present. It also became the basis of the TUC courses from 1964 onwards and for the education programmes of most, if not all, individual unions.

At this time, in 1953, there were two major concerns for the Education Department. The first one was to find a settled home for the summer school programme, and the second was what to do with the 'follow on' students who had passed through the summer schools and needed a more advanced level of study. This was the first recognition of a system of progression in TGWU education, and grew as more students entered the system. At the end of 1952, Ellen McCullough reported that she was trying to find 'a suitable centre somewhere in the middle of England which can be used for all four weeks of our schools. This will not only be more economical from the point of view of payment of fares, but will be much easier to organise on the trade union side. At the time this report is being prepared we are negotiating with the governors of the Royal Agricultural College at Cirencester. If it is possible to secure the use of these premises, we shall have an ideally-situated centre in which each student will have a separate study bedroom and at which there will be good teaching rooms and library facilities'.[43] The plan for 1953 for this school was to book the whole of August for approximately 250 students, recommended by regional secretaries. These students would each stay for one week.

The 1953 Cirencester school was held from 1 to 29 August. Professor H. Dickinson (University of Bristol) was the Director of Studies. Tony Corfield was one of the tutors, along with Allan Flanders and Vic Allen (Oxford), Douglas MacRae (LSE), 'Billy' Hughes (Ruskin) and other economists, political scientists and WEA tutors. Ellen McCullough was in charge for the union, along with Bro. Hills (Regional Secretary Region 8), Len Neal, and J. Mitchell from the Education Department. The theme was 'Can We Maintain Our Standard of Living?' and the school included 15 separate seminars on the same theme. Students were advised to 'bring your ration book, soap and towel, notebook and pencil'.[44] One of the advantages of

Cirencester was its position in central, rather than southern, England, and as a result the northern school was abandoned, provoking a complaint from Region 8 to the GEC.[45]

The second problem, of providing a follow-on system for selected students who had completed the 'basic' schools, was more complicated, as it involved the selection of appropriate students and finding a venue and suitable time-period for the courses which would be distinct from the 'ordinary' schools at Cirencester. The first such course for advanced students was held at Fircroft College for one week in April 1953. There were 34 in attendance, recommended by their tutors from the 1952 summer school, and approved by their regional secretaries. The syllabus was deliberately heavy, with three hours a day in tutorial groups, and two hours for reading and preparing papers. Half the teaching time was spent in role-playing an industrial situation to give the students experience in collecting and presenting materials and in conducting negotiations and reporting back. There were three full-time tutors at the school, who had all previously taught TGWU students. George Brown MP (then Chair of the TGWU Parliamentary Group) also addressed the students. The general theme of the school was 'Trade Unions and the State'.[46]

There was a need to hold these courses at a different time from the 'ordinary' summer schools, because they involved some of the same tutors and senior officers of the union. It was therefore decided to use Beatrice Webb House, which, unlike Fircroft, was a residential adult education centre rather than a 'working' college with its own students who would have been in attendance during term time. These courses would be for members who had done exceptionally well at the summer schools and had been recommended by their tutors. These advanced courses were organised from Easter until Whitsun 1954 to cater for approximately 300 students over the period. The first course began on 24 April 1954, to great excitement in the union.

The school consisted of eight successive courses each lasting one week, beginning in April and ending in June. Six of these were for branch officers and two were follow-on courses for students selected from the 1953 summer school. There were four separate and related syllabuses for shop stewards, secretaries, chairmen (sic) and committeemen delegates (these last being mainly from the bus industry). In addition there was a special syllabus for the follow-on students. The key theme was 'Trade Union Organisation'. Three hundred students were in attendance over the eight-week period. Students who attended the school were paid fares, 'loss of time' and expenses as if engaged on union business. Before arriving on the course, students were expected to write an essay concerned with the particular problems they had as shop stewards or branch officers. Students and tutors also filled in a report on each other and on the course, and the report on the student also indicated whether he or she was thought to be suitable for follow-on training courses and for full-time scholarships. The tutors on these courses in 1954 were Vic Allen as Director of Studies, and WEA tutors Noel Williams and Robert Davies. Apart from McCullough and Corfield, several other TGWU officers took part in the programme, including Bro. Hills, and Arthur Deakin, who was fulsome in his praise for the courses, regarding them as 'an unqualified success'.[47]

In 1955 the pattern was repeated between 23 April and 7 May – the final two weeks had to be cancelled because of a rail strike. Due to the strike, the Communications and General Courses were held from 6 to 20 August at Cirencester. Over 300 students attended at Beatrice Webb House and 98 at the Cirencester course. The forced move to Cirencester in August 1955 brought home to the Education Department the unnecessary rigidity of the division between the 'basic' Cirencester schools and the Branch Officers' follow-on courses. The communications course which was moved to Cirencester was originally intended for younger members and those who were not office-holders in the union. However, because of the special circumstances, many of the students were, in fact, branch officers, and the places were filled in practice with those who had been unsuccessful in applying for the earlier series of branch officers' training courses. It became clear that the most sensible and practical arrangement was to focus all the union's energies on one centre during one period – the summer – at one venue – Cirencester – and integrate the 'follow-on' programme into the overall summer school curriculum. From 1955 onwards, this was the system adopted by the union, and remained unchanged into the 1980s.

Therefore, for the 1956 courses, the long-term pattern was established. The tutors on the courses beginning in 1954 through to 1956 provide a veritable who's who of adult education for the period. The Director of Studies was Tony Corfield, Ellen McCullough was the resident union officer and during seven weeks in July, August and September 1956, there were 30 visiting tutors including Vic Allen, now transferred from Oxford to the LSE, Fred Bayliss and Arthur Marsh among many from Oxford, H.D. (Billy) Hughes, Principal of Ruskin College, and Henry Smith, the Vice-Principal, Alex Kelly, J.F.C. Harrison and Bill Pritchard from Leeds University and Geoffrey Stuttard and Jim Carruthers from London University as well as other tutors from universities and WEAs. Edna Wilderspin (WEA) and Miss R. Saran (Hillcroft) were the only female tutors. Later schools included husband – and wife Eric and Mrs R Rowe, Harry Newton[48] and Tony Topham.

During the period 1950 to 1956, therefore, the union established the prototype of its National Members' School, which became the proving-ground for several generations of TGWU activists and full-time officials. The system evolved from TWI and the experiences of a number of the key tutor-organisers, not least Fred Horne, Tony

Corfield and Vic Allen. The focus on practical industrial problems coupled with active learning methods suited TGWU activists perfectly, and the courses never lost their popularity, becoming an 'institution' and continuing as a central feature of the education programme even after regional educational programmes overtook them in volume in the 1980s and 1990s.

WOMEN'S EDUCATION IN THE POST-WAR PERIOD

In 1945, despite the commitment given a year earlier, the enthusiasm of the leadership towards organising women workers began to cool as the country returned to the 'normality' of men in work and women in the home. By March 1946, the membership of the union was 1,019,069. However, there were 159,090 women compared with 215,199 at the end of 1944, a reduction of 56,049,[49] at a time when the union was growing overall.

On 4 March 1946, Muriel Rayment became the first woman to take her seat on the GEC, representing the Metal, Engineering and Chemical Workers Trade Group. Rather quaintly, reports to the GEC now began 'Dear Sirs and Brothers (Madam)'.[50] Muriel Rayment, a woman of outstanding personality, worked for HMV in Southall. She was promoted by Fred Horne, her Regional Trade Group Secretary and was a member of the Communist Party. She was in her early thirties at the time when she sat on the GEC, and was a particular thorn in the side of Florence Hancock, by now very much an establishment figure – Chair of the TUC General Council, with an OBE and then a CBE. By contrast, Muriel wore men's clothes, smoked and drank, and was at home with the rough language of the shop floor, which she delighted in using in front of Florence Hancock.[51] Also significant at this time were Pat Turner, who became the assistant to Ellen McCullough in the Education Department, and Vi Taylor, who came from Morgan Crucible, and in 1952 became the second woman to be elected to the GEC.[52]

The General Executive Council elected in 1950 reverted to being all male, until Vi Taylor was elected for the period between 1952 and 1954. It is possible that Muriel Rayment was not elected because she fell foul of the ban on Communist Party members holding office in the union introduced at the 1949 BDC. However, there is no firm evidence for this.[53]

Some of the post-war generation of women activists took the opportunity to develop themselves through union education. One of the first was Sis. I. Martin of the London Passenger Section, who in 1946 was awarded the Bryn Mawr American travelling scholarship from an outside source, which made provision for an eight-week stay in America at the summer school near New York. A special grant of £10 from the GEC was given to this member.[54] In 1947 the GEC decided to award six scholarships for the new TUC training courses, but restricted them to Area 1. They had 26 applications from Area 1 members, two from officers and three from staff. Vi Taylor was awarded one of the scholarships, and in 1948 she attended the LSE, and Miss Alexander from the Central Office Education Department was awarded a place at Ruskin College at the same time.[55] Ellen McCullough also tried to encourage women in the union to build on their increased wartime role and to extend their involvement in the union's education programme. In 1945 she was elected as a member of the council at Hillcroft College for women, and began to encourage the involvement of women TGWU members in the college, as well as giving a short course of lectures on 'Trade Union Principles and Practice' to the Hillcroft students. At this time, the syllabus at Hillcroft included history, English literature and composition, psychology, economics, logic and the history of art. There was also painting, tennis, dramatic work, dancing and netball. At this time there were two TGWU members attending the college, Sis. D.M. Collins of Area 5 and Sis. G. Wolstenholme of Area 6, both on external funding, but on Ellen McCullough's request, a small grant was given to them. Ellen McCullough also accepted an invitation to become a trustee of the Mary McArthur scholarships. In March 1950, Jessie Murray was appointed to the position of Woman Organiser in Region 7 and became, in practice, the Education Officer for Scotland, combining the roles of course organiser and tutor.

Apart from Region 7 and a regular TUC programme of women's schools, the union provided only a smattering of women's courses at this time. For example, a special school for women was held in Birmingham in February 1951. However, the main drive in the immediate post-war years came from the radical Region 1 Regional Committee and the rising generation of officers in the new industries. In March 1955, a resolution was sent to the GEC from Region 1, recommending the council to sanction the holding of a one-day conference of women collectors, stewards and key workers. The curriculum was to deal solely with organising problems. The regional committee favoured a central conference. The GEC, however, was distinctly lukewarm, and recommended that conferences were to be held on a local basis. The proposal was referred back to the Region 1 Committee for further examination, and it accepted this view.[56] However, no systematic programme of conferences was held.

Region 1 returned to the fray in 1958 with a resolution to the GEC directing attention to the difficulties associated with the problem of developing organisation amongst women in industry:

> If this union wants to effectively compete with other trade unions in this particular field, then there is a need to make concessions in regard to contribution rates and other respects.[57]

The suggestion of a lower rate of contribution for women was not accepted by the GEC. A year later the region sent a further resolution following an earlier one from Region 10 asking for a lower rate of contribution for women members. The GEC took the view that the fact that other organisations had a cheaper rate for women could be overcome through efficient servicing by the TGWU.[58] At national level, once the Cirencester programme was established, the lack of women's involvement in the Branch Officers' courses became apparent. An analysis carried out in 1955 showed that by far the largest number of students came from Passenger Transport with three times the number of the next highest trade group, General Workers. In those days, the bus industry was overwhelmingly male, with some local TGWU branches even holding out against the 'dilution' resulting from hiring females. From more than 267 students on the Branch Officers' training courses in 1955, only three were women. On the other follow-on courses, no women members attended out of 83 students. On the general communications course, out of 98 students, only three were women.[59] This was repeated in 1956; 72 students enrolled on the follow-on courses but no women members attended. On the Branch Officers' and Communications courses, out of 336 students, only eight women attended. In 1958 the situation was improved with the establishment of a course exclusively for women members dealing with their special problems of organisation and recruitment; however, the tutor was usually a man.

As the 1950s drew to a close, so did the career of Florence Hancock, still the National Women's Officer. She was by now even more part of the Establishment, involving herself in events such as the first Duke of Edinburgh's Study Conference on Human Problems in Industry in 1956 where she represented the TUC on the conference organising council and addressed the conference. In that year she was also invited to join the Board of the BBC. This was a part-time salaried position for a period of five years. Her retirement from the union would take effect from February 1958 and she wanted to serve on the BBC Board but retain her association with the union until that time. The GEC agreed that she could take up her position on the BBC Board.[60] She was also the President of Hillcroft College Council.

The GEC had to consider whether or not to replace her when the time came. Women's membership in the union had been growing steadily throughout the 1950s. Overall union membership at the end of 1956 was 1,328,820, only 8,240 short of the figure for 1951 which was the highest membership in the union's history. Women's membership was 155,260, an increase of 3,433 over the previous year,[61] and by early 1957, women's membership was 163,361, an increase of 8,101 compared with the end of 1955.[62] In 1957 the GEC agreed to a replacement for Florence Hancock and defined the post as 'dealing with the development of union organisation amongst women in industry and conducting national negotiations on their behalf where appropriate'.[63] In January 1958 the GEC interviewed candidates for Florence Hancock's replacement, who included Vi Taylor and Sis. J. Stevens, the Region 13 Finance Administrator, and appointed Ellen McCullough from 10 February 1958. Tony Corfield was appointed Secretary of the Education Department, in which position he was required to report directly to the Council, but was not given the status of National Officer. This was not the only time that Ellen McCullough moved from being in charge of education, without actually leaving completely, and we can speculate that she was appointed by an all-male GEC and a traditionalist general secretary (in this field at least) as a 'safe pair of hands' for a role which they did not completely understand or sympathise with.

METHODS AND OBJECTIVES IN THE POST-WAR PERIOD

It has already been noted that the significance of the TWI scheme was not only that it provided a new focus on the shop steward and workplace relations as central to the union's education mission, but that it was also the vehicle for the introduction of new active learning methods, in particular role-play and participative techniques. This was fully recognised at the time, as was the contrast which these methods provided with the pre-war approach of the NCLC and WEA. Harold Clay had occasionally experimented with interactive sessions, but most trade union education in the earlier period was based on the lecture and question-and-answer session for any active members who turned up. The same was true of the TGWU correspondence course, described by Tony Corfield as 'desperately dull',[64] and the wartime programme of John Price generally followed the 'liberal education' model. A flavour of both the value and the limitations of this type of school can be seen from this report to *The Record* in 1948 of a WEA school at Beatrice Webb House:

> Some 70 students were in residence. An international air pervaded the school. There was Walter Stude, a Swiss; a schoolmaster from Hanover and his three German compatriots, one a Fraulein flown straight from Berlin; our dark brothers from the West Indies, with much knowledge of racial discrimination; Vernon, the Ceylonese; Jack and a friend from Nigeria – Jack knew a thing or two about ground nuts. Chicago University as well as Toronto were worthily represented by adept and voluble individuals; 'The Vivacious Mademoiselle' was an asset, and lastly but by no means least, was the lady from Jerusalem and the disciples of Marx and Engels.[65]

Whilst it was clearly beneficial for TGWU members to meet such a wide cross-section of society, and clearly all were having a good time, there inevitably would have been very little focus on the workplace role of the shop steward at such a school. The debate on how to overcome this contradiction was being argued out in the WEA at this time, and led Ellen McCullough in 1951 to call for the Creech-Jones inquiry into trade union education in the Association.[66] By the time the Cirencester summer schools had become established, in the mid-1950s, teaching methods in the TGWU had been completely changed as a result of the different approach of Corfield's generation of tutors. The summer schools used WEA tutors who were essentially younger university lecturers in the 'extra mural' tradition, many of whom had a specific political commitment to trade unionism. The syllabus was in two sections. The morning consisted of training in practical skills such as report-making, note-taking and representation. In the afternoon there were sessions concerned with the union's wider responsibilities with employers, the Labour Party and the Labour Movement. While these may sometimes have been lectures, Corfield was a great believer in structure and practical outcomes, and there were documents for each section of the course. There was also role-play, public speaking inside and outdoors, and practice work in small groups, as well as general sessions such as branch meetings with exercises based on resolutions.

The background to the new approach was well described by Ellen McCullough:

> At our summer school in 1953 we tried a new method. The academic work was unchanged, but instead of supplementing this by lectures on various aspects of union work, we provided the students with papers relating to real or fabricated industrial situations, and set them to 'act out' the resulting chain of events. The tutors sat as assessors, criticising the performance after each session. In the planning of this course we had four ideas in mind. First, we believed that courses especially designed to help branch officers in their work would meet with a much better response than those of a non-specialist nature. Second, we resolved to make the teaching as practical as possible. Third, we determined not to narrow the syllabus to cover techniques only. We wanted students to learn not only how to do various union jobs well, but also why they should do them at all. Fourth, we wanted to devise methods which would make use of our students' maturity and practical experience, to overcome the difficulties they had as a result of poor education.[67]

When the first follow-on Branch Officers' training course was introduced in 1954, *The Record* gave it a full feature, with an emphasis on method:

> The TGWU has just embarked on what is probably the most ambitious educational experiment undertaken by any trade union in this country.

> Four hundred union members have been attending courses at Beatrice Webb House ... The course is thoroughly practical and as modern as tomorrow. A tape recorder is used to illustrate the pitfalls to avoid in making a speech, moving a resolution or presenting a wage claim. Many of the students have been fascinated to hear themselves as others hear them ... The students are probably the hardest worked of any in this country. They work a seven-hour day, reading, writing and hammering out problems. The tutors are Tony Corfield, Robert Davies, Noel Williams and Vic Allen.[68]

Allen was fully aware of this new development in union's education. He made the point when he opened the school on the first day. It had developed beyond the 'old-time' summer schools where the accent was on academic quality and where principles rather than practice were taught. This new approach concentrated on practical training for workshop organisation. He praised Fred Horne for his work in creating this new outlook, and referred to the experimental course in 1953 at which the methods of co-ordinating practical and academic training were perfected.[69]

A good example of the difference in approach was an article in *The Record* in July 1958, an 'interview' between Fred Horne and one of his stewards, Arthur Barnett, Secretary of the 1/693 branch, Murex Welding Processes. The discussion was about the practical training courses run in Region 1. Bro. Barnett was quoted as saying:

> On the Region 1 weekend schools our own officers take us, and we are already on close terms with them and are happy about asking them questions. Naturally I felt more at home with Jack Lucas as a tutor for I deal with him all the time. Graham Wootton my (WEA) tutor at Cirencester was a nice chap but we had not got the same close interests. He knows a lot about the British Legion (he has written a book about it) and the Labour Party, but on shop floor issues he didn't seem to be any better informed than, say, a lay member.[70]

That the union felt comfortable in publishing this rather brutal criticism, as well as the name of the hapless WEA tutor, is significant in itself. Throughout the 1950s and 1960s, the Education Department tried to build on this approach by developing a combination of 'drills' and active learning methods with educational aids of various kinds, in particular filmstrips, tape-recorders, and dedicated teaching manuals. Fred Horne's Region 1 Engineering and Chemical Workers Trade Group began experimenting with the use of films and filmstrips as early as 1951.[71] By 1952 the union had produced two filmstrips, one on the union's history and one depicting the situation leading to an unofficial strike. A third, on the union's structure, was completed in 1955. The TGWU was the only British trade union using filmstrips at this time. Each had about 60 frames or pictures, together with a recorded commentary, and ran for about half an hour.

By the mid-1950s all the regions were equipped with projection apparatus, and towards the end of 1955, better versions of the film-strips were completed, with a commentary on gramophone records dealing with the union's organisation and structure. By the 1960s, they had become dated in both method and content: innovators like Jack Jones were calling for the use of television in promoting and educating trade unionists, and the first TV programmes for trade unionists began to be made.

Another development grew out of the need to make sure that tutors teaching on TGWU programmes were 'on message' in terms of the union's policies and approach to students, and that they had relevant teaching material to support them in their task. During the 1950s, the Education Department attempted to standardise this aspect of the programme. The first step was to review the Home Study course. By the 1950s this course had been running for more than ten years, without serious revision. It will be recalled that from the earliest days of the course, the Education Committee adopted a rigorous standard, expecting detailed reports on each student essay, and only rarely awarding a certificate 'With Distinction'. By 1951, it was recognised that this approach had disadvantages, particularly in the case of the large number of inexperienced students who, working in isolation, found the writing of essays daunting. An alternative scheme was introduced under which students were asked to study the six course booklets carefully and to complete a test paper in the form of a questionnaire, rather than write essays. The adoption of this scheme led to an increase in the number of students who, having enrolled for the course, then completed. For example, of the 342 students completing the course in 1949 and 1950, 4.1 per cent applied for certificates, and of these 23.4 per cent gained 'Ordinary' certificates and 2.2 per cent certificates 'With Distinction'. Of the 579 students completing in 1951 and 1952, 43 per cent applied for certificates and of these 29.6 per cent gained 'Ordinary' certificates and 11.7 per cent certificates 'With Distinction'.[72] On the other hand, of course, it could be said that the course had been 'dumbed down', but the Department was unapologetic about reducing 'academic' content in the union's courses. The course continued steadily throughout the period, passing the 1,000 student mark in 1949, 3,000 in 1954 and 4,000 in 1956. In the early 1950s about 1,200 students enrolled each year, and about half of these completed the course. About 30 'With Distinction' certificates were issued each year.[73]

A second innovation which grew out of Corfield's practical approach to methods was the development of the teaching manual as a strict guide for tutors and students. Apart from its general appeal as the basis for active and participative learning methods, the teaching manual was also an attempt to solve the perennial problem of who was to tutor the union's courses, and was intended to be linked to the extension of the union official's role into this field. The objective of the Department was to extend the role of officers in the education programme, but this could only be done if tutors' materials were standardised, as officers had neither the background nor the time to act like traditional WEA or university tutors. As Fred Horne put it when comparing himself with Tony Corfield: 'The difference between you and me as teachers, is that I only teach what I know'.[74]

The development of teaching manuals also grew out of concern that many of the union's regional weekend schools were being conducted on 'liberal' WEA lines. It was becoming clear that whilst the union's national programmes were moving towards targeted shop steward and branch officer training, in the regions the WEA was still covering quite general issues and the NCLC was still focused on politics and current affairs. In 1955 the Education Department carried out a review of weekend schools in an attempt to bring them into a more standardised pattern. Ellen McCullough wanted to make sure that the weekend schools were using materials that were directly relevant to the roles of shop stewards or other branch officers. Union weekend schools were divided into two types: one for shop stewards and other branch officers where tuition was given on trade problems; 'these we do not propose to disturb'.[75] In other cases weekend schools consisted of lectures with questions and discussion. Because of the cost it was proposed that these should be restricted and that organisers should make sure that courses followed particular rules, making sure that:

> Proceedings during the weekend are connected courses, not just two or three lectures, and every student present has the opportunity to take an active part including making a speech ... There should be instruction papers, what we would call 'course materials', so that the students go away with a permanent record of what has happened.[76]

It was the intention of the Education Department to apply this rule to all regions and to make sure that the local officers were trained in using these methods. It was logical therefore that training manuals be developed to assist this process and to standardise the course content. This process was underway by 1958, and Tony Corfield used *The Record* to promote the use of officers as tutors:

> The trade union official in the second half of the twentieth century seems to be taking off his cloth cap and replacing it with a mortar board ... In the TGWU, at least 50 officials regularly teach in weekend schools. And the union is planning to place a greater reliance upon them as they extend the basic training programme for their active members.[77]

He was unapologetic about the union using officers as tutors; indeed he championed them in this role:

> To the professional tutor in adult education, such developments must look uncomfortably like dilution of labour. The skilled man is pushed out and unqualified teachers are taking over ... (However) I would go so far as to say that much of the recent advance in teaching methods throughout the adult education movement derives from experiments carried out by these full-time officers.[78]

During an internal debate on teaching methods within the WEA, Corfield made the link between the educational process on the courses, and focused trade union objectives:

> Over the four years during which we have been applying this method, every major controversial issue facing the union has been thoroughly aired – the size of the TGWU, the problem of breakaways, unofficial strikes, political tests for office-holding, the block vote, the power of full-time officials, and compulsory trade unionism; these have all been the subject of exercises ... The object of our schools is not merely to throw open the doors to academic study. It is more than this. It is an attempt to demonstrate that, by searching study, more effective answers can be given to the daily problems which arise for trade unionists ... [and] to demonstrate to our students that even after as little as three weeks' study of a particular problem they will be in a better position to give leadership on it.[79]

By the end of 1958, eight regions had completed briefing sessions for officers wishing to teach using the basic training manuals, and four others had made a commitment to do so. The manuals covered areas such as making branch policy, the wider links between the union and the Labour Party, the work of the shop steward, and the legal responsibility of branch officers. By 1962 there were six booklets on which the basic training was based.

THE DEBATE ON LONGER COURSES

By the mid 1950s, the basic pattern of the union's education programme was to use the Home Study course as the first stage, and then to encourage students to attend the summer school, where they would be trained using the teaching manuals. After that, they could attend the follow-on course, which was sometimes held away from Cirencester. In 1958, 40 selected students attended the follow-on course at Beatrice Webb House at the beginning of June. Normally, however, all the courses took place at Cirencester. At the same time as a student was following the theoretical course for chairmen or shop stewards, he, or rarely she, would also be undertaking practical training in skills. These might be opening and closing meetings, the rules for procedure, controlling debates, holding committee meetings, taking notes or making speeches. Shop stewards would also be trained in interviewing, preparing and presenting a case and reporting back to the members. He/she would also receive training in the proper procedure following an accident at work, in letter writing and report-drafting. The follow-on course focused on recent developments in wages policy. This was quite a theoretical course looking at the study and analysis of wages policy, wage restraint, and general economic issues. Ellen McCullough summed up the essence of the approach in 1956:

> A syllabus in effect has two main aspects – an inward-looking one into the special skills required for trade union action, and an outward-looking one into the political and economic environment in which action takes place. Students are given the opportunity of seeing their daily problems in the round – as problems calling for specialist skills and for a good general knowledge.[80]

Throughout the post-war period, the union had continued to send students to Ruskin College, Coleg Harlech, LSE and Hillcroft, in no great numbers, but with a high profile. In 1949 the F&GP agreed that the sum of £2,000 should be given to the Ruskin College Golden Jubilee Fund to support the expansion of the college. This proposed that two rooms in a new college building should bear the name of Ernest Bevin and Ben Tillett.[81] In 1951 the union agreed to make a contribution of £1,000 per annum over a period of seven years by entering into a deed of covenant for Ruskin College, and in 1957 the union decided to renew this deed of covenant to Ruskin College for a further seven years. In 1951, the college invited the union to appoint a further representative in addition to Creech-Jones to serve on the governing council, and the GEC appointed Ellen McCullough. In 1956 Tony Corfield prepared a short pamphlet *How to be a Student* to assist Ruskin College students.

By the mid 1950s, however, the focus of the union had shifted completely towards teaching the skills and issues associated with the role of branch officer and shop steward, and some of the active members began to question the value of supporting TGWU students at higher education colleges, arguing that scarce resources should be directed towards the union's own education programmes. At an individual level, the questioning of the value of sending TGWU students into higher education was increased by the example of Region 1 full-time official Len (later Sir Len) Neal. In 1952 the GEC was asked to support Bro. Neal, who had been awarded a scholarship for a degree in economics at Cambridge University for three years. The GEC granted him the equivalent of a full-time scholarship. It was noted at the time that it was his intention to continue in the service of the union, but the GEC felt that it would not be practicable to guarantee reinstatement to his then position of Assistant General Workers Group Secretary but only as Group Organiser.[82] After his three years at Cambridge, Len Neal was awarded a first-class honours degree. In June 1955 he returned to be General Workers District Officer at Clapham Road office. The August 1955 *Record* was full of praise for his achievement: 'Heartiest congratulations to Bro. Len Neal, awarded a first-class honours degree in economics at Cambridge University. He is probably the only British trade union official to graduate from university 26 years after leaving school'.[83] However, things were to go wrong almost immediately. Clearly Len Neal's achievement had made him feel that he deserved recognition and a higher position in the union, and in the summer of 1955 he stood against Frank Cousins for the post of Assistant General Secretary, but did not make the shortlist. He resigned from his position as full-time official in November 1955, not only leaving the union but going over to the 'other side', and ultimately becoming chairman of London Transport.

Len Neal's example goes to the heart of the dilemma facing the advocates of higher education for trade unionists. On the one hand, the union wants to provide higher education opportunities for its members. On the other hand, the union also wants to make sure that advancement in the organisation is open to all and is mostly dependent on building up a record of involvement within the organisation and serving time on committees and in the workplace. Higher education should not be seen as short-circuiting this process. As it happens members who have been to college often see their real choice frustrated, or leave the union to enter management or the professions – exactly what happened to Len Neal. This in turn raises questions amongst the remaining membership as to the value of spending the union's resources on such people.

This issue came to a head at the 1957 BDC and an ensuing 'great debate' during 1958. At the BDC one of the delegates openly criticised the fact that union money was spent to send TGWU members to college as full-time students:

> It is not my purpose to criticise the actual (education) expenditure ... I am chiefly concerned with the amount spent on scholarships at the LSE, Coleg Harlech and Ruskin College and I draw attention to the fact that in Region 1 we have educated several people and spent considerable sums of money in sending them to the LSE and Ruskin College and when they have achieved their object they leave the union and go to the other side ... a bus worker was sent to the LSE for two years and he went to Canada. What he is doing in Canada I do not know, but I can assure you he is not driving a bus. If we are going to concentrate on

> education as we should, we should concentrate on the form of education which will be of value to our organisation and not to the other side … I am not attacking Miss McCullough as such, I will say this, that what we need is more short-term education such as one-day schools, weekend schools and weekend scholarships. This is the form of education of most benefit to our movement and not the vast sums of money which are being spent to educate our people and then they go and work for the other side.[84]

Frank Cousins intervened to advocate caution: 'As to those who use the LSE and Ruskin College as a jumping-ground as betterment for themselves, let us remember the others who went to those places and used them as a medium to help others. Let us not get it out of perspective'.[85]

Despite Cousins's intervention, this incident opened a hornets' nest, and throughout 1958 there was a debate in *The Record* about whether full-time education for trade unionists was a waste of the resources of the union. A typical example was an article in February 1958 'Workers at College', written by Tony Corfield:

> No one who attended the BDC at Torquay last summer and who listened to Bro. Benny Cohen's criticisms about full-time education for trade unionists can be left in any doubt that this is a controversial question. Is it the job of the union to send members to college? And even if it is, oughtn't we to begrudge spending money which could otherwise be used on weekend and one-day schools to benefit a large number of members on full-time education or a very small minority?[86]

This debate was intriguing in that it touched a nerve, and the amount of energy spent on it by Tony Corfield and Ellen McCullough was a classic case of 'protesting too much' over what amounted to an insignificant number of students and a minimal expenditure by the union. It is apparent with hindsight that Corfield and McCullough saw this type of 'workerist' criticism as a threat to their strategic goal of leading the most able TGWU members into higher education. They were both, after all, firmly rooted in the WEA and were 'improvers' through and through. They recognised that once working-class people had left school, it was almost impossible for them to engage in higher education, unless they could be brought into the longer courses such as those provided by the WEA through the trade union route. The difference between them and many others in adult education at that time was that they understood that conventional academic teaching methods were unsuitable for trade union students on the short courses and would have turned them off further involvement in education. This was noted at the time by Jack Lucas, who remembered Ellen McCullough as a very good teacher, who would say about conventional academics 'I don't call them academics, I call them dirty dogs'.[87] Although this was tongue-in-cheek, Ellen McCullough did draw a strict line between the unions' business and the academics' business when it came to mainstream trade union education. For example, in 1951, whilst she was proposing to the WEA annual conference a motion calling for the WEA to set up a committee to study the direction in which trade union education should go with the WEA, she was also snubbing the involvement of other academics in the same question. In her own words:

> Some weeks ago I received from Nuffield College an invitation to take part in a private conference convened to discuss the future of trade union education. The invitation was a personal one from Mr H. Clegg and others at Nuffield College, from Mr Pickstock of the University of Oxford and from Mr H.D. Hughes. I am strongly of the opinion that discussions on the future development of trade union education are better conducted inside our own movement, and I therefore declined the invitation on these grounds. I have since been informed that others invited acted similarly, and the conference has therefore been abandoned.[88]

However, this was more a rejection of outsiders' interference in the policy and purpose of trade union education rather than a rejection of academic study itself. In other respects, Ellen McCullough was a firm supporter of the wider 'lifelong learning' aims of the WEA and the extra-mural movement.

Tony Corfield's own firm rejection of vague academic methods for the short courses has already been noted. However, he was also keen to introduce longer study-based courses in the union such as the 'Busmen's Long Course' at Transport House. This represented something of a pet project for Corfield, and beginning in 1953, was his first significant work outside of the summer schools. This was a three-year class and all students had to write essays regularly. Tony Corfield was formally attached to the University of London to act as tutor and the General Secretary authorised the use of a committee room at Transport House. The inaugural meeting of the tutorial class was held at on 2 November 1953, with 50 students in attendance. The course covered subjects such as the functions and structure of trade unions, economic problems and trade unions and politics. In order to tailor a long course to meet the needs of shift workers, it was decided that the class would meet on Tuesday mornings and also in the evenings. Identical classes were given at both sessions on each day so that students on shift work could attend at least one of them.[89] This proved an innovative and successful course, and lasted until 1959.

This commitment to a long traditional university extra-mural course and Corfield's personal involvement in it showed that the traditional WEA goal of personal improvement through adult education was still there, and in response to the challenge to it, all hands went to the pumps to defend academic education for trade unionists. To some extent, McCullough and Corfield had a tiger by the tail, because it was they who had so strongly advocated the value of 'drill' and role education in contrast to the 'liberal academic' approach of the pre-war WEA. Their approach had proved extremely popular within the union, and TGWU members were increasingly confident of their ownership of the union's education methods and their superiority over elementary school and higher academic approaches to learning.

Corfield's article in *The Record* in February 1958 went on justify TGWU students attending longer courses:

> One of the most widely-held complaints against sending students to college is that many of them are afterwards lost to the Labour Movement. A recent survey of the subsequent careers of union scholars shows a healthier picture. Of the 92 members who received scholarships from the union between 1946 and 1956, 11 have been appointed full-time officials, 2 full-time members of the staff, 4 as officers of the WEA, and 1 an officer of the TUC, all of whom are union members. Thirty-eight have returned to their previous industries and kept up membership, no fewer than 33 holding some lay office in the union. Six became schoolteachers and are now members of the NUT. Two have entered other occupations and hold office in their appropriate unions, 1 has become unemployed, 4 have changed their occupations and now belong to no union. Two have married and left paid employment, 2 have died, 3 have entered the Colonial Labour Service, 2 have emigrated, 7 are still studying and contact has been lost with the remaining 7 members, most of whom were awarded their scholarships in the period from 1946 to 1948.[90]

The article then invited correspondence on the subject and the debate continued in the pages of *The Record*.

Vi Taylor, formerly a member of the GEC and by this time a member of Region 1 Committee for six years and a member of the union's parliamentary panel, and 'Billy' Hughes, Principal of Ruskin College, staged an 'interview' in the record to advocate students attending longer courses either at LSE and particularly at Ruskin College. Vi Taylor put her case:

> I am not saying I found everything perfect at Ruskin, but on the basis of my own experience I most emphatically favour sending trade unionists to college. It gave me the chance to tackle the more fundamental problems facing us in the sphere of wages, organisation and politics, without feeling, as I often did before, that I was out of my depth. I came back a

> keener, and I hope more efficient trade unionist. My year at college was a most stimulating intellectual and social experience, and one in which I made and have kept some sterling friendships. What I got out of my year at college I have tried my best to give back to the union.[91]

One of the best contributions to the debate was a letter from C.B. Ward of 8/250 branch:

> I believe I am the only existing officer who has been appointed after attending a full-time course of study at Ruskin College, and ... I am taking this opportunity of stating why I believe it is in the interest of the union to continue to provide facilities for full-time study for interested and active members ... There is an old English saying which goes 'he who learns by experience is intelligent but he who will only learn by personal experience is a fool' ... The value of any full-time course is that it enables one to devote one's full time to studying the experiences and opinions of others.[92]

Whilst the debate itself faded from the pages of the journal, it had the effect of prompting Ellen McCullough and Tony Corfield to ask the GEC in September 1958 to institute a review of education provision, and to adopt an Executive Statement on the structure and objectives of the programme, the first since the 1949 BDC. The GEC was keen to deflect any criticism which might come at the 1959 BDC. In March 1959, therefore, the GEC made it plain that 'future union educational policy was to be primarily based upon a desire that there should be a greater emphasis on the development of a service more widely related to the internal needs of the membership'.[93]

However, this was defined in such a way as to maintain the existing system beginning at a practical level linked to the workplace, using officers as tutors and instruction manuals, and progressing through more liberal and discussing methods, summer schools and onto full-time academic education for an appropriate and self-selected few. The only new emphasis was that the regions were to be asked to be more systematic in their approach to education provision. The Home Study course would continue to operate in its existing form, with the booklets being revised and brought up to date, and students would continue to be steered onto WEA and NCLC correspondence courses.

However, when it came to what was called 'Liberal Studies' in the regions, any future work in conjunction with outside educational bodies was to be limited to a pre-determined budget. The regions were given responsibility, but these activities were to be incidental to the main purpose, which was workplace-based. The one-week union training and follow-on courses were to continue as before; however, an educational qualification for entry was instituted, based on enrolment for the Home Study course. With regard to full-time studies, regardless of the 'great debate', the present system was to continue unchanged.[94] All of this represented a victory for Tony Corfield, and made sense in practical terms. It did, however, cause some resentment in the regions. Former Administrative Officer Sid Forty commented: 'Support for regional education diminished when the Education Department was under Corfield, as he thought all education activities were the prerogative of Central Office, hence there were grounds for conflict'.[95] It also represented another nail in the coffin of the NCLC and the WETUC, soon to be absorbed into the TUC education scheme, and it also set the scene for the extension of regional education programmes, local initiatives and company-based courses which were to flourish in the 1960s.

MANAGING THE PROGRAMME, 1945-1959

Arthur Deakin never deviated from enthusiastic support for the union's education programme in general and Ellen McCullough in particular. Apart from Florence Hancock, Ellen McCullough was the only female senior official of the union, and often had to work with an all-male GEC. She was one of those women who is comfortable in a male-dominated environment, and clearly had the ability to make the men feel comfortable with her. Jack Lucas described her as 'very much one of the lads',[96] and Deakin's own attitude was demonstrated at the 1949 BDC when one of the delegates stated that it was 'very difficult in this conference to launch an attack upon a department of this union which is controlled by a member of the opposite sex'. Deakin intervened immediately: 'Don't you hesitate brother!', which caused laughter in the conference. The speaker persisted that 'Even in the hurly-burly of this conference, a certain gentleness is shown towards the ladies ... ' However, Ellen McCullough would have none of it, and to more laughter insisted: 'Mr Chairman and friends: may I begin by telling the first questioner that I am not particularly frail or in need of gentleness'.[97] Deakin went on to say to the conference – to great applause and shouts of 'hear, hear', 'I do not think that this union suffers by reason of the fact that a member of the female sex is in charge of our educational side ... and there is no trade union in the country that is more liberal in making provision for its members than this union of ours'.[98]

As noted earlier, Deakin took a long-term view of the benefits of education:

> Money spent on education, though not always bringing results immediately, must be regarded as a necessary commitment if an organisation such as ours is to hold its own and play its proper part within a democracy. In other words, if we are to prepare our people for the acceptance of greater responsibilities, then we must accept the commitment and expand our educational programme to the fullest possible extent.[99]

One of Deakin's final statements was at the 1953 BDC – his last – in answer to a question on the cost of education. He simply said 'Nothing is too much to do – our aim is full educational development'.[100]

His record in supporting the growth of the programme is difficult to challenge. The point has been well made by Vic Allen in his biography of Deakin:

> In 1942 the sum of £10 was distributed as educational grants; this had increased to £744 for year ending 31 December 1947 and to £34,764 for the year ending 31 December 1954 ... Arthur Deakin nor any other official of the union attempted to control the manner in which the individual tutor tackled his syllabus or what he taught. The spirit of liberal education remained unimpaired ... It is always difficult to assign credit to individuals on the achievements of the organisation. The pioneering work was led by the Secretary of the Education Department (i.e. John Price) but it could not have been done at all without Deakin's support.[101]

That Deakin was serious in this was shown with the financial commitment for the second leap forward for the education programme following the 1949 BDC. Overall expenditure on education in 1945 had been £1,502, in 1947, £8,605, and for 1948, £9,473, reaching the £10,000 mark in 1949 (£200,000 at today's values) The estimate of the additional expenditure involved for the new scheme in 1950 was in the region of £25,000 per annum (£500,000 at today's values) – an enormous sum in those days – excluded the general administration costs associated with the Education Department.[102] Expenditure remained at £25,000 during 1951 and 1952, rising to £30,000 in 1953. By 1955, the financial allocation had been increased to £32,500 (£450,000 at today's values) and it remained at or around this level throughout the rest of the 1950s, being slightly reduced in 1956, and again slightly increased. Contemporary estimates of the actual total cost of the programme, including the cost of administration, varied between £65,000 and £100,000 (£800,000 to £1,200,000 at today's values).[103]

Throughout the immediate post-war years, student numbers rose in response to the extension of education facilities.[104] An analysis of TGWU students in 1948-49 showed that 1,583 students were enrolled for correspondence courses with all bodies, and that a total of 630 students had attended day and weekend schools, including 450 on the union's own schools.[105] By the early 1950s, the Department was claiming an annual student number of around 10,000. This was partly due to an extremely inclusive way of counting students attending WEA, NCLC and similar external bodies, and also treating each student place as a 'new' student, whereas students would attend more than one course. Nevertheless, the increase was still impressive.

TGWU student numbers 1951-54 and 1955-56

Year	Total Students	Short Courses	B/O Students
1951-52	19,026	1,983	1,957
1953-54	19,484	3,711	2,878
1955-56	19,154	2,315	3,185

Source: TGWU Education Department Reports. Branch Officers Course Students

Arthur Deakin died on May 1st, 1955 whilst addressing a May Day rally in Leicester. Those prepared to stand for General Secretary on Deakin's retirement were Charles Brandon, Alf Chandler, Frank Cousins, Harry Nicholas, Tim O'Leary, and Arthur Tiffin. In the subsequent election Arthur Tiffin came first with 267,000 votes, followed by Charles Brandon with 146,000, Frank Cousins with 74,000 and Harry Nicholas with 44,000. However, although elected in the summer of 1955, Tiffin was never able to take up his position because of illness, and he died on 27 December in the same year. Although often overlooked because of his extremely short time as General Secretary, Tiffin, appointed AGS in 1948, also had an involvement in education. He began his working life as a railway clerk and joined the Railway Clerks in 1912. He served in the 1914-18 war and rose to the rank of Captain, a title he was still formally entitled to, and was wounded in action and discharged in 1918. In 1919 he became a London bus driver and a member of the union. He was appointed a district officer in 1932 and took over the membership on the country services of the London General Omnibus Company. He chaired the London Labour Party and the London Trades Council and represented WETUC on the national executive of the WEA. There is no doubt that had Tiffin lived to fulfil his role as General Secretary, he would have continued Deakin's support for the education programme.

Among the candidates for Assistant General Secretary were Frank Cousins, Jack Jones, Len Neal and Harry Nicholas. The two short-listed candidates were Frank Cousins and Harry Nicholas and Frank Cousins was appointed from 6 August 1955. Because of Tiffin's illness, Frank Cousins had to take full responsibility almost from the start, assisted by his unexpected champion, Alf Chandler.[106] Cousins was very different from Deakin, and not at home in the area of union education. He had had very little involvement with the WEA or NCLC, and although extremely interested in science and technology and in education and training in general, was associated with the industrial and political aspects of the union, rather than with its education programme, and indeed made very few public statements on the subject. Frank Cousins joined the WETUC committee after taking up his duties as AGS, but the pressure of other duties prevented his attendance.[107] On the other hand, Cousins was generally supportive, as show here in 1958 while addressing one of the union's branches:

> In our early days in trade unionism there was no education for us, but there is now for our younger members. Our Education Department is a very important part of the union, and I am glad to say that some of the members of this branch are availing themselves of the facilities. That is what we want, fully trained members in branches, because whatever we at Central Office try to do, we cannot achieve anything without our members.[108]

Along with the other senior officials, Cousins strongly supported Ellen McCullough, and she retained her place on the TUC General Council during Cousins's term as General Secretary. She in turn relied heavily on Tony Corfield as the brains behind the new education ideas. She was a generation older than Corfield, and would habitually refer to him as her 'boyfriend' (with the meaning of the present-day 'toy-boy').[109] Corfield was always kept slightly at arm's length by the leadership, and was in some ways rather too middle-class and radical for some officials and GEC members. They respected his enthusiasm and knowledge, but some of the more right wing of the leadership had an uncomfortable relationship with Corfield – similar to that of conservative working-class parents with a progressive grammar-school teacher. A good example of this is an article written by Corfield himself in the WEA journal *Trade Union Education,* reporting on the 1955 summer schools. In it he notes that 'in the afternoon the chairmen (sic) took part in an exercise in controlling a debate. The subject of the debate was on a motion to end the practice of using the block vote at the TUC and Labour Party conferences in the interests of securing a more just representation of the views of the membership on general policy'.[110] No safe bureaucrat would have introduced such a debate on a TGWU school at that time, or, if he had, certainly would not have publicised it in that way.

When, therefore, in February 1958 Ellen McCullough replaced Florence Hancock, Corfield was not appointed as her direct replacement by the Executive Council and was referred to as Secretary rather than National Secretary, i.e. staff rather than officer. He still had to report to the GEC, making his first appearance in March 1958. This slightly uneasy relationship was to affect Corfield's position in the 1960s and contributed to the circumstances of his resignation from the union in 1969. Generally speaking, both the Department and the course programme were well managed by McCullough and Corfield, and they were always keen to use *The Record* to publicise the courses available.

The great success of the immediate post-war period was the introduction and consolidation of the branch officers' summer schools based on active learning methods. As the 1960s evolved, these began to be equalled in importance by local initiatives based on day-release. As the 1960s approached, Ellen McCullough could look back at the progress made in the 15 years since the war, and her own and the Department's achievements:

> We are proud of the educational service we give. We believe it is the most comprehensive offered by any union in the country, and over the last ten years we have built up a wealth of experience which we believe will enable us to improve and vary the provision from year to year. We are now able to say that we have a clear view of our members' wishes and needs in the educational field, and good means of judging changes in these wishes and needs as they take place in the future.[111]

Thus ended one of the most consistently creative periods in the history of the union's education programme, reflecting the shift from the more bureaucratic, staid union of Bevin and Deakin to the more open, left-leaning TGWU of Cousins and Jack Jones. If, as has been said, the key to the change was the development of plant and company bargaining, and the recognition of the key role played in this process by the shop steward, then the education programme played a vital part in this development through the summer schools and through the focus on branch officers' and shop stewards' skills which was central to these, and central to the thinking of Tony Corfield, Ellen McCullough, Fred Horne, Tom Wylie and the other tutors and organisers described in the narrative. A major difference in this respect between the development of the union as a whole and within the education programme was that in the latter case progress was firmly supported by Arthur Deakin, often seen as the most bureaucratic and reactionary of general secretaries. He may have had his own reasons for giving support, but there is no doubt that it was genuine, and that in his period of office significant resources were diverted into the education programme. The hard work of the late 1940s and 1950s put the TGWU in a strong position to take advantage of even more radical change and opportunity available in the 1960s, the period which saw the rise of Jack Jones, the spread of day-release, the beginning of the TUC shop stewards' education scheme, but also the departure of Tony Corfield from his position in the union.

NOTES

1. Report of the Political, Research and Education Department, 16 August 1946.
2. Report of the Political, Research and Education Department, 18 November 1946.

3. Memo from A.J. Chandler to E. McCullough, 14 March 1946.
4. Minutes of the F&GP, 17 January 1946, Minute No 47, p10.
5. Minutes of the Education Committee, 15 August 1946, Minute No 332.
6. General Secretary's Report, 1946, p314.
7. GEC, 18 September 1947, Minute No 112.
8. GEC, 6 December 1946, Minute No 1262, p303.
9. F&GP, 8 May 1947, Minute No 463, p113.
10. Report of the Education Secretary dated 8 May 1946.
11. Meeting of the Education Committee, 17 May 1944.
12. Ibid.
13. Ibid.
14. Reports of the Secretary dated 8 May 1946 and 22 April 1947.
15. Education Committee, 22 April 1947.
16. Minutes of the GEC, 20 September 1945, Minute No 932, p203.
17. Minutes of the GEC, 23 May 1947, Minute No 700, p156.
18. GEC, 3 December 1947, Minute No 1416, p307.
19. *The Record,* March/April 1947, p221.
20. *The Record,* September 1947, p78.
21. Ibid.
22. *The Record*, June 1949, p17.
23. *The Record,* March 1949 and June 1949. The optimistic spirit and joint approach associated with the nationalised industries can be seen in this small example. In 1949, the London Transport Executive had an opening of a war memorial for members who died during the war, and organised a concert with many TGWU people in attendance including Arthur Deakin and Harold Clay. The entertainment was compiled by Bill Owen and the artists included Petula Clarke, Dinah Sheridan, Jon Pertwee, Richard Attenborough and Jack Warner.
24. R. Fieldhouse and Associates, *A History of Modern British Adult Education*, London: NIACE, 1996, p338.
25. See Corfield, op. cit., pp106-7.
26. Fred Horne's report to the Education Committee, 8 May 1950.
27. Interview with Jack Lucas, 22 January 1999.
28. BDC, 15 July 1949, pp349-352 of Verbatim Minutes.
29. Minutes of the Education Committee, 16 November 1949, Minute No 558.
30. Appendix to the Minutes of the GEC submitted by the General Secretary for the extension of the Union Education Facilities, 15 December 1949.
31. It should be emphasised that although shop stewards were increasingly important in the workplace, they were still not acknowledged in the TGWU rulebook.
32. Education Committee, 8 May 1950.
33. Report of the Political, Research, Education and International Department, 26 May 1953, p7.
34. *The Record*, February 1953.
35. See John Burrows, *University Adult Education in London: A Century of Achievement:* University of London, 1976, p104.
36. Report of the Education Secretary, 5 November 1951.
37. Ibid.
38. Ibid.

39. General Secretary's Report, 2 March 1953, p53.
40. Interview with Tony Corfield, 26 March 1998.
41. 'Education Notes' by Tony Corfield, The Record, April 1968, p19.
42. A. Corfield and E. McCullough, *Trade Union Branch Officers' Manual*, London: Chapman and Hall, 1964, pv.
43. Report of the Political, Research, Education and International Department, 3 December 1952, p7.
44. WEA, Programme for the 1953 TGWU National Residential Courses.
45. GEC, 12 June 1953, Minute No 446, p106.
46. Report of the Political, Research, Education and International Department, 26 May 1953, p6.
47. General Secretary's Report dated 20 September 1954, p181.
48. Later accused of being an agent for MI5.
49. Acting General Secretary' Quarterly Report, March 1946, p64.
50. See, for example, report of the Political, Research, Education and International Department, 2 September 1949.
51. Conversation with Sid Forty, 28 January 2001.
52. Interview with Jack Lucas, 22 January 1999. Up until the 1980s, Trade Group representation on the GEC came from the relevant National Committee, whereas 'territorial' reps were directly elected by the members. So Muriel Rayment and Vi Taylor would have come to the GEC via this route.
53. It is thought she then worked in London Transport. Conversation with Sid Forty, 26 January 2001.
54. Minutes of the Education Committee, 15 August 1946, Minute No 320.
55. Meeting of the Education Committee, 23 June 1948, Minute No 467.
56. GEC, 4 March 1955, Minute No 238, p51.
57. GEC, 3 June 1958, Minute No 347, p89.
58. GEC, 5 June 1959, Minute No 402.
59. Report of the Education Secretary, 9 November 1955.
60. General Executive Council, 14 June 1956, p88.
61. Acting General Secretary's Report, 5 March 1956, p54.
62 General Secretary's Fourth Quarterly Report, 4 March 1957.
63. GEC, 17 September 1957, Minute No 548.
64. Interview with Tony Corfield, 26 March 1998.
65. *The Record*, September 1948, p73. Harold Clay and Ernest Green both spoke at this school. The reporter was Herbert Woodhead, from Halifax.
66. See Corfield, op. cit., pp104-122.
67. Education Secretary's Report, 13 August 1954.
68. *The Record*, July 1954, p46.
69. *The Record*, May 1954, p324.
70. *The Record*, July 1958, pp45-47.
71. Report of the Political, Research, Education and International Department, 30t August 1951, p6.
72. Trade Group Departmental Review 1951, pp182-187.
73. TGWU Correspondence Course. Numbers enrolling: 1951-52, 1,343; 1953-54, 1,281; 1955-56, 1,127. Number Completing: 1951-52, 579; 1953-54, 821; 1955-56, 694. Number of students awarded 'With Distinction' Certificates: 1951-52, 29; 1953-54, 29; 1955-56, 31.
74. 'Trade Union Officials as Instructors' by Tony Corfield, *The Record*, July

1958, p41.
75. Education Secretary's Report, 9 November 1955.
76. Ibid.
77. Tony Corfield, *The Record*, July 1958, op. cit., p41.
78. Ibid.
79. A. Corfield, 'A Reply on Teaching Methods', *Trade Union Education,* No 5, March 1957, pp10-13.
80. Trade Group and Departmental Review for 1956, p198.
81. The first recipient of the Ernest Bevin Second Year Memorial Scholarship was Bro. R.H. Carmichael of 8/489 branch, General Secretary's Report, 15 September 1952, p173.
82. F&GP, 24 April 1952, Minute No 224, p63.
83. *The Record*, August 1955, p60.
84. Bro. B. Cohen, Region 1, BDC 1957, first day, 8 July 1957, Verbatim Minutes pp68-69.
85. Ibid., p70.
86. *The Record,* February 1958.
87. Interview with Jack Lucas, 22 January 1999.
88. Education Committee Report, 26 April 1951.
89. See *The Record,* December 1953, p181.
90. *The Record,* February 1958.
91. Ibid., p28.
92. *The Record*, June 1958, p43.
93. GEC, 3 March 1959, Minute No 134, p29.
94. Appendix to the GEC Minutes: 'Basis of a plan to govern future union educational policy as referred to in Minute No. 134', 3 March 1959.
95. Letter from Sid Forty, 29 January 2001.
96. Interview with Jack Lucas, 22 January 1999.
97. BDC, 12 July 1949, Verbatim Minutes, p140.
98. Ibid., p144.
99. General Secretary's Report, 12 December 1949, p273.
100. *The Record*, August 1953, p80.
101. Allen, *Trade Union Leadership*, op. cit., pp243-245.
102. GEC, 15 December 1949, Minute No 1100, p257.
103. See, for example, Press Policy Statement from the GEC, 28 February 1955, p61, and Trade Group and Departmental Review for 1956, pp194-202.
104. The student statistics are taken from the annual Education Department reports for the period.
105. Report of the Political, Research, Education and International Department, 20 May 1949, p3.
106. See G. Goodman, *The Awkward Warrior: Frank Cousins: His Life and Times*, London: Spokesman, 1979, especially pp80-113.
107. Report on the Union Education Scheme, 1955.
108. *The Record*, February 1958, p37.
109. Interview with Jack Lucas, 22 January 1999.
110. Corfield, 'Report on the TGWU Training Courses in 1955', op. cit., p16.
111. Trade Group and Departmental Review for 1956, p200.

Chapter 5

The Regions and Day Release 1945–1969

This chapter looks at the growing involvement of the regions of the TGWU in the education programme, which began in earnest in the immediate post-war period. The union had been strongly 'federalist' since its inception, with area secretaries being amongst the most powerful officials, and the education programme inevitably reflected area/regional diversity. The chapter looks at this process, and at particular innovations at the local level in various parts of the union. It also considers the important developments which began in the 1960s and which were to fundamentally affect the TGWU programme. These were the establishment of a centralised TUC education scheme in 1964, and the introduction of the principle of day release, embodied in the 1964 Industrial Training Act, which led to the increasing importance of workplace-based courses and joint courses with employers.

THE RISE OF THE REGIONS

We saw earlier that in 1943 John Price had put forward the view that the future of TGWU education lay in the regions (then called areas), and that at some point this would call for the appointment of someone of sufficient seniority to oversee and develop the education programme in each area/region. In the immediate post-war period, the implementation of this was delayed for a number of reasons. First of all, by leaving the union, John Price was not able to carry the plan through in the face of resistance by the area secretaries, who generally preferred education to be organised through their own offices, with the assistance of an administrative grade member of staff. Secondly, Ellen McCullough and Tony Corfield focused their attention on developing shop stewards' education through the national summer school and follow-on system, where they could directly influence content and quality, and make sure that their progressive active learning methods were implemented consistently across all the union's membership, whatever their region. However, we should note that regional and local education programmes continued throughout this period, and began to gain in strength during the 1960s. By the 1970s, the demand for a systematic regional approach to education was such that by the end of that decade most of them had appointed an 'Education Specialist' or Regional Education Officer, and by the 1980s the centre of gravity of the education programme had shifted decisively towards the regions.

The issue of local provision came up immediately after the war, at the 1945 BDC, when a resolution was submitted in the name of branch 9/4 (Rotherham and Sheffield Passenger):

> That this branch, realising the strength and importance of the union both politically and industrially, realises also that leadership of the union branches have a great responsibility. We, therefore, seek the support of conference in urging the GEC to extend direct educational facilities in the areas, during the immediate post-war years, in order that we may be equipped to carry out our duties intelligently.[1]

In the debate it was pointed out that an adequate scheme designed to develop the union's education facilities was already in operation, and this scheme made provision for a wide measure of flexibility. The view was expressed that a scheme based on the areas would probably have the effect of tying the hands of the GEC in carrying through the education policy of the union; in other words, it was felt to be better to have the GEC in control rather than some of the area secretaries. On this argument, the motion was lost. The issue was raised again at the 1949 conference, when both Area 3 (South-West) and the Power Workers' Group, both long-time advocates of education, submitted resolutions. Area 3 sought to replicate its own system throughout the union:

> That this conference agrees to the appointment of a full-time education officer in each area, and that more funds be made available to each area for educational purposes. Further, that Social and Educational Councils in each area shall have greater facilities and funds to further social activities for educational purposes.[2]

The Power Workers' resolution came from the Rogerstone branch:

> That full-time education officers shall be appointed in each district for the purpose of giving lectures to shop stewards, branch officers and active lay members, on such important issues as the functions of trade unions, the political and economic structures of modern society, legislation affecting trade unions, Industrial Injuries Act etc.[3]

These were two of the resolutions withdrawn at the 1949 BDC in response to Deakin's commitment to implement the national scheme which went on to become the Cirencester schools, and to encourage education in the areas.

The issue had also been raised on the GEC immediately after the war, for example in March 1946 when Area 4 asked for the appointment of a specialised Area Education Officer. The GEC view was that administrative work should be in the hands of one or more of the existing officers or senior members of the staff, and therefore it did not support the proposal.[4] The Welsh did not take this lying down, however, and at the next GEC, in May, Area 4 reaffirmed its earlier request for an education officer, saying it was unreasonable to expect an existing officer or member of staff to undertake the administrative work involved, in addition to their normal duties. The GEC asked the Education Committee to take note of the views expressed during the discussion and consider the advisability of giving further guidance to areas in relation to their education activities.[5] The matter was taken up at the Education Committee, and in November 1946 Ellen McCullough reported that contact officers or members of staff were functioning in all areas. On the other hand, the Committee accepted the view that there was a need, at least in the case of certain areas, to co-ordinate the education activities and stimulate interest, as there was unevenness.[6]

The Education Committee took the view that whilst financial provision and publicity should be met from Central Office, 'the real work of encouraging members to take full advantage of such facilities must, of necessity, lie with the respective area offices'.[7] The area secretaries were asked to approach 1947 with particular targets:

1. Bringing the facilities for correspondence courses to the notice of members – particularly new members and those returning from the forces.
2. Making sure that branches understood that if they wished to organise a class or course of lectures, the resources of the WETUC were at their disposal.
3. Bringing the scholarships available for full-time instruction to the notice of members who were most likely to take full advantage of them.
4. Organising one-day or weekend schools for members, particularly in relatively remote areas where educational opportunities were scanty.
5. Maintaining contact with local offices of the WETUC.[8]

Each area reported on the current state of education publicity and organisation as follows:

Area 1: There was no special sub-committee or machinery for educational purposes. Arthur Tiffin as Area Organiser tried to encourage and stimulate interest in education matters in the area. Harry White, Kent District Officer, was organising schools.

Area 3: The Bristol Educational and Social Council carried out education work 'both formal and informal'. In 1947 six residential weekend schools were being organised.

Area 5: Although an industrial officer in the Birmingham district, Tom Wylie was described as 'Area Education Officer', one of whose responsibilities was putting the educational facilities before the branches in his district. One-day schools for union members, conducted by district officers, had been organised in Birmingham, Nuneaton, Worcester, Coventry and Leicester.

Area 6: (North-west) This area had established an Educational and Social Council which organised several one-day schools.

Area 7: (Scotland) No special committee had been formed, but the area secretary and his clerical assistant informed interested members as to opportunities.

Area 8: (Northern) No special committee had been set up, but at the area committee and at other committees special attention was drawn to educational facilities provided by the union. In several cases WETUC classes had been run exclusively for union members. A very large number of one-day schools was organised in this comparatively small area, and Bro. Hills (Area Secretary) and Miss Grieve (clerical assistant) made sure that members, even in isolated places, had the opportunity to take advantage of the facilities.

Area 9: Two education committees had been set up in the area, in the Sheffield and Leeds districts. The first meetings had been held and plans were in hand for a series of schools and educational conferences.

Area 12: (Merseyside) The area committee had set up a sub-committee charged with the duty of promoting the cultural, social and education facilities.

Area 13: (North Wales) The area committee had instructed the area secretary to establish a fund for further education purposes.

No information was received from Areas 2, 4 and 10, and Area 11(Ireland) reported that 'at the moment we feel that our members take very good advantage of courses available through the WEA and the NCLC'.[9] It is easy to see that many of these replies were bureaucratic attempts by area secretaries to give an indication that ambitious plans were afoot, whilst not giving any specific information on activities which, in some cases, did not in fact exist. The historical evidence clearly indicates that in this period just after the war, only Areas 3, 5 and to a lesser extent 8 and 9 had a systematic approach to local courses. The other areas, if they did anything, imported the day-schools from the National Education Department. Areas 1, 2 and 7 were to develop their programmes towards the end of the 1940s and into the 1950s, and Areas 10, 4 and 6 had little provision into the 1960s.

These reports also show the wide range of area/regional diversity throughout the union, and how difficult it was going to be to try to establish any form of standardisation through an area-based mechanism.

From October 1950 the term 'area' was changed to 'region' in the reports of the Education Committee, and I shall henceforth use that term. The emphasis on the Centre meant that regional development was patchy throughout the 1950s. In some cases, such as in Region 1, great progress was made, in others, virtually none.

Some of the difficulties were practical, such as the quality or enthusiasm of particular officers, the relationship with local colleges or other providers, or administrative problems within the region. In 1956 the Education Department undertook a review of the payment of 'loss of time' to branch officers on weekend schools. The Department proposed to the regions a scheme whereby a sum was made available at the beginning of the year for day and weekend schools, based on the whole amount available to the union for this purpose and apportioned amongst the regions on a basis roughly equivalent to their proportion of membership.

This represented the first attempt by the Department to allocate budgets to the regions, and to try to set some minimum standards of administration and education methods. Previous to this, regions had 'imported' a school of national standard, or the arrangements had been left in the hands of regional secretaries or enthusiastic local officers.

The report of the Education Scheme for 1957 includes for the first time an allocation of the amount for each region, and £5,000 total expenditure was allowed on this basis:

Region	Allocation £	Amount spent £
1	1,650	1,444
2	300	87
3	350	239
4	250	0
5	600	335
6	300	55
7	450	415
8	300	250
9	150	106
10	100	0
11	250	44
12	200	0
13	100	0

Of the total allocation of £5,000, the amount actually spent was £2,980. It was noted at the time that Regions 4, 12 and 11 relied on the WEA rather than on their own courses.[10] It is significant that several regions spent no money on education at this time, whereas Region 1 spent far in excess of any other region, a pattern which was to continue for many years.

Take-up under the new system was slow. In the first full year, 1959, Regions 1, 2, 9 and 10 and the Power Workers' Group took up their allocation for expenditure on directly-sponsored weekend schools. On the other hand Regions 4, 6, 10, 11 and 12 spent less than half their allocation, and Region 11 only spent 30 per cent of its allocation.[11] In 1961, whilst Regions 1, 5 and 7 spent their whole allocation, Regions 4 and 8 spent little or nothing.[12]

Region	1961 expenditure £	1962 expenditure £	1964 expenditure £
1	1,960	2,529	1,862
2	355	569	462
3	515	665	330
4	340	326	0
5	980	1,415	176
6	450	607	649
7	555	687	312
8	355	318	42
9	340	333	245
10	195	188	238
11	465	442	250
12	305	333	25
13	205	188	198
Total	7,000	**8,600**	**5,789**

Source: Supplements to Education Committee Reports, 1961, 1962, 1964

Apart from the obvious concern about the great variation in regional provision, and the fact that some regions were spending very little or even nothing on education, the overall pattern at this time was an under-spending of the allocation. For example, in 1964, as the table shows, £5,789 was spent, but the allocation was £7,000.

By the mid-1960s, a more complex pattern had emerged, with some regions over-spending, and some under-spending.

Region	1965 estimate £	1965 actual £
1	1,855	3,830
2	350	236
3	525	903
4	336	295
5	1,120	1,196
6	476	330
7	546	528
8	315	329
9	322	501
10	196	155
11	455	256
12	315	135
13	199	208
Total	**7,000**	**8,922**

Source: Appendix to the Education Committee Reports, February 1966

The estimated expenditure totalled £7,000, with actual expenditure £8,922, but removing the balance of £1,974 paid by Region 1 leaves £6,948.

At the extremes were Region 1, who supplemented their expenditure significantly from regional funds, and Regions 10, 12 and 13, who sometimes spent nothing at all.

This variation in provision and expenditure continued throughout the decade. In 1967 the estimated expenditure for Region 1 was £1,968 but the region paid a further £2,285 on top of this allocation. By this time, all regions were spending something on one-day and weekend schools. In 1968, Region 1 was allocated £1,968 and spent £3,046, £1,078 on top of the Central Office allocation. At the other end of the scale Region 9 was allocated £392 and spent £22. Allocation for Region 1 in 1970 was £1,888 but the region's actual expenditure was £3,066. All other regions spent less than their allocation and Regions 10 and 11 had an allocation of £248 and £520 respectively and spent nothing.[13]

Whilst not being a complete measure of provision, as some regions used external providers more than others, every activity incurred some cost, and this analysis of expenditure shows just how uneven the provision was. It is difficult to identify precisely why the diversity was so significant, and why it has remained a factor throughout the union's existence. Clearly factors such as the personality and commitment of key officers and committees, the place of education in the priorities of the region, and the industrial base of the region must play an important part in the outcome; but there are also other factors such as the influence of outside institutions and individual educators, the attitude to expenditure within a region, and personalities amongst the lay members who would or would not have demanded education from the union. It is interesting that although personalities have changed over the years, the diversity, and even the balance within this diversity, has changed very little, showing that regional tradition, once established, is hard to change. We will now look at the detail of regional provision up to the late 1960s.

THE SOUTHERN REGIONS 1, 2 AND 3

The extensive commitment which Region 1[14] (London and the South-East) made to education by the 1960s was the product of a long history of involvement in the post-war period. Some of the work of Fred Horne has already been noted, and he was clearly one of the 'stars' of TGWU education during this period. The region also produced other significant personalities whose names have already been mentioned in our story – Charles Brandon, Regional Secretary during the 1940s, Ted Sheehan, in the same position during the 1950s, Harry White, District Officer in Maidstone, and Jack Lucas, Fred Horne's leading disciple, who became Regional Organiser in the 1960s and ran the region's education programme. Region 1, through its progressive and politically-conscious regional committee, in which Communists played a significant part, continually pressed the union to expand its education programme.

By this time, Charles Brandon was Regional Secretary and Ted Sheehan Regional Organiser, the responsibility of which included education. Both officials were keen educationalists. Charles Brandon's background has already been noted. Ted Sheehan joined the union in January 1922 on entering the employment of London County Council Tramways, and within a year of joining he was co-opted onto the branch committee at New Cross Tram Depot. He was also a member of the London District Tram and Trolleybus Committee, Region 1 Passenger Committee, and the National Passenger Committee. With a background in the radical London Bus Section, Sheehan had a thorough political education, and a clear understanding of the strategic objectives of the education programme, as he set them out in an article in *The Record* in 1959:

> In our region we commence from the angle that the huge majority of our members have but little interest in our basic function and purpose, primarily because, relatively, their position is not too bad, secondly because they get such good value for such a small premium. This uninterested class could be a real, positive danger, if there was a serious turn

> of the economic tide in the wrong direction, which of course, is always on the cards within the system of capitalism. We have tried every means to get at this mass but without success, so we are now turning to the bulwark of the working-class movement, branch officer, secretary, chairman, committeeman, steward, representative, etc. Concentrate on this section so that it becomes an intelligent and able bulwark, fully understanding our position, and to be relied upon to meet any circumstances, adverse or favourable.[15]

Following the proscription against Communists introduced at the 1949 BDC, Sheehan was banned from holding office and had to resign his position and return to the bus industry in Catford. In 1952 he contested the decision, and it was agreed by the GEC that if the Region 1 Committee were satisfied that he was no longer a member of the Communist Party, it could restore his membership and be eligible to hold union office.[16] In September 1952 Region 1 formally requested that he be allowed to hold office within the union, and in 1953 the GEC lifted the ban, beginning with the 1954-1955 electoral period. By this time Sheehan had become an Inspector on London Transport.[17] Sheehan returned as Regional Organiser and in July 1959 he followed Brandon as Regional Secretary. He retired in 1962 and died in 1972.

In the early 1950s, the main function of the two senior officers in the region was to provide a supportive regime for the activities of Fred Horne and other industrial officers who used education as a key part of their organising programme. Apart from Fred Horne's Metal and Engineering Group, schools were also held for dairy workers and building workers in the late 1940s, sometimes using Beatrice Webb House. Fred Horne would most often take shop stewards from his group to Bexhill-on-Sea or Clacton, using the officers as tutors, as in this example in 1953 where fifty students attended and where Horne was assisted by Jack Lucas, Barney Nertney, Reg Lamb (Assistant Trade Group Secretary), Harry Kendrick, Frank Ashley and George Parker: all officers from his group. Sid Forty, the future Administrative Officer of the union and then a Region 1 staff member, led a session on administrative duties. Horne's courses were largely concerned with workshop practice with particular reference to 'time and motion' study. These courses continued through the 1950s, and regular 'time and motion' study courses were held at the regional office, Southend, Eastbourne, Enfield, and Bedford. The Eastbourne school in 1953 was held at Victoria Court, Grand Parade, only yards from where, twenty years later, the union's own education centre would be built.

A similar but less ambitious programme was also organised by the General Workers Group through its senior official, Bert Roullier. In 1958, the systematic approach of the two trade groups was combined with the TUC for the simultaneous running of an introductory and a follow-up course on 'time and motion' study at the College of Aeronautics, Cranfield. Two representatives of the Production Department of the TUC took nearly 40 shop stewards from the two trade groups through an intensive weekend school.[18]

Other groups had a more irregular provision. The London Cab Section held their first-ever weekend school at Hillside Guest House, Godalming, on 10 and 11 April 1954. The school was attended by 48 branch officers and stewards, the Cab Trade Committee and four Labour councillors. Jim Francis,[19] Section Secretary, acted as chairman and the two lecturers were Ted Sheehan and George Haynes, Passenger Trade Group Secretary.[20] In 1958, at Beatrice Webb House, 40 building trade stewards from all over the region took part in a two-day school organised by the Trade Group Committee. This was the first venture into this type of education activity by the Trade Group. The lecturers were Ted Sheehan and Building Group district officers.[21] Repeat schools were held in 1959, with one school attended by Tony Corfield with the training manuals.

As has been noted, the large and influential London Bus Section had its own special long course based at Central Office during the 1950s, but there were also weekend schools for bus workers. This example of one held in the Albion Hotel, Ramsgate, in April 1961, gives a flavour of the type of education and the issues of the day:

> The tutor was Mr John Ireland from Oxford. The evening session consisted of making a three-minute speech on subjects:
>
> 1. Why I am a Trade Unionist;
> 2. Why you should be a member of a Trade Union;
> 3. Why Trade Unions should be members of the TUC.
>
> Later there was a debate on Sunday morning. Topics for debate were:
>
> 1. That this union refuses to support any further increases in one-man operations.
> 2. That this union welcomes and supports the introduction of high-capacity buses.
> 3. That bus workers should receive a substantial increase in wages.[22]

In the early 1960s, courses on bus scheduling were given by Larry Smith, who later became an Executive Officer of the union, but at that time was Schedules Officer and also Trade Group Officer. When Jack Lucas became Regional Organiser in the 1960s, the Trade Group organised a large number of courses in various bus garages,[23] and in the later 1960s this work was taken over by Terry Allen, Central Bus Section Schedules Officer, who later became Trade Group Officer. By this time the Central Bus Section held a monthly one-day school for branch representatives and committeemen (sic) responsible for schedules and roster.[24]

In the districts, local one-day and weekend schools on general subjects continued on an *ad hoc* basis, and co-existed with WEA and NCLC provision. Harry White continued to provide the occasional course in Maidstone and Kent, such as in May 1953 when Ted Sheehan took part. White stood unsuccessfully for Parliament in 1950 and 1951, but in 1952, on medical advice, he informed the GEC that he would not be standing again. At the end of 1961 he took early retirement on the grounds of illness. Activity in Kent continued in the later 1950s, for instance in November 1957, when 1/167 Dover branch arranged a one-day school for all the TGWU branches in the area. Reg Prentice was the speaker on The Labour Party and Pensions.[25] The Dover branches had been quite active in education immediately after the war, holding regular classes on issues of the day, often with MPs as speakers. Some courses were held in Cambridge in the early 1950s, sometimes with Len Neal taking time off from his studies to act as a tutor. The first weekend school organised by the South-East Essex District Committee was held at Southend-on-Sea in March 1955.

In March 1962 Ted Sheehan retired, and Bert Fry, Regional Organiser since 1959, was appointed Regional Secretary. His place as RO was taken by Jack Lucas. Ron Todd, later Regional Secretary and General Secretary, was appointed Metal, Engineering and Chemical Group Organiser to follow Jack Lucas. Jack Lucas's background was in the Engineering Industry. However, he was originally an apprentice in the fur trade in the City of London but joined the union when he moved to Sagamow Weston Engineering in Enfield during the war. He built the union there to 100 per cent and became a shop steward. He was then elected to the Region 1 Chemical Trade Group Committee, became the Chair, and also sat on the London Trades Council. He joined the CP during the War. In 1949 the proscription on Communists removed some excellent officials who were CP members, but Lucas refused to follow this line and leave the union and, therefore, left the CP as he felt it was more important to work within the union. During this time he joined the WEA to learn more about the Trade Union Movement and began his involvement in TGWU education. He was appointed an officer in September 1946 in Stratford, with Harold Clay chairing the interviewing panel. His first responsibility was in Ford, and he worked under the authority of Fred Horne. Fred Horne encouraged all his officers to attend the TWI scheme and Jack Lucas and another officer, Charlie Jordan, went to the ministry for a week during 1948 and 1949, and followed this up with teaching on the courses.

As Regional Organiser, he was not officially in charge of education, which was the responsibility of the regional secretary. However, Bert Fry had little interest in it, and Lucas was given some time off from other duties to organise and teach in the education programme.[26] He was of the view that the variation in 'Education grew up mainly depending on particular people and officials who wanted to do it'.[27] He was certainly one of these, and continued his involvement in TGWU education for a decade following his retirement in 1978. Jack Lucas enjoyed a happy and active retirement until his death on 10 September 2002. One of the virtues of Jack Lucas was that he was a creative thinker as well as an amusing and enthusiastic teacher, who also saw the link between education and union organising. Bevin and Deakin had stressed the importance of education in the understanding of the union's structure and purpose, and Ellen McCullough and Tony Corfield had used it to develop the key skills of the branch officers and shop stewards. The two Jacks, Jones and Lucas, saw education as a vital *organising* tool, and it was that which made them the most creative of the senior officers in their use of union education. Jack Lucas used education to extend the union into new areas. For example, in early 1965 Region 1 held a weekend school at St Leonards-on-Sea with 56 delegates from nine different trade groups, including 8 women. Particular attention was paid to the problem of organising women and Lucas used education extensively to build women's organisation in the region.

One of the first innovations in the new decade of the 1960s was the Diploma Scheme, which was piloted in Region 1, with courses also held in Liverpool and Aberdeen. This was aimed at improving numeracy, calculation and statistical methods for trade unionists. Tony Corfield promoted the diploma, telling the membership 'The language of a trade unionist needs to be one of figures as well as one of words'.[28] The pilot course met in Region 1 for two hours, one evening each week, for 26 weeks from October 1959 to April 1960. Of the 25 students who began in 1959, 15 sat an examination in the spring of 1960. The region presented successful students with a slide-rule and a diploma signed by the general secretary, the regional secretary and the regional chairman. The first of the diplomas was formally presented in November 1961 to Bro. Ron de Ritis at a meeting of his branch, 1/49.[29] The scheme was specialised and difficult, and was integrated into the basic TUC courses from 1964 onwards. By the end of the 1960s, the region was funding a significant amount of this activity from its own regional funds, and providing substantial education opportunities for its membership.

The characters of 'old' Region 2 (Central Southern England) and 'old' Region 3 (the South-West)[30] were very different from the London-centred Region 1. They were strongly influenced by the defence industry and by the membership in the military bases in Portsmouth, Aldershot, Plymouth, Aldermaston, and around Hampshire, Wiltshire and Dorset. The main industrial centres were Southampton and Bristol, with significant docks, road haulage, bus/passenger and manufacturing membership. Region 2 also contained the Channel Islands where in 1947 the WETUC sent three officials to restore adult education following the Nazi occupation.[31]

In 'old' Region 2, the two most important contributors to TGWU education in the immediate post-war period were J.S. Brandie, initially the Salisbury district officer, and E.G. 'Ernie' Allen, from 1961 Regional Secretary. Brandie came from the 2/99 branch in Portsmouth and completed the Home Study course in 1948, and was one of the successful applicants for a full-time scholarship at Ruskin College in 1950. He was a naval reservist and at the time of this award he expected to be called up (possibly to Korea) and therefore deferred his attendance at Ruskin. It is not clear what happened, but in the event he was appointed as Salisbury District Organiser from 4 June 1951. He immediately instituted a programme of education in his district, with courses in Andover and Basingstoke as well as Salisbury. Brandie had a difficult job, as he was operating in a district where no education had taken place previously. He began to build something of a following, and his education programmes ran from the Autumn of 1951 until 1955 when he was appointed combined Portsmouth District and Regional Government Workers Trade Group Secretary. Examples of his programme show that in early 1953, 30 members attended a school in Salisbury at which Ellen McCullough spoke on workers' control; and in the spring of 1954, 20 members attended a Government Workers' shop stewards' school with a showing of the union's filmstrip *Our Heritage*. One of his winter schools in 1955 saw 40 members in attendance to listen to Ben Roberts, Director of Trade Union Studies at LSE.[32]

Brandie's replacement, Bro. L.G. Broomfield, continued where he had left off, and in the winter of 1956 Ernie Allen lectured on the subject The Duties and Responsibilities of Shop Stewards.[33] Activities continued in Salisbury into the 1960s, for example in February 1961 when there was a joint meeting for women members of 2/166/213 branches at Porton, addressed by Ellen McCullough. In the afternoon of the same day she addressed 100 girls at the St Edmond's Secondary Modern Girls' School in Salisbury and in the evening the Salisbury and District Trades Council on the organisation of women in industry.[34]

Little more is heard of Brandie's educational activities, but Ernie Allen carried his through to the leadership of the region, and became one of the prime movers of the Southampton Educational and Social Council, set up in 1950. The council kept an eye on the Salisbury courses, and Ernie Allen used his base in Southampton to extend shop stewards' courses to the most important industries in the district. He reported to *The Record* in 1959 under the title 'Planned Training in the South':

> Over recent years we have been experimenting with shop stewards' courses. As a result of our experiments we have now got down to a

> programme which we feel meets the requirements of the shop stewards so far as training is concerned ... two such courses have been held, one at the Fawley Refinery and the other at our Southampton regional office. The one at Fawley was solely for refinery stewards, whereas at the one held in the regional office stewards came from a number of industries in the engineering field.[35]

Allen was totally committed to the celebrated Fawley productivity deal, which he negotiated and which opened the era of 'productivity bargaining', and he used the education programme to test these ideas in the preliminary stages.[36] In April 1961 he was appointed Regional Secretary and continued to support shop stewards' education, regularly using the regional office as a venue. The first shop stewards' course on the Isle of Wight was held in the Fountain Hotel at Cowes on the 14 and 15 November 1962. Tony Corfield led a school in Guernsey in April 1967 on the implications of joining the Common Market. Allen particularly used the growing extra-mural department at Southampton University, in particular Basil Bye, one of the new generation of trade union tutors, and John Cronin, a law lecturer with a particular interest in industrial relations. The growth of a systematic programme of shop stewards' training in the region really began after Allen's retirement, but in a region not known for its heavy industry or its militancy, he at least established the principle that education was a central part of trade union activity.

In 'old' Region 3, the model of the Educational and Social Council was at its strongest. In addition to the Bristol Council, in 1947 an Educational and Social Council was established in Bath, and the first weekend school organised by the Plymouth District Social and Educational Council was organised in March 1953 in Torquay. Yeovil established a similar body in 1961, holding its first weekend school in the spring with the local district officer as the tutor. These councils organised a WEA-type programme of useful general topics, but they were not targeted on particular industrial groups of the union, and were therefore ultimately overtaken by a new generation. They tended to organise weekend schools with senior officials or MPs. This June 1948 weekend school was typical; it was held at Penscotts Guest House, Somerset. The lecturer was Bro. W.S. Plummer, Regional Claims Manager, speaking on workmen's compensation. It was followed by a lecture on new social insurance legislation by George Oliver, MP.[37] This was very much the pre-war WEA approach, and a generation behind Jones, Wylie, Horne, Lucas and Corfield.

The Bristol Council continued its activities with enthusiasm in the immediate post-war period. In 1953 its 19th Annual Festival was attended by Arthur Deakin, and more than 2,000 members and friends were at the Colston Hall to greet him.[38] Also in 1953, the first school organised by the Exeter District was held at Teignmouth with 53 students in attendance, and the Regional Secretary as lecturer.[39] In the later 1950s, the new Regional Secretary, Ron Nethercott, supported the education programme without directing it to a definite purpose. Under the first years of his regime, the programme was mainly centred around weekend schools, such as one held by Bath Educational and Social Council on 7 and 8 December 1957, dealing with the structure of the union and methods of industrial negotiation and arbitration. Full-time officers took the school. The first shop stewards' weekend school to be arranged in the Swindon District took place at the Ball and Castle Hotel, Marlborough, in the summer of 1959. The tutors were Les Kealey, Engineering National Secretary, and P. Stanford, Regional Engineering Group Officer.[40]

Once the TUC programme of shop stewards' day-release courses got underway in the mid-1960s, these councils lost their function, and began to be integrated into the TUC programme, and they also became more focused on industrial and political issues. By the end of the 1960s, Regions 2 and 3 had become closely integrated into the TUC shop stewards' programmes, with Southampton University, Slough College and Gloucester Technical College becoming centres for TUC education.

THE MIDDLE REGIONS 4, 13, 5 AND 10

There is little evidence of systematic educational work in Region 4 (South and Mid-Wales) in the immediate post-war period, although, as has been seen, in the early years of the union, Wales was a strong centre of education, with Jack Donovan, Arthur Deakin and other officials making their mark. After the refusal of the GEC to grant a Regional Education Officer in 1946, the region seems to have taken it on itself not to develop a systematic programme, and this was one of the regions which spent literally nothing in the late 1950s, when the first budgetary allocations were made. In the early 1950s, noting that 'next to nothing was being done in the area of trade union education', Port Talbot was selected as one of the WEA special areas for trade union studies, and the WEA put on a range of courses in 1956 and 1957, mainly for steelworkers using the Extra-Mural Departments of Cardiff and Swansea Universities.[41] Region 13 (North Wales and Cheshire) had some involvement in the early years, but nothing significant in the immediate post-war period. The region held a one-day school for its agricultural and rural members at Llangefni, Anglesey, in 1948, and occasional courses at Shotton and Chester, sometimes using Ellen McCullough or other national tutors.

In Region 5 (East and West Midlands) however, the situation was very different. We have already seen how effectively Jack Jones and Tom Wylie had used education as a tool, and they established a strong tradition in the region which was then taken up by Les Kealey. The comprehensive provision for shop stewards in the Coventry and

Birmingham areas set up by Jones and Wylie continued into the post-war period with schools held in Coventry, Leicester, Birmingham and Wolverhampton in the winter of 1946. Tom Wylie's courses were at their peak: courses organised with the WEA in this period included one at Birmingham University, 'Industrial Relations and the Trade Union Movement', which was attended by 90 students. In 1946, a one-day school for Birmingham Trades Council on Trade Unions and the Future attracted 85 students in Birmingham in September and 80 students at King's Norton in October.[42]

In Coventry, Jack Jones and Harry Urwin, who followed Jones as District Secretary, Regional Secretary and then became Deputy General Secretary, carried on the wartime work and in 1951 established the Dalgleish Study Centre in Coventry (named after the Engineering National Secretary Arthur Dalgleish), which held courses for shop stewards on issues such as joint consultation, productivity, time study and incentive schemes.[43] Weekend schools organised by Jones and Urwin in the early 1950s regularly had 40 or 50 stewards in attendance. In April 1955 Jack Jones left Coventry to become Region 5 Metal and Engineering Group Secretary, and he became Regional Secretary in February 1956. However, the education work continued, as shown by an article in *The Record* in 1961 with the intriguing title 'Gay Evening at Coventry', an event attended by over 150 members. The main speakers were Dr W.F. Frank, Head of the Department of Management and Business Studies at the new Lanchester College of Technology, and Jack Jones. Jones said that the union spent more money on education for its members than in paying dispute benefit, and this was a testimony to the fact that the union was trying to do a constructive job.[44] Other parts of the region provided courses intermittently. For example, 30 members of the Northampton District, and 6 members from Leicester, took part in the first school held in the Northampton District in November 1957. The lecturers were local district officers and the subjects were 'The union, what is it?' by Bro. Waldon; 'The union, what can I give it?' by Bro. Bromley and 'The union, what can it give me?'[45]

Les Kealey was one of the officers who began to organise a systematic programme in the region in the early 1950s. He was actually referred to as the 'Education Officer', and through this work he became a member of the local WETUC, a member of the advisory committee to the Birmingham Technical College, and a governor of Fircroft College. During this period, the region was able to offer quite a comprehensive programme to its members and stewards. In 1951, for instance, it organised a twelve-lecture course for shop stewards on the functions of trade unions, the duties of shop stewards and industrial relations.[46] In the mid-1950s, Region 5 also had a regular programme based around management techniques and problems in the car industry.[47] A good example of a local district programme operating at that time is that for the western side of the region for 1955/56. This offered general schools open to all members three times a year, linked schools for chemical and engineering membership three times a year focusing on work study and management techniques, and another three on economics and growth of industry. There were schools for shop stewards in trade sections eight times a year, a school for road haulage commercial members once a year, a school for particular districts four times a year and a weekend branch officers' course. Many of these were two-day courses and often weekend schools. There was also a special weekend school for women members once a year, conducted by Ellen McCullough, and in April 1955, a special school for Midland Red garage representatives was held in Bromsgrove. Venues included Moreton Paddox, Cottage in the Wood, Malvern, Brandon Hall, and Avoncroft College.[48]

By the 1960s, the region's programme was concentrated on large manufacturing plants then at their peak, and companies such as IMI Tubes, Rover, and other engineering and car companies all had union or joint company-union courses on a regular basis. Region 5 courses also targeted transport, breweries, chemicals, Typhoo Tea, Parkinson Cowan and many other large employers. Companies such as Michelin also had a regular education programme in this period, and well-organised branches such as the 5/188 (Stoke on Trent) appointed a Branch Education Officer in 1960 and advocated the same for every branch throughout the district and an education officer on the district committee to co-ordinate the work.[49] As the TUC training programme grew in the later 1960s, the Midlands became a major centre for TUC shop stewards' courses.

Region 10 (Hull and East Coast) was another of the educationally weaker regions in the immediate post-war period, and another 'zero spender' at the end of the 1950s. An occasional school was held in the 1950s, such as a shop stewards' school at Cleethorpes in November 1954. However, no systematic programme was provided up to the early 1960s.

In the main centre, Hull, matters had already improved by the mid-1960s, thanks to a combination of new officials like Peter Grant and a new generation of tutors, led by Tony Topham of Hull University. The first venture, in 1963, was to follow Region 1 in the Diploma in Statistics Within Industry, which was offered as a night class in conjunction with the WEA, at the College of Technology. This was a 24-week course with 20 students in the class tutored by Tony Topham.[50] Topham organised a number of courses during this period, usually on a day-release basis, and was influential in developing a core of TGWU activists around the courses, in particular in manufacturing and the docks, where leading activists such as Walter Greendale, who later became chairman of the GEC, extended their involvement into bodies such as the Institute for Workers' Control, making contact with Ken Coates, Tony Benn, Michael Barratt-Brown and Mike Cooley.[51] The Hull Docks stewards' course at Hull University in the late 1960s was the most important of Topham's courses. This programme was jointly sponsored by the union and Hull port employers. The courses dealt with the history and structure of the union, national and local dock agreements, payment systems, shop stewards' duties, the structure of the port employers, the NDLB and safety on the docks. Officers such as the then Regional Secretary, Dave Shenton, Jack Ashwell, Brian Barker, and management representatives[52] all took part in the programme.

Some attempts were made at this time to extend to other parts of the region. For example the first shop stewards' course to be held in Peterborough was held in March 1963, with thirty stewards from branches covering London Brick, Hotpoint, Metal Box and Wittersley Brick. Peter Grant led the course along with Tony Corfield.[53] Hull, however, remained the only significant centre.

THE NORTHERN REGIONS 9, 8, 6, AND 12

Region 9 (Yorkshire) had maintained a connection with the union's education programme ever since Harold Clay became its first area secretary at the amalgamation in 1922. Branches such as Sheffield Trams and Leeds Transport had particularly been involved in union education in the inter-war years. The region began its post-war programme in May 1947 with a weekend school at Tonn Hall, Drighlington, with 58 students in attendance. The lecturers were A.J. Heal, the Regional Secretary, and Florence Hancock, who lectured on the economic position of women with special reference to the report of the Commission for Equal Pay.

The region was fortunate to have both Leeds and Sheffield universities within its geographical area, as these institutions became centres for adult and trade union education in the post-war period. Their principal link was with the NUM, but TGWU members also became involved.[54] For example, in 1954 the union supported a special one-week course at the University of Leeds in 'Trade Union Problems and Practice', taught in part by the staff of the university and in part by Tony Corfield. In January 1955, as part of the special trade union studies pilot schemes established in Teesside, Tyneside and Port Talbot by the WEA, a one-week course was held at Leeds University called Scientific Management and Trade Unions, looking specifically at new management techniques. There were 30 students on the course, mostly from Teesside, with a significant number from ICI. The union paid the residential costs, and jointly tutored the course with the WEA.[55] Vic Allen also established himself at Leeds in the late 1950s and kept in touch with the union.[56] As it was, the region moved steadily into the era of day-release. The future long-serving Regional Secretary Mike Davey was a supporter of education, having himself been sponsored by the union to attend LSE in 1963.

The Northern Region, Region 8, began its programme immediately after the war, and a union school was held in Penrith in October 1947 mainly for members employed in transport and agriculture. A one-day school was held in Berwick in the same month with Bro. Hills, the Regional Secretary, and a weekend school was held at Dalston Hall, Workington, in March 1948. In the immediate post-war years, the region tended to organise weekend schools in country houses on topical issues, often led by MPs with the regional secretary in the chair. Schools were also held in Stockton and Carlisle on a regular basis. The WEA special pilot project in the early 1950s had a significant impact on Region 8, as both Tyneside and Teesside were pilot areas. There were many WETUC schools in the region during this period, and also exclusively TGWU schools. In Tyneside, for example, three linked schools in 1955 were provided for 27 students.[57] In Teesside, students in the projects came mainly from ICI and Middlesbrough docks.[58] The region was to come more into its own in the period of day-release, when large companies like ICI, based in the region, led the field in joint union-management courses.

Region 6 (North-West) and Region 12 (Liverpool and Merseyside) were steady local contributors to the programme. In 1948 it was noted that an Educational and Social Council was operating in Region 6 and had arranged three conferences to deal with the problems of the coal crisis, the first one being on 17 January in Blackburn. Florence Hancock was in Burnley on 21st February, and Arthur Deakin in Oldham on 10 April. The WEA and NCLC were quite strongly organised in the North-West, and many TGWU members received their education through this means, particularly in Liverpool and Lancashire.[59] A series of 6 TGWU schools was organised in Liverpool from November 1948 through to April 1949. Liverpool, as always, was highly political, and the education programme reflected this; for example Region 12 held a school on 'The Union and Politics' in the spring of 1962, when this subject was a rarity in the union as a whole.

SCOTLAND AND IRELAND: REGIONS 7 AND 11

The first post-war union weekend school in Scotland was held at the WEA guesthouse in Dunoon on 18 and 19 October 1947. There were 50 delegates present, and the lecturers were Bros. Patterson, Sullivan and McKay; all TGWU officers. A boost to education in the region came in March 1950 when Jessie Murray was appointed to the position of Woman Organiser (sic). She established a systematic programme of education, including courses for women members such as a women's school held at Bridge of Allan in September 1952 with female tutors.[60] Women's schools were regularly organised in the region, and regular courses were held at Bridge of Allan, Aberdeen, and other venues throughout the 1950s, meriting a special feature in *The Record* in 1958, including describing innovations, for instance that students on courses had to make an open-air speech advising a group of striking workers to join the union.

Jessie Murray retired in April 1961 and was not replaced. One of her disciples, however, was Jimmy McIntyre, branch secretary, 7/144 branch, and later Dunfermline District Secretary and Regional Organiser. McIntyre took over education, introducing new arrangements such as that in 1969 with Fife County Council Adult Education Department to run a day-release course on industrial relations for the membership employed in the Rosyth Dockyard. McIntyre was to combine the role of Regional Organiser with Education Officer into the 1980s, giving the region a traditional emphasis in its education somewhat longer than other regions.

Region 11 (now Region 3) covers the whole of Ireland, and given that part of the region is a separate state, has always had a 'semi-detached' relationship with the TGWU as a whole. The Irish region's education programme was therefore influenced by its connection to other bodies such as the Irish Congress of Trades Unions, but, nevertheless, Irish members took part in the TGWU's UK-based programmes such as the Cirencester schools. One of the first certificates to be awarded in the Republic of Ireland from the correspondence course was awarded in 1953 to Bro. Dennis O'Rourke of branch 11/61 near Waterford. Courses based in the region sometimes covered issues specific to Ireland, for example a school held in Malahide in January 1957 on Banking and Credit and one in Bangor in April 1957 on Northern Ireland and Her Neighbours.[61] As early as 1961, the Dublin Education Committee had arranged a series of courses, one on European integration, long before this issue was discussed in the UK. In the late 1950s, education in the region was organised by Joe Cooper, permanent secretary of the 11/2 Belfast branch, the 'Carters' Branch', formerly the Belfast Carters' Union, and one of the first amalgamating branches into the TGWU. In the early 1960s the ICTU suggested to its affiliated unions that they should set up an Education Committee in each union, and Congress itself had appointed a full-time education officer. The region held occasional schools in this period, including women's schools. However, a perennial problem was that a substantial part of the material included in the UK-based courses was not applicable in Ireland, as the legislation and industrial relations system was so different.

THE INFLUENCE OF DAY-RELEASE

In the immediate post-war period, the great majority of TGWU members attended courses at weekends, in their own time, or were supported by the union 'as if they were attending normal union business', with a 'loss of time' payment. Those receiving paid release had been very few. However, during the 1950s a number of developments took place which brought paid release into centre stage and set the scene for a significant expansion of shop stewards' education. One source of progress was the nationalised industries. The most extensive schemes were those drawn up between the National Coal Board, the NUM, and Nottingham, Sheffield and Leeds Universities, which provided courses up to three years based on day-release.[63] Innovative officials also put pressure on individual employers to introduce day-release. Jack Jones, when he was Midlands Regional Secretary, first suggested day-release courses in 1958 specifically for shop stewards in the British Motor Corporation. The courses which began in Birmingham and Coventry that year were a direct result of his proposal.[64]

During the 1950s and early 1960s a number of trends came together to create a new approach to training policy, the most important being the continuing influence of TWI and training methods, the demand for qualifications, the growth of directed management training and the joint approach of the CBI and the TUC to a more deliberate training system.[65] The result was the Industrial Training Act of 1964, which introduced the practice of day-release for apprentices and trainees, and the principle was easily extended to shop stewards. This in turn led to a mushrooming of 'in-plant' and joint courses with employers, and the establishment of the TUC shop stewards' training courses from 1964 onwards, also generally based on day-release, increased the volume of trade union education still further.

Within the TGWU, these developments were closely watched, particularly by Tony Corfield. In *The Record*, he raised the issue in a special article, arguing that trade union representatives 'have a duty to ensure that no opportunity is missed of pressing employers to extend day-release to their young workers'.[66] In April 1963 the TUC and the British Employers' Confederation issued a joint statement. In it they agreed that there was 'a need to increase the amount of training so that more stewards can obtain a broader understanding of their functions and responsibilities ... it is in the interests of employers that stewards should represent their unions and the members of those unions effectively ... there should be more courses of an appropriate nature, for attendance at which stewards might be released with pay'.[67] The TUC had taken the view that 'where day-release with pay is granted for this purpose the syllabuses of courses should be agreed with employers'.[68] However, in the TGWU, this provision was nominal, as Corfield reported to the Education Committee in 1964:

> Initially the intentions were that the emphasis on shop stewards' courses assisted by the employers should be upon broader courses giving background information. This was the gist of the joint TUC and

> BEC statement. A substantial proportion of the courses which had actually been held appear to have been prepared and tutored exclusively by the union.[69]

Whether or not programmes were formally agreed with employers, there is no evidence that they interfered significantly with either the content or the teaching of these courses. 'In-plant' courses became a trademark of individual TGWU education provision as distinct from the TUC shop stewards' training, which was almost exclusively day-release and college-based. Some of the earliest of these type of courses were in 1963, with 'in-plant' provision for TGWU members at British Drug Houses, Parkestone (Region 2), Magicoat (Berger) Paints, and Van Den Berghs and Jurgens (Unilever) at Purfleet (Region 1). This became a long-running programme, and the next year a joint course for shop stewards and management took place, organised by Jack Lucas.[70]

In 1964, the Education Committee noted that at many one-day and two-day schools in the regions, employers were paying 'loss of time' to shop stewards for attending and that this had led to a substantial increase in the number of shop stewards able to train.[71] However, the Committee took the view that:

> these courses could never entirely replace the union's own education system. There were certain problems in which the union had a separate interest and outlook from the employers and we would need freedom to be able to give instruction in these. On the other hand there was much common ground between the two parties in terms of knowledge of procedure and working arrangements which could beneficially be taught in employer-financed courses.[72]

By the mid-1960s, courses were being organised at Shell Petrochemicals, ICI and British Nylon Spinners in Gloucester, the latter tutored by Tony Corfield and J.C. Woldridge, District Secretary. Corfield also taught ICI members at Wilton on Teesside and at the ICI paint factory at Stowmarket, Manchester and in Scotland. He was joined by the TGWU Chemical Group National Secretary and also the ICI divisional personnel manager.[73] By 1968, Frank Cousins had sent out a circular encouraging regions to extend one-day training schools for their shop stewards as widely as possible. The union preferred these to be held during working hours where arrangements could be arrived at with employers. The union also became aware of the fact that the new Industrial Training Boards were prepared to finance shop stewards' courses, and prepared a standard form for regions to fill in to provide information about day-release courses for their shop stewards. However, a new complicating factor was that most day-release courses were now run by the TUC at local level and

TGWU regional secretaries did not always know about them.[74] This was to be a growing problem in the coming years.

Meanwhile, the years from 1965 onwards represented an explosion in locally-based 'in-plant' courses and day-release courses for shop stewards. There were courses in almost all the major oil, chemical, and food-processing companies such as Fry's, Birds Eye, ICI, Shell, Austin's, Midland Red, Lucas, the docks, Waterford Glass and Courtaulds. *The Record* supported the development enthusiastically:

> Day-release is expanding rapidly and that already these courses outnumber directly-sponsored union ones by 3 to 1. This means you have three times as much chance of getting a place on a day-release course as on a residential union course.[75]

There was also 'a major responsibility on the unions to see that they keep some sort of control over it. More and more district officers will be called upon to advise in the drawing up of syllabuses to help select tutors, and to take part in the instruction themselves'.[76]

THE TUC SCHEME

The original decision to establish a centralised education provision for the movement through the TUC was taken in 1925, but because of the General Strike, the depression, the war and divisions within the movement, particularly between supporters of the WETUC and the NCLC, it was not implemented until 1964, when both the NCLC and the WETUC were merged within the TUC. Ellen McCullough played a key role in the establishment of this scheme, when she was seconded from the union to the TUC as Head of the Department of Education from November 1962 to October 1965. McCullough was seen by George Woodcock as a 'safe pair of hands' who would control the influence of the NCLC and the university extra-mural departments in the new scheme, and replicate the functional trade union approach to shop steward training already established in her own union and in other unions in partnership with the WETUC. The details surrounding the development of the TUC scheme have been described elsewhere, so I will concentrate on the effects of the new scheme on the TGWU.[77]

In May 1961 the union set out its view of the new scheme, which it expected to be fully-funded by affiliates' contributions to the TUC:

> The Education Committee felt that new schemes should be operated on the compulsory principle on the grounds that educational services should be as far as possible uniform throughout the Trade Union Movement. For this reason they did not approve of the idea of a two-part tariff scheme with a compulsory basic contribution and optional additional services. The Education Committee considered that a per

capita contribution of 2d per head should be the financial basis upon which the TUC scheme should operate.[78]

The TUC Congress in September accepted that the cost of financing the new scheme should be included in the affiliation fee and not raised by a separate financial arrangement.

In June 1961 the GEC confirmed the decision to associate the union with the establishment by the TUC of a national scheme, and supported the acceptance of the principles of the scheme at the 1961 TUC Congress.[79] When the scheme was launched in 1965, Tony Corfield promoted it in *The Record* and called it a

> major breakthrough for the British Labour Movement ... The educational organisers are no longer outside looking in, they are on the inside. There will be professional educational organisers as members of the Regional Education Advisory Committees. They will be in the mainstream of authority and influence inside the Trade Union Movement ... We can now look forward literally to every branch within the Trade Union Movement having its own educational programme.[80]

The Record continued to promote the scheme throughout the summer of 1965; while this is understandable, it did gloss over the major difficulty created by the scheme, which was the loss of control by the union, and the confusion as to whether TGWU students were enrolled as union or TUC students, and whether the union even knew of their participation in a TUC course.

Corfield tried to resolve this problem during the first two years of the new scheme, with little success, as in 1966:

> I have still been unable to obtain from the TUC information about TGWU participation in their programme of one-day and weekend schools. It is impossible, therefore, at this stage to estimate how fairly the scheme is working. At informal meetings of education officers at the TUC, I have pointed out the importance the union attaches to relating the TUC's regional activity to our own educational programme.[81]

In 1967, therefore, in response to this problem, Corfield used *The Record* to let members and branch secretaries know that the union could not keep a record of TGWU students as applicants for TUC courses if they only needed the endorsement of a branch secretary. As a result, 'In the TGWU a member needs also the endorsement of his regional secretary and applications will not be sent forward if a member has left a previous course unfinished. The TGWU insists that district officers should approve applications from our union before they are accepted'.[82]

Nevertheless, the £18,000 contributed to the TUC by the TGWU and similar contributions from other unions led to an increase in day-release courses and the entry of the technical colleges and universities into the system of trade union education on an unprecedented scale. It also enlarged the scope of union education and led to both the union and the TUC expanding their services, even if the union was not exactly sure how many of its members took part in TUC courses. By the end of 1965 the union was co-operating with a much wider range of providers than ever before. These included, in Region 1, Balham and Tooting College of Commerce, Slough Training College, Brighton Technical College, and Thurrock Technical College. In Region 2, Highbury Technical College and Southampton Technical College, and later Southampton University. In Region 3, Bristol University, and in Region 4, Cardiff University. The WEA was used in a number of regions, including 4 and 5. Region 8 used the university extension centre of Leeds University based in Middlesbrough and Billingham Technical College, and Region 10 the University of Hull and WEA. Region 13 used the Industrial Society and the West Cheshire Central College of Further and Higher Education. By the end of the 1960s the two new streams of 'in plant' courses with companies and day-release courses with colleges were coming together in a vastly expanded programme, sometimes as single-union courses, sometimes jointly, and sometimes through the TUC.

Student numbers reflected the surge in course provision. By 1968, the union's day and weekend schools showed a substantial increase as compared with 1965-66, largely brought about by the extension of day-release courses for shop stewards. Union sponsored schools of one, to or three days showed an increase from 3,636 students in 1959-1960, to 4,062 in 1965-66 to 5,790 in 1967-68. TGWU students on courses lasting one, two or three days with day-release increased from 2,223 in 1969 to 2,827 in 1970 and 3,187 in 1971. As for members taking part in TUC regional education work, in 1968-69, so far as the union had an accurate record, TGWU students in linked weekend courses were 872, single weekend courses 1,697, linked day courses 422, day schools 951, evening classes 513, and day-release courses 1,439; a total of 5,884.

The 1960s came to an end with the union's education programme transformed yet again. On the one hand, the centre of gravity had moved substantially from the Centre to the regions, and day-release, productivity bargaining, the expanded role of the shop steward and the introduction of the TUC scheme had led to an acceleration of growth and a widening of the scope of course provision. On the other hand, control of the programme and its strategic direction and purpose had become confused, and had even been abrogated to some extent to the TUC and the colleges. This contradiction was to be exacerbated and partly resolved in the 1970s. For the TGWU the decade is associated particularly with one man, Jack Jones, who, apart from leaving his mark on the history of the union as a whole, now had his greatest opportunity to influence its education programme.

NOTES

1. 'Area Education Facilities', BDC 1945, Minute No 82.
2. BDC 1949, resolution 755, branch 3/211.
3. BDC 1949, resolution 756 from Rogerstone branch (Power Workers Group).
4. GEC, 5 March 1946, Minute 170, p44.
5. GEC, 28 May 1946, Minute 510, p116.
6. Minutes of the Education Committee, 13 November 1946, Minute No 349.
7. Minutes of the Education Committee, February 1947.
8. Ibid.
9. 'Education in Working Areas', Appendix to the Report of the Education Committee, 30 April 1947.
10. Union Education Scheme Annual Report, 1957.
11. Appendix to Education Secretary's Report, February 1960, p2.
12. Supplement to Education Committee Report, February 1962, p1.
13. Appendix (e) to the Education Committee Report, November 1970.
14. I will now only use the term 'Region', whatever the reference date (i.e. even if before 1950).
15. *The Record,* February 1959, pp44-46.
16. GEC, 10 June 1952, Minute No 352, p93.
17. GEC, 9 June 1953, Minute No 359, pp86-87.
18. 'Combined Operation' by F. Horne, *The Record*, June 1958, p42.
19. Francis was the holder of a British Empire Medal for outstanding service as a Regimental Sergeant- Major (WO1) in the REME.
20. *The Record*, May 1954, p325.
21. 'Building Workers' School', *The Record*, June 1958, p42.
22. The Record, June 1961, p46.
23. Interview with Jack Lucas, 22 January 1999.
24. *The Record,* June 1969, p27.
25. *The Record,* January 1958, p45.
26. Interview with Jack Lucas, 22 January 1999.
27. Ibid.
28. Tony Corfield 'Our Union's Diploma Course', *The Record,* December 1960.
29. *The Record*, December 1961, p41.
30. In 1992 'old' Regions 2 and 3 (South-West England) became Region 2. 'Old' Regions 8, 9 and 10 (the North-East, Yorkshire, and East Coast) became Region 8, and 'old' Region 11 (Ireland) became Region 3.
31. Education Committee, 11 February 1947, Minute No 375.
32 *The Record*, March 1955.
33. *The Record*, March 1956, p233.
34. *The Record*, February 1961.
35. 'Planned Training in the South' by E.G. Allen, *The Record*, January 1959, p45.

36. See A. Flanders, *The Fawley Productivity Agreements*, London: Faber and Faber, 1964.
37. *The Record*, August 1948, p52.
38. *The Record*, April 1953.
39. *The Record*, May 1953, p321.
40. *The Record*, August 1959, p22.
41. See Clegg and Adams, *Trade Union Education*, op. cit., Chapter 1.
42. Report of the Secretary dated 8 May 1946.
43. *The Record*, July 1951, p53.
44. 'Gay Evening at Coventry', *The Record*, July 1961, p20.
45. 'Northampton School', *The Record*, January 1958, pp44-55.
46. *The Record*, March 1951.
47. Report of the Education Secretary, 9 November 1955.
48. Avoncroft College was at Stoke Prior near Bromsgrove, and regularly used by the WETUC and the WEA. The Cottage in the Wood, Malvern, was a private hotel, and Moreton Paddox was a guesthouse run by the Workers' Travel Association. Western House, Barford, was a residential college in Warwickshire run by Warwickshire County Education Committee and Birmingham University Extramural Board. Oakfield Conference House, Worcester, was owned by Worcester County Local Education Authority.
49. *The Record*, June 1960, p45.
50. *The Record*, March 1963, p27.
51. See K. Coates (ed), *Can the Workers Run Industry?*, London: Sphere, 1968; K. Coates and T. Topham, *Workers' Control*, London: Panther, 1970.
52. *The Record*, June 1968, p54.
53. *The Record*, June 1963, p52.
54. See the themed articles, 'Reflections on Adult Continuing Education' looking at work in various universities, in *The Industrial Tutor*, Vol. 5 No 4, Autumn 1991.
55. J. Malling, 'Report on Work with Trade Unionists in the Extra-Mural area of the University of Leeds', in *Trade Union Education* (WEA), No 1, January 1955. See also G. Mitchell, 'Responsible Body: the story of 50 years of adult education in the University of Sheffield', University of Sheffield 2000.
56. When in 1964 Allen was arrested in Nigeria for allegedly acting with others against the Government, Region 9 sent a resolution to the GEC asking that he receive 'assistance as required in providing his defence and all the help which the British High Commission could give to a British Subject placed in such circumstances', GEC, 25 September 1964, Minute No 670. Sheffield had a brief moment of excitement when in 1960 Frank Cousins attended a dinner of the Sheffield and District branches and shared the platform with Paul Robeson.
57. C. H. Hocking, 'The Tyneside Project', *Trade Union Education* (WEA), No 4, April 1956, pp9-15.
58. G.F. Sedgewick, 'The Pilot Scheme in Cleveland', *Trade Union Education* (WEA), No 4, April 1956, pp1-8.
59. See for example M. Cohen, 'The Labour College Movement between the Wars' in B. Simon, *The Search for Enlightenment*, op. cit., pp137-152.
60 *The Record*, February 1953, p231.
61. Education Secretary's Report, 7 May 1957, p2.

62. Education Secretary's Report, August 1968, p1.
63. See J. McIlroy, 'The Triumph of Technical Training?' in B. Simon, *The Search for Enlightenment*, op. cit., pp208-243.
64. The Record, January 1968, pp30-35.
65. For more discussion see John Field, 'Learning for Work' in R. Fieldhouse, *A History of Modern British Adult Education*, op. cit., pp333-353.
66. 'Training in Industry for the Non-Craftsman' by Tony Corfield, *The Record*, April 1961, pp52 and 53.
67. Halford, *Union Education in Great Britain*, op. cit., pp78-79.
68. Ibid, p79.
69. Education Secretary's Report, 19 February 1964, p5.
70. *The Record*, August 1965, p13.
71. Education Secretary's Report, 18 November 1964, p7.
72. Education Secretary's Report, 19 May 1965, p5.
73. The Record, January 1965, p22.
74. Report of the Political, Education and International Department, May 1968, p2.
75. The Record, October 1967.
76. *The Record,* July 1967, pp29-31.
77. See Holford, *Union Education in Great Britain*; Corfield, *Epoch in Workers' Education*, and Simon, *The Search for Enlightenment*, op. cit.
78. Education Secretary's Report, 26 May 1961, p5.
79. GEC, 8 June 1961, Minute No 440, p115.
80. *The Record*, March 1965, pp44 to 45.
81. Education Secretary's Report, May 1966, p2.
82. *The Record*, February 1967, p19.
83. Education Secretary's Report, Appendix (d) May 1966.
84. During 1968, for example, Region 1 courses were held at the South-West London College, Thurrock Technical College, Harrow College, Borough Polytechnic, Isleworth Polytechnic, and at Central Office and jointly with Phillips Mills Limited, Bird's Eye Foods, Lowestoft and Guinness, Park Royal. In Region 2 with universities and technical colleges at Salisbury, Southampton, Isle of Wight, Poole, Farnborough, Portsmouth, and Basingstoke and with the War Department dockyards, local authorities, hospitals, chemical, tyre and rubber firms, brewers, engineering, electricity boards, brick makers, tilers, and timber merchants. Region 3 courses were arranged with universities at Bristol, Avonmouth, and technical colleges at Bridgwater, St Austell, Filton, Bath, Yeovil, Gloucester and Trowbridge. Employers who co-operated were Westland Aircraft, Normalair, Marglass (Sherbourne), Unigate Creameries, Drakes' Textiles, ICI, the haulage industry, W.D. & H. Wills, British Cellophane, Bonded Fibre Fabrics, Bookwell Industries, Shellmex & BP, Alcan, Tate & Lyle, Bristol Omnibus Company, RAF, RAMC Iflex and John Laing. Region 4 courses were arranged with the Universities of Swansea, Cardiff, Liverpool, Wrexham Tech. and the WEA. Employers included BP, Richard Thomas & Baldwin, Aluminium Cable Works, British Steel and Ford's. Region 13 used Flintshire Technical College. Region 5 companies included Lucas, BSA, Girling, Triplex, Rists Cables, GEC, and AEI. Regions 6 and 12 courses were with the TUC at various venues including Manchester University, John Dalton College, and Moston College.

Companies included Courtaulds, Michelin, Shell, and the Royal Ordnance Factory. Region 12 had a docks course in Liverpool. Region 7 included Rolls-Royce. Region 8 technical colleges included Sunderland, Middlesbrough, and Newcastle, and employers included ICI, Dorman Long, and Newcastle Transport. Region 9 technical colleges included Doncaster, Richmond, and Leeds. Employers included Leeds Corporation. Source: Appendix (e) to the Education Committee Report, May, 1969.

85. Report of the Research, Production and Political Department, 1968.
86. Appendix (I) to the Education Committee Report, February 1972.
87. Trade Group Departmental Review, 1970, p119.

Royal Agricultural College, Cirencester, cricket on Tuesday afternoons

Refectory at Cirencester, c. 1960s

Training aids for the mass meeting, Cirencester, 1950s

Union WEA course, 1940s

Shop Stewards and Branch Officers from the bus industry at a Union lecture during a one week course set up with the University of London, 1950

T&G Union students at LSE, early 1950s

Northern Summer School, early 1950s

A discussion group, Bexhill on Sea 1950

Summer School, Cirencester, August 1953

Jack Jones and his wife Evelyn Jones with a group of tutors in the 1960s, also in the picture Marie Patterson (sitting far left) and Tony Corfield (third from the right, standing)

Presenting of certificate, home study course, early 1960s

Ellen McCullough 1958

John Price 1930s

Jack Lucas with students, late 1950s

Teaching aid: Tony Corfield demonstrates the slide rule, 1950s

Harrow Road Training Centre, early 1970s

Summer School at the Royal Agriculture College Cirencester, 1976. Among others in the group are Ollie Jackson, Pete Batten, Ray Collins, Frank Cosgrove

L to R Harry Lees (Education Officer of old Region 3),
Neil Kinnock and Frank Cosgrove

New Officers outside the Education Centre in Eastbourne in the early 1980s with Moss Evans the General Secretary in the middle

First Distance-Learning course Region 1, June 1984, R to L: Pat Harris, John Fisher Duncan Warmington, Larry Smith, Bill Horslen, Brendan Gold, Frank Cosgrove, Ken Fuller, Paul Bonython, Bill Donald, Mick Alleway, Gordon White, Barry Camfield, Larry Marson

First TGWU National Women's Course, 26 to 31 October 1980, in the picture among others Pete Batten and Margaret Prosser

First group of Regional Women's Organisers, 1990, from L to R: Sylvia Greenwood, Carole Rowe, Muriel Mayor, Yvonne Strachan, Diana Holland, Margaret Prosser, Lindy Whiston

The Education Officers, mid 1990s (absent is Gordon Pointer, Region 2). **Front row L to R**: *Chris Russell – Region 8, Ann McCall – Region 6, Jim Hunt - Region 5 Regional Secretary, Bill Morris – General Secretary, Mary Edwards – Region 4.* **Back row R to R**: *Liam McBrinn – Region 3, Bob Sissons – Region 5, Pete Batten – Region 1, Lesley Sutherland – Region 7, John Fisher – Director of Education*

Chapter 6

The Jones Era 1960–1979

This chapter looks at the 1960s and 1970s. Jack Jones, General Secretary for most of the period, played a key part in the development of the union's education programme. Jones's innovative approach to education has already been noted, and from a position of power he was able to move the programme forward in a number of ways, in particular in the areas of full-time officer training, health and safety, equalities and in the regions through the appointment of the first Regional Education Officers. He was also the prime mover behind the building of the Eastbourne education and holiday centre, which gave the union an all-year-round base for residential courses. Jack Jones's period as GS coincided with the high-point of TGWU membership in the century, and the extension of legislation on paid release and the rights and duties of shop stewards and safety representatives, all of which added a new impetus to the union's education programme.

We left the national programme in 1959 with a new policy of making sure that TGWU education directly assisted the union's workplace representatives as much as possible and that it should be firmly rooted in the day-to-day activities of the union's growing number of shop stewards. The person best placed to implement this policy to the full was Jack Jones. In his Coventry days he had used education as an organising tool and as a way of recruiting and developing shop stewards. Now, in the early 1960s, he was in a position where his core ideas were also in tune with the times. By the end of the 1970s, Jack Jones had laid the groundwork for an education 'specialist' in each region, and had also restructured the national leadership of TGWU education following the end of the McCullough/Corfield period.

By the early 1960s, Jack Jones had been Regional Secretary of Region 5 (Midlands) for seven years, the same length of time as Frank Cousins' stewardship of the union as a whole. The TGWU had entered a period of growth and change in the boom period of that time, and in March 1963 the GEC accepted a recommendation from the General Secretary for the need to appoint a third executive officer in order to bring some relief of the union's administration at this level 'in view of the constantly increasing pressures relating to the membership'.[1] Cousins was beginning to tire, and his deputy, Harry Nicholas, was himself unwell and not up to taking on extra responsibilities. Although the decision to have a third executive officer was taken slightly earlier at the suggestion of Alf Chandler, its realisation was strengthened by the fact that Cousins had suffered a heart attack, and was already preparing for the time when he could no longer carry out the exhausting task of General Secretary. Jack Jones had built his reputation in the Midlands, he and Cousins were in tune politically, and were also personal friends. Although reluctant to move to London, Jones agreed to run for the position with Cousins's support.[2] There were nine candidates initially, and Jack Jones and Bob Davis (General Workers' National Secretary) were shortlisted to appear before the GEC with the recommendation from the F&GP for the appointment of Jack Jones to the position of Assistant Executive Secretary. He was duly appointed on 21 August 1963, almost 24 years to the day since he first became a TGWU officer. Harry Urwin was appointed to replace Jones as Region 5 Regional Secretary from 24 September 1963. The list of activities to be carried out by Jack Jones was extremely wide-ranging and included the preparation of introductory pamphlets for new members, material for an illustrated history of the union, and the extended development of courses for officers and shop stewards on the general problems associated with work study, bonus schemes and management techniques. He also had a remit to review *The Record* and union communications generally.[3]

Jones had just begun his work when Labour won the 1964 general election, and in October of that year Cousins announced that he had been invited to accept the position of Minister of Technology in the new government. The GEC granted leave of absence to Cousins and from 19 October 1964, Harry Nicholas took up the position of Acting General Secretary and Jack Jones moved to the position of Acting Assistant General Secretary. In July 1966 Cousins returned to the union, having resigned his ministerial position. However, he never again took firm control of the union. In September 1968, at the age of 63, Harry Nicholas accepted the position of Secretary-General of the Labour Party, and asked to begin the process of retirement, from 2 November 1968. Because of these developments, Jack Jones became the dominant figure in the TGWU leadership even before his formal election as General Secretary, going into the election in the autumn of 1968 as a strong favourite. There were initially a large number of names put forward for the position, including Tony Corfield, Jack Lucas, and Larry Smith, the former London busman and main right-wing rival to Jones. Many nominations were declined at the initial stage, including that of Corfield. However, ten candidates were accepted for the ballot paper including Lucas and Smith. The result was an overwhelming victory for Jones, with 334,000 votes. Bob Davis polled 28,000, Jack Lucas 19,000, and Larry Smith 22,000.

One of the casualties of the Jones campaign was Tony Corfield. When Ellen McCullough returned from her secondment with the TUC Education Department at the end of 1965, her job as National Woman Officer (sic) had been taken by Marie Patterson, and Tony Corfield was in charge of Education and Research. In a typical move in favour of McCullough, the Executive created a new Production and Research Department with her at its head, and from February 1966 she began reporting to the GEC, officially on matters linked to productivity bargaining and company information, but in fact covering many of the areas in her real priority; trade union education. Her first report included references to participation in adult education, lecturing to trade union studies courses at LSE, productivity bargaining and assistance rendered in the field of industrial training.[4] Throughout her period as National Woman Officer, she still maintained her former role as one of the officers on duty at Cirencester. All this must have created frustration for Tony Corfield, who never enjoyed the same easy supportive relationship with the GEC as Ellen McCullough.

Some of Corfield's frustration came out in his backing of Larry Smith, the main challenger to Jones for the general secretary's position. Although no great advocate of education, Smith may have offered Corfield a way out of his unsatisfactory situation. Corfield began to promote Smith, for example in an article in *The Record* of April 1967 titled 'Comments on Union Education from Two Well-Known Students'. This was an interview between Tony Corfield, Larry Smith and Len Squire, RTC National Officer.[5] When the campaign for general secretary got underway the next year, Corfield challenged the near-certainty of Jones's victory by publishing a pamphlet entitled *Collective Leadership for the TGWU*, which called for a 'rotating' GS every four years and generally challenged the dominance of the general secretary's position.

Corfield took the GS election as his starting-point: 'The members of the TGWU have the chance to choose, not between people, but between principles. They are asked not just to exercise an option as between the suitability of one person or another for general secretary, but to judge whether the position as we have known it in the past should be allowed to continue. In my submission the power vested in the man who becomes general secretary in this union has increased, is increasing, and ought to be diminished'.[6] After this devastating start, Corfield went on to set out the 'three disadvantages of personal leadership':

> The first disadvantage of vesting executive authority on one person for life is that it stands in the way of further union amalgamation ... The leaders of other unions are unlikely to submerge their own personal pre-eminence by joining a union in which leadership and prestige are monopolised in one top position ... Its second disadvantage is that it

> tends to discourage the governing committees in the union from exercising their full responsibilities. The more all the important decisions tend to be concentrated in the hands of one man, the less the various governing bodies can feel genuine responsibility for the proposals they suggest ... Its third disadvantage is that it tends to insulate the general secretary, however well-intentioned he might be, from the feelings of his members. Because he is there for life, he has less need to take a close day-to-day account of the wishes and needs of the rank and file.[7]

For a senior member of staff to make such points at that particular time was unforgivable, and the issue was raised at the F&GP in October, where his pamphlet was described as 'containing a definite bias towards one of the candidates not named involved in the ballot'.[8] Tony Corfield was summoned before the GEC in December 1968 and attempted to justify his action in publishing the pamphlet, asserting that he had, in no way, been in breach of the rules and constitution of the union.[9]

At the close of the review, during which many GEC members voiced strong disapproval of Corfield's action, the matter was referred back to the F&GP for its January 1969 meeting, a clear sign that he would be dealt with by the General Secretary in the meantime, with the backing of the F&GP. Corfield was in effect dismissed, although both he and Jack Jones claim that he resigned. Cousins would still have been the one who administered the disciplinary action, and Jones says that he was particularly incensed by the pamphlet. Jack Jones also says he respected Corfield's right to his opinion, made it clear at the time, and would have worked with him had he remained.[10] For his part, Corfield claims that he was not actually told to leave but that he was told he would be excluded from future TUC and Labour Party conferences, and generally kept out in the cold. On this basis he decided to leave.[11]

Corfield had written his last 'Education Notes' for the March 1969 edition of *The Record*, as at the beginning of February he had taken up an appointment with the WEA as director of their newly-established Service Centre for Social Studies. Corfield had remained very close to the WEA. Throughout 1967 and 1968 he had acted as convenor for the WEA working group setting up the Service Centre, as well as being on all the key WEA committees, so there may be some truth in the view that he had decided to leave the union of his own volition. 'Education Notes' was taken over by Ellen McCullough, who was re-appointed Secretary of the Education Department at the March 1969 GEC meeting.

So ended the direct association between the TGWU and the person most responsible for the character of the Cirencester summer schools and the active, role-oriented teaching methods throughout the union's education programme. It was a sorry end to a very significant career with the union, but Corfield had always been kept slightly at a distance by the union's leadership, and his frustration had clearly been coming to a head before the final incident. He remained at the WEA for a short time, then became the principal of Fircroft College, Birmingham, for 5 years, where he became embroiled in a bitter dispute with students, staff and governors in the mid-1970s, during which he lost his post at the college.[12] Corfield remained a TGWU member and the union supported the request for a full public inquiry into the Fircroft dispute.[13] He then became co-ordinator for the National Health and Safety Groups Council. At the time of writing, he is retired but alert and active, and has continued to be a member of the ACTS section of the union.

EXPANDING THE BASIC PROGRAMME

Courses on the Industrial Relations Bill were being held in most regions during 1970 and 1971, organised as part of a TUC campaign against the Bill. TGWU involvement with colleges and universities, mainly as part of the TUC scheme, continued to grow. Also, the expansion of union-only and joint company-union shop stewards' courses, which began in the 1960s, continued apace into the 1970s. TGWU students at courses lasting one, two or three days using day-release grew from 2,223 in 1969 to 3,187 by 1971.[14] In that year courses were held for the first time in a number of companies, including in the East Anglian Brewery Company Greene King, Metal Box (Winsford), Rockware Glass (Greenford), Albright & Wilson (Widnes), Manchester Corporation, UG Glass Limited (New Cross), ICI, Courtaulds (Preston), Fords and Shell (Shell Haven).[15] During the period 1971-1972, major agreements giving paid release for shop stewards' training were concluded with employers. These included local government, the docks, and the passenger transport industry.

During the first quarter of 1972 in-plant courses were held at Guinness (Runcorn Brewery), BXL (Newton Aycliffe), Greene King, ICI (Wilton) and Shell Haven. Discussions on shop stewards' training were held with the United Kingdom Atomic Energy, Wanda Limited, Walls Meats, BP, Midland Red and Tetley Brewery. In-plant courses during 1973 and 1974 included five courses held at ICI Fibres (Gloucester), Lansil Limited (Lancaster), Bachelor's Foods Limited (Sheffield and Worksop), Courtauld's (Preston), and EPS (Manchester). Courses of particular interest during this period included one at the Central Office Training Centre on job evaluation for former Chemical Workers Union members, one of the first on this subject. The union also provided three two-day crash job evaluation courses for stewards with special problems at Amalgamated Oxide Limited (Dartford), and Long & Hambly Limited (High Wycombe). London Transport platform staff also had customised courses. Most of these courses were held in accommodation provided by the employing company, usually in their own training centres with audio-visual aids provided.

One unusual in-plant course was held in April 1973 at Sheffield University, the first ever in-plant course arranged for non-teaching staff. Over half the students on the course were women and the course programme included sessions designed to develop skills in communications, grievance handling and so on. Four linked courses were held at Fry's (Bristol), and at British Nuclear Fuels, where the programme included one of the first uses of closed-circuit television and videotape recordings in some of the role-play exercises. At the 1973 in-plant course for Greene King Brewery from 30 April to 4 May, there was a break for May Day so that students could attend demonstrations.[16]

By 1974 the number of company courses had expanded yet again, to include Bowyer's, Avon Rubber, ICI Fibres and Organics, Courtauld's, UG Glass and BSC. Some positive effects beyond education were noted at the time:

> One result of the in-plant course for shop stewards and supervisors at the Greene King Breweries has been the organisation into membership of most of the supervisory staff and the union organisation of the small brewery at Furneaux Pelham where previously there was no membership.[17]

The provision of in-plant courses continued throughout the later 1970s for a number of companies including British Steel and Clyde Paper. In 1975 there was an in-plant course at the Clatterbridge Hospital complex in the Wirrall, one of the first courses to include health and safety at work and the Trade Union and Labour Relations Act and Employment Protection Act as well as industrial democracy, trade unions in the Common Market, and workers' participation. There was a further course at Metal Box Limited, Worcester and the first in-plant course to be held in Region 10 was at Capper Pass in Hull. Other courses in 1975 included Batchelor's Foods at Sheffield and Worksop; ICI paints at Stowmarket and Slough; Food Industries Limited, Brombrough; Brylcreem at Maidenhead and British Airways at Heathrow. Boots and United Distillers all had in-plant courses at this time.[18] In the whole of 1975 15 five-day in-plant courses were held in the Central Office Training Centre. In the later 1970s in-plant courses were held for other companies, including Gilby Vintners, Scholl's, and in Region 2, Dimplex, Mullard's and Courage's. Region 5 had a one-week residential course for senior stewards at Fircroft College and a course at Greenshield Stamps. Region 8 held an induction course for safety reps at Shield's Packaging and Region 11 provided in-plant courses at Guinness's. Many of these companies continued to run in-plant courses on a local basis into the 1980s, and some of them such as ICI and the oil companies moved to residential courses, often using the union's Eastbourne Centre.

Jack Jones soon made his influence felt in the national programme. He and his wife always attended the summer schools, where he normally addressed the whole student gathering, and in July 1972, he circulated to the regions a list of union publications which were to be used in the education programme. These included the *Shop Stewards' Handbook*, *Plant and Productivity Bargaining* by Harry Irwin, *Plant Level Bargaining*, and the Home Study course. The programme also used *Figure It Out*, a book on the basics of arithmetic, *Trade Unionism in the 70s* by Jack Jones, *Women's Rights in Industry*, *The Right to Participate,* based on a talk by Jack Jones, *Here's Your Tool Kit,* a leaflet about the education programme and *The Law and You*, a basic legal manual. It became normal practice for the GEC Education Committee to meet during the summer school and for its members to participate in sessions with the students.

He also organised a joint Anglo-American trade union study course looking at the problems of the motor industry; 21 leading officials of the UAW, AEF and the TGWU met at Cirencester in July, 1969. Jack Jones and Leonard Woodcock (UAW President) presided over the conference, which took place at the same time as the Branch Officers' training course and the American visitors took the opportunity to have 'ball sessions' with groups of TGWU students during their free time.

By 1971, about 10,000 shop stewards and branch officers had attended courses at Cirencester since 1953. In that year, out of 35 tutors invited to the courses, about half were TGWU members who had taken advantage of the union's education facilities after having formerly attended Cirencester as students. The other half were WEA and university extra-mural tutors, the great majority having a link with the Labour Movement, or at least sympathy with it. A small minority were management studies tutors giving themselves a different perspective by teaching trade union students. Tutors at this time were paid £60 for the week, and in 1977 the GEC agreed that their fees be subject to annual review. By the early 1970s, usually around 500 students participated in the Cirencester courses. The programme was much as before, focusing on the skills and issues relevant to branch officers and shop stewards. In 1972 the total attendance at Cirencester courses was 573, the largest ever in a five-week period. From 1973 the school included a general session on safety and health at work, provided in later years by Harry Moore, the Eastbourne Centre Education Officer, using 35 millimetre slides, very much the 'new thing' at that time. In 1974 it was noted that an encouraging trend was that a high proportion of those attending were under 40 years of age; in that year 311 out of 479, or 65 per cent; 136 were under 30, almost 30 per cent of students, showing that a new generation was coming through. In the Jones era, the 'all school' evening debates were also extended in their political range; in 1975, for example, covering the issues of public ownership, inflation, the Social

Contract, multi-racial workforces, and workers' control of industry. The Cirencester course library was brought up to date, Arrow Books presented their new industrial relations series and each student was given a copy of the history of the union and of the *TUC Health and Safety at Work Guide*.[19] As a result of these improvements, and as a sign of the times, the number of applications for 1976 was the highest ever, a total of 767 applicants and 601 students. Sixty-six per cent were under 40 years of age.[20] Up to this time, recommended students from the summer schools had attended a course at the TUC but from 1976 the TUC training college had ceased taking follow-on students and the union, therefore, tried to increase the number of places at Cirencester. The demand for follow-on training remained persistently high and the courses in 1975-1976 were adjusted to permit the concentration on the new legislation coming in at that time. These courses were subsequently allocated to Eastbourne.

The other core course in the national programme was the Home Study course, which continued throughout the Jones era. In 1962 Tony Corfield published a list in *The Record* of the most active branches for the year 1959-1961 whose members took part in the course. The best branch was 4/162, the Pontypool Factory of British Nylon Spinners. The second best branch was 5/37, Midland Red Bus Garage, and the third best 8/160, ICI Billingham Riggers' branch. The 6/60 branch, Blackpool Passenger Commercial Road Transport, had the highest number of students in Region 6 to complete the course between 1959 and 1961.[21] This remained an active education branch right up to the 1990s, with one of its members, the late Larry Marson, serving on the GEC Education Committee in the 1980s. In the mid-1960s, the booklets which made up the course were completely revised, and it was agreed that members who had already completed the course would be able to take it again if they wished. Numbers enrolling on the course in this period increased from 3,803 in 1961-1962 to 4,031 in 1965-1966. However, numbers completing decreased from 2,050 in 1961-1962 to 1,996 in 1965-1966.[22] Numbers declined in the late 1960s perhaps because of the expansion of direct collective involvement in shop stewards' and in-plant courses. Numbers enrolling for the course in 1967-1968 totalled 4,297, and in 1969-1970, were 4,050. Those completing the course in 1967-1968 were 436, and in 1969-1970 were 608.[23]

In 1967 Tony Corfield wrote an article on the revamped course, describing the three stages:

> Anyone who can fill up a football coupon can tackle the first stage. Each student gets a booklet on questions sent to him each month for six months. The questions are simply to be answered yes or no.[24]

Stage 2 involved written answers to six questions, for which the material was all contained in the booklets provided.

> The third and final stage is more exacting. Members wishing to complete this must demonstrate an ability to relate the theory about the union to their own experience. This stage is intended to demand a high standard from members taking it and those completing it to the satisfaction of the Education Committee receive a certificate 'With Distinction'.[25]

The old title *The Union, its Work and Problems* was phased out in 1970, and the revamped course was called *The Union in Action*. Whereas the original course had concentrated on understanding the objectives and structure of the union, the new one concentrated much more on the field of collective bargaining and services to members. Book 1 concentrated on the structure, benefits and services, Book 2 on negotiating techniques and procedures and Book 3 on the union's relationship with wider political and industrial movements. In 1976 the course was reviewed once again, and the more active and relevant nature of the course increased student enrolment and participation. Whereas in 1971-1972 4,478 students enrolled and 2,458 completed, by 1976, 5,729 had enrolled and 2,643 completed. By the later 1970s the level of participation in the Home Study course was the highest ever attained, although it must be remembered that the level of the union's membership at this time was nearing the two million mark.[26]

HEALTH AND SAFETY AT WORK

Another issue which came to the fore in the Jones years was health and safety at work, and the beginning of the systematic training of union safety representatives, today a core element of all trade union education provision. Before the 1970s, although safety was always a trade union issue, such training did not specifically feature in TGWU education programmes. In 1950, the NCLC had introduced a new postal course on industrial injuries insurance, and dealing with accidents and claims was a standard part of shop steward training. TWI also included a safety training element aimed at supervisors. Once again, it was Jack Jones who in March 1960 first raised the issue in an article in *The Record* entitled 'Trade Unions and Safety at Work', in which he said that 'there should be less talking at the workers and more talking with the workers'.[27]

In 1961 the union associated itself with the Campaign for Industrial Safety and made arrangements to publicise the campaign throughout the union through letters, statements, press releases and leaflets. One of the reasons for supporting the campaign was the serious increase of industrial accidents in 1960.[28] The pressure was maintained with an article 'Trade Unions and Safety' in *The Record* in October 1961 which made the point that 'safety is a matter of such importance that both sides of industry must bury the hatchet together to find the right answer'.[29] The next month's edition featured a double-page spread

'The Challenge of Industrial Safety' by Frank Cousins, proposing the strengthening of the trade union role:

> A lively effective joint works safety committee can play a major part in this but only a small percentage of the establishments covered by the Factories Act have them and some of these are very limited in the scope of their activities. If the committees are to be respected by the workers and have the enthusiastic support of trade union representatives, they must be given real responsibilities and enough powers to do an effective job of work.[30]

In the spring of 1962 the union had initiated a campaign for industrial safety with the distribution of publicity to branches and with discussions on the issue with the TUC and the government. The government and the Chief Inspector of Factories had asked whether the trade unions were doing their share to make workers safety conscious and if information was available to indicate the effect of industrial safety campaigns. The Chief Inspector of Factories expressed the view that works safety committees were increasingly coming into effective operation and 'will play a big part in future safety activities'. This view was supported by the Executive, who authorised various articles in *The Record* in support of the campaign.[31]

By 1968 the union's Legal Director, Albert Blyghton, was writing in *The Record* on works safety committees and arguing that they should be compulsory.[32] When Jack Jones moved up to the position of Assistant Executive Secretary, he again promoted the safety issue, and in March 1968 *The Record* published an article by him called 'Industrial Safety – Joint Control is the Answer'. This set out some of the principles later to be included in the Health and Safety at Work Act 1974; for example:

> In Sweden legislation provides that in all workplaces with five or more workers a safety delegate should be elected. Where 50 or more are employed, joint safety committees have to be set up. This could be of a far-reaching character, giving worker representatives a right to stop unsafe working, inspect and determine what are or are not safe working methods including layout and equipment ... Better training is needed but training itself is not sufficient.[33]

The issue of health and safety was given a great boost with the establishment of the Robens Committee in 1970. Following the publication of the Committee's report in July 1972, the TUC held a conference on health and safety at work in October, in which the TGWU participated. The GEC stated that the Robens' report was 'far-reaching and concerned future organisation and administration of safety and health at national and workplace levels; drew particular attention to the failure of existing arrangements; and emphasised the need for greater involvement in safety at the workplace'.[34]

In the period between the passing of the Health and Safety at Work Act in 1974 and the introduction of the Safety Representatives and Safety Committees Regulations in the autumn of 1977, the union developed its policy and its training provision for a new constituency. In 1973, Region 1 had sent a remit to the GEC calling for the union to give a much higher priority to this issue, and asking that any proposals for a non-enforceable voluntary code for safety and health at work should be rejected.[35] In terms of training, the key issues were independent trade union safety courses and the right to paid release for safety representatives. This issue came up at the Confederation of Shipbuilding and Engineering Unions in 1976 when some local employers' associations advised constituent firms not to agree to paid release for TUC courses on health and safety at work on the grounds that the syllabus of training had not been mutually approved. The employers were not prepared to be involved until the regulations came into force. The General Council of the TUC called a conference of affiliated organisations in March 1976, and advised that shop stewards should not attend any training courses on health and safety at work unless they received payment for any 'lost time' from their employers.

Following this TUC conference, Jack Jones sent a letter to all TGWU officers setting out the union's policy:

> You will be aware of our union policy in regard to health and safety reps in that where shop stewards are being elected it should be understood that they are also being elected as the union safety rep. It is also our union policy that this particular issue should be followed as strictly as possible, recognising that there may be odd occasions where we have active members who may have specialised in this field in whom our members generally have every confidence and they too might be considered'.[36]

Health and safety was included for the first time in the 1975 Cirencester programme and the union considered a new industrial law course to also include other recent legislation such as the Trade Union and Labour Relations Act and the Employment Protection Act. The EPA's provisions on time off for paid release for union training came into force on 1 April 1978. This gave trade union representatives the right to paid time off for industrial relations duties and activities and union training. By the summer of 1978, the GEC asked that there should be an earlier meeting of all regional education officers and staff to ensure a co-ordinated and consistent approach to this training being provided and claiming the maximum financial assistance from public funds.[37] In July the Education Committee urged all regions 'to concentrate on urgent training in respect to the provisions of the Health and Safety at Work Act'.[38]

Thus the scene was set for the massive expansion in health and safety at work courses which would follow in the next few years, and for the establishment of health and safety as a key element in TGWU education. Courses for safety reps became the norm in the 1980s, and were included as a core requirement for TGWU education in the 1990s. Accredited partnerships also gave both tutors and students the opportunity to achieve technical qualifications in health and safety such as IOSH and NEBOSH, and to adapt courses to new legislation such as COSHH and the EU 'Six Pack'. In the 1990s the union also introduced a new national course, Trade Unions and the Environment.

FULL-TIME OFFICER EDUCATION AND TRAINING

One of Jack Jones's particular interests from the start of his appointment as Assistant Executive Secretary was the training of the union's officials. He took the view that training and education benefited everyone, not least full-time officials faced with pressure from all sides in an ever-changing industrial and political environment, and in the mid-1960s he set about organising the first systematic national programme for TGWU officials. He was entering a complex part of the union's education programme. Whilst the need to educate and train lay representatives has always been clearly understood throughout the history of the union, the relationship between education, training and the corps of full-time officials has been, and remains, uneasy. In some parts of the TGWU there is the view that to become an official is the end of a long involvement with the union, even a reward for services, and that 'if a person needs training, s/he should not have been appointed an official'.[39]

These comments represent a basic insecurity, and for some officials to admit that they need training or education can involve a loss of face. Others take the view that with limited resources, the union should not divert too much to those in the fortunate position of being in employment with the union, and should concentrate on the lay membership. It has always been a cherished part of the union's constitution and culture that its officers should be recruited from the ranks of the membership. In a manual union, however, this meant that most of the candidates would be unqualified for the administrative, legal and professional side of their job and, for the reasons mentioned above, unwilling to submit to professional training or continuing education.

The issue had been raised as early as 1926 when the ACTS National Committee and the Area 8 Committee sent a resolution to the GEC calling for professional qualifications for the union's officials:

> ... This Trade Group Committee feels that while there are a great number of officials who have a very wide knowledge of the industrial situation and who are capable propagandists and negotiators, it is their

> opinion that it is likely that many of the administrative posts in the union are filled by people without administrative knowledge or training and it would be to the general benefit of the membership that the administration of the union should be closely examined and as vacancies occur care should be taken that officials placed in administrative posts should be men or women with administrative training and ability, and it is their opinion that money might be saved and efficiency increased if this were done.[40]

This touched a nerve, and a rather shirty GEC reminded the two committees that it appointed people who in their opinion were fully qualified for their positions.

Very little was done in the inter-war years to give any educational support to the union's officials, but when in 1939 education came to the top of the agenda with the development of the correspondence course, John Price raised the matter with Bevin and Alf Chandler:

> It was reported how many of the newly-appointed officers desired to take up study courses to help them in their work, and who asked for useful books to read in connection with their work. It was felt that newly-appointed officers might usefully spend a week or so at Head Office, studying methods, examining forms of agreements etc, and it was decided that consideration be given to this point.[41]

Nothing came of this suggestion in the war years, and although there was a debate in the union immediately after the war on the question of officers' representation in the union, as far as their education was concerned, no national TGWU scheme was introduced, and the matter was left to the TUC, TWI and the regions. By June 1952, 104 TGWU officers had been sent on the TUC one-week course in production management and 'time and motion'. Officers continued to use the TUC for this type of training.

At the regional level, the provision for officers was patchy, as it was for the lay members. In the 1950s the most active regions were 1, 5 and 7. The Region 1 officers' programme began in 1951 and was organised by Ted Sheehan, and involved a series of one-day schools held on Saturdays in the London district. The lecturers were from the London WEA and around 40 officers attended. The school was divided into groups to consider these questions:

> (a) What do trade union officials mean by Industrial Democracy?
> (b) Should trade unions be a part of management?
> (c) What is meant by joint consultation?[42]

These day-schools were supplemented by regular weekend schools, and during 1951 and 1952 six day-schools were held on Saturdays, followed by a weekend school, attracting an average of 50 or 60 people. In the winter of 1963, 60 officers were in attendance at St Leonard's-on-Sea to hear Frank Cousins give a lecture on wages policy and the NEDC. The regional secretary also took part in the weekend school, which was organised by Jack Lucas.[43]

Beyond this untypical provision, most officers were left to their own devices until Jack Jones's appointment. Jack Jones attended those officers' courses currently in operation, but he also began to look at a systematic programme of officer training, and the Education Committee at its quarterly meeting in February 1966 agreed to introduce an experimental one-week course for full-time officials. It was decided to use Cirencester in the period immediately following the summer schools, but before the regular agricultural students returned. The first one-week officers' course was therefore held between 10 and 17 September 1966, and following its success, a further course was arranged at Coleg Harlech from 14 to 21 March 1967, and a third course for the summer of 1967.

Forty-five newly-appointed officers attended the first school, including one from Gibraltar. Frank Cousins gave the initial address, and two members of the union's parliamentary group, Trevor Park, MP for South-East Derbyshire, and Lewis Carter-Jones, MP for Eccles, acted as tutors for the political part of the school. Harry Urwin, then Midlands Regional Secretary, conducted an exercise in negotiating an incentive scheme, Ellen McCullough led a session about research and sources of information, and Bill Wedderburn from LSE gave a talk on trade union law. Jack Jones attended throughout, focusing mainly on productivity bargaining and union organisation. The second school followed a similar pattern, with the same tutors and speakers. An addition was that a reporter from the *Liverpool Echo* attended to give a special report on the school. This was transformed into a written exercise with each officer being asked to prepare a press release on the school, stressing its local significance for readers in Wales.[44] The course ran from 5pm on the Tuesday through to 6.45pm on the following Monday, and 47, mainly new officers, attended. The third school returned to Cirencester from 9 to 16 September 1967. This last course had an adjusted programme to include teaching methods, reflecting that the expansion of shop stewards' training was making a new demand on officers as tutors. Jack Jones also encouraged debate amongst officers on how to deal with productivity bargaining, the key industrial relations practice in this period. He organised a conference of national officers and regional secretaries at Rewley House, Oxford, on 21 and 22 May 1966, to examine the application of union policy on productivity bargaining both locally and nationally. Hugh Clegg and Allan Flanders provided the main discussion document, with Jack Jones winding up with the implications for the union.[45]

Regional provision for officers also expanded in this period. The course in Region 2 in February 1967 has been noted in the previous chapter, and in the early summer of 1968 Jack Jones conducted a weekend school for officers in Regions 8, 9 and 10. In Region 1, Jack Lucas extended the existing provision into new fields. In June 1966, 65 regional officers attended the annual weekend course at St Leonard's. Bob Harle, a management consultant, lectured on wages development, and Bill Wedderburn gave a lecture on the law.[46] Seventy-five officers attended the 1969 school to hear Jack Jones, and Region 1 also introduced an on-going officers' school in the spring of 1968. This consisted of an evening class on teaching methods for officers in the General Workers and Municipal Trade Groups. The course lasted for twelve sessions, and was held weekly at Transport House from April to July. The purpose of the class was to assist officers to teach shop stewards.

Following this initial burst of activity, officers' education continued into the 1970s in an *ad hoc* manner, with Jack Jones calling conferences of officers together when an important policy issue needed to be confronted. There was, however, no systematic programme of officers' education either at national or regional level, and the regions remained uneven in their provision. In September 1976 the Region 1 Committee sent a remit to the GEC calling for improved facilities for the training of officers, advocating a systematic approach, including a period of induction for newly-appointed district officers, more modern and comprehensive office facilities, staff training regardless of age, paid release and 'opportunities for established officers to get education and training or to do research in their specialist areas, including the opportunity to publish their results'.[47]

The resolution was too radical for the Council, who recognised that most of the education provision was in the hands of regional administrations, and most regional secretaries would not have engaged in so extensive a programme. The remit was received and noted. By the mid-1970s, the main source of officer training continued to be the TUC, and in 1972, for example, a total of 34 full-time officers attended TUC courses mainly on negotiation, management techniques and teaching methods.[48]

THE EASTBOURNE CENTRE

Another major development in the union's education provision was the establishment of the union's holiday, convalescent and education centre at Eastbourne, which opened in 1976 and which provides a lasting monument to Jack Jones' leadership. The establishment of such a centre had always been an aim of Jack Jones; in 1962, during his period as regional secretary, the GEC was sent a resolution from his Region 5 Committee calling for the conversion of the union's convalescent home at Buxton into an educational centre and the closure of both existing homes and 'the establishment of a modern convalescent home and holiday centre at a suitable seaside resort'. The resolution was received and noted but the GEC was reluctant to take the step.[49] The issue, however, did not go away and in 1967 the TGWU joined the GMWU and AEF in looking at the possibility of using Cliveden House, the former home of the Astor family but then owned by the National Trust, as an education centre. This matter was left in the hands of the General Secretary but was not viable because of the costs of adapting a National Trust property to public access.[50] In January 1969, *The Record* published a letter calling for 'a full-time school based somewhere within 25 miles of London with accommodation for at least 100 students'.[51] The issue was debated at the 1969 BDC – which marked the formal transition to Jack Jones's regime – and a resolution was carried unanimously:

> That this Conference, noting the need for a more comprehensive education service, instructs the GEC to reorganise existing union educational services to meet this need.[52]

The 1969 BDC reflected the growing demand for union education throughout the working year, and raised the question of the union's own residential facilities. While the education programme consisted essentially of the Home Study course and the concentrated series of courses grouped together around the summer schools, it was possible for Cirencester to act as a temporary, seasonal 'home' for TGWU education for a few weeks each year. However, as the education programme became more comprehensive, the limitations of having a residential centre available only in the summer became obvious, and increased the pressure to establish an all-year-round education facility. As a consequence of this pressure, the union took advantage of its merger with the National Association of Operative Plasterers in 1969 to use NAOP's former HQ, a large residential house in Harrow Road, Wembley, called 'Clanrye' as an education centre. The first course – for road haulage drivers – was held in June 1969, and further courses were planned for workers from different industries, the second group being rubber workers. In November 1969, a four-day study course for national and regional officers was held, directed by Harry Urwin. In late 1969 and early 1970, four schools were held at the Wembley Centre for shop stewards in engineering, road haulage, freightliner and cold stores, with about 50 students in attendance. The union met all the students' costs and the employers were asked to pay loss of earnings, which they recovered from the training boards. However, despite Ellen McCullough's assertion that the Wembley Training Centre was 'very pleasant and suitable for the purpose',[53] it became apparent quite quickly that the building was unsuitable in both its location and its facilities, which had been designed for residence and converted into offices. Its use as an education centre was discontinued in the summer of 1970 and the building was sold.

Following the closure of the Wembley Centre, a new training facility was established at Central Office in the autumn of 1970, using a room near Transport Hall. This, of course, was non-residential, but proved very popular. In the period up to the opening of the Eastbourne Centre in 1976, the Central Office facility was fully booked for most of the time. In 1973, for example, ten courses were held, eight of which were general courses, one was for shop stewards in the chemical industry and the other for shop stewards employed by Wander Limited. The total attendance was 152.[54] With the opening of Eastbourne in 1976, the room at Central Office ceased to be used as a classroom on a regular basis, and instead was used as a space for the production and collation of education materials for the Department's courses.

When Jack Jones became General Secretary he was able to pursue the idea of a permanent and purpose-built education centre, and in 1970 Jack Lucas, as Region 1 Regional Organiser, was made responsible for selecting the site when Jack Jones asked for one somewhere in Eastbourne or in that vicinity on the south coast. Jack Lucas felt that Eastbourne was 'a blue rash area for London', but the General Secretary favoured the south coast because of the holiday and convalescent aspects of the new centre.[55] In June 1971 the GEC visited and approved the proposed site, and in late 1971 tenders were invited from selected builders. Eight tenders were received, the lowest of which was £1,826,244 and the highest £1,971,443, with the completion of the work varying from 117 weeks to 143 weeks. The Council agreed to the acceptance of the lowest tender, submitted by Walter Llewellyn & Sons Ltd. Acceptance was subject also to conforming with the union's stipulations regarding the employment of trade union labour, and in addition, the inclusion of a clause in the contract expressly prohibiting the use of labour-only subcontracting.[56] The target set for the foundation stone-laying ceremony was early 1974 and an appeal fund was opened so that regions, branches, and members could identify themselves with the project through a donation. The stone-laying ceremony actually took place on 18 September 1974. The agenda of the GEC was adjourned for the day and the Council and Executive Officers were joined by union officials, former Executive members, the Mayor of Eastbourne, the press, and members of a fraternal delegation from the Bulgarian Trade Union of Transport Workers. Jack Jones made a speech in which he said that

> The Trade Union Movement is part of the very fibre of British life and we hope to demonstrate that it has a very human face. Perhaps what we are doing here is the best answer to the prophets of gloom in Britain. We in the TGWU have confidence in the future and we know that the great heart of our people beats soundly in the knowledge that the stronger the

> Trade Union Movement the better will be the future for our country and our people.[57]

The message set into the foundation stone itself said:

> This stone was laid by Jack Jones, General Secretary, on 18 September 1974 to inaugurate the construction of the first Holiday, Recuperation and Conference Centre for the Transport and General Workers Union dedicated to the working people of all lands.

The Centre was built to a high specification, on a prime site overlooking the sea, and the great majority of bedrooms had a balcony and a sea view. There were 130 bedrooms and a capacity for 240 residents. The facility included a conference hall for around 150 people and three seminar rooms – also overlooking the sea – which could be converted to four or five smaller rooms. The restaurant and bar facilities were also first-class. Compared with existing trade union and Labour Movement education centres, and at that time the residential facilities normally experienced by TGWU members on holidays or at conferences, the Centre was far superior. It is still an excellent facility, and now includes an IT training centre. New generations expect a purpose-built crèche and some sporting or relaxation services such as a gym or sauna, and the Centre lacks these. However, it has been great value for money and is still rightly regarded as the pride of the union.

In April 1976 the GEC agreed to the appointment of an administration manager for the Centre, and in July W.A. (Alan) Simpson, then Carlisle District Secretary, Region 8, took up his post. The official opening of the Centre was 4 September 1976, although occupancy did not take place until late October. The first three courses were arranged for the weeks of 1 to 5 November, 15 to 19 November and 6 to 10 December. The Education Committee took the view that the Centre could be used for joint union/company courses, comprising shop stewards and supervisors, under full union control of both content and tutors, which could also involve the participation of national officers. Other priority areas were to be industrial democracy and tutor training. These first courses were for new full-time officials and senior stewards, and were essentially *ad hoc*, with the officers' course mixing a thorough examination of industrial democracy with a short burst of tutor training provided by George Clark of the TUC.[58]

During the summer of 1977, an international shop stewards' seminar under the Ernest Bevin International Study Group scheme was conducted at Eastbourne for shop stewards from road haulage and engineering and their counterparts from the Danish Union SID. Also in that summer, agreement was reached with BP Oil, Esso and Containerbase on joint courses to be held at the Centre, another programme which ran well into the 1980s. As a result, two courses were held for Containerbase and BP Oil in October. By 1978 Eastbourne was being used by Esso, BP, Beechams, and UK Atomic Energy. It was also heavily used by Region 1 for trade-group-based weekend courses for Central Bus, Building Trades, Public Services, Hotel and Catering and ACTS.

Inevitably the pressure grew to consider appointing regular tutorial staff, not only to teach the courses but also to maintain the trade union element in joint courses with companies. Jack Lucas retired in 1978 and was asked to take part as a tutor in the joint courses on a regular basis. In March 1978 the GEC agreed that there should be an education and training officer based at Eastbourne. This officer was to be responsible for developing and organising company-financed and union-organised courses. The committee appointed Harry Moore, District Secretary in Swindon, Region 3. Harry Moore's early life had been spent in the Royal Navy, and he had then become a senior lay representative at the Dunlop Tyre factory in Inchinnan, near Renfrew, where he had been involved in organising joint international action with trade unionists in Pirelli. In the late 1960s he attended Ruskin College and was subsequently appointed as a district officer. He took up his position at the end of July 1978, the only education officer to be appointed to the Centre.

Harry Moore's appointment led to an expansion of provision at Eastbourne; for example in the last quarter of 1978, 23 courses were held, of which the great majority were company courses largely financed by the employers, particularly oil companies, and taught mainly by Harry Moore, Jack Lucas and Frank Cosgrove, the Director of Studies. In 1979 the union also targeted the issue of information technology with a Microprocessor Training Programme, teaching officers about the new technology.

On-going concerns were the small number of women students, the lack of regular professional tutors and the issue of whether the summer schools should be transferred from Cirencester to Eastbourne. On the issue of tutors, Harry Moore was expected to minimise the need to employ outside tutors and in the first year on only one occasion, due to an emergency, was it necessary to employ a tutor to cover. However, as the range and specialisation of provision increased, this was to remain a problem for the Centre, which did not have a tutorial staff in the manner of a residential college. The Education Committee also agreed to transfer follow-on students from the summer school to Eastbourne. This was to begin in the off-peak period 1981. Thus the pattern of the first few years was established, using the Centre for company courses, specialist and officer training, and for the summer school follow-on courses.

WOMEN'S EDUCATION IN THE JONES ERA

We left the development of women's organisation and education in 1963 with Ellen McCullough, in one of her various roles, this time as

National Woman Officer, being seconded to the TUC to steer through the introduction of the TUC education scheme. The GEC decided to replace her and in January 1963 Marie Patterson was appointed. Patterson was an 'insider' from Central Office, who had been employed as a specialist clerk for the previous six years, mainly administering the affairs of the Education Department. She had been involved in further education, taking a degree and a diploma in Sociology at Bedford College whilst in the employement of the union. It seems likely, therefore, that she was recommended by Ellen McCullough.

The reason why the GEC wanted to move rapidly in this area was that they recognised the changes in industry and the growing importance of women in the labour force. The year 1963 closed with a total membership of 1,412,603, the highest the union had ever reached up to that time, an increase of 42,885 during the year. Women's membership stood at 174,222, an increase of 9,160.[59]

Marie Patterson made a good start. In the May 1963 edition of *The Record* she started a page mainly for women members – something which had not been done since the days of Mary Carlin in the 1920s. This page also promoted particular women who had completed the Home Study Certificate and named them. Patterson also used these pages to be photographed for the first time with all the women delegates at the 20th BDC in July 1963. The issue of women's involvement in the union was high on the agenda of this conference, and resolutions which called for greater women's involvement were not only carried, but supported by an Executive Statement and by the Assistant General Secretary on its behalf:

> That this conference, aware of the lack of trade union organisation amongst women in industry, instructs the GEC to inaugurate a women's recruiting campaign during the next biennial period, and to add to or amend the union department responsible so that such a campaign can be brought to a successful conclusion.[60]

Another motion went further:

> That this conference, perturbed at the lack of women officers, asks the GEC to give serious consideration to the appointment of more women officers.[61]

Whilst giving full support to these resolutions, the AGS ominously pointed out that the enforcement mechanism was essentially through the regions, thus paving the way for the usual unevenness in both appointments and education provision. One of the best regions in this respect was the London Region. As ever, Jack Lucas took a positive, energetic approach and made organising women one of his priorities. In November 1963 the region held a special one-day conference for women at the regional office, the first conference held following the debate at the BDC. At a district organising conference called in Region 1 earlier in the year, out of 80 delegates, only six were women. At this women's conference there 50 delegates and the number of applications initially exceeded 90.[62] Arising from this conference, the region devised its *Plan for Women*, led by Lucas and enthusiastically supported by Marie Patterson. The plan aimed at doubling the women's membership figure and increasing the number of women holding office.

Jack Jones also included the organisation of women in his brief as Assistant Executive Secretary, and produced a special recruitment broadsheet to organise 'women and girls' (sic) into the union.[63] *The Record* also began to carry articles of particular interest to women members, such as in January 1965 when it featured an article on cervical cancer. Marie Patterson became the union's representative on the TUC Education Committee, and her appointment encouraged the establishment of women's courses at Cirencester. In 1964 a special women's course was established, and there is a photograph in *The Record* of the group with their tutor who is a man, and Jack and Evelyn Jones are also featured with the women's group.[64] Overall, however, women's involvement in the summer schools was disappointing; in 1965 there were only 22 women altogether attending the courses, eleven of them on the special women's course. This compared with a total attendance in 1964 of 19'.[65] Thirty women attended in 1966; this dropped to 18 in 1967 and rose again to 31 in 1968.

By 1970, women's membership in the union totalled 213,524, an increase of 13,252 over the year. By 1974, total national membership was 1,857,308, an increase of 72,524 over the year. Women's membership reached 286,829 for 1974, an increase of 20,767 over the year. This was also the year of the death of Florence Hancock, officially referred to as Dame Florence Donovan,[66] who died on 14 April. By 1979 the two million mark had been passed, with membership at the end of 1978 reaching 2,072,818. Women's membership had risen to 329,534, an increase of 11,627 over the year, totalling 15.7 per cent of the whole membership.

In the mid-1970s, Jack Jones continued to promote the recruitment and organisation of women into the union as an essential policy for future growth. In a 1975 pamphlet *Equal Pay and Equal Opportunities* he stated: 'We want more women as shop stewards and more women as officials of the union. The trade union movement will have to become more representative of the female membership if it really wants to progress along the road of equality for women. We also want male shop stewards to make the demand for women's rights one of their priorities'.[67]

However, despite political encouragement from the leadership and the Education Department, there was still precious little sign of an increase in women's involvement in the education programme. In 1977 the Education Committee noted that a disturbing feature of the year was the decline in the number of women members participating in the summer schools, and by 1979 there were 31 women attending the summer schools, a mere 6.9 per cent of those attending.[68] The Committee was also concerned at the lack of women's involvement on courses held at the Eastbourne Centre and it was noted in May 1979 that since September 1978 only three women representatives had attended.[69] In 1978, at an Education Committee discussion of the TUC Charter *Equality for Women in Trade Unions*, it was agreed that the union should consider childcare facilities at union meetings, particularly at the union's next BDC. However, no childcare facilities were available at Eastbourne for some years.[70]

MANAGING THE PROGRAMME IN THE 1970s

With the departure of Tony Corfield, Ellen McCullough returned to her previous role as Head of Education. However, she was essentially a 'safe pair of hands', and she was very near retirement. In April 1970, as part of Jones's plan to re-launch *The Record* as a newspaper rather than a journal, he proposed that the Assistant General Secretary should accept overall responsibility for the paper and that Bob Rolfe should be transferred to the Education Department in the capacity of Senior Assistant.[71] Rolfe concentrated on filling one of Corfield's roles as the main organiser for the summer schools, but did not take over the administration of the Department. Ellen McCullough exercised her option to retire from 5 March 1971. At the time she was 62 years of age and had completed 45 years service with the Workers' Union and the TGWU. Her reasons for retirement were stated as 'personal considerations', coupled with the acceptance of an invitation from the WEA to take charge, on a part-time basis, of their research centre in trade union and social studies. Ever popular with the GEC, she was given a rousing send-off from the union at the March 1971 Executive, and a £500 ex-gratia payment. Jack Jones said:

> Her contribution has been outstanding. Here is a woman who has championed many trade union causes over the years, was identified with Ernest Bevin's trade union philosophy and clearly she faithfully developed that through the Education Department. Not only the members of the Executive, but thousands of members of the union appreciate the great contribution she has made to the education system of the union.[72]

Ellen McCullough directly inherited the mantle of John Price and Ernest Bevin, and although she encouraged innovators like Corfield, she always kept a firm grip on the politics of TGWU and TUC education, and linked it closely with the WEA and the Labour Party centre. Ellen McCullough died on 19 May 1985.

Jones now cast around for a suitable replacement, one who would drive his ideas forward, and yet who understood the principles of education. The short-listed candidates for the position of National Secretary of the Education and Research Department were Frank Cosgrove, Peter Hopson, (both then Region 1 district officers), Ray Padley, Bob Rolfe, Fred Silberman, and Norman Willis, all from the Research Department. The unsuccessful candidates included B.J. (Mick) Connolly, also a district officer and later Secretary of the South-East Region of the TUC. Norman Willis was appointed to the position from 24 May1971. Willis came from within Transport House, with very little industrial experience. He had attended Ruskin College and Oxford on leaving the RAF, but had no record as an educator. When the opportunity came for him to join the staff of the TUC, Jones did not stand in his way. In December 1973, Willis joined the TUC as Assistant General Secretary, and later became General Secretary. He gave his last report to the GEC on 5 December 1973.

Bob Rolfe himself was not interested in taking on the role of Director,[73] and the Committee agreed to replace Willis with someone who would work with Rolfe. In February 1974 interviews took place for the post of National Officer of the Education and Research Department. Included in the list of 12 candidates were Ray Padley, Tony Gordon, and Fred Silberman, all of the Research Department; Frank Cosgrove and Peter Hopson; and Regan Scott, then a journalist on *The Record.* The Committee were unable to make an appointment amongst these candidates, and therefore resolved that fresh applications should be received from the whole of the union. For the interview in June there were 22 candidates and they were shortlisted down to seven. Frank Cosgrove was not shortlisted and neither were Regan Scott nor Fred Silberman. In the event Bob Harrison was appointed from 1 July 1974.

Given the fact that both Cosgrove and Scott later took charge of the education programme, and that Harrison was an outsider, it seems likely that he was a candidate who 'came through the middle'. Bob Harrison was a New Zealander who had previously been a District Officer in Coventry, which may have positively influenced Jones and D.G.S. Harry Urwin. He had had no particular involvement with the union's education programme, but at some stage had undergone teacher-training. Because of the need to cover his allocation in Coventry, Harrison actually took up his position at the end of September, and attended his first GEC meeting in November 1974. In March 1975, however, Jack Jones was again raising the issue of the impending retirement of Bob Rolfe. His compulsory retirement date was not until October 1976, but the Education Committee and the GEC agreed to create a new position with the appointed person working with Bob Rolfe prior to his retirement, particularly on the branch officers' training courses at Cirencester.[74] During the summer of 1975 Jones prepared the ground and in December he recommended that Frank Cosgrove,

> Who having expressed an interest and been fully consulted, should be transferred to operate from Central Office in the capacity of Director of Studies responsible for the shop steward and other training within the educational provisions made by the union. In the special circumstances it was further recommended that Brother Cosgrove should retain his status as a permanent officer at his existing salary.[75]

The GEC agreed the proposal for Frank Cosgrove to transfer to Central Office from 26 January 1976. Cosgrove was an Irishman who came to the UK from Dublin in 1949. He then worked in London Transport and joined the union in 1956, taking part in the 1958 bus strike. He took NCLC correspondence courses and in 1965-66 attended LSE as a full-time student on a TUC bursary, and in 1967 he was appointed to the position of Region 1 Passenger Service Group Inside Staff Organiser. Cosgrove was energetic, and had not only taken part in the Region 1 education programme as a student and tutor, but had encouraged his garage reps into training and education. On the other hand, he was not an academic, and it was these qualities which appealed to Jones, who wanted somebody practical rather than theoretical in charge of education. Frank Cosgrove was seen as someone with direct industrial experience rather than a bureaucrat.[76] The position of 'Director of Studies' related back to Tony Corfield's day, the difference being that whilst Corfield remained as a staff member, Cosgrove was already an officer. This anomalous position was to dog Cosgrove's relationship with the union's administration throughout his career, for despite been effectively head of education from the late 1970s until his retirement in 1992, he was never placed on Grade 1 of the officers', scale, appropriate to all other national secretaries.[77]

Bob Rolfe retired on 27 February1976, and the first time Frank Cosgrove appeared before the Executive was 4 March 1976, accompanied by Bob Harrison and Neil Kinnock, then Chair of the TGWU Parliamentary Group. However, for the September 1976 meeting of the GEC, only Bob Harrison and Neil Kinnock were in attendance, not Frank Cosgrove – the first sign of his anomalous position. In October 1978 the GEC appointed Harrison as National Secretary of the Food, Drink and Tobacco Trade Group, and he took up the position from 1 January 1979. At a special session of the GEC in January 1979, it was agreed to appoint a National Secretary of Education and Research to replace Harrison. Candidates for this position included Mel Doyle, a TGWU member and later Deputy General Secretary of the WEA, Regan Scott, Tony Gordon and Frank Cosgrove. Regan

Scott was appointed from 29 January 1979. Scott came from a Socialist background (his father was a journalist who had been a member of the union before the war). He had joined the staff of the union in 1969 as a journalist on a contract basis to work on *The Record,* when Jack Jones wanted to transform the journal into a popular newspaper.

At the regional level, Jack Jones implemented his aim of expanding the education programme in both quantity and scope in a number of ways. In 1970 the procedure was changed so that TGWU courses could be organised straight through a district official rather than regional secretary, no doubt reflecting Jones's own experience in Regions 12 and 5. An important corollary of this greater professionalism in the union's administration of its education programme was the need to have a dedicated officer in each region responsible for the administration, organisation and development of the programme. It became clear in the 1970s that the tremendous opportunities for expansion, coupled with the need for professionalism, meant that this situation would have to be rationalised. Jones turned his attention to this in 1974 and proposed that the 1974 allocation for day and weekend schools be increased to £10,000 and a suitable programme be drafted, aimed to stimulate and organise an education campaign in each region. He also won the position that a draft training programme for shop stewards with tutors' notes and visual aids should be prepared for use in the regions.[78] For 1975 the sum was increased by 25 per cent, bringing the total to £12,500, and the overall allocation for 1975 to £62,500 rather than £50,000 as for 1974.[79]

On 19 November 1974, Jones called a meeting of national officers and regional secretaries where he took the opportunity to raise the issue of the provision of education, and where he made it clear that regions would have to standardise their organisation and administration. In particular, it was agreed that at least one officer in each region should be a specialist and should be given the responsibility and the resources to develop the organisation of union education and training. In January of 1975 and 1976 he also wrote to all branches drawing attention to the services available, and urging maximum participation; this letter was accompanied by a folder describing the services in 1975 called *Here's your Tool Kit* and in 1976 *Help Yourself*. He was also concerned that the expected expansion of trade union education and training should be fully under the control of the union, and not be employer-led. Joint training courses were being promoted by organisations such as the Industrial Society, and were growing in popularity. Jones laid down a firm guideline to the GEC on this issue in 1976:

> The Education Committee are particularly anxious to ensure that our educational facilities, which are now very extensive, should not lose sight of the rank-and-file member and the branches ... As it becomes apparent that some students and officers had been participating in shop

> stewards' training schemes, prepared and controlled by management, I found it necessary to stress to regional secretaries during the quarter that the union is against this practice, as in our view shop stewards' training is essentially a matter for union control.[80]

However, if courses organised by the union were to be under full union control, this raised questions about the course content, organisation and provision of tutors. In November 1976 Jones called a meeting of all regional secretaries, along with regional officers and staff involved in union education, to discuss questions of developing education services for the members. The purpose was to examine future developments and deal with in-plant training and the role of district officers; and also the general question of co-ordination, administration of in-plant training in the regions and the provision of teaching aids. This meeting gave a further boost to the idea of 'education specialists', and each regional secretary was asked to give consideration to the appointment of such a person within their region. However, at this time Jones was still thinking in terms of an *existing* officer taking charge of education.

In the area of administration, funding was a vital issue, and although it has already been seen that budgetary allocations had begun in the 1960s, these were not strictly enforced. As the opportunities for expansion increased, the management of these budgets became more important. It was clear that the total money available to fund an expansion of the programme would need to be substantially increased, particularly if there was to be a quantum leap in provision with the advent of safety reps, along with training in the new legislation and new technology.

The issue was raised at the 1975 BDC, through a resolution calling on the union to protect or maintain the existence of the TUC weekend schools. Jack Jones dealt with the issue himself:

> The TUC have come to the conclusion, which is identical to the view of the union, that our resources have first and foremost to be put into shop steward training and training for branch officials, and secondly, full-time officials' training. In other words those who directly represent the membership in all of our negotiations. We have to say straightaway that the T&G is delighted to see that the TUC Education Committee endorses our view of the situation. There has been a switch of resources in an expanding programme away from weekend courses to make more funds available to those areas which we think are most necessary.[81]

In 1974, the F&GP agreed that Jack Jones should make an approach to the Minister of Education and the Secretary of State for Employment to obtain an increase in grants for adult education, particularly as any reduction in the adult education programme would have an effect on training within industry.[82] This was the beginning of the process which would lead to the introduction of public funds in 1976. Jones realised that if the union began to be in receipt of public funds in any significant quantity, then the consequences would not only be the opportunity to massively expand both the provision and the administration of the programme, but also that accounting and record-keeping would have to be put onto a much more professional basis. In 1975 he therefore began the process of requiring regions to arrange a quarterly summary of their education courses to be sent to the Education Department at Central Office. This need had been confirmed by the GEC at their meeting in December 1975, but so far these reports had been received only intermittently from some regions. At their meeting in February 1976 the Education Committee decided to recommend to the GEC that regional committees be requested to arrange for the receipt of a quarterly report on regional education activity at each of their meetings and that a copy of this report be forwarded to the National Education Officer. This recommendation was endorsed by the GEC at the meeting held in March 1976. This has remained the practice to date.

Later in the year the regions were requested to budget (that is to say to provide an estimate of proposed expenditure) for their 1977-1978 educational requirements and to submit such budgetary proposals to the Education Committee. This was not a 'capped' but an 'open' budget, designed to bring visibility and professionalism into the administration of education rather than to exercise financial restriction.

Public funds became available from 1976-1977. Funds were allocated to the extension of the TUC day-release programmes, residential training courses organised by individual unions (a boost for the TGWU and Eastbourne courses), development and departmental work by the TUC, and tutor training. The initial figure was £600,000, then £1 million, rising to £1.5 million, to be claimed through the TUC. In 1977-1978 the union received £39,000 on its reclaim of public money, and the following year £78,000 – double the previous year's figure. TUC statistics in 1979 showed the TGWU to be providing one of the largest number of short courses for any affiliated union, double the student places of the GMWU.[83]

At the time, there was concern in some quarters that state funding represented an undue interference in trade union education,[123] but it should be recalled that it was the unions who pushed for such funding, and it was felt that a Labour government would not seek to control the content of courses, and that trained union representatives would gain more respect, and therefore more influence, with employers.

THE APPOINTMENT OF REGIONAL EDUCATION SPECIALISTS

The logical next step along this road of expansion and specialisation was for the regions to respond to Jack Jones's suggestion and to request the GTC to allow them to appoint dedicated education 'specialists'.

This term was used, rather than the term 'officers', because not every region requested an appointment of a person of officer status.[85] Frank Cosgrove had argued for a Grade 4 officer position, above the lowest levels, and later felt that the appointment of 'specialists' was 'half the battle won'.[86] Indeed, the job description, and the job itself, whilst being mainly concerned with education of the union's members, has not been standardised to this day. Some REOs (Regional Education Officers) also have a general membership allocation, like every other officer. Some are pensions or health and safety officers and others are involved in staff training. For some years, one or two regions refused to have an officer in this post at all. By the beginning of 1978, when the first REOs were appointed, the union had seen an increase in regional education activity of 50 per cent compared with 1976. Although the picture was very uneven, a number of individuals had already begun to specialise in education work in the regions. Steve Grinter (later a TUC REO and then an official with the Textiles International) was employed in the Northern Region Education and Research Department, Tom Cook and Alan Tuckwood worked for the Midland Region, Tom Carlyle was staff member in Bristol and regional organisers such as Jim McIntyre in Scotland and Les Shorter in London had education as part of their duties.

In November 1977, Region 9 Committee submitted a recommendation to the GEC for the appointment of a 'Regional Education and Information Officer'. Knowing that Jones was behind them, the regions had the bit between their teeth, and in January 1978 the F&GP endorsed the appointment of a 'District Officer for Research, Education and Training' in Region 2. Bob Purkiss was appointed from 2 January 1978.[87] Although *The Record* referred to Purkiss as a 'former docker'[88] he was in fact mainly a former seafarer and employee on the Isle of Wight ferries from Southampton. Bob Purkiss, along with Bill Morris, was one of the first prominent black activists in the union. He was born and raised in Hampshire, and after becoming involved in the union through Basil Bye's courses at Southampton University, he was employed by the Industrial Society training shop stewards, and was seconded to Jamaica for a year. Purkiss later became National Race Equalities Officer of the union, and the chair of the TUC Race Equality Committee and member of the TUC General Council. He retired from the union in 2000 on health grounds, but is still active in the CRE.

Applications for appointments now came thick and fast. In June 1978 Region 11(Ireland) asked for sanction for the appointment of a district officer with responsibility for shop stewards' education, training and research within the Republic of Ireland.[89] By November, an arrangement was worked out with the Irish Congress of Trade Unions (ICTU) setting out the basis of the financial assistance to be given in connection with this appointment. The agreement was that the officer would be designated 'ICTU Training Officer', and the union would be responsible for 50 per cent of the costs incurred in organising courses. The appointment was largely supported by the ICTU from public funds.[90] As a result, an Irish Executive member, J. (Sean) Morrissey, was appointed to the position of Education, Research and Training Officer from 30 October 1978. In December, Morrissey resigned from the GEC on being appointed. Morrissey had a background in the Irish Republican Movement, but then had joined the Communist Party of Ireland, and extended his involvement in trade unionism. Despite the terms of his appointment, he operated from the start as much in Northern Ireland as in the Republic.

In July 1978 the GEC was requested to endorse the appointment of an Education and Research Officer in Region 1. This was agreed by the Council, and in November the interviewing committee appointed Barry Camfield. Camfield became a District Officer in East London in May 1975, at 24 one of the youngest officers ever appointed. His background was in the rubber industry, but as a 'bright boy' he was picked out as having potential both as an officer and as an REO. Camfield later became Regional Secretary and later Assistant General Secretary of the union. In August, the GEC also agreed to the earlier request from Region 9, recommending the appointment of an education officer. However, in December, the Committee was unable to choose from the candidates, but after a further interview they selected Phil Scott who took up the position on 10 September 1979. Scott was a South Yorkshire busman with little educational experience. After some good work with schoolchildren, but limited success with shop stewards, he later reverted to being a district officer on the merger of Regions 8, 9 and 10. In December 1979, Region 10 (East Coast) also asked for the appointment of an additional officer in the capacity of 'regional education, research and general duties'. In response, Chris Russell was appointed from 9 April 1979. Russell was unusual in the union at that time in that he had been to polytechnic and had a degree. He became involved with the union as a Hull bus worker and stepped quite naturally into the REO position. Russell was a REO for many years but in 1999 he became Regional Organiser of the merged Region 8. Courses in the 'old' Region 8 were mainly provided by staff member Steve Grinter who employed officers as tutors. This region requested an REO in December 1979. Eventually, Tom Nesbit was appointed from 1 December 1980. Nesbit was a bus worker from Richmond, who also had an extensive involvement with the WEA.

In Region 6 (North-West), a complicated situation prevailed where the region was split into 3 divisions, with nominally an officer in each responsible for education and devoting 50 per cent of their time to it. To a certain extent, in the Merseyside Division, this was a mechanism for giving 'light duties' to certain officers who could no longer carry a full load of work, and the region as a whole provided very little education.

Such was the case in the early 1980s with Frank Murray, a district official working out of the Accrington office, who suffered a heart attack; he was brought into the regional office and referred to as 'Education Officer', but he never tutored nor did he prepare any course materials, although he was able to help with course administration.[91] In Region 6 the tutors were mainly officers such as Bill Hayward, Gerry Flaherty and Doug Farrar, the Regional Secretary. Margaret Casey, Finance Administrator, also took part in the courses. Jim Mowatt was appointed REO from 12 January 1981. Mowatt was at that time employed as a regional education officer by the TUC. Mowatt's intention was to approach education on a region-wide basis from the Merseyside Division. However, existing officers in the other divisions also had responsibility for education. These were Brian Dawson (Northern) and Martin Howard (Southern), so the situation was somewhat untidy. Mowatt later became TGWU National Secretary for Power and Engineering, and then Chemical, Oil and Rubber.

In the remaining regions, which did not apply for the appointment of an education officer, various practices prevailed. In Region 3 (South-West), Tom Carlyle continued to organise education from a staff position, mainly using the TUC. In Region 4 (Wales), Keith Jones was appointed as a district officer in December 1977, and he took over a number of duties in the regional office, including education. In Region 5 a comprehensive programme was carried out by a mixture of staff and officers under the supervision of the Regional Organiser, Ron Marston. Staff included Alan Tuckwood, based in the northern part of the region in Nottingham, and Tom Cook, based in the regional office and covering the West Midlands. Tony Corfield also ran courses for the union from his base at Fircroft College. In Region 7 (Scotland), Jim McIntyre, the Regional Organiser, ran the programme using mainly officers as tutors.

Most of the new generation of union educators and administrators were brought together in a landmark conference on 26 September 1979, when the essential pattern of TGWU education for the next decade was established. Seventy REOs, staff and associated officers attended. Frank Cosgrove was in the chair, along with Regan Scott and Regional Organisers Ron Marston and Les Shorter. The conference looked at the funding of education, in a climate where public funds, new rights to time off and a membership of 2 million made the problem one of how to organise expansion rather than how to control costs:

> The question of annual budgets being drawn up by regions was raised, and after discussion it was suggested that these might be dropped, since they dated from a period before proper reporting procedures had been started. The question was raised as to why they were called 'budgets', as in effect they had not been implemented, since the officers and staff concerned did not have budgeted funds set aside on an annual basis'.[92]

From then on, until the 1990s, the union did not refer to education budgets as the basis for the financial administration of education.

Other emerging issues were raised. The first concerned the tutoring of courses. Little thought had been given to this in the new climate. In the period when the summer schools were the main educational activity, the members of the Education Department, with the exception of Tony Corfield, and later Bob Rolfe, had essentially been administrators, and the course tutors had been recruited from the WEA and university extra-mural departments for the six weeks or so of the school. With a year-round and much more comprehensive programme, this was not possible, and some REOs had found that their regional secretaries had expected them to shoulder the whole teaching burden. Others had assumed that regular district officers would become tutors, and yet others talked of using 'lay tutors' – usually senior stewards from well-organised workplaces – taking paid release to teach other stewards.

Overall, the decisions taken at this conference set the pattern of much of the union's programme over the next few years. It was also agreed that from 1981 the follow-on courses from the summer school would automatically be transferred to Eastbourne, and that the use of video recording equipment would be available for education along with a video library. It was also agreed that there should be an annual conference of Regional Education Specialists, officers and staff on the lines of this conference, a pledge that was kept on an intermittent basis. Despite the earlier comments, regions were being asked to submit budget estimates for 1980, but as a guide rather than a control mechanism. A significant decision was to move forward the idea of 'lay tutors', and, following this conference, each region was asked to draw up a panel of senior lay members whose experience in the union would be made available for tutoring work on courses.[93]

In receiving the very positive report from this conference, the Education Committee showed its constructive attitude to the new generation of TGWU educators and gave them every encouragement for the future:

> The Committee wished to make it clear that there should be no inhibitions in any region about promoting educational activity – this was an area in which the General Executive Council continually emphasised should be given utmost priority.[94]

Moss Evans was elected to replace Jack Jones as General Secretary from 29 March 1978. On 20 February 1978 a union festival was held, similar to the 1972 Jubilee celebration but also to allow the changeover from Jones to Evans; 2,600 people attended, 1,250 from the Centre and 1,300 from the regions. These included a 'thousand officers and wives', (sic), 80 members and former members of the GEC, union trustees and wives, 40 members of the TGWU Parliamentary Group and wives, 80 Central Office staff, and 50 invited guests. Foreshadowing the next stage of Jack Jones's political involvement, a testimonial of £10,000, subscribed by the membership, was used for the continuation of the pensioners' campaign and for the benefit of retired members of the union.

The Jones era was the beginning of a golden age for TGWU education. All of the changes of the Jones era – the appointment of specialist officers and staff; the new rights for paid release for time off under the new laws; the growth in safety reps; public funds for courses; and the Eastbourne facility – encouraged either the growth or the potential for growth in the education programme. In 1971 union membership was 1,638,686, a new record, and the increase from 1970 was the highest ever achieved in a normal year. By the end of the decade it had passed the 2 million mark, standing at 2,060,315 at the end of the first quarter of 1980. Regional education expenditure increased from £23,164 in 1977 to £54,773 in 1978; Region 7 increased from £3,781 to £13,544, Region 11 from £546 to £2,899 while Region 2 went from £1,479 to £7,838. They did not know about the Thatcher years to come, and they looked forward to the next decade with optimism.

NOTES

1. GEC, 8 March 1963. Minute No 254, p51.
2. See Goodman, 1979, op. cit., pp358-359 and Jones, 1986, op. cit., pp152-153.
3. Assistant Executive Secretary's Report, 2 March 1964, p61.
4. GEC, 28 February 1968, Minute No 148, p39.
5. *The Record,* April 1967.
6. Tony Corfield, *Collective Leadership for the TGWU*, Sidcup: R. Brierly, 1968, p2.
7. Ibid., pp2-3.
8. F&GP, 10 October 1968, Minute No 724, p217.
9. GEC, 4 December 1968, Minute No 881, p248.
10. Interview with Jack Jones, 28 May 1998, and supplementary note from Jack Jones, September 2002.
11. Interview with Tony Corfield, 26 March 1998.
12. See *Report of a Committee of Inquiry into the problems of Fircroft College under the chairmanship of Andrew Leggatt, QC*, House of Commons, April 1976. Also Bob Houlton (ed) *Residential Adult Education-Values, Policies and Problems*, Society of Industrial Tutors, 1977.
13. Report of the Education Committee of the GEC, 31 July 1975, Minute No 1255. He also wrote the controversial book on the Midlands TGWU, *The Rule of Law*, Birmingham: R. Brierly Publications, 1982.
14. Appendix (I) to the Education Committee Report, February 1972.
15. Minutes of the Education Committee of the GEC, 11August 1971.
16. Education Secretary's Report, August 1973.
17. Report of the Research, Education and Parliamentary Department, May 1974, p3.
18. Report of Research, Education and Political Department, March 1975 to

May 1975, p3. Education Committee of the GEC, 4 November 1975, Minute No 1260, p3.
19. Appendix (d) to the Education Committee Report, 31 July 1975.
20. Appendix (e) to Education Committee Report, November 1976.
21. *The Record*, May 1962, pp28-30. Other good branches were 1/909 ; 2/207; 3/19 ; 6/60 ; 7/230 ; 8/94; 9/65 ; 10/79 ; 11/30 ; 12/41; 13/07 and the Power Workers' Group Attercliffe branch.
22. Report on the Political, Education, and International Department, 1966.
23. Trade Group and Departmental Review, 1970, p187.
24. *The Record,* September 1967, pp43 to 45.
25. Ibid.
26. Trade Group and Departmental Review, 1976. Among those to complete at this time were B. Theobald, 1/1265; J. Britton, 9/336, both of whom became full-time officers, and a distinction to M.J. Carden, 6/567, who later served on the GEC.
27. 'Trade Unions and Safety at Work' by Jack Jones, *The Record*, March 1960, pp20-21.
28. GEC, 7 December 1961, Minute No 918, p236.
29. 'Trade Unions and Safety', *The Record,* October 1961, pp7-8.
30. 'The Challenge of Industrial Safety', The Record, November 1961, pp32 and 33.
31. GEC, 20 September 1962, Minute No 698, p168.
32. *The Record,* November 1968, pp14 and 15.
33. 'Industrial Safety – Joint Control is the Answer' by Jack Jones, *The Record,* March 1968, pp13-14.
34. GEC, 5 December 1972, Minute No 879, p237.
35. GEC, 8 March 1973, Minute No 202, p48.
36. Letter from the General Secretary to all officers, June 1976.
37. GEC, 8 June 1978, Minute No 482, p117.
38. Education Committee of the GEC, 31 July 1978, Minute No 1411, p5.
39 A comment made to this author at the start of a TGWU new officers' course at Eastbourne.
40. Resolution from ACTS National Committee (endorsed by Area 8 Committee) GEC, 18 November 1926, Minute No 1002, pp265-6.
41. Meeting on 24 January 1939 between Bevin, Chandler, Price and Miss Saunders, Ernest Bevin Collection, Modern Records Centre, Warwick University.
42. *The Record*, December 1951, p175.
43. The Record, January 1963, p26.
44. *The Record,* May 1967, pp8-10.
45. The Record, July 1966, p4.
46. The Record, July 1966, p15.
47. GEC, 22 September 1976, Minute No 657, p177.
48. Appendix (h) to the Education Committee Report, February 1973.
49. GEC, 3 December 1962, Minute No 861.
50. F&GP, 9 November 1967, Minute No 821, p219. Also GEC, 29 May 1968, Minute No 431, p113.
51. *The Record*, January 1969, p41.
52. Minutes of the 23rd BDC, 14-18 July 1969: motion 247, Minute No 77, p35.

53. Education Secretary's Report, February 1970.
54 Appendix (f) to the Education Committee, February 1973.
55. Interview with Jack Lucas, 22 January 1999.
56. GEC, 8 March 1972, Minute No 214, p47.
57. *The Record,* October 1974, p5.
58. Interview with Barry Camfield, 11 September 1999.
59. General Secretary's Report, 2 March 1964, p51.
60. Minutes of the 20th BDC, July 1963, Minute No 89 in the name of branches 1/289 and 1/816.
61. Ibid., motion 327 in the name of branch 7/106.
62. *The Record,* January 1964, pp22 to 24.
63. *The Record,* March 1964, p15.
64. *The Record,* October 1965, pp20-21.
65. Education Secretary's Report, October 1965, appendix (d) p3.
66. She had married Jack Donovan, former Docks Group National Secretary.
67. Jack Jones, *Equal Pay and Equal Opportunities*, TGWU, 1975.
68. Appendix C to the Education Committee Report, November 1979.
69. Education Committee, 8 May 1979, Minute No 1445, p3.
70. Education Committee, 6 November 1979, Minute No 1469, p3.
71. F&GP, 9 April 1970, Minute No 285, p67.
72. *The Record,* April 1971, p4.
73. Interview with Frank Cosgrove, 23 March 2001.
74. GEC, 6 March 1975, Minute No 207, p45. An interesting footnote at this point is that in April 1975 Norman Richards, Senior Education Assistant, retired after 49 years service. His son Gareth Richards commenced work as an assistant in the Education Department at the beginning of 1975 and is still employed as Senior Education Assistant.
75. GEC, 1 December 1975, Minute No 745, p201.
76. Interview with Jack Jones, 28 May 1998.
77. In 1979 Frank Cosgrove asked for his grading to be advanced from Grade 3 to Grade 2 of the Officers' Salary Structure. This was not supported by the GEC, but referred to the General Secretary for an examination. The General Secretary advised the Committee that the application had been subjected to an in-depth examination after which the application was withdrawn. In 1982 he again put in a request for upgrading, and the General Secretary was asked to look at the whole structure of the Department and report back. The result was that whilst agreeing that Frank Cosgrove be upgraded to Grade 2 of the officers' salary structure, the position would not be that of National Officer, but would retain the title of Director of Educational Studies. This is how he remained.
78. Education Committee of the GEC, 6 February 1974, Minute No 1167, p3.
79. The figures broke down as follows: Grants to colleges etc. £4,250; day and weekend schools £12,500; Cirencester and Training Centre courses £41,250, full-time bursaries £4,375, ICTU £125. Total £62,500.
80. General Secretary's Report, September 1976, p191.
81. BDC, 30 June 1975, Statement from the General Secretary. Verbatim Minutes p11.
82. F&GP, 1 May 1974, Minute No 311, p82.
83. Report of Research and Education Department, June to August 1979, dated 4 September 1979.

84. See the debate in the Introduction.
85. I will use the acronym REOs for all those carrying out the regional education function, but leave in RESs or Specialists if quoting.
86. Interview with Frank Cosgrove, 23 March 2001.
87. F&GP, 12 January 1978, Minute No 22, p5.
88. *The Record,* April 1978, p8.
89. GEC, 6 June 1978, Minute No 442, p109.
90. F&GP, 2 November 1978, Minute No 871, p225.
91. Interview with Jim Mowatt, 1 November 1999.
92. Appendix (f) to the Education Committee Report November 1979.
93. Letter from Regan Scott and Frank Cosgrove dated June 1979.
94. Education Committee, 6 November 1979, Minute No 1471, 'Regional Education Specialists' Conference'.

Chapter 7

TGWU Education in the Thatcher Years 1980–1992

This chapter looks at the development of the TGWU education programme through one of the most difficult periods in the union's history. Just at the time when the great investments in education had been made in the Jones period, the tide turned as the union began to lose membership and resources at a disturbing rate, leading to a financial crisis in the early 1990s. One of the responses to the new conditions was the development of explicit political education, as part of a belated recognition that not enough had been done in this area in the 1960s and 1970s. Another was the attempt to increase the union's involvement in the Manpower Services Commission and the training schemes which mushroomed in the 1980s.The union also developed lay tutors, and began for the first time to develop education programmes linked to pensions, equalities and diversity. By this time, the regions were providing the bulk of the education provision, and their activities in the period are dealt with in the next chapter.

The union entered the new decade apprehensive about what lay in store for the movement with the election of the first Thatcher government, but also angry at the drift to the right of the Callaghan government, especially its abandonment of progressive policies such as industrial democracy and the Social Contract, and the inept decisions which had led to the 'Winter of Discontent' in 1978-79. However, this anger and apprehension were tempered by a confidence that the trade union movement had grown to an all-time peak of membership and influence, and could weather any storm. As we shall see, by the mid-1980s this confidence had been seriously undermined. In terms of TGWU education, the late 1970s had been a period of solid investment, and the 1980s began with the need to establish the mechanisms to extract the maximum benefit from this investment.

MANAGING THE PROGRAMME, 1980-1992

The enormously expanded programme which followed the appointment of the REOs placed an inevitably greater strain on resources. During

1980 the regions reported a total throughput of students of approximately 10,400, with Cirencester having 460, the Home Study 1,938, and Eastbourne 1,628. With an estimated TGWU participation in TUC courses of 3,000, the annual total reached 17,426 students. In the same year the GMB, the TGWU's nearest equivalent, only catered for 2,096 students. Excluding TUC courses, education expenditure for 1980 totalled approximately £428,000.[1] It should be recalled that in a period where TGWU membership reached more than two million, the main policy was to increase expenditure on education in ways which would benefit the union, rather than, as a decade later, to look for ways in which expenditure could be reduced. Nevertheless, on a day-to-day basis, it was always better to spend someone else's money rather than one's own, and the main source of external funding continued to be the reclaim from public funds via the TUC. The money recovered for 1979-1980 amounted to a record £114,104, with the previous year's figure being £79,000.[2] However, in 1980-1981 the union received £248,958 from its reclaim, and in 1981-1982, £316,879,[3] and the expansion continued into the mid-1980s. The regional course throughput for 1982 saw a record of over 12,000 students, an increase of 20 per cent over the previous year. In the last quarter of 1982 there was a throughput of 3,076 students.

The regional student total for 1983 declined to 11,337 and for 1984 to 11,361. Although student numbers rose again in 1985, the weight of expenditure was now falling more directly on the union. As early as 1981, Frank Cosgrove had predicted that the growth in public funds was unlikely to be maintained, as the union had probably reached its peak in regional and residential provision, as some public funds allocated to the TUC were redistributed as supplementary payments in this year, and because the government had increased funds at less than the rate of inflation. Also, as more unions developed education facilities, this would result in a thinner redistribution.[4] Although this process was delayed for two years, it nevertheless proved to be an accurate prediction. The amount received from public funds for 1982-1983 was only £183,017, due to the reduction in the grant from £1,850,000 to £1,600,000 by the government. For 1984 the figure was £139,236. The net result of this process was a continuing rise in net education expenditure, from the 1981 figure of £438,598 to £554,954 in 1982, £633,988 in 1983, and £656,860 in 1984. This situation was exacerbated by the general deterioration in the economic and political climate. In 1981 the Education Committee noted that there had been a cutback in courses by the oil companies, as joint training was overtaken by the new Human Resource Management philosophy, which put less of a premium on working with the trade unions, and began to see them as an obstacle to be circumvented or even removed.[5] It was noted that there had also been a reduction in the number of students attending Cirencester in 1981 compared with 1980, as employers became less willing to agree to paid release.

However, the union was still trying to look forward. The 1981 BDC carried a resolution on long-term support for education:

> In order to maintain effective trade union education, in the event of an election of a Labour Government, legislation should be established to ensure that paid release is given automatically to employees on recognised trade union and TUC courses.[6]

This set the scene for a joint publication between the union and the Society of Industrial Tutors, which the F&GP agreed to sponsor with £1,500. Published in 1988 as *The Impossible Dream?*, it looked at detailed policies on PEL, and included a foreword by Ron Todd.[7]

Of course, the Thatcher government was moving in precisely the opposite direction, and a further twist in financial pressure on trade union education was instituted in 1984 when the government amended its classification of public fund support with the introduction of 'Change at Work' supplementary funding. The government was keen to reduce the element of independent trade union control over courses (and also to placate its own backbenchers), so for the year 1983-1984, £1.5 million was allocated to the TUC for the public fund reclaim, with an additional grant of £200,000 for short-term courses on 'Change at Work' which required employer endorsement. The message was that all public funding might cease if the 'Change at Work' element was ignored.

This policy created a dilemma for the TGWU. The union had no doubts about its opposition to the *principle* of this new formula. In practice, however, there was some disagreement between Frank Cosgrove and some REOs. Frank Cosgrove was essentially a pragmatist, and whilst not allowing potentially hostile employers (such as British Leyland) to gain control over course content, he was willing to avail the union of access to this money where employers would be happy simply to counter-sign the forms and allow the union to determine course content. This applied to some private employers where there was a long-standing relationship (such as Grants of St James's, British Sugar Corporation, Remploy or the RAC), or public sector organisations such as British Waterways, where many managers were union members. At national level, Frank Cosgrove organised a number of 'Change at Work' courses in partnership with these supportive employers, and also tried to put pressure on REOs to do the same. In July 1984 he sent a letter to all REOs urging them to use the money:

> At the Education Committee meeting held on 14 May 1984, the Executive expressed concern at the lack of take-up on 'Change at Work' courses, and felt that efforts should be made to utilise this source of funding ... The Executive are aware of the fears expressed by some offi-

> cers as to this special category type of course, but feel that, where appropriate, courses can be set up to qualify for this funding – without encroaching on our control of the course.[8]

Some of the REOs were opposed as a political principle to touching any of the money. This was the view of Barry Camfield, for example:

> Once again defending the independence of union education has proved to be a difficult, but achievable, task if the effort is made. Some companies, notably multinationals like Glaxo, are demanding heavy participation in shop stewards' courses on a paternalist basis. The key to defending independent provision is a clear purpose about why we provide education and what we seek to achieve from each course. If trade union education becomes a tool by which management influences our shop stewards to their priorities and their strategies, then it is no longer independent and no longer trade union education.[9]

In 1984 the Mobil Oil Company was asked to pay for a residential course at Eastbourne for workers at the Coryton refinery. Initial talks were positive, but a further meeting with the company indicated that the price of a residential course was a heavy presence and involvement of the company. Barry Camfield and Fred Higgs, the industrial officer, considered the company's request unacceptable. The company, though refusing to pay for the stewards to use the Eastbourne Centre, nevertheless conceded that the course should take place locally and be run by the union.

What actually happened is that the response from the regions to the utilisation of these funds was patchy, with the 'left' regions preferring not to hold courses under this heading. In trade union education, the balance of the relationship with the employer was normally that the trade union had a key role in determining course content, primarily because in most companies shop stewards would not attend what they saw as a 'company brainwashing' session controlled by their employer. Despite this attempt to pressurise trade unions to allow the employers a greater say, the reality was that 'Change at Work' was never implemented, not only in the TGWU, but in other unions; as a substantial amount of money was returned by the TUC to the Department of Education and Science as a result of the low take-up on behalf of a number of unions. Courses remained either exclusively trade union, or were joint courses based on mutuality of interest and content between the employer and the union, expressed through a process of negotiation, and directly funded by the employer. It was this type of course, rather than those funded through the government's mechanism, which grew in importance in the 1980s and 1990s.

EDUCATION TUTORS

At the beginning of the 1980s, one of the first problems for the REOs to overcome was the provision of course tutors. Although Harry Moore was appointed to Eastbourne with a teaching brief, and REOs were expected to teach, they soon became overwhelmed by the difficulty of organising and administering courses and course materials, whilst being required simultaneously to teach full-time. This became literally impossible when more than one course was being held during any week. It was not easy to call in WEA and FE tutors to fill the gap. Whilst they may have been available during the summer period, they could not work for the union throughout the year, as many of them were committed to TUC courses, or even non-union work such as management studies or university teaching. Neither was it economical to employ teaching staff throughout the regions who might only be called on for a few weeks a year. The first thought was to use existing full-time officers as tutors; and this, of course, had always been done, and some officers tutored on a regular basis. Regardless of this, there was also the key problem that an officer's first duty was to his or her industrial membership allocation, and if a dispute or serious problem occurred at the same time as a course, then it was inevitable that the officer would have to cancel or leave the course. In the 1950s and 1960s, most of the courses had been held at weekends, where this problem was less likely to arise, but by the 1970s, with the spread of day-release, courses were increasingly held on working days.

The solution was felt to be the 'lay tutor'; typically a senior active lay member with a good knowledge of the union who could obtain day-release for him or herself to take part in courses as a tutor. In practice, convenors often took the lead in running in-plant courses for their junior colleagues, and many would have had to cover for the officer if he or she was called away. During 1978 Frank Cosgrove persuaded Jack Jones to give the go-ahead for tutor training courses, initially for shop steward and health and safety training.[10]

The main pressure was coming from the increasing use of Eastbourne, where there was only one member of staff on duty, Harry Moore. The Education Committee noted the situation:

> Bookings for education courses, especially on health and safety, are now so heavy at Eastbourne that two courses in parallel and occasionally three are frequent. It is self-evident that Brother Moore needs assistance, above and beyond that provided for the full-time officers who, frankly, are finding it difficult to undertake adequate cover. The Education Department is therefore seeking approval for normal tutorial fees to be paid as and when necessary for courses at Eastbourne.[11]

During September and October 1979 it had been necessary for Frank Cosgrove himself to assist Harry Moore with the workload. The

Education Committee felt that there should be support from officers and that 'efforts should be made to set up a panel of active lay members who could assist as tutors and generally more should be done to train lay members as tutors to back up regional education specialists'.[12]

It was agreed to begin a programme of tutor training during 1980, and the responsibility was given to Dr John Fisher of Surrey University.[13] John Fisher had worked as part of Basil Bye's trade union studies group based at Southampton University from the early 1970s, mainly teaching and developing courses in Region 2. In 1977 he was appointed Lecturer in Adult Education at Surrey with a particular brief to develop Industrial Studies. In this capacity he assisted Region 2 and then, on Barry Camfield's appointment in 1978, Region 1, to develop their regional course programmes. He was also one of the first tutors to teach the national courses at Eastbourne and, as a formally qualified FE teacher, was asked by Frank Cosgrove to train the lay tutors. In the summer of 1980, Frank Cosgrove sent out a letter advertising the course, and the choice of candidates was based on observations made at Cirencester. This was a mistake, as it later became clear that if tutors were to be mainly used in the regions, then the REOs must make the recommendations, not the summer school tutors or the Education Department. From the very first course, the selection of tutors by the Centre provoked a reaction. As early as July 1980, Ron Marston of Region 5 wrote to Frank Cosgrove pointing out that the two names put forward from his region were unknown to the regional education department:

> I would wish to make it clear to you that if it is the intention to have lay member tutor training we feel that prior to being an invitation or nomination to the course, that the region should be consulted, otherwise, if the invitation is made at national level and the member informed, any regional objection could cause embarrassment to the member.[14]

There were 12 students on the first tutor training course, which was held at the end of September 1980. The course looked at active and passive learning methods, course planning and preparation and used closed circuit TV to record mock teaching sessions. John Fisher set out the basic approach of the course in a report to the Education Committee:

> The requirement is similar to that in all areas of trade union education, namely we are dealing with people who do not have a great deal of formal schooling and very few paper qualifications, but who nevertheless have a great deal of experience and ability in leadership and articulation. This would call for a very specialised approach, not too 'academic' but also not insultingly basic. A practical course using the

> experience and ability which is already there and geared to practical usage.[15]

The course was very successful and Frank Cosgrove approved a regular programme of two or three courses per year. John Fisher made a recommendation on each student's suitability as a tutor, and Frank Cosgrove passed these on to the regional education officers. Before long, it was the REOs who were taking a lead in nominations, although some still came via the summer schools and follow-on courses. Although about 100 lay tutors were trained in the first two years, there was still a problem of how to employ them. It was not possible to give them staff jobs in the union, and in some regions they were hardly used at all. On the other hand, the individual lay tutor felt that the course had given him or her a step forward, and usually left Eastbourne full of enthusiasm.

In order to investigate what was happening to the lay tutors, in July 1981 John Fisher produced a report for the Education Committee based on a questionnaire to those people who had attended the tutor training courses. The investigation found that most of the respondents combined extensive trade union experience with both a limited personal education and experience of trade union tutoring, though not of experience as students on TUC and TGWU education programmes: 87 per cent had over 10 years trade union membership, 78 per cent had 4 to 10 years experience as trade union representatives whilst 17 per cent had over 10 years experience. Almost all (83 per cent) had left school at 15 and only 1 had continued schooling beyond the age of 17. Those who had attended a shop stewards' day-release course were 92 per cent, 65 per cent had attended a branch officers' course and 92 per cent had attended the Cirencester summer school. Thirty-nine per cent had taught before whilst 61 per cent had not; 95 per cent found the tutor training course very useful and most of them had attended TGWU courses as tutors after the course. However, only 61 per cent of the lay tutors had been able to apply their training. It appeared that Regions 10, 7, 8, 6 and 9 expected to use their lay tutors following training, whilst Regions 1, 2, 3, 4 and 5 had no machinery for the use of lay tutors, or did not support their use in practice.[16]

It was only when the REOs strictly controlled nominations that the regional take-up of lay tutors improved, as candidates were only nominated when it was expected that there would be a role for them in the region after the course. It became accepted by the REOs that they would not employ lay tutors unless they had been through this course, and it became an important development route for many future tutors, activists and officers of the 1990s generation.

For the TGWU national programme at this time, the term 'outside tutors' primarily referred to the group organised by Basil Bye at Southampton University, and the group led by John Fisher at Surrey.

John Fisher and his main tutor, Pete Batten, worked with Region 1 and part of the national programme. Basil Bye's group remained with Region 2 and provided tutors for another part of the national programme.

However, in September 1981 Frank Cosgrove made it clear that he preferred John Fisher and Pete Batten to play the major part in tutoring the follow-on courses. Basil Bye's national tutors were to be Peter Emery, Les Ford (both later became staff members of the National Education Department), and Jeff Beattie. From May 1983, the responsibility for Peter Emery was transferred to John Fisher and Pete Batten at the University of Surrey. Jeff Beattie became a tutor in Region 4, and Les Ford also joined the Surrey group shortly afterwards. From that time, John Fisher's group became the main tutor group teaching national courses, along with Jack Lucas and members of the Education Department such as Gareth Richards. As we shall see, the regions also slowly began to build their own tutor teams.

EASTBOURNE NATIONAL COURSES

From the late 1970s onwards, Eastbourne was regularly used as the base for company-sponsored courses. In 1982-1983, for example, 286 stewards attended Eastbourne company-sponsored courses and produced a direct input of £36,180 to the Centre.[17] In volume terms, the oil companies – Shell, BP, Esso, Conoco and Mobil – regularly used the Centre for health and safety and shop stewards' training, which included technical training in industrial safety procedures. Frank Cosgrove, Harry Moore, and right up to the late 1980s Jack Lucas, usually took care of the shop stewards' courses, with the younger generation of tutors such as John Fisher, Pete Emery or Pete Batten concentrating on the union-only courses. Other regular companies using the Centre at this time were Young's Breweries, Grants of St James's, British Sugar, BOC, Bejams, Sainsburys, Walker's Crisps and Containerbase, although there were many others. The oil companies reduced their involvement towards the end of the decade, but other companies such as Blue Circle, Geest, TI Desford and IDV took their place.

The union-only courses were more varied, and tended to reflect the demands of particular trade groups or officers. In the early 1980s Clive Woffenden and Ken Reid were still working on ESI courses which they had established in the 1970s. The first shop stewards' course for Civil Air Transport cabin crew was held in January 1984 with John Fisher and CAT district officer Eddie McDermott, later Region 1 Regional Secretary, as tutors. In 1984, at a Public Services Trade Group course in December, MOD members had put pressure on the Department to run courses on the issue of defence and job conversion, and the Education Committee agreed a pilot course on this issue. Also, in 1987, in response to requests from the Power and Engineering and Public Services Trade Groups, two special courses were designed for senior stewards working in nuclear energy industries. A national course for hotel and catering workers was held in Eastbourne in December 1985, and again in early 1987. In January 1986, an Industrial Democracy course with 23 students was organised, with John Fisher and Les Ford as tutors, the last national course to date organised by the union on this subject, once a centre-piece of the union's strategy.

One of the regular national courses established at this time involved training the union's pension trustees. With the growth of company pension schemes in the 1970s and 1980s, there was an increasing demand for specialist training. In 1981, in response to this pressure, Barry Camfield wrote to Frank Cosgrove asking to deal with issues on a national basis.

This topic was raised on the GEC and at a meeting of REOs in autumn 1981, and in the summer of 1982 a list was compiled of 84 members who occupied positions as pension trustees. The first pensions course was held at Eastbourne from 13 to 17 December 1982, attended by regional pension specialists and pension trustees including Executive members Larry Grogan and Brian Nicholson. Tutors included Albert Blyghton and Jim Moher from the Legal Department, and Doug Gowan from the TUC. Gareth Richards acted as course co-ordinator, and was responsible for the development of the documents for the course. Because of the demand, a further two courses were arranged in January and March 1983. Both the pensions course and the tutoring of the courses by Gareth Richards have continued to date, with up to five courses each year at Eastbourne, plus occasional courses in the regions.

At the end of the decade, the management of the Centre changed. The first manager, Alan Simpson, retired in January 1989, and was replaced by Jack Douglas, a former catering worker in the Royal Marines. Both he and his successor left very soon under a cloud, but the management of the Centre stabilised in the 1990s with the appointment of Robin Hodson, with Wendy Banks as course organiser. In January 1992 Harry Moore, the Centre's only Education and Training Officer, retired and was not replaced.

THE SUMMER SCHOOLS

Throughout this period, the Cirencester summer school remained a central part of the national education programme. However, as the regions began to take up more of the basic shop stewards' and safety reps' induction training, the Education Department looked to develop Cirencester as one step beyond the introductory two or three-day induction. The first change was to develop an intensive bargaining skills course to be called 'Bargaining in the 80s' (later the 90s). Frank Cosgrove asked John Fisher, Pete Batten and the TURU group at Ruskin College to develop materials and case studies. From 1981 a new health and safety course was included in the summer school programme, but the main changes were introduced in 1982, with the summer school retaining the basic courses 'Workplace Representation', 'Shop Stewards' and 'Union Work' at Local Level', but also introducing the new courses 'Bargaining in the 80s' and 'Workplace Organisation'. Attendance at the schools began to decline in the early 1980s. For example, figures for 1983 were 12 per cent down on 1982. In response it was decided to reduce the school from three weeks in July, three weeks' break and two weeks in August and September to a condensed period of four weeks in July 1983 and three weeks in July 1984. This was on the basis of increasing the places available to 150 per week in 1983 and 200 per week in 1984.[18] A further change was to the venue itself. In early 1983, Frank Cosgrove reported that the College was now run on more commercial lines, forcing costs up at a faster rate than before, and it was recommended that the Department investigate the NUT college at Stoke Rochford. An invitation had been extended to the Education Committee to visit the college to attend a special evening on 19 March 1983. Following this visit, the General Secretary, Executive Officer Larry Smith, and Chair of the GEC visited Stoke Rochford on 17 and 18 September 1983, and at the September GEC Moss Evans recommended that the union continue to use Cirencester for the summer of 1984 and move to Stoke Rochford in 1985. This was agreed by the Council.[19]

After the long relationship of 30 years, the union left Cirencester with regret:

> This will be the last meeting of the union's summer school at Cirencester. No doubt many experiences and memories will be recalled, testifying to a long and satisfactory relationship between the TGWU and the Royal Agricultural College. It is not so long ago that the Cirencester school was the jewel in the crown of union education, and despite the terrific expansion in regional provision and Eastbourne courses, the summer school has maintained its status as the second rung in the union's educational ladder.[20]

Nevertheless, this regret was short-lived, as Stoke Rochford showed itself eminently suitable; it was centrally placed, on the A1 near Grantham, and in its own grounds adjoining an excellent golf course. It also had swimming and sports facilities, and first-class childcare arrangements. Particularly following the construction of a residential block of higher specifications, such as *en suite* rooms, Stoke Rochford became well liked. By 1986, summer school applications were running at record levels, with the proportion of women increasing to around 16 per cent of the total.

In January 1981, the follow-on courses from the summer school moved to Eastbourne. Twenty members were invited to attend each course, with the aim of having 15 to 16 participants, and 154 members took part in the first year. The course looked at general topics relevant to the union, and changed with the times. The 1988 programme, for example, covered the economic situation, proposed changes in trade union law, 1987 BDC policy, and organisation in the community, with special exercises to emphasise the Link-up and Low Pay campaigns.[21] The follow-on course was abandoned in the early 1990s when the summer school itself was split up into the three 'seasonal' courses. Eastbourne had not been used for the summer schools, as it was also a holiday venue, and it was expected that holidaymakers would fill the Centre in the summer period. However, in 1990, as the financial crisis facing the union became more apparent, it was decided to look into the feasibility of a transfer of the summer school to the Eastbourne Centre.[22] In 1991, the decision was taken that from 1992 the summer school would be transferred to Eastbourne, and would be re-christened the *National Members School*, run throughout the year on three separate weeks, summer, autumn and winter.[23] This pattern continued into the new century.

THE HOME STUDY COURSE

In the 1980s, the Home Study course continued as the basis for entry into the summer school, and at the start of the decade followed a now-established pattern of a very high level of completion for the first stage with a sharp falling-off in the following stages. The figures for 1979, for example, show that enrolments totalled 3,155, with completions at 1,828 for the first stage, 359 for the second stage and only 25 for the third.[24] This pattern continued into the mid-1980s; the corresponding figures for 1983, for example, were: first stage, 1,234; second stage, 179 and third stage, 39.[25] In March 1984, a decision was taken at the conference of REOs and Executive members to revise the course and base it on two booklets. It was hoped that the material would be ready for early 1985. The first book was to cover how the union worked, and the second book wider issues. Book One was ready for 1985, but Book Two entered a process of delay which lasted more than a decade.

The book was still being promised in 1991; it was never produced and was combined with the former Book 1 in the next incarnation of the course in 1998. Another difficulty was the style of the new book. Traditionally, the course had been based on individual private study, but the 1985 edition tried to encourage group discussion through study circles, and for that reason was more complicated than earlier versions.

By 1989, the course had become a much smaller operation than in the 1970s, with 976 enrolments and 218 completions. This had declined by 1993 to 497 enrolments and 109 completions. In 1995, the course was completely redesigned into one book incorporating the former Book 1 and the subject-matter for the never-finished Book 2; in other words a single book covering the history, structure, benefits and services of the union, and also looking at key policy areas such as recruitment, equalities, training and pay. For the first time, the course was produced using information technology, allowing for regular updating every two or three years. Two levels were set: Level 1, where the answers were essentially in the text, and Level 2, needing more thought and analysis. When the new course was launched in January 1998, enrolments underwent a surge, with 948 enrolments for the year. However, completions were much lower: 19 for level 1 and only 4 for level 2. For the first three quarters of 1999 there were more than 600 enrolments but less than 70 completions. It was clear that the new book was being used as a resource about the union rather than a course book, and that the comprehensive nature of the new course meant that completion was a difficult task. The Education Committee were keen for the course to be made a compulsory entry-point for all TGWU education,[26] and in 2000 it was decided to produce a smaller, simpler version which could be more easily completed. This course became operative in early 2001.

LONGER COURSES AND 'DISTANCE LEARNING'

Throughout the period of innovative developments in short courses in the 1960s and 1970s, the aspect of TGWU education relating to longer courses and academic study remained virtually unchanged. Essentially, the union's education programme was built on courses which were practical and role-orientated and which usually lasted no longer than five days, or ten days if provided through the TUC. In a period when the Open University was in its infancy, and part-time modular degrees a rarity, TGWU members wishing to study for longer periods could only enter Ruskin College or one of the other residential colleges on an individual basis with a small union bursary for financial support.[27] At a time when Warwick and other business schools hardly ever had contact with trade union students, the LSE course was the only other recognised course providing longer academic study, apart from the specialist programmes for the NUM at Sheffield or Leeds.

Ruskin in particular still retained a pre-eminent place in the hearts of union executives, and the TGWU was no exception. The basis of the relationship with Ruskin was a Deed of Covenant of £1,000 per annum, renewable every seven years. This was renewed in 1965, 1972 and 1978, and lasted into the 1990s. The union also supported special appeals and projects from the college, for example giving £15,000 to the adult residential colleges in 1964 and a mortgage loan of £10,000 to Ruskin in 1968 in order to purchase six houses.[28] In 1970 the union agreed to support the new research unit (TURU) being formed at Ruskin College with a financial commitment of £2,000 per year, and agreed to take part in a special project on the Ford Motor Company looking at parity of earnings in the car industry.[29] However, the union also responded to requests for support from other similar colleges. In 1968, the GEC agreed that in response to a development campaign fund request from Coleg Harlech, a delegation would visit the college, and in 1970 the union agreed to sponsor a TGWU room in the college's new hall of residence at a cost of £3,000, most of which came from the regions.[30]

In 1979 Regan Scott, Frank Cosgrove, Yorkshire Regional Secretary Mike Davey and a GEC member visited Northern College, and it was agreed that the union should extend its bursary award scheme to include that college.[31] The relationship grew closer and in 1985 the GEC accepted an invitation from the college and nominated Walter Greendale, Chair of the GEC, for membership of the Management Board.[32] In 1987 Gwent College put in a request to be included in the bursary scheme and it was agreed to include the college for a trial period of one year.[33] Gwent offered a diploma in Trade Union and Social Studies based on four core subject areas: Industrial Relations, Sociology, Political Economy and Labour History. No formal academic qualifications were required for entry to the course. The union had promoted the one-year full-time Trade Union Studies course at Middlesex Polytechnic in *The Record* from 1974, and in 1989 a visit from Frank Cosgrove, Ken Reid, Region 1 Regional Secretary, and Pete Batten, REO, led to a recommendation to include the college in the bursary scheme.[34]

Although the range of opportunity increased through the inclusion of more colleges in the bursary scheme, the essential formula of residential study remained virtually unchanged from the pre-war period, with students studying in effect a pre-university one-year or two-year academic course. TURU had been set up to make the work of Ruskin College more directly relevant to the unions, but this was a separate unit within the college.

When the TGWU's regional education programmes got underway in the early 1980s, there was an enormous expansion of short courses, particularly at the 'induction' or introductory level, and very soon, REOs were responding to demands for 'follow-on' courses. As a result, the problem of what to do for further advanced study was intensified. Thus there was a 'niche' for a type of course which would be more advanced and thorough, but which would not involve the student leaving his or her existing union activities. In TGWU terms, this dilemma was first identified by Barry Camfield, and in 1981 he asked John Fisher to design a course which would meet the need. John Fisher developed the concept of a course which was a hybrid of individual study and supervised project work, along with regular group and residential education. Because the union already had its Home Study course, and to avoid confusion, Camfield and Fisher agreed on the title 'Distance Learning' for the project. Although there were elements of distance learning in the scheme, it was not pure distance learning *à la* the Open University, but the name was convenient and it stuck.

The basic concept of the course was that each individual student would study a 'core' and an 'option' programme. The core was collective, and involved ten monthly day-long group sessions at the regional office, plus an initial weekend school and a final week-long residential summer school. The option programme involved each student selecting a project topic to study in depth throughout the year, and being allocated a supervising tutor on a one-to-one basis. The tutors were volunteers who came from colleges, the WEA and universities throughout the Region. The course was jointly supervised by a board, which included two GEC members, and the university published the students' projects. The course was not accredited, but a joint University of Surrey/TGWU departmental certificate was awarded, signed by the General Secretary and the Professorial Head of Department at Surrey.[35]

John Fisher and Barry Camfield were invited to attend the meeting of the Committee in May 1982 to discuss the scheme. The key point put to the Committee was that 'this course caters for members who want to be educated to a high level and still retain their position in the union'.[36] The Committee agreed that the nominees from the TGWU to the course board would be GEC members Bill Donald (Chairman), and Larry Marson, along with Frank Cosgrove and Barry Camfield. John Fisher, Pat Hayes (of Southampton University), Pat Lyons (a trade unionist then on secondment to the University of Surrey, and Pete Batten (then a Surrey tutor) represented the university on the board. The project was relatively cheap; the total expenditure on the first course was £7,337, an expenditure of £1,191 on each student, which was offset by a return from public funds of approximately £1,000. Thus the actual cost was similar to that of the union bursary.

The union also gave the course a fair amount of publicity, with a feature in *The Record* entitled 'Distance Learning Breaks New Ground', identifying the course as 'an exciting new concept of trade union education', thereby promoting the concept throughout the regions.[37]

The first meeting of the Region 1 course board was held on 11 December 1982 and in April 1983 it interviewed 17 applicants at the regional office. Thirty students had originally applied, and 10 were ultimately accepted. The core and option elements of the course were followed through the winter of 1983-1984. The core programme covered the history and development of trade unions, principles of industrial relations, basic economics, law and rights at work, class and inequality, industrial democracy, women and black minorities in unions, and trade unions and politics. Of the ten students who began the course, seven completed. The students' option subjects included *The History of London Busmen*, by Ken Fuller, later published by

Lawrence and Wishart,[38] *Demarcation Disputes in the Shipbuilding Industry*, *Workers' Co-ops and the Trade Union Role*, by Brendan Gold, who later became a TGWU officer, *The Role of Law as it Affects Trade Unions*, and *Political Ideology and its Effect in Industrial Disputes*. The summer school was held in July at Wansfell College, Essex. Larry Smith presented the certificates and DGS Alex Kitson and GS Ron Todd also attended to address the students.

The Education Committee reviewed the course at its November 1984 meeting and resolved to circulate a recommendation to set up similar courses to all regions.[39] Region 1 was allowed to run further courses, and opted for one every two years. Meanwhile, other regions looked at the model and developed their own Distance Learning courses with modifications and with varying degrees of success.

In 1983 the union made a grant to Tony Kinder, TUC tutor at Falkirk College of Technology, to organise distance learning courses in the remote areas of Scotland, where members were unable to attend TUC or TGWU courses.[40] In May 1985, Region 8 expressed an interest in developing a course based on the Region 1 model and a meeting was held with Tom Nesbit (REO) and Doug Miller from Newcastle Polytechnic.[41] The course was officially launched on 16 January 1986 at Newcastle Polytechnic and attended by Joe Mills, Regional Secretary, Regan Scott and Tom Nesbit. The course began on 12 January 1986 with a weekend school in Darlington, with 16 students present, ran through to December 1987 and finished with another weekend school. The presentation of the awards for the course was combined with the opening of the new regional office in Newcastle in January 1987, and the region began its second course later in that year. Region 6 also took up the idea of a longer course, based on a partnership with John McIlroy of Manchester University and Alan Campbell of Liverpool University. The initial weekend school for the Region 6 course took place in September 1986 at Manchester University, and 14 students were selected from 35 applicants. The first course ran through to June 1987 when the final school was held at Hollyroyde College, Manchester. By July 1991 the region had run four such courses.

Region 9 also ran a course beginning in 1987, in co-operation with Keith Forrester, Bruce Spencer, Marie Stinson, Val Smith and Andy Morgan of Leeds University. However, they preferred to run a two-year course, as they felt that the one-year course was too concentrated for the students. There was also an established tradition at Leeds University of two-year, longer courses for trade unionists. In co-operation with the TGWU Leeds bus branch, and particularly Ronnie Morrison (later a full-time officer), the university established a two-year Leeds Busworkers' course. The immediate catchments were through attendance on TUC courses, then students exclusively from the TGWU would look at economic, political and industrial issues with a focus on the bus industry. An important product of this course was the report on stress in the industry, one of the first health and safety reports to focus on this issue. Other former students such as Aileen Larson and Jim Mckenna progressed to Northern College, and then played a subsequent role in adult education. The first introductory session of the 2-year Distance Learning course was held on 9 to 11 October 1987. The Region 9 course was quite formal, and included a Distance Learning Monitoring Committee consisting of the Regional Education Sub-Committee, Education Officer, Regional Secretary, Director of Education, two tutors, an Executive member and two students.[42] Thirteen students completed the first course and the presentation of the certificates was made by Ron Todd and Mike Davey on 7 July 1989, in Bridlington.

The courses in Regions 8 and 9 vanished with the merger of Regions 8, 9 and 10, as it was clear that their cost could not be sustained. The Region 6 course disappeared with the resignation of Tom Hart, the REO. Only the Region 1 course was sustained, but in a new form linked to the accreditation of courses, which became a major feature in the 1990s. The TGWU distance learning courses were an important innovation, in that they brought the concept of sustained learning into the union's programme as an alternative to residential college study. They also laid the groundwork for the idea of accredited courses and lifelong learning as an integral part of union education, and helped to break down the barriers between traditional trade union 'role education' and academic study. In that sense they were ahead of their time, and also in tune with the expectations of a new generation of trade union students.

Other innovations were attempted during this period. At the end of the 1970s the Department was using a tape/slide programme entitled *This is the TGWU*, which had been produced by Basil Bye in Southampton. Also in 1979, the Committee was given a demonstration of video equipment by the Region 5 Organiser Ron Marston. By 1984 the use of video had become commonplace, and in February Gareth Richards put the case for a VHS video recorder for use in the Education Department. The next step was for the union to begin to produce its own videos. The issue of control was uppermost from the start, and in March 1984 the GEC took the view that 'in the event of the union commissioning video films for education purposes, then these should include a statement of union policy made by the General Secretary, as should any other educational material issued to members'.[43] A young person's video, *Day One,* was produced in 1986, and an organising video, *User Friendly*, in 1988, and by the later 1980s there were a number in preparation.

The videos which achieved wide circulation were *Women of the T&G, Moving the Goalposts* (on new management techniques), and

This is Branch Life. In 1991 a regional initiative was taken by Pete Batten (Region 1 REO) who 'uncovered' the two filmstrips from the 1950s *Stranger in the Pub* and *Our Heritage*, and had these early visual aids transferred to video.[44] Although the use of video became standard practice, for financial reasons none were produced by the union at national level after 1992.

POLITICAL EDUCATION

The union had entered the 1980s with some confidence, and treated Margaret Thatcher as a temporary aberration who would soon be forgotten. As the 1980s progressed, however, it slowly woke up to the seriousness of the situation and the realisation that it might be a very long and hard road to return to a Labour Government or even 'Heathite' Tory policies. The first sign of danger was the rapid about-turn in membership growth. After years of uninterrupted expansion, membership at the end of March 1980 totalled 2,060,315, a decrease of 20,966 compared with the previous quarter and 23,564 compared with the March quarter of 1979. At the end of the June quarter, membership was 2,004,245, a decrease of 56,070 compared with the previous quarter; and by December, membership stood at 1,943,440, a decrease of 60,805 compared with the previous quarter. In the course of the year to September 1980 the union lost 142,000 members.[45] By March 1982 membership stood at 1,695,818, a decrease of 32,411 over the previous quarter and 191,153 over the year.[46] The rate of loss was moderated during 1982 mainly because there were important mergers in that year. The Agricultural and Allied Workers became part of the union from 1 May 1982, and the National Union of Dyers, Bleachers and Textile Workers and the National Amalgamated Stevedores and Dockers also merged with the union. As the Thatcherite policies unfolded to ever greater dismay, and trade union members showed their willingness to vote Tory and against a Labour Party seeming to want to self-destruct, the TGWU leadership looked to raise the profile of political education in the union.

The attitude towards political education in the union had always been rather curious. There had never been any question that the TGWU was inseparably linked to the Labour Party, and that it was every member's duty to support, vote for and even join the Party. Bevin, Deakin, Cousins and Jones had all been key Labour Party figures; and two of them, of course, went straight from being General Secretary to Cabinet Minister. On the other hand, there was a reticence about running explicitly political courses as a normal part of the education programme. It was perhaps felt that the role of the union's education programme was primarily industrial, and that explicitly political education should be the business of the Labour Party, regardless of whether or not they actually carried it out. The view was that TGWU education was 'implicitly' political, as if by osmosis. This view was typified by Tony Corfield in 1962 in an article 'Political Education in our Union':

> Our union has a record of political education which can compare with any in the country. Every single member who has passed through the union's Branch Officers' training courses ... has been instructed upon his responsibility to help build the working partnership between the union branch and the Labour Party.[47]

However, as we have seen, the summer schools were primarily industrial, and any political session, if included, would normally consist of a speech from an MP. Members of the Parliamentary Panel such as Lewis Carter-Jones and Neil Kinnock regularly attended Cirencester, and Jack Jones himself always injected a political edge into his speeches. On the other hand, there were no explicit political courses in the education programme. Some regions held political schools during the post-war period, with Scotland providing the most.

An example of Region 7 work was a joint TGWU/Labour Party school organised in September 1981 at Stirling University. There were 54 members in attendance from various districts, including councillors and full-time officials. Gordon Brown outlined the importance of North Sea Oil and the difference between the Norwegian and British Government's approach. Sam Aaronovich's book *The Road From Thatcherism* was standard on the course, and Aaronovich also led a session on the Alternative Economic Strategy. Region 1 had also begun to run two political training courses, 'Trade Unions' and 'Politics and The Tory Attack'. The region also included explicit political content in trade group courses, with a session on the economy, and in the course 'New Technology, Jobs and Conditions'.[48] For the rest, the picture was mixed. Region 2 had courses on the Economic Crisis; Region 6 had a political weekend school linking the union and the Labour Party, and Region 8 had held one school in 1979. Regions 3, 4, 9, 10 and 11 had no specific political courses. Cirencester had an evening meeting with an MP and at Eastbourne the follow-on course had what was described as a 'semi-political' session.[49]

In the later 1960s and 1970s, the style of trade union education became dominated by the TUC courses. On the positive side, this meant the use of active learning methods and a clear focus on role education rather than theory or academic study. On the negative side, it meant the virtual elimination of politics from the curriculum, so that by the end of the 1970s a generation of shop stewards had been made to feel that it was acceptable to be a shop steward and have no link with politics or even to combine the role with voting Tory. Coupled with the wider changes in the society which led to the growth of Thatcherism, it meant that TGWU education had not included any systematic political courses in the immediate pre-Thatcher period.

In January 1982, as a pledge of support to the Party, the TGWU, GMWU, ASTMS and SOGAT agreed that they would make available their college facilities with a view to training 300 trade union officers, lay agents and Party activists in more effective election procedures between then and the next general election. It was also noted that the TUC was going to institute a major education campaign against the Tebbitt Trade Union Bill called 'Tackling Tebbitt', mainly in 1982 and 1983.[50] The two TGWU courses for the Labour Party were held in October and November 1982 in Treesbank and Eastbourne, supplemented by regional meetings.

Little more was done up to the 1983 election, which was more of a shock to the union than 1979, as it showed that Thatcherism was well-established, and that it would be a long road back for the Labour Party. At the July 1983 Education Committee, a discussion took place on the need for the Education Department to look at political membership education in the light of the general election result, and it was agreed that Frank Cosgrove would draft proposals for consideration by the Committee. A paper was presented to the October 1983 meeting of the committee, and at last faced up to the scale of the problem:

> Following the disastrous election result in June 1983 and the continuous hostility of the media to trade unions, it is essential to make the general membership more aware of the value of trade unions and the need to protect the facilities gained over the years, such as 100 per cent agreements, check-off system, and the need to maintain the political levy ... The defeat of the Labour Party at the general election, and the clear indication that a majority of trade unionists voted Tory, in spite of the appalling economic record of the Tory government, emphasises the necessity for the continued maintenance and expansion of education for active members, shop stewards, branch officers and representatives, and underlies the necessity to extend this facility to the general membership where possible ...

In May 1984 the Committee also agreed to organise a week's national political school to serve as a pilot scheme for the second stage programme and recommended to the Executive that two members from each region and a quota from the GEC should attend.[51] At the next meeting, Regan Scott set out the aims of the school:

1. To foster closer liaison between the industrial and political wings of our movement.
2. To stimulate an interest in basic Socialist ideas and thinking.
3. To develop our lay tutor training programme to cover political education work.
4. To develop a TGWU guideline for political education, so that the

expansion of regional political education programmes can have a common reference point.

5. To develop materials in order of priority for issues which will enable us to target other political work more accurately.
6. To develop a deep understanding of the reasoning behind TGWU political policies and views.[52]

It was proposed that the broad subject areas would be the politics of the British economy, trade unions and Socialism, the unions' relationship with the Labour Party, international perspectives, peace, solidarity and the Third World, and civil liberties and the state. Approval was given to the Department to organise the school in the week beginning 21 January 1985. The course was introduced by Ron Todd (then GS Elect), who led the first day's discussion on the political aspects of the 'Alternative Economic Strategy'. The Deputy General Secretary, Alex Kitson, introduced the second day's discussion on international issues and Bill Wedderburn introduced the third day, on the legal attack on unions. Jim Mortimer, recently retired as Labour Party General Secretary, led the fourth day, on the issue of rebuilding the Party. Twenty-four members attended and the Education Department staff carried out the tutorial work.

Whilst it was agreed that this had been generally successful, the Committee took the view that while a single annual school might serve a valuable purpose, TGWU political education should become an integrated part of the overall education provision. It was agreed to recommend 4 to 6 schools per year, paid for out of the Central Political Fund, and 5 national political schools were booked for 1986.[53] Frank Cosgrove asked John Fisher to be the core tutor, working with Jenny Pardington to develop the programme.

The first school took place at Eastbourne from 1 to 6 June 1986. This was an outstanding success, with Tony Blair (then, of course, a back-bencher) being the first MP to attend. For the on-going programme, John Fisher and Jenny Pardington and later her replacement, Sue Rubner, attended every course. Pat Hayes from Southampton University led a session on Inequality and Social Policy, and on the first courses Jim Mortimer sometimes attended to present a session on the crisis in the Labour Party. Mike Gapes (later an MP but then on the Party staff) occasionally led a session on international issues, and Roy Lewis, then at Ruskin, sometimes led a session on the law and politics. A TGWU-sponsored MP usually attended, and apart from Tony Blair, some of the lesser luminaries of 'New Labour' crossed swords with the TGWU students, including Margaret Beckett, Ian McCartney and Tessa Jowell. Others were backbenchers such as Ken Livingstone, Maria Fyffe, Joyce Quinn, George Galloway and Kevin McNamara. When available, the course ended with a session from an Executive Officer such as Larry Smith or Bill Morris.

In 1987 it was agreed by the GEC that Executive members should attend these courses on a rota basis. Due to pressure of business, members could not always oblige, but they made a valuable addition to the course, which also gave them first-hand experience of the union's education programme.

In May 1990 the Committee considered a paper on the national political schools called 'Developing T&G Political Education'. It was concluded that recruitment to the schools would need to be targeted in terms of key people who were to play opinion-forming and organisational roles in relationship to the various political challenges facing the union.

It was proposed that the union adopt a new procedure which would ask the regions to draw up 'a panel of nominees, to be supplemented by national nomination, of members already active politically, and possibly including members of the Parliamentary Panel, local authority councillors and candidates and elected members drawn from the union's committee structure, such as regional political committees, and full-time officers'. Other, more specific, political education was also undertaken at national level at this time. The union had run an ongoing campaign against deregulation in the passenger transport industry, which although essentially campaigning rather than educational, had included serious political debate. In 1988 a Local Government briefing pack had been developed with the University of Surrey as part of the campaign against CCT and privatisation. Regional courses were held for active lay members, and officer-training seminars were run at three venues, Transport House, Stoke Rochford and Glasgow, involving 50 officers from all regions. This represented a serious and systematic attempt to use the education programme as a way of directly influencing a major government policy which was felt to be detrimental to the interests of the union.[54]

POLITICAL EDUCATION IN THE REGIONS

During the Thatcher period, the union also sought to encourage the regions to undertake more political education at the local level. Some regions, particularly Regions 1 and 7, needed no such encouragement. Region 1 held a range of new Law on the Shop Floor courses in April, May and June 1985. Region 2 held a weekend course in June 1985 at Easthampstead Park, Wokingham. Other regions held similar political fund workshops and employment law briefings. Region 6 held 24 courses covering 26 days and attracting 1,243 students, and Region 7 had a very large programme on the political fund issue and employment legislation throughout March, April, May and June 1985. Region 9 held 22 political fund seminars and Region 10 ran 24 courses with 521 students.[55]

In Region 1, political weekend schools were introduced in 1981 and by the end of the decade the region had run 48 courses with 1,567 students. The region developed the model that was later adopted by the national schools, based around John Fisher, Jenny Pardington and Pat Hayes. Jack Dromey (later Services National Organiser) attended the weekends for the first two years, and Barry Camfield also attended. The MP who attended most frequently was Tony Banks, and later Ken Livingstone was a regular participant. Region 2 occasionally used the Marsham Court Hotel, Bournemouth, for courses organised by Basil Bye. In the North-East, Region 10 periodically used Stoke Rochford for political weekends, beginning in 1984, and this venue was also used by the Midland Region for occasional political schools. Region 8 had intermittent courses, usually linked to election campaigns, such as a series of courses in March 1987 in the election run-up period. Region 7 ran occasional political courses such as one in June 1983, a three-day course 'Political Aspects of Trade Union Work' held in Grangemouth, Dunfermline and Aberdeen.

The political programme at national level was seen as a long-term rebuilding of the political awareness of the membership, rather than as an immediate fire-fighting operation which would somehow reverse the wider political situation which the union faced. The proposals made in 1991 to change significantly the recruitment process for the national course were overtaken by the union's crisis of 1992, and by the review of union sponsorship of MPs which was instigated by the Nolan Committee and by the new Blairite leadership of the Party, which abandoned the Hastings Agreement that had governed union-party links for many years. In the late 1990s the union took part in reviewing its relationship with the Labour Party, and considering the establishment of Constituency Development Plans and regional support for MPs and councillors. It also considered a 'Public Office Panel', of those union members sitting as councillors, school governors, health trust members, and so on; the future of national political education will be bound up with educational support for that proposal.

TGWU WOMEN'S EDUCATION IN THE THATCHER PERIOD

We have already seen how the Jones era saw the strengthening of the demand from TGWU women to play a greater role in the union, and to specifically benefit from the union's education provision. The 1979 BDC clarified the demands which would take forward women in the union into the next decade. The key resolution was as follows:

> That this conference supports the policy for equal pay for equal work and on all employment conditions. It recognises the special problems faced by women workers and female trade unionists, particularly the lack of confidence of many women at union meetings and conferences, and the extra difficulties imposed by the domestic burdens of some women. The union should, therefore, develop training programmes specifically for women in the union in the form of one-day schools

> and/or short courses; introduce special courses and schools on equal pay, sex discrimination, and maternity legislation; ensure that as wide publicity as possible is given to women at all levels in the union about education facilities available; introduce the provision of crèche facilities at conferences and meetings; examine the contracts of employment of some of the women in the union, particularly in respect of maternity leave, pay during sick leave, hours of work; look at the wages of some of our women members in the traditionally 'female' occupations. Committees should be set up either nationally and by each region and develop programmes to encourage women's participation.[56]

The next TGWU Women's Conference, held the following January, began to show signs of rising expectations amongst women members. The conference recognised the commitment of the union to involve women members at all levels and note was taken of the education courses aimed at women members and the development of course materials on women's issues for wider use, the gathering of information on collective agreements of specific interest to women and parents, and the use of *The Record* in promoting women's rights.

In implementing these demands within the education programme, the first decision was to hold a national course specifically for women. In the traditional programme, women remained a tiny minority. For example, at Cirencester in 1980, only 33 women took part – just 8 per cent of those attending.[57] Therefore it was decided to hold a special women's course in October 1980 at Eastbourne; 16 members attended the course and it was widely seen as a breakthrough for women in the union. Among the students were Margaret Prosser, later National Women's Secretary and Deputy General Secretary, and other women who were to play an important role in the union. The course syllabus essentially covered how the union worked and some of the key principles and skills of being a trade union representative, plus special sessions focusing on the role of women in the union. The core tutor was a man, Pete Batten, but female speakers and officers such as Marie Patterson also attended.

The 1980 course established a regular pattern of women's courses both nationally and in the regions. Following this course, in 1982, Theresa Murphy, a professional tutor, was seconded from Slough College under a lecturers' scheme for three months to revise the *T&G Women's Handbook* and develop teaching materials.

National courses were held about four times a year, sometimes with a 'special' variation, such as an ILO course on women workers in 1984. In the first half of 1983 12 women's courses were held in the regions, particularly in Regions 1, 4 and 6, and another national women's course was held at Eastbourne during the first week in October. In April 1990 the basic women's national course was supplemented by a Women's Advanced Course with Diana Holland as the core tutor, but with specialist sessions from John Fisher on the economy and Barry Camfield on the union's organising agenda. This course also included a session encouraging and training women to apply for officer's jobs, and a conference procedure exercise.

A step forward for women in the union occurred in June 1983 with the appointment of Margaret Prosser to the position of district officer for the Public Services Group in Region 1. Margaret Prosser, along with Sylvia Greenwood, from Sheffield, and Kriss McQueen, from Blackpool, was the most significant of the 'new generation' of female officers in the union who were determined to make the 1979 BDC resolution a reality. Although from a working-class background in South London, Margaret Prosser had worked in a law centre and was an articulate spokesperson for women as a distinct group in the union. She was joined in Region 1 by another female officer, Jaqui Ford, who was appointed to the position of District Officer, Woolwich, from 16 July 1984, and later by Margaret Holmes, serving mainly agricultural members.

Another step forward was taken with the election of Joan Burbidge to the GEC in March 1984. Joan Burbidge was the first woman to sit on the Executive since Vi Taylor in the early 1950s. She was full-time convenor at Carnaud Metal Box, Wisbech, and sat for the southern part of Region 10, which included Grimsby, Lincoln, Boston, Peterborough and her own district, Kings Lynn, from 1984 to 1988. She was elected primarily on her industrial record. Joan Burbidge was joined on the committee by Maureen Twomey, from Liverpool, who was elected in 1986 to represent the ACTS Trade Group. Sis. Twomey sat on the GEC throughout the early 1980s and 1990s before becoming a district officer in Region 6 in 1996. She was also the first woman to sit on the GEC Education Committee, and took part in many key decisions affecting TGWU education in the 1980s and 1990s.

In October 1984 Marie Patterson decided to marry and tendered her resignation from the service of the union with effect from the end of the year.[58] Although the F&GP agreed to a replacement, the position was advertised as 'National Officer' rather than 'National Women's (or Woman) Officer', and two out of four of the candidates were men, Livie Reid (Region 3) and Alan Wilson (Region 1).[59] The two women candidates were Margaret Prosser and Sylvia Greenwood, and Margaret Prosser was appointed from 10 December 1984.[60] She very quickly took her seat on the TUC General Council and on the TUC Trade Union Education Committee, and began the task of building on the 1979 resolution and its re-affirmation at the 1983 conference.

In 1983 and 1984 national women's courses were tutored by Kim Burridge,[61] who was employed as the librarian in Central Office, and was interested in becoming more involved in education. In December 1985 she moved to the TUC National Education Centre and then became an education officer for the Civil Service union PCS. Kim was replaced as the union's national women's tutor by Janice Winder. She was then working for the NCCL Rights for Women Unit and was already a TGWU voluntary sector member, and in April 1985 joined the staff at Central Office as education assistant. Other women tutors beginning to make their mark in the regions were Maria Smyth (Region 6), who later became a district officer; Diana Holland (Region 1), who was to follow Janice Winder into the Education Department and then, via Region 1, to follow Margaret Prosser as National Women's Secretary; and Avila Kilmurray (Region 3), who was to become Regional Women's Organiser before returning to community work and political activity around the Irish peace process.[62]

The years of 1984 and 1985 were spent in working on the constitution of the National and Regional Women's Advisory Committees. In March and April 1984 the GEC agreed the terms of reference for the National Women's Advisory Committee, the first meeting of which took place on 30 October 1984. Members included Janice Winder, Ann McCall, Jane McKay (later the first women's representative on the GEC), Yvonne Strachan, Marie Vannet (later Public Services rep on the GEC), and Monica McWilliams from Ireland. Marie Patterson was ex officio, and Ron Todd (National Organiser) and Alex Kitson (DGS) attended at the start. Jane McKay was elected chair of the committee. At this meeting the committee expressed the hope that 'the excellent women's courses would be continued at national level', and raised the matter of crèche facilities on courses.[63]

In September 1986 Bill Morris addressed a meeting of the REOs and argued that there was a need to use education as a vehicle to develop equal opportunities, for example on the follow-on course at Eastbourne, and he asked REOs to look at course materials to ensure that equal opportunities received a higher profile.[64] A major problem was still the tiny proportion of women who attended the regular programme; for example, the 1984 summer school was attended by only 36 women, representing only 6 per cent of those who attended the school. In order to meet this problem, in 1985 one of the weeks in August was designated 'Women's Week'. Margaret Prosser and the Regional Women's Advisory Committees were asked to publicise the special week, 'drawing to their attention the excellent crèche facilities available'.[65] Neither Eastbourne nor Cirencester had offered crèche facilities, but Stoke Rochford was owned by the National Union of Teachers, whose membership was overwhelmingly female, and was expected to provide this facility, unlike the TGWU, where women's membership had never risen above 20 per cent. Providing high-quality childcare was recognised as a key to increasing the involvement of women in the education programme, but it was also extremely costly, and an almost all-male GEC and Executive Officer corps contained some who were not prepared to meet the cost.

The issue rumbled on until 1988, when the Education Committee recommended the establishment of permanent crèche facilities within the Eastbourne Centre.[111]

Some of these changes began to show results. At Stoke Rochford a purpose-built and professionally-staffed crèche was available for children up to six years old, and the Education Committee made arrangements for playgroup facilities to cater for older children for 1986, 1987 and 1988.[67] In 1988, 435 students attended the summer school and out of this number 82 were women, the highest number for women members ever recorded. Out of 36 course tutors, six were women. The crèche facilities were used by 14 students; 10 women and 4 men. In 1990 the GEC agreed to an overall policy on childcare, following a remit from Region 6. It was agreed that childcare allowance should be paid to members with childcare responsibilities who attend statutory committees of the union, and arrangements would be made for day-care for children of students attending Eastbourne and Stoke Rochford.[68] The issue was to come up again in the 1990s, following the refurbishment of Eastbourne and the closure of the crèche. In the 1980s, however, the principle of childcare for union education courses became established for the first time.

WOMEN'S EDUCATION IN THE REGIONS

A key part of the structure set out in the 1979 BDC resolution was the establishment of Regional Women's Advisory Committees, and a regional infrastructure, including education and training, was essential if the project of increasing women's involvement and membership was to be realised. Local courses were underway in several regions by 1983, using a variety of formats, but usually based around the issues of sexual harassment at work, part-time workers, equal pay for work of equal value, and negotiating equal opportunities.

In Region 1, a women's course with seven members was held in January 1983 with Barry Camfield, the REO, as tutor. At this time it was not yet the norm to employ a female tutor on a women's course, but hostility from the women students, including a 'picket' of the training room at the regional office soon made itself felt, and the London Region began to look around for a suitable woman tutor. The first to make her mark was Diana Holland, later National Organiser for Women, Race and Equalities. Diana had joined the union in Brighton whilst working on the Youth Opportunities Programme, and had risen quickly through the regional education programme to become a tutor, initially on YTS courses. Region 1 established an on-going programme of women's weekend schools and day-release women's courses throughout the 1980s. The region increased its percentage of women students attending courses from 8.4 per cent in 1983 to 21 per cent in 1984; and maintained a figure of around 20 per cent through the rest of the period, in line with the proportion of women in the union.

The Irish Region, Region 11, also made a good start in women's education. The region ran a programme of courses around the theme 'Women in the ATGWU',[69] in May and June, 1983. At the end of that year two women's courses were run, one in the Fairways Hotel, Dundalk, and the other held at Drogheda and reserved for female members in the Irish Women's Country Association. Marie Patterson stayed with this course for two days. Courses were held in Waterford, Dublin, and Dundalk, usually one-day schools bringing women trade unionists together. The momentum was increased following the establishment of the RWAC in 1984-1985. This was an exceptional committee, consisting of Margaret Redmond (Chair), Anne Nolan, Shirley Hobson, Monica McWilliams, Helen Gray, May Blood, Brenda Irvine, Catherine Colton, Liz White, Eileen Weir, Doris Johnson, Anne-Marie Powell, Avila Kilmurray, Teresa Kelly and Anne Connolly. Some of these women have continued to play an important part in Irish politics as well as in the trade union movement, including a key role in the Irish peace process as part of the 'Women's Coalition'.

At this time, 40 per cent of students in the region were women, twice the rate in the union as a whole. The climax of this first period of activity was the organising of a week of trade union activity in Derry from 10 to 14 November 1986. As the report rather quaintly noted: 'This proved highly successful in the Londonderry area and amongst those participating was Margaret Prosser, National Officer for Females'.[70] The momentum was maintained at the end of the decade following the appointment of Avila Kilmurray as Regional Women's Officer. A seminar was held for the linen industry with mainly female workers in November 1990 and a course 'Women in a Changing Economy', with 14 students, was held in November 1990 in Waterford. A weekend school 'The Role of Women within the ATGWU' was held in Dublin in December 1990 with the Regional Women's Committee.[71]

Region 6 also began its women's courses at this time. A women's seminar was held in June 1984 with 31 students and Clare Stanley as tutor. Clare Stanley was originally a barmaid who had become involved with the union as a full-time recruiter and then an official. A shop stewards' women's course was held in the Liverpool office in March 1985 with 37 students. The tutors were Liz Smith[72] and Jenny Sanderson, both from the WEA, and Margaret Prosser. In August 1987 the region also ran a four-day school in Liverpool for contract cleaners with 14 in attendance, and a women's bridging course was held in September 1987 in the Liverpool office with 5 students tutored by Muriel Mayor, later to become the Regional Women's Organiser.[73]

Region 10 held a joint weekend school for new women shop stewards in conjunction with NUPE at the Delmont Hotel, Scarborough, in April 1983. Because of the interest shown, a second school, wholly for the TGWU, was organised at Stoke Rochford the following September. This became a regular feature: for example a course held in

February 1985 'Women in Trade Unions', with 38 students and tutor Janie Glenn from Hull University, and lay tutors Val Burn (later on the GEC and Education Committee), Irene Cave and Lesley Sharp (later Regional Women's Officer). Ruth Winterton and Jean McCrindle from Northern College also assisted the region as women's tutors in the 1980s. The region also held a pilot course 'Equal Pay and Job Evaluation' in Peterborough in November, 1984, beginning a regular series of women's weekends and day schools, such as one in Hull in December 1987 on maternity rights.[74]

In Region 4, a women's course with 9 students was held in November 1983 in the Osborne Hotel, Swansea, with Marie Patterson and Sylvia Greenwood from the Yorkshire Region (one of the few female officers in the union at that time) as tutors, with another one on 23 and 24 November in Colwyn Bay.[75] Another women's course was held in Swansea in October. Kim Burridge attended the women's course in September with Anne Clwyd MP.[76] A women's political course with 23 students was held in March 1985 at the Imperial Hotel, Llandudno, with speakers including Margaret Prosser. A women's school was held in Cwmbran in October 1987 which included Margaret Prosser and Janice Winder as tutors, and there was another one in November 1987 in Llanrwst, with tutors including Sylvia Greenwood.[77] Women's schools were also held in Rhyl and Cardiff in the same month. The Cardiff school included Janice Winder and Ann McCall, later Region 6 REO, as tutors. However, for a shop stewards' course Women at Work, held in September 1988 at Cardiff, all four tutors were men.[78]

By 1987, other regions had developed courses for women members, such as one held in West Bromwich (Region 5) in October and a women's health and safety course in-plant in Lawtons, Birmingham in November.[79] From 1984, Region 3 ran courses with themes which would appeal to women members. Examples were a Health and Safety for Women residential weekend school held in October 1984 at the Manor House Hotel, Okehampton, with Pam Tatlow (TUC) as the tutor, a 'Facing up to AIDS' evening course of five evenings at the Imperial Hotel, Exeter in 1987, and a 'Women in the Labour Movement' weekend residential school in October 1987, again at the Manor House Hotel, Okehampton. Guest speakers included Dawn Primarolo, later Bristol MP and minister. The region also ran cancer screening one-day seminars in 1987 with Pam Tatlow. Region 2 courses were taught by Carole Rowe, who later sat on the GEC and for a short time became the Regional Women's Organiser in the merged Region 2/3. One of the first courses was held in Slough in February 1986.

Region 9 began its programme in 1984 with a women's course of three days in November 1984 in the Swallow Hotel, Wakefield, with 15 students and Sylvia Greenwood as the tutor. In April 1987 a weekend school for the unusual combination of women and the building section was held at the St Nicholas Hotel, Scarborough, with 32 students, and Sylvia Greenwood, Margaret Prosser, and Margaret Beckett MP as the speakers.[80] These courses continued intermittently; for example in October 1990 a women's course was held at the Monarch Hotel, Bridlington, with 17 students, and Sylvia Greenwood was joined as tutor by KP Rotherham senior shop steward Alison Daykin, later a member of the GEC.[81]

Region 8 held its first women's course in March 1986 at the Crest Hotel, Newcastle, with Margaret Prosser and Stella Guy as the tutors. In July 1993, Stella Guy became Regional Organiser of Region 8 and in 1999 Regional Secretary of the merged Region 8/9/10, the first woman to reach the position of RS. A *Women's Health in Employment* conference was held on 30 January 1987 in Newcastle. A women's weekend with 47 students was held at the Imperial Hotel, Newcastle, on 17 and 18 November 1990, with Deborah Leon, Stella Guy, and fellow-officers Mick Brider and Alan McGuckin as tutors.[82]

THE APPOINTMENT OF RWOS

All this activity increased the pressure to realise another key component of the 1979 resolution, the appointment of a Women's Organiser in each region. The Scottish Region had established a long tradition of women's education going back to Jessie Murray, although by the 1980s it had been overtaken by other regions. In May 1984, a women's course was held at Treesbank, part of an established pattern at this time, and in November that year the region held a half-day women's conference in the Edinburgh District office with 15 students. The tutors were Yvonne Strachan and Irene Kinder, daughter of Alex Kitson, then TGWU Deputy General Secretary. Jane Mackay, as Chair of the NWAC, was also putting pressure on her region, especially on the Regional Secretary, Hugh Wyper, to set an example in the area of appointing RWOs. As a result, in April 1984 Region 7 asked the GEC for the appointment of a Women's Organiser, and in November 1984 it was agreed that this should be a full-time officer's position.[83] Yvonne Strachan was appointed to the position of Women's Organiser from 22 April 1985. She was completely different from the usual male, industrial, traditional officials in the region. Prior to becoming an official, Yvonne was active in the Edinburgh Voluntary Sector branch, District Committee and Regional Women's Committee. She trained as a primary school teacher at Aberdeen College of Education and became involved in student politics, as President of the SRC. She worked for the Anti-Apartheid Movement in London, then as International/Overseas Students Officer, then Research Officer for the National Union of Students in Scotland. After 15 years with the TGWU, she left the union in 1999 to head the Equalities Office in the new Scottish Parliament.

Other regions followed suit. The Irish region formally requested a women's officer in 1989 and Avila Kilmurray was appointed to the position from 8 January 1990. She had a background of involvement in community work, in fighting sectarianism and encouraging the involvement of women in this activity.

Muriel Mayor was appointed to the position of Women's Co-ordinating Officer, Region 6, from 12 March 1990; Deborah Leon was appointed to the position of Regional Women's Organiser, Region 8, from 27 August 1990,[84] and Diana Holland was appointed Regional Women's Co-ordinating Officer, Region 1, from 10 September 1990. This was a year of other steps forward for women in the union. Carole Rowe from Region 2 was appointed to the F&GP in April, the first woman to achieve this position. Also in April, Maureen Twomey was appointed to the GEC Education Committee. In November, the F&GP supported Yvonne Strachan's claim to be upgraded to Grade 4 of the officers' scale from 5 November 1990, thus recognising the women's officer as a senior regional position.[85] By 1991, the GEC included three women: Maureen Twomey (ACTS), Carol Rowe, and Margaret Cassidy (Textiles).

Thus the scene was set for further steps forward in the 1990s. Women's education had become an established part of the union's programme, and by the third quarter of 1990 the number of women members on courses was brought to an approximate *pro rata* position of 20 per cent of the total.[86]

RACE EQUALITY

Race equality was given less prominence than women's equality during the 1980s. From the 1950s onwards, when significant numbers of black and ethnic workers began to join the TGWU, it was assumed that union members would not be racially prejudiced, and that the general message of worker solidarity would overcome xenophobic or racist feelings. On the other hand, there were clearly sections of the union's membership, most famously the Powellite dockers, where racism was strongly embedded. Although the union's leadership always promoted good race relations and condemned prejudice, it was the rise of Bill Morris (supported by Bob Purkiss) which led to a clear focus on a positive agenda in the 1980s, and TGWU education played an important part in this process.

The first TGWU black or ethnic member ever to have his or her picture in *The Record* was Brother Charn Singh, a Newcastle bus driver from 8/34 branch who had been awarded the certificate With Merit from the Home Study course in February 1962. Brother Singh came from the Punjab to Britain in April 1958 as a Warrant Officer with the Royal Signals.[87] The first article in *The Record* that explicitly attacked racism was published in January 1963 and was called 'Hiding Behind our Ideologies'. It was written by John Stevens of 1/382 branch, a member of the Central Road Services Committee and later an officer. The article condemned those who attack immigrants.[88] In 1967 *The Record* also published an article by Mary Biswas of the 1/128 Central Office branch about the campaign against racial discrimination to which the branch had affiliated.[89]

The shock of the sight of TGWU dockers marching for Powell[90] led the Education Department to specifically include race issues in its education programmes from the late 1960s onwards. In the final session of the Cirencester summer school, at which students participated in a mock branch meeting, one of the items on the agenda was a discussion on racial prejudice. In preparation for this debate, members of the school were given the NCCL's brochure *Twenty Questions About Immigrants*; 1,000 of these pamphlets were distributed to the students on the course each year.[91] At the local level, some TGWU courses tried to deal with racial issues, particularly where it was felt to be a significant factor in industrial relations. For example, in 1974 one of the features of the joint course at UG Glass Containers at New Cross (South-East London) was a discussion with the Race Relations Board's industrial specialist.[92] Also in 1974, in the TGWU Southall office, the union began running a pilot course in English for the Indian women cleaning staff at Heathrow Airport. The union paid for the teacher and provided accommodation for the course, which was run in co-operation with the local Community Relations Officer.[93]

In 1984, the Education Department began work on a race relations brochure, setting out the union's policy background on this issue, and providing advice and educational information. Bill Morris opened an REOs' conference on equal opportunities held in Transport House in July 1986, intended to raise the status of equalities within the education programme. The Regional Education Officers assembled again at the Eastbourne Centre in December 1986 to develop programmes and materials to implement the union's policy on equal opportunities.

In March 1988 the GEC discussed a paper outlining proposals for the union's policies on equal opportunities for ethnic minorities and people with disabilities. This had been drafted in line with BDC policy as outlined in Composite No 13, carried at the 1987 conference. A working party was established consisting of representatives from appropriate Central Office departments and one delegate from each region.[94] Frank Cosgrove was the chair of the working party which drew up the paper, but the bulk of the background work was carried out by Diana Holland, then an Education Assistant in the Department, and Bob Purkiss. The Race Advisory Committees began to be established in 1989, first in the three pilot Regions, 1, 5 and 8, then in 2, 6, 7, 3 and 4. A further step forward was taken with the appointment of Bob Purkiss to the position of National Equalities Officer in December 1989.

Bob Purkiss had already been attending the summer school on a regular basis to lead a special session on race relations at the workplace. From 1989 the summer school included on all courses case studies on equal opportunities and racial discrimination. The theme of the 1990 summer school was 'Equality at the Workplace'. A special general session on each Wednesday morning looked in detail at these issues, with special emphasis on race discrimination awareness at workplace level. Bob Purkiss attended and lectured on these sessions assisted by active lay members from the National Race Advisory Committee, and from 1991 an Equality course was run every week on the summer school with assistance from Bob Purkiss. Outside the summer school, there have been *ad hoc* national courses, one of the first being an Equality at Work course in April 1991, with the late Bryn Hazell (Solihull FE College and racism campaigner) Bryony Smith and Bob Purkiss as tutors.[95]

In 1990, Region 1 conducted 5 one-day race awareness courses for some 50 officers and tutors. The first black and ethnic members' weekend was conducted from 1 to 3 June 1990 at Eastbourne; 23 members attended, three black lay tutors and Bob Purkiss. The region tried to link its equalities education with targeting specific groups of ethnic workers. A shop stewards' course for Turkish textile workers was carried out on six consecutive Saturdays in October/November 1988 in the Islington Turkish Workers' Centre. Translation was provided by Enver Bekar, a TGWU member working for SWAAP, a service workers' community development group.[96] An Iranian workers' day-school was held on 29 September 1990 and a Turkish workers' day-school on 30 September 1990 at the regional office with eight students attending each.

In Region 5, a special course on Trade Unions and Racism was held in the Nottingham District in October 1984. Speakers included Bill Morris and other race relations specialists.[97] Region 8 also began courses on race awareness in the early 1980s, and was one of the leading regions in this respect. In the summer of 1983, the region ran a weekend school on combating racism, drawing participants from several industries and cultures. One of the highlights was a visit on the Saturday evening to Gujurati New Year celebrations.[98] In 1984, a joint school for the TGWU and NUPE was held in Darlington,[99] and in 1986 the region ran a series of day-schools on equal opportunities to promote and encourage union activity amongst members who were young, black, women or disabled. After the appointment of Deborah Leon, the region ran a regular Bargaining for Equality course, such as the one held in January 1991 with Doug Miller (Newcastle Poly) and Deborah as tutors.[100] In Region 9, a race awareness course was held in April 1991 in the Monarch Hotel, Bridlington, with 20 students and Bob Purkiss as the tutor.[101] Although patchy across the regions, these courses established race equality as a mainstream subject for TGWU education, and in the 1990s the inclusion of equalities as a core subject, which was a mandatory teaching requirement in all regions and the national programme, led to the continuing inclusion of this subject in the education programme.

TRAINING AND YOUTH

In the period of the 'New Deal' and relatively full employment, it is difficult to appreciate the profound impact on the union and the trade union movement in general of a combination of mass unemployment and drastic membership loss as occurred in the early 1980s. Union leaderships began desperately casting around for solutions, and looked to extending trade union involvement in the world of the Manpower Services Commission and so-called 'training schemes', with the objective of making contact with what seemed almost a whole generation of youngsters who, it appeared, would grow up without the conventional workplace contact with the trade union movement. Making contact with these 'trainees', and with the rising numbers of the unemployed, became part of the brief of trade union education services, and the TGWU was no exception.

In the earlier Thatcher period the union joined in a special one-day TUC conference to discuss the overall trade union strategy for the unemployed. The TGWU itself called a conference on MSC schemes on 1 December 1982. The union was caught in the dilemma that on the one hand, it condemned the Tory government's use of 'training schemes' as a way of camouflaging unemployment, whilst on the other, a boycott of involvement would remove any chance of positively influencing the training content and overall quality of 'schemes', including the opportunity to recruit young workers.

In March 1983, in response to this debate, the GEC approved a remit from the Building Crafts Section calling for maximum representation on MSC Boards,[102] and following a debate at the 1983 BDC on Youth Training schemes, YTS leaflets were prepared and sent to all regions, together with a request to designate one officer who would be responsible for organising YTS schemes within the Region.[103]

In 1985, the Rules Conference decided to offer 10p per week membership to YTS trainees on the basic allowance,[104] and the Research Department produced a detailed handbook on YTS for TGWU negotiators to coincide with this decision. In November 1983 the union produced the first issue of the *YTS Bulletin*, which was intended to keep officers in touch with the latest developments of national policy and local problems and successes. It was produced intermittently through the 1980s primarily by Shane Enright, a member of the Education Department staff, who later went via the International Department to the ITF.

The GEC agreed to the convening of a conference of all TGWU members and officers on Area Manpower Boards, and officers who had been allocated responsibility for MSC schemes in their region, on 15 November 1984.[105] At the instigation of Frank Cosgrove, Larry

Smith requested training for AMB representatives to help equip them in carrying out their role effectively, and to assist them to understand the variety of schemes put to them for approval. The first of these courses was held in January 1986 with Harry Moore and Peter Emery as tutors, and with 14 students, mainly officers.

In June 1987 the GEC, following a remit from Region 1 on the Job Training Scheme, asserted its total opposition to the JTS.[106] In June 1988 Ron Todd resigned from the Training Commission because the government's proposals were unacceptable, and because the tripartite principle in the Training Commission, formerly MSC, was being undermined.[107] Also, at the BDC in June 1989 the union launched a comprehensive pack of training resources, including a model training agreement, negotiators' guide, and directory of information sources. A new *National Training Bulletin* was also launched at the conference. The union also co-operated with the GMB in producing a publication, *Training For Britain's Economic Success,* calling for each worker to have the right to 5 days training per year. This was posted to 2,000 UK personnel managers. In 1997 this exercise was repeated with an updated book *Training For Success.*

Some regions attempted to link this activity around training to develop a youth strategy. In 1982, Region 7 was the only region which held a course specifically for young members. Region 1 introduced YTS courses in 1985, using Diana Holland as the tutor. Other regions tried to link training with the development of youth policy in the union, and with education sessions provided for schoolchildren, which was particularly important in Region 9 and Region 1.

In 1986-1987, the GEC established a system of youth forums in regions in the form of a varied weekend of activity and discussion. This was intended to lead up to a National Youth Forum from which delegates would be expected to report back to the regions. This proposal included regional youth education courses. Publicity and information material, aimed specifically at young people, was authorised, together with support material for visits to schools and YTS courses. Various steps were taken regionally and nationally to implement this decision, and often involved education departments, who were seen as natural vehicles for carrying the policy through. The video *Day One,* starring Tony Robinson, was issued in September 1986 with an education pack *Young People Need Trade Unions* to accompany the video. This pack had practical activities, case studies, discussion questions and information pages on the union at work, the TGWU and young people, and union services to members. Tutors' and speaker's notes gave guidance on structuring a session on trade unions for young people, using the video and pack materials.

The union also established closer working relationships with SCIP. The acronym originally stood for Schools Council Industry Project and had been established under the 1970s Labour Government to promote the world of work and industry – and trade unions – in schools. The Tories abolished the Schools Council but retained SCIP, re-christening it Schools Curriculum Industry Partnership. The project had 110 LEA appointed 'co-ordinators' via a system of national, regional and local meetings. The idea was to involve TGWU lay tutors and/or other TGWU members in SCIP's programme of national and regional conferences, workshops and teacher training. In 1988, the GEC gave its approval for a national youth school, which was held in August at Eastbourne. The tutors were Diana Holland, who had been co-ordinating this work in the Education Department, and Steve Turner, one of the University of Surrey/Region 1 tutors who later became a district officer. The national youth school was intended to supplement existing youth activity within the regions, put a national perspective on youth issues, and complement the union's commitment to wider youth involvement at all stages of the union structure. Although successful, the school did not become a regular feature, as Diana Holland moved on in 1990, and youth courses suffered from under-recruitment in the regions, thus failing to create a sufficient pool for national courses.

In Ireland in the early 1980s, Liam McBrinn, who later became the REO, was mainly teaching on the Youth Training Programme courses. A youth school was held at the Derry office for young members within the YTP, and a regional school was held for women members and youth members in Dublin in December 1987, which Bill Morris attended. This was repeated the following December. In Region 1, a youth weekend with 21 members aged under 25 was held in November 1983, the first course in the region. Fortunately, Jack Jones was in the Eastbourne Centre at the time of the course and was very well received when he was invited to speak to the course members.[173] This was repeated in 1984, when 15 attended, and on through the 1980s. The region also developed a comprehensive programme of school visits and at the end of the decade the region was reaching over 10,000 school students each year. Nowhere was the focus on school students and YTS trainees more marked than in Region 9, Yorkshire. The REO, Phil Scott, provided one of the smallest regional programmes for TGWU representatives, yet attended a school or training centre almost every working day to speak to young people on the benefits of trade unionism. For example, in the summer quarter of 1988, only three shop stewards' courses were organised, but there were 28 separate YTS and school visits. This programme reached about 1,000 school students and leavers each quarter.

OFFICER AND STAFF TRAINING

We have seen how the imaginative programme of officer training established by Jack Jones in the late 1960s progressed in an *ad hoc*, intermittent fashion with the occasional course at Eastbourne, but that no systematic or comprehensive officer training programme was instituted. By the early 1980s, officer training was reduced to a single new officers' induction course of one week, which, mainly because attendance was not compulsorily enforced by regional secretaries, often included some officers who had been in post for up to two years, as well as brand new appointees; and some new officers never attended at all. For the established officers, the very occasional specialist course such as AMB or pensions training had to suffice. By and large, the assumption made by the union was that, in the words of the Education Committee, 'officers should already be in possession of the skills and understanding necessary to perform their duties at the time of appointment'.[109]

One other option at this time was the Coleg Harlech Fellowship Scheme for officers, which had been established in 1982. This allowed an officer to attend the college for a month's study. Ian Stewart from Region 6 (later MP for Eccles) was awarded the 1982 fellowship, followed by Alan Wilson (Region 1) who studied pensions. By 1984, however, Larry Smith had to write a letter to the regions asking for nominations and the Education Committee noted that there were no positive inquiries for an officer to take up the scheme even though all regions had been contacted.[110] In these circumstances, the Committee was persuaded that it should support some analysis of officers' training needs, and in July 1982 the union commissioned John Hughes and Tony Smith of Ruskin College to conduct a survey. Their report noted that officers expressed their training needs as primarily

1. Collective bargaining issues.
2. Employment law.
3. Negotiating preparation.
4. Recruitment of members.
5. Office management.
6. Unions and the political economy.[111]

The induction course at that time included the role of the Research Department, using the press and media, office administration, management techniques, current and proposed trade union legislation, medical appeal tribunals, practical teaching methods, TGWU policies and the role of the full-time officer. A session on TGWU organisation was given by the National Organiser, and one on TGWU policies by an Executive Officer.

The recommendations of the report were as follows:

1. Newly-appointed officers should be introduced to their job through a period of systematic induction or planned job experience;
2. A basic course on collective bargaining should be provided for all district officers to prepare them for their negotiating role;
3. Issues and skills not provided for in the basic course should be

> included in a number of specialist short courses, which could be taken selectively at intervals by officers who had previously attended the basic course and gained some experience in their work (p11).

In May 1984, the paper was presented to regional secretaries and their views were sought by the Education Committee. It was noted in the responses from the regional consultation that many officers were concerned at the amount of detailed administration work they had to undertake and the increasing number and complexity of industrial tribunal cases. During the latter part of 1984 the Education Committee tried to turn this exercise into a substantial change in officers' working conditions. They proposed that all full-time officers, on appointment, should be entitled to four weeks' paid training leave within their first two years of appointment. Central Office induction courses should continue to be mounted where new officer numbers justified them, and all officers should be able to visit Transport House, to be instructed about the various services, such as Research, Education and Legal. It was recommended that such entitlement be incorporated in the terms of contract (in letters of appointment) of all new full-time officers.[112]

This represented a high-point of recommendations for officers' training, and very quickly, after consultation with regional secretaries, the entitlement of 4 weeks' training was removed and the emphasis placed on the officer being required to seek training from the Education Department and his/her regional secretary. It was argued that to specify a precise number of weeks as a training release 'right' might be too formal, and consequently more stress would be placed on management's (i.e. regional secretaries') responsibility to initiate training. In practice, the system reverted to the annual induction course.[113]

Another detailed investigation into officers' training took place later in the decade. In 1986, Surrey University was awarded a grant of £10,000 from the government under the PICKUP scheme, and John Fisher and Diana Holland proposed that this project look into officer training in the TGWU and compare it with that in other unions. Frank Cosgrove accepted the proposal and the project began in June 1987. The report was presented in June 1988 and proposed a comprehensive officer training programme:

1. An integrated approach to education and training from appointment, through induction, to updating and continuing education, and including a requirement to attend courses, and procedures for release and cover;
2. That officers themselves be involved in identifying their own training needs, for example with a questionnaire after 9 months in post;
3. That a comprehensive and integrated induction programme be estab-

lished, including hands-on induction within the officer's region from day 1 and a mandatory one week's national induction course for all new officers;

4. That a comprehensive and integrated continuing education updating programme be established including 3 specialist national courses; Industrial Law and Tribunals, Computers and Research, Advanced Recruitment, Organisation and Representation. Encouragement for officers to attend existing advanced courses available to lay members, *ad hoc* national courses as appropriate, and pre-retirement education.[114]

Although the union did not implement a systematic programme of officer induction and training as a result of this project, it did lead to a brief introduction of wider educational opportunities for officers. In 1990, three new full-time officers' courses were introduced; one on industrial law and tribunals, another covering the officers' role in the light of new developments such as HRM and equalities legislation, and a third on the use of research, bargaining information and computers. These new courses were held in April, October, and November 1990.

In the 1990s, Bill Morris took the view that officer training should be the responsibility of the Personnel Department rather than the Education Department. At the time of writing no systematic officer training programme is in place at national level, although some training is carried out in the regions under the authority of regional secretaries.

There were also some hesitant attempts at staff training during this period. In general, the staff had the same facility as other members of ACTS, but no special training programme. The training agreement did not specify any greater rights to staff than to the membership. Following further pressure to set up an induction programme for Central Office staff, between November 1989 and January 1990, seven training courses were held for the members of staff in Central Office, who were Region 1 members, and were trained in the region rather than at Central Office, in order to take them away from their normal duties. The courses covered the history and structure of the union, working for the union, agreements and procedures, Transport House organisation, the skills of putting the union's case and dealing with members, staff representation, the union's administration and organisation, and a session on further union courses. The tutors were John Fisher and Diana Holland, with sessions led by the chair of the Staff Committee, Administrative Officer Ray Collins, and Education Officer Pete Batten. Although Frank Cosgrove reported that these courses had been very successful and 'it was hoped to extend this to all staff throughout the union',[115] no regular programme was established on the other side of the crisis of 1992 and the election of Bill Morris.

In the late 1990s, some training for staff in Information Technology was established under the authority of the Heads of Personnel and Training.

CONCLUSION

In one sense, the TGWU education programme responded positively and enthusiastically to the challenge presented by the Thatcher years. It introduced new and relevant national courses such as the political schools, tutor training, pensions and multinational companies. It also extended the union's involvement in the equalities agenda, especially in the area of women's education, and built up a strong base with a number of companies through joint training. Innovations such as 'distance learning' broke new ground in trade union education. In the regions, the REOs went from strength to strength, in some regions building a thoroughly comprehensive education provision, particularly in the fields of health and safety at work and basic shop stewards' role education.

On the other hand, it could be argued that some of those in education 'fiddled while Rome burned', and continued to advocate ever more education expenditure at a time when the union was losing up to 200,000 members in some years, and lost 1 million members through the 1980s. Those in education, of course, argued that only by a positive response to the challenge could the union avoid a cycle of 'managing decline', and that the union's education programme stemmed an even greater decline, but there was no particular focus on an organising agenda, and this attitude in part left the education service vulnerable to the charge of putting its own interest first.

To some extent, bad luck played a part in this situation, as it was to be expected that the great investment in education personnel and facilities made at the end of the Jones era would come on stream in the 1980s, and lead to a 'virtuous circle' of comprehensive union education coupled with growth and expansion in the TGWU and in the trade union movement as a whole. It was unlucky that just when the ship was launched, the current turned violently in the opposite direction, leaving the vessel in danger of being stranded. As the union moved towards its crisis in the early 1990s, the education programme was unable to maintain its momentum and was inexorably drawn into the fundamental review of union organisation and services which the crisis provoked.

NOTES

1. Education Committee, 12 February 1981, Minute No 1530, p2.
2. Education Department Report, 31 January 1983.
3. Education Department Report, July 1980, Education Committee, 24 July 1981, Minute No 1561.

4. Education Department Report, February 1981, Minute No 1562.
5. As happened in Shell later in the decade.
6. BDC 1981, Composite 24, Minute No 17.
7. *The Impossible Dream?*, London: SIT/TGWU, 1988.
8. Letter from Frank Cosgrove to REOs, 5 July 1984.
9. Region 1 Education Report, January/March 1986.
10. Letter from Frank Cosgrove to Harry Moore, 30 November 1978.
11. Education Committee, 2 March 1979, Minute No 1439, p4.
12. Education Committee, 6 November 1979, Minute No 1469, p3.
13. This author, but as this is a history and not a memoir, I will refer to myself in the third person.
14. Letter from Ron Marston, 21 July 1989.
15. *Report on Tutor Training Courses*, appendix C 1 to the Education Committee Report, July 1981.
16. Ibid.
17. Appendix C to the Education Committee Report, May 1981.
18. Appendix C to Education Committee Report, November 1981.
19. GEC, 22 September 1983, Minute No 646.
20. Education Department Report, 18 July 1984, p3. The move also coincided with the retirement of Jack Russell, a long-term member of staff in the Education Department, who personified Cirencester to generations of TGWU students.
21. Education Department Report, 4th quarter 1990.
22 Education Committee Report, 18 November 1991, Minute No 2481.
23. Education Report, November 1988.
24. Appendix (a) to the Education Committee Report, July 1980.
25. Appendix (a) to the Education Committee Report, February 1984.
26. GEC, March 1998, Minute No 145: 'The Council reiterated the Education Committee's decision that the completion of the course be made a mandatory requirement for further access to T&G national courses as well as applicants for T&G bursary'.
27. The amount ranging from about £100 p.a. in the early 1970s to £900 in 2000.
28. F&GP, 13 August 1970, Minute No 566, p134.
29. GEC, 1 June 1964, Minute No 351; F&GP, 2 May 1968, Minute No 297, p87.
30. F&GP, 9 April 1970, Minute No 284, p67.
31. GEC, 6 June 1979, Minute No 436.
32. GEC, 25 July 1985, Minute No 594, p155.
33. GEC, 2 December 1987, Minute No 934.
34. Education Committee, 16 February 1989, Minute No 2243.
35. See J. Fisher and B. Camfield, 'Missing Link in Trade Union Education?', *The Industrial Tutor*, Vol. 4, No 4, Autumn 1986, pp30-36.
36. Education Committee, 17 May 1982, Minute No 1625.
37. *The Record,* November 1983, p13.
38. Ken Fuller, *Radical Aristocrats: London Busworkers from the 1880s to the 1980s*, op. cit.
39. Education Committee, 8 November 1984, Minute No 1889. See also Fisher and Camfield, op. cit., pp30-36.
40. Region 7 Education Report, December 1983.

41. Education Department Report, Appendix C, May 1985, p2.
42. Education Report, 11 November 1986, Minute No 2062.
43. GEC, 13 March 1984, Minute No 152, p32.
44. Appendix (g) to the Education Committee, February 1985.
45. General Secretary's Reports, June, September and December 1980.
46. General Secretary's Report, 1 March 1982.
47. *The Record*, February 1962 pp23-24.
48. Letter from Barry Camfield to Frank Cosgrove, 22 June 1981.
49. Appendix C to the Education Committee Report, November 1981.
50. NEC/TULV Conference, 5 and 6 January 1982.
51. Education Committee, 14 May 1984, Minute No 1841.
52 Education Committee, August 1984, p1.
53. Minutes of the Education Committee, 22 February 1985 Minute No 1903.
54. Education Report, 3rd quarter 1988, p4.
55. Regional Education Specialists' Conference, July 1985.
56. BDC, 1979, Minute No 15, pp8-9.
57. Appendix (e) to the Education Committee Report, November 1980.
58. She was marrying a journalist from the 'Tory' press and it appears that she felt that this may have been incompatible with her union position, although there is doubt that this would have been the case.
59 Apparently the two men treated the occasion as a joke. Interview with Frank Cosgrove, 23 March 2001.
60. F&GP, 27 November 1984, Minute No 869, p210.
61. Daughter of Tom Jackson, General Secretary of the Post Office Workers.
62. She later became Director of the Northern Ireland Voluntary Trust, a very important body in channelling funds, especially from the UK and USA, to community projects assisting the peace process.
63. Minutes of the NWAC, 30 October 1984, Minute No 7/8, p4. To commemorate the 15th anniversary of the establishment of the NWAC, these minutes were re-presented to the National Women's Committee by Diana Holland on 26 October 1999.
64. GEC, 17 March 1988, Minute No 107.
65. Appendix C to the Education Committee Report, May 1985.
66. Education Committee Report, 9 February 1988, Minute No 2168.
67. GEC, 6 March 1989, Minute No 128.
68. GEC, 18 September 1990, Minute No 630.
69. ATGWU stands for Amalgamated TGWU, the Irish name of the union.
70. Region 11 Education Report, January 1987.
71. Region 11 Education Report, December 1990.
72. Liz Smith then worked with the TUC Education Service, including playing an important role in the success of the Union Learning Fund. Jenny Sanderson later worked for the Open College Network on Merseyside.
73. Region 6 Education Report, December 1987.
74. Region 10 Education Report, July/September 1984; Region 10 Education Officer's Report, September/December 1987.
75. Region 4 Education Report, December quarter 1983.
76. Education Report, Region 4, July/September 1984.
77. Region 8 Quarterly Report, final quarter 1990.
78. Region 4 Education Report, December quarter 1987.
79. Region 5 Education Report, final quarter 1987.

80. Region 9 Report, June 1987.
81. Region 9 Quarterly Report, December 1990.
82. Region 8 Quarterly Report, final quarter 1990.
83. F&GP, 1 November 1984, Minute No 841, p202.
84. Deborah Leon was tragically killed in an air crash in the Himalayas on 27 September 1992.
85. F&GP, 1 November 1990, Minute No 758. Margaret Prosser's application to be regraded to Grade 1 (National Secretary) was agreed, effective from 7 December 1987.
86. Education Department Report, 19 November 1990.
87. *The Record*, February 1962, p45.
88. *The Record,* January 1963, pp13 and 14. John Stevens was a bus driver with a long history of progressive politics, who was influenced by Sid Easton and briefly joined the CP. He began serving as an officer in August 1965 and died in service in March 1986. I am grateful to GEC member Pat Hicks for this information.
89. *The Record*, February 1967, p29.
90. There has been some debate as to whether the racists were in fact TGWU dockers, but it seemed to be the case at the time.
91. Report of the Political, Education and International Department, December 1968, p3.
92. *The Record*, April 1974, p16.
93. *The Record,* January 1974, p7.
94. GEC, 10 March 1988, Minute No 206.
95. Another Solihull tutor, the late Mervyn Ishmael, was another regular black tutor on the union's summer schools.
96. Region 1 Education Officer's Report, October/December 1988. Brian Theobald was a participant on the very first national tutor-training course in September 1980.
97. Region 5 Regional Education Report, September quarter 1984.
98. Region 8 Education Report, last quarter 1983.
99. See P. Flynn and D. Miller, 'Racism Awareness Training for Trade Unionists – Report from the North East', *The Industrial Tutor,* Vol. 4, No 1, Spring 1985, pp23-29.
100. Region 8 Education Report, 1st quarter 1991.
101. Region 9 Education Report, June 1991.
102. GEC, 10 March 1983.
103. GEC, 20 September 1983, Minute No 584, p151.
104. GEC, 2 December 1985, Minute No 966, p256.
105. GEC, 18 September 1984, Minute No 688, p158.
106. GEC, 16 June 1987, Minute No 518.
107. General Secretary's Report, September 1988.
108. Region 1 Education Report, October/December 1983.
109. Education Committee, 21 February 1984, Minute No 1801.
110. Education Department Report, 18 July 1984.
111. Tony Smith, *T&G Full Time Officer Training: Rusking College Research Report*, March 1984.
112. Education Department Report, 31 October 1984.
113. Minutes of the Education Committee, 22 February 1985, Minute No 1901.The proposals were also opposed by Frank Cosgrove, who did not

want Ruskin College in control of TGWU officer training, and 'kicked it into touch'. Interview with Frank Cosgrove, 23 March 2001.

114. J. Fisher and D. Holland, *Training for Full-Time Officials of Trade Unions*, University of Surrey, 1988.
115. Education Committee, 22 May 1990, Minute No 2335.

Chapter 8

Crisis, Budgets and Accreditation 1992–2000

This chapter brings the national programme up to 2000. The 1990s were a period of radical change in TGWU education, with three different directors and a change from Tory to Labour governments. They began with a financial crisis, and a restructuring of the union from which the education service could not be immune. The early 1990s brought a strict system of budgetary control, but also produced policy guidelines which defined and institutionalised the provision of education in the union, and thus gave it a solid base from which to advance. The withdrawal of government funds was met with a creative response through the establishment of accredited partnerships with colleges and universities, which enhanced both the quality and range of the courses, and gave employment status to the core of lay tutors. The equalities and diversity agenda was expanded, and subject areas such as Change at Work, *the environment, joint training with employers and information technology training were expanded through the decade.*

THE CRISIS OF 1992

By the end of the 1980s, membership of the union continued to plummet, and this increased the call for tighter financial controls over education (and all other) expenditure. By 1989, TGWU membership totalled 1,312,853, a decrease of 35,859 compared with December quarter, 1988, and at the end of the June quarter 1992 it had declined to 1,080,638, a decrease of 93,104 compared with the June quarter, 1991. From being beyond the 2 million mark in 1979, the union was on the brink of dipping below the 1 million mark only a decade later. This critical period coincided with the election of Bill Morris as General Secretary, who formally took over from Ron Todd in March 1992. Morris made the establishment of financial stability a top priority and instituted a thorough review and reorganisation of the union to meet the new circumstances and stem what was seen as a haemorrhaging of the membership.

In October 1991, following his election as General Secretary-elect, Bill Morris had proposed to the F&GP that it should establish a special working party with terms of reference 'to draft a financial strategy to resolve the current deficit situation of the union, and to review the organisation of the union and make recommendations bearing in mind future statutory meetings and conferences'.[1] This Executive Working Group was to have access to all senior officers, staff and committees of the union and all relevant information. A special meeting of the GEC to consider union finances was held on 5 November 1991, at which the Working Group proposal was accepted. The Council was also addressed by an American organisational consultant, Adam Klein, who had acted for several major trade unions in the USA. The Council agreed to offer Klein & Co. a commission, with a target date of March 1992 for completion.

The result of the Klein consultancy and the Working Group report was far-reaching for the union as a whole; it meant reducing the number of regions, offices, officers and staff, and introducing a tighter system of financial management, especially following the appointment of a financial and information technology specialist, Peter Regnier (later Executive Finance Director) in the summer of 1992. A special Rules Conference on the restructuring of the union was held on 17 and 18 December 1992 in the Winter Gardens, Eastbourne, and before this at a special meeting of the GEC that was held on 12 and 13 November 1992 the basic principles of the Klein investigation were agreed to as follows:

> To adopt the principle of a single corporate identity in the re-launch of the public image of the union; to seek legal advice and financial control; to investigate other sources of revenue for the union; to rationalise branch structure; to move the union towards information technology and links between branches and the centre; to reduce the number of regions from 11 to 8; to undertake a review of trade group representation; to introduce clustering amongst offices; to restructure departments at Central Office; to appoint a health and safety specialist; to look at the composition of constitutional committees; to introduce personal communications, electronic mail, freephones, etc; to improve the identification of shop stewards and lay reps; to look at personnel policy in the union; courses should be held on the role and responsibility of full-time officers, and there should be a programme of induction courses for new employees and members of the Council should receive appropriate training; there should be a national training strategy.[2]

Although some of the last points in the statement were to impact on the union's education provision, the most important result of the crisis of 1992 for TGWU education was the introduction of much stricter financial controls, and a much more standardised and systematic approach to the organisation, administration and delivery of the service. These changes manifested themselves primarily in the introduction of budgetary systems of control, and in the creation of the *1992 Guidelines*, which set out the key objectives for the education programme and for the Education Department and REOs.

EDUCATION BUDGETS

The 1980s period was paradoxical in that whilst it brought a drastic reduction in union membership, it also led to a significant expansion of education provision, as the enthusiastic education officers and tutors launched themselves into new areas of education and engaged with newly available numbers of trade union students. Without tight budgetary control, the result was ever-increasing education expenditure. Direct course expenditure reached a total of £810,000 in 1986, with total expenditure going over £1 million. The balance, taking into account a slightly increased TUC grant, settled at approximately £850,000.[3] In 1987 the balance of expenditure exceeded £1 million for the first time, and in March of that year Frank Cosgrove sent a letter to regional secretaries, finance administrators and education officers pointing out that the increase in residential costs was most worrying and requesting that regions looked at a reduction in weekend courses,[4] made sure that all programmes met the requirements under public funding for a minimum of 15 hours, and ensured employer endorsement where possible.[5] However, with the return on public funds to the TGWU remaining at around £180,000 per annum, even maximising the reclaim would not have significantly improved the overall expenditure situation. By 1989, the total amount recovered by the TGWU from public funds since 1977 was £1,500,000. However, the maintenance of public funding could not compensate for the huge growth in expenditure and the demands of stewards and safety reps which continued to increase despite the loss of membership.

Expenditure rose again by 25 per cent between 1988 and 1989 to £1,015,394, and the REOs were called to a meeting on 30 March 1989 at Transport House, where Bill Morris, then Deputy General Secretary, took his first opportunity to meet them as a group. Whilst re-affirming the union's support for education, he also insisted that education expenditure needed to be examined, in line with the general review of expenditure throughout the union, and outlined proposals to reduce costs. Thus began the process which by 1992 would lead to the introduction of a strict budgetary system for education expenditure.

Different budgeting approaches were examined, such as allocation of expenditure on the basis of pence per member per region, but this was felt to be only one of several choices. This was the fundamental dilemma of introducing a budgetary system: on the one hand, the logical principle was simply to allocate funds per member, but on the other hand the regions were not starting from the same base, as some (such as Regions 1 and 8) had developed a comprehensive provision, whilst others (such as Regions 4, 5 or 7) had only a rudimentary programme, and/or relied much more heavily on the TUC to provide their courses. To allocate only on membership would therefore have penalised the better regional programmes without necessarily benefiting the weaker ones. In the event, the principle adopted was to take into account previous provision, the average cost of course provision, the number of shop stewards in a region and 'move towards' allocating on the basis of membership over 3 or 4 years.[6]

The new Acting Head of Education and Research, Joe Irvin, started a consultation exercise which both clarified the key objectives and organisation of the education programme, and set out the principles and the mechanism for the introduction of a strict budgetary system. Irvin had to resist pressure from some quarters not only to cut back on expenditure, but also to 'rein in' the REOs and education in the union, which was seen by some as an alternative locus of influence. The key to his approach was to be much more systematic and focused on areas such as 'core' course provision; standardisation of provision across the regions; cost; and the identification, training and overall standard of tutors.

In the 1980s, many of the practices in the education programme had grown up as a response to demand and to new ideas from the REOs and their external associates, in an *ad hoc* and even haphazard way, and had not been codified. In fact, following the appointment of REOs, a document was produced in March 1980 by Regan Scott and Frank Cosgrove which attempted to lay down the policies set by the Education Committee and endorsed by the GEC.[7] Some of the points in the 1980 document were definitive and were carried over into the 1990s; for example

> to see that all *reasonable* demands for courses from the membership are met; to stimulate a major expansion in existing provision within the regions; to see that all shop stewards, staff representatives, branch officers and safety reps have basic training made available to them, ideally within six months of their appointment ... Broader social and political education courses are particularly recommended on issues such as sex discrimination, equal pay, microtechnology, and current economic and political policies'.[8]

Although this document remained in the background during the 1980s, and was not linked to specific budget allocations, it essentially determined the way the Department was run under Frank Cosgrove, and some of the principles were carried over into the new document produced by Joe Irvin with the assistance of REOs, in particular Pete Batten of Region 1 and Chris Russell of Region 8. The document, *T&G Education in the 1990s: Guidelines for Education Officers*, was approved by the GEC in March and issued on 6 May 1992. It became universally known as the *1992 Executive Guidelines* on education, and set the pattern for the rest of the decade.

The document covered a number of key areas necessary for a comprehensive and professional education programme. The first section was called *Encouraging Participation*, in which it was required that there should be a target for all new shop stewards and safety reps to be enrolled on a course within 6 months of appointment, and that paid release should be the basis of their participation. The second section was *A National Service to Members*. This section defined the role of the REO: 'Regional Education Officers are full-time officers of the union. Their primary function is to act as organisers and promoters of union education and training courses, bringing together members and tutors in coherent and structured courses'.[9] The duties of the REO with regard to tutors, materials, expenditure and reporting were all set out in detail. The duties of the National Education Department were also delineated, in particular its role in producing standardised course materials and processing the financial arrangements of the programme.

The quality of provision was also covered in the document, especially the quality of course materials, assessment and tutors. Three categories of tutors were approved: full-time professional tutors dedicated to TGWU work; occasional (that is to say, specialist) professional tutors, and lay-activist tutors.

The substance of the union's education provision was identified as a 'core' of shop stewards, safety reps and branch officials. Advanced shop stewards' and officers' courses were also encouraged. In addition it was spelt out clearly that 'courses to improve the involvement of women members, and other under-represented groups, are also a priority for core provision'.[10] Residential advanced courses were allocated to the National Department and became more focused; for example, there were fewer generalised trade group residential courses. The achievement of maximum funding from employers for joint courses was encouraged, whilst maintaining union control over content.

An important section, and an additional document, covered the financial mechanism under the title *Cost Effective Education*. Its principles were to develop high volume on-site and local induction courses in every region at low cost, to maximise support from employers and from public funds. Both the National Education Office and the regions were required to operate within annual budgets from the year commencing April 1992. Relatively expensive residential courses were explicitly discouraged, and a minimum of eight students was set for each course. Fares and expenses to TUC courses were not to be paid.

In August 1992 the Department produced a document, *T&G Education in the 1990s: Guidelines for Full-Time Officers*. This was intended to explain the new system to officers, and to encourage them to involve their members in the union's education programme. The

Guidelines for Full-Time Officers also set out the new structure of education, looking at company-sponsored and employer-endorsed courses and the funding system; and a *Negotiators' Guide for Time Off* was included to encourage officers to secure paid release for their stewards.

These documents represented a landmark in the history of TGWU education. Not only did they set a systematic pattern for the future, but also they represented an accumulation of much of the good education practice which had been built since the appointment of REOs more than a decade before. They were logical, clear and rational, and based on practical experience of real work in the regions. By allowing REOs to recycle externally-generated funds rather than returning them to the Centre, they encouraged innovation and new approaches, so that by the end of the decade, whilst the TUC programme had declined significantly, TGWU education had expanded, yet it had become less of a drain on central funds, which by that time provided a minority share of overall direct education expenditure. The Guidelines also provided a virtual job description for the REO when most officers in the union did not possess one, and clearly identified the REO as the manager of the budget, tutors and course materials, subject to the formal authority of the regional secretary and GEC. In this sense they greatly enhanced the status of the education service, locating it as a central part of the union's overall activities, and explicitly not as an 'add-on'.

In general, REOs supported the substance of the review, and felt it gave them a stronger base and some protection from opponents of education. They also were aware that the union could not afford for its expenditure to run out of control. The key architect of the policy, Joe Irvin, commented:

> What I brought to the party was a systematic approach and some ideas as to how we could reconcile conflicting demands – e.g. budgetary constraints and a degree of pluralism and autonomy for REOs ... 'Let a thousand flowers bloom' might well have been the best approach for the 1970s and early 1980s, but by 1990 we did need to be assured that we were acting in a way which helped achieve our overall aims. This did require a more systematic approach. In a way I think we saved the education service from the sort of restrictions and rigid control which falling membership would have otherwise dictated.[11]

The issue of education budgets again came to the fore in 1999 when, following a remit to the GEC from Region 2 asking for more funding, Peter Regnier carried out an investigation into Region 2's education finance. A paper was produced in the summer of 1999, which sought to base budgets on membership levels, and which would have also weakened the REOs' ability to make accredited partnerships. Following a consultation exercise, in November 2000 the Education Committee approved a revised paper which established the principle of linking funding with membership, but was much more positive on accredited partnerships.

MANAGING THE PROGRAMME 1992-2000

A further step in this process was a change in the management of the Education Department. One of the initial reactions to the financial crisis was the trimming-down of the officer and staff complement through a voluntary severance scheme. In July 1991, Frank Cosgrove informed the GEC that he wished to retire from October of that year.[12] Bill Morris had decided that he would not be replaced, and took advantage of his leaving to restructure the Department. In early 1992, Regan Scott was re-allocated to the position of European Co-ordinator, and in April 1992 Joe Irvin was asked to take over the duties of 'Acting' Head of a merged Education and Research Department. Joe Irvin had initially worked for Courtaulds in Preston and the TUC, but had joined the TGWU as a researcher in 1980, had worked very closely on policy work with Ron Todd and Bill Morris. At the time of his appointment he was the head of a small group known as the Executive Policy Support Unit (EPSU), which was mainly concerned with drawing up policy documents and preparing speeches for the union leadership.

Given the support of the General Secretary, it would have been reasonable to expect that Joe Irvin's position as 'Acting' Head would soon lead to his formal confirmation as Head of Education and Research. However, this was not the case. A year after taking up his post, in May 1993, the Executive Officers, whilst accepting the Klein recommendation that all Central Office service departments should be headed by professional directors, nevertheless recommended that the GEC sanction the appointment of a replacement position entitled National Secretary for the Research and Education Department. This recommendation was rejected by the Council, which called for a report on the status of Heads of Department.[13] This was an embarrassment to Bill Morris, and a severe blow to Joe Irvin. The Council may have felt that the General Secretary was showing disregard for the principles of the Klein Report in asking for a national secretary position at this stage.

In December 1993, the Council decided to designate the Heads of the Education and Legal departments as Directors and to maintain the existing recruitment procedure for the interview and decision-making by the whole of the GEC. Directors would also be of equal status to that of national secretaries, being paid the same grade with all associated conditions and benefits. On 13 April 1994, the GEC interviewed a number of applicants, including Pete Batten, Tom Hart (considered in his absence) and John Fisher, and Joe Irvin was appointed the first Director of Education and Research. Joe Irvin took up his post on 18 April 1994. He was to last less than one year.

On 6 March 1995, Bill Morris informed the GEC that Joe Irvin had resigned and had accepted a position as Parliamentary Officer for the Royal Society for the Protection of Birds (RSPB).[14] This was surprising for someone who had been at Transport House for more than 15 years and had just reached one of his goals as a national official. It is difficult to identify the precise reason for the resignation, but perhaps it was to move towards a political career. The RSPB position was to last a only short time, and Joe Irvin was soon offered the job as political adviser to John Prescott, Deputy Leader of the Labour Party, then Deputy Prime Minister, where he remained up to the election of 2001.[15]

In March 1995 the F&GP shortlisted four candidates: John Fisher Hugh Kirkbride, a member of the Research Department; Dennis Gregory, of Ruskin College; and Tom Wilson, then an official of the AUT (later of NATFHE and then the TUC). John Fisher was appointed to the post of Director of Research and Education from 29 May 1995.[16]

Following the resignation of Joe Irvin, the range of duties attached to the Director's position, which had included education, research, non-EU international and parliamentary affairs, including liaison with the Labour Party and TUC, was reduced as extra policy staff were employed, and in 1999 the research element of the Department was attached to the new industrial and equalities sectors. The Education and Research Department then became the Education and International Department, and John Fisher became its Director.

INFORMATION TECHNOLOGY

During this period the education programme began to incorporate the new information technology. In the union's education service, awareness of the possibilities of information technology began to be raised in the early 1980s; for example, in December 1984 the REOs stressed the importance of good record-keeping and stated that computerisation could be very valuable for lists of tutors and students attending courses. Along with its supposed benefit to administration, the education service also looked at the use of IT in the process of education.

The major breakthrough in the provision of IT education was carried out by Ann McCall, Region 6 REO, in 1996. Ann had been a TUC IT tutor in Liverpool and took the opportunity presented by external employer funding to establish an ITC training centre in the new Salford regional office. She also offered training in IT for TGWU representatives and members. This was highly popular, and Bill Morris promoted the idea of IT centres throughout the union, partly to save money on administration, and partly to put the union in the forefront of information technology training. By 2000, 15 IT centres had been established throughout the country, and the union was offering training to members (and staff) in these centres. The centres also prompted applications to the Labour Government's Union Learning Fund at this time, nationally in partnership with Stagecoach, and locally in Regions 6, 5 and 8. From 1999, the National Members' School also offered IT training in the new Eastbourne IT training centre. IT training was being offered in most regions by 2000, and in the case of Regions 6 and 8, fully accredited at CLAIT and IBT2 level, as part of those regions' accredited partnerships. By 2000 discussions were taking place as to how the union might offer its Home Study course or other courses via IT-based distance learning.

THE STATUS OF TUTORS

It was noted above how the union established its system of lay tutors from the early 1980s onwards. Whilst in theory the idea of using the union's own active and experienced members as tutors was sound, in practice the concept contained contradictions. If, on the one hand, only senior stewards fully-employed in industry were to be used, the problem was that as education programmes expanded, it would become impossible to meet tutoring needs with part-timers who, as the 1980s progressed, were finding it more difficult to secure paid release. Also, as joint courses with companies became more important, employers wanted to know that union tutors were fully qualified and professional. On the other hand, once full-time tutors began to be used, the question of their employment status arose, and in the absence of full-time employment as union staff, they became effectively casual labour, in a period when the union was opposing the spread of casual and agency employment.

The subject came up in 1989-1990 over the regular use in Region 10 of an effectively full-time tutor, Mick Bond (later Region 8 REO) when 'The Committee expressed concern that Regions 2 and 10 had not made sufficient use of lay tutors. In Region 10, only one name appeared on the list of tutors'.[17]

Chris Russell had to defend his position:

> It is my opinion that the Committee has taken a myopic view of the role of tutors without looking at the overall provision of education in the region. It will be necessary to find additional tutors, and some lay members may well have the potential to develop the necessary skills. The required tutor training needs to be gradual but intensive. The training of suitable tutors is not limited to a five-day course at Eastbourne, and would have to recognise the needs of the regional programme. Initial contributions made by such new tutors on any issue will inevitably be limited – both in time and responsibility.[18]

The real issue, here, of course, was the definition of 'lay tutor'. The Committee were still assuming it would be an experienced active member fully employed and released, probably on pay, to teach two or three times a year, whereas Russell was acting on the new reality that for a comprehensive programme, the region needed at least one tutor who would be fully available and expert – in other words a full-time tutor.

In the event, Russell expanded his team without undermining Mick Bond, and was able to absorb more tutors with the merging of Regions 8, 9 and 10 in 1992. The status of tutors was further affected with the introduction of accreditation for trade union education following the 1992 Education Act. In February 1993, Joe Irvin submitted a paper prepared by John Fisher and himself entitled 'TGWU Education; Tutor Assessment'. This document initially proposed a joint validating system to be established between the union and the University of Surrey, involving some form of joint certification. It also included the extension of the tutor-training course into a post-course probation year for new tutors with assessments and reports, and a programme of in-service training and appraisals for existing tutors.[19] A viable scheme of accreditation for TGWU tutors was established with the Surrey Open College Federation. The scheme was based on three stages: involvement in the union and in its courses; successful completion of the tutor-training course at Eastbourne; and an 'apprenticeship' system, usually lasting about 18 months. Mel Doyle, Deputy General Secretary of the WEA, acted as moderator for the programme. This system was introduced in the autumn of 1994. At the same time, existing tutors began to be assessed, usually by John Fisher, but also by Pat Hayes of Southampton University, and by the REOs.

A regular system of 'Advanced Tutors' Briefings' was introduced in Eastbourne, covering issues such as updates on health and safety (1995), or Assessment Techniques (2000). However, none of this support altered the fundamental problem of the employment status of tutors. At the same time, the Inland Revenue was cracking down on 'bogus self-employment', making it more difficult for tutors to register as self-employed 'consultants', particularly when all, or almost all, of their work was carried out on behalf of one organisation.

The issue came to a head in 1994-5 over the 'dismissal' of a Region 1 tutor who had been involved in an incident which led the REO to declare his unsuitability to act as a tutor for the region. The tutor instituted an employment tribunal case claiming he had employment status with the TGWU, and the union for its part argued that employment status was with Surrey University, and the tribunal ruled in favour of the union's argument. The problem was noted by the Education Committee in November 1995. At this meeting, Bill Morris asked for a review of the basis on which tutors carried out work for the union.[20] As a result, guidelines were produced by the Legal Department which required tutors to acknowledge that they were not union employees and that they were being paid for services, but such a disclaimer was not really tested in court.

ACCREDITATION

A more substantial attempt to tackle the problem of tutors' employment status was the establishment of accredited partnerships with colleges and universities, through which agreements could be made which took into account the employment of tutors. The union's education programme had traditionally been set within the field of 'liberal adult education', closest to the WEA philosophy, and this implied 'role education' rather than vocational or academic education, and therefore was not normally associated with formal qualifications. An advantage of accreditation was that it was said to provide the possibility of measurement of standards.

However, in the Russell Report of 1973, trade union education continued to be defined as non-accredited 'role education' and the expansion of trade union education in the 1960s and 1970s remained firmly within the non-vocational sector. In 1991, however, the government issued a set of White Papers on education and training which formed the basis of the 1992 Education Act. This made a distinction between 'accredited' courses, which would qualify for public funding, and 'non-accredited' courses, for which full fees would have to be paid. Trade union education was attached to the latter group, representing a threat to its survival. At the same time, the government began a phased process of reducing direct public support for trade union education to zero over four years to 1996.

In 1993, in response to this threat, the TUC began a process of linking trade union studies courses to learning credits. At the Education Committee in May 1993, it was noted that the TUC had put forward proposals to use these standards as the basis of National Vocational Qualifications for full-time officers and subsequently for shop stewards and safety reps.[21] The Committee was concerned about this development and in September 1993 Alan Grant, Head of Education at the TUC, was invited to address the members of the Education Committee on standards for full-time officers and lay reps, and attended the Committee in February 1994.

The effect of Alan Grant's visit and of the government's actions was to propel the union into exploring a number of possibilities linked to accreditation. At the end of 1994 Joe Irvin had visited South Birmingham College (SBC) to discuss the granting of learning credits for 'Rover Learning', an employee development programme established following negotiations between the company and unions led by the TGWU. At this meeting, SBC also offered to effectively 'franchise' the TGWU education programme so that the union's courses would be acknowledged by the college, leading to joint certificates. This arrangement was supported by the Education Committee so that members undertaking courses would have 'something to show' for their efforts, and evidence of undertaking training and education in a particular subject. Each student would receive a certificate issued by the TGWU, but also recognised by SBC. Although this was not a formally accredited system, the financial element was irresistible to the union, at a time when courses might have been sacrificed as public funds via the TUC were withdrawn. In the first year, the college received £6.50 per unit of study at the 1995 rate. Of this £5.85 was passed on to the union, and therefore for each student on a three-day course the union received £48.00. On an average claim for about 3,000 students in a year this amounted to £143,910. In February 1995, the Committee agreed to support the scheme, subject to its being reviewed at the end of the academic year to 31 July 1995.

This agreement provided a new and unexpected financial benefit to the union at an otherwise difficult time. The final year of public funding for trade union education in its non-accredited form was 1995-1996. However, the union did not claim for that year because the franchising arrangement provided a larger return. In other respects, however, the agreement proved contentious. In May 1995, the franchising arrangement was raised by Alan Grant at a meeting of National Education Officers. He alleged that the TGWU was undermining trade union education by deregistering students from existing colleges and registering them with SBC, and that the union could deliberately steer students away from TUC courses and towards SBC.

In fact the arrangement was short-lived. The FEFC discovered that some FE colleges were entering into 'bogus' franchising agreements where the college had no quality control over the programmes, which often amounted to a state subsidy for work which organisations should have been funding themselves. Although this criticism did not apply to the SBC/TGWU agreement, the DfEE ruled out public support for agreements which did not actually produce formal learning credits. Accordingly, SBC informed the union that from 31 July 1996 they would no longer be able to operate the agreement without courses being accredited.

The TUC circulated a consultative document in August 1995 regarding its own proposals for accrediting TUC courses with the Open College Network, and in December John Fisher called on each REO to consider finding a means of accrediting their courses, preferably with a partner who would complement regional identity. The fact that by 2000, seven out of eight regions had achieved a successful regional partnership, proved the correctness of this approach.

Region 1 had maintained a good relationship with Surrey University after John Fisher had left in May 1995, and the union's favoured candidate, Pat Hayes, was appointed. Shortly after Pat Hayes took up his appointment, however, a new departmental administration at the university decided it would only accredit the higher level courses, leaving the lower levels unaccredited, and therefore not funded. Early in 1996, the region was still in discussion with the university to achieve a final agreement, but by then the union had been approached by the University of North London (UNL)[22] with a more suitable offer.

The region terminated its agreement with Surrey University and opened an agreement with UNL, and Pat Hayes transferred his appointment from Surrey. The General Secretary, Regional Secretary and the UNL's Vice-Chancellor signed the formal agreement with UNL, with a launch on 16 July 1998. The University of North London also agreed to fund eight tutor posts for TGWU education work, thus contributing significantly to employment security for tutors.

In Region 8, good progress had been made with Hull University, where there had already been a decade of co-operation, particularly with Daniel Vulliamy, and also with Colin Thorne and Keith Forrester at Leeds. In the summer of 1994 it was agreed that the two TGWU modules on basic training for shop stewards and safety reps would be adopted as an accredited programme towards a University Foundation Award (UFA), a pre-degree qualification designed to enable students to lay the foundation for further study. Five accredited modules were piloted between September 1994 and June 1995. Each module carried ten credits, which students used towards obtaining a certificate (120 credits at Level 1), a diploma (240 credits at Level 2), and a degree (360 credits at Level 3). By the summer of 1995, almost the whole of the region's provision was accredited. However, after the first flush of students who had been waiting for this type of opportunity, the take-up of students completing assessments began to slow down, and by the end of the decade the relationship with Hull University had become dominant, and little if any Level 1 work was being completed with Leeds.

Other regions began to follow suit. In the winter of 1995-1996, Region 5 initiated an accredited partnership with South Birmingham College. This was the first FE-based partnership and quickly led to the employment of two tutors, Nick Price and Jerry Vernon, by the college. In early 1997, Region 6 initiated a fruitful partnership with Manchester City College. MCC were able to offer not only accreditation but also IT courses and various favourable offers for TGWU members and their families in accessing courses such as GCSE. The partnership became active in early 1998 and by the summer of 1999 four tutors had been awarded contracts of employment, and the college also agreed to pay the wages of part-time lay tutors teaching on accredited courses.

Region 3 established a partnership with North-West Institute of HE, Derry, in November 1999 and at the same time Region 4 and Region 2 signed similar agreements with Llandrillo College, North Wales, and Southampton City College of FE respectively. All these agreements made provision for accreditation and tutor financial support and development in various ways. In 2000, approaches were being made to Scottish colleges and the devolved Scottish administration to secure an agreement for the one remaining unaccredited region, Region 7.

The creative response of the wider trade union education service in affiliates like UNISON and the TGWU and within the TUC itself, coupled with the election of a Labour Government in 1997, meant that accreditation became not only popular with trade union members, but added to provision in terms of quality and finance.[23] The flexibility and regional autonomy of the TGWU REOs meant that they could make agreements which directly benefited their programme, and maximised the scope and financial return to the union. This was estimated by REOs to be worth more than £500,000 per annum, greater than the earlier form of direct public funding support through the TUC.[24] It also met the government's objectives of extending Lifelong Learning to those who would not normally engage in adult education, and met the union's objective of maintaining a wide range of good-quality education opportunities as well as providing a greater degree of employment security to TGWU tutors, short of being able to offer them full-time positions on the union's staff.

RESPONDING TO HUMAN RESOURCES MANAGEMENT

In the union's industrial work, the growth of Human Resource Management (HRM) was the major issue of the 1980s and 1990s. The 1980s were characterised by high unemployment and a buyer's labour market, an aggressively right-wing political climate, and the arrival of globalisation and of a new breed of Japanese companies apparently sweeping all before them. At company level, management consultants were proposing fundamental changes in working practices, including teamwork, continuous improvement, lean production, 'customer first', outsourcing and Total Quality Management (TQM). The initial reaction of the union was curiosity, followed by opposition, then by a more sophisticated response of 'constructive engagement' later in the decade. The union's education programme was to play a key role in the evolution of the union's response to HRM.[25]

TGWU members in the Automotive Group began to take note of the 'Quality Movement' in the early 1980s. In 1982, the Ellesmere Port Vauxhall shop stewards invited Mike Parker, author of *Inside the Circle*, one of the first books on quality circles, over from the US to address them. The introduction of this new form of industrial relations was also being noted in the regions at this time. In September 1984, for example, a course on quality circles and 'union busting' was held in the Region 3 Bristol office with Les Ford as tutor.[26] Region 10 was co-operating with Northern College in the mid-1980s looking at single union deals, 'concession bargaining' and 'de-recognition', and Region 4 was focusing on 'Japanisation'. In 1987, Region 1 was trying to deal with *de facto* de-recognition at the Westway plant of Unigate Dairies, formerly a 100 per cent unionised company, and the Irish region was confronting a wave of new management techniques at Waterford Glass and at Du Pont in Derry.

In September 1984 the Automotive group requested the GEC to issue guidelines to active members, shop stewards and officers. In December, Ron Todd submitted a report to the GEC on employee involvement. As a result the Council issued a warning of the dangers of 'so-called Employee Involvement and Quality Circle schemes' on the following basis:

1. That they should not be introduced without union scrutiny and consent.
2. Representatives should be chosen in line with union representative machinery.
3. That where they exist such schemes should be brought in line with union structures and under union control.
4. In no case should they be allowed to undermine union structures or collective bargaining. The Research Department was to draw up a booklet drawing to attention the dangers of employee involvement and quality circles being introduced without the control of the union.[27]

A booklet on employee involvement and quality circles was issued in July 1985 incorporating these views. This initial 'oppositional' position was difficult to sustain in the light of the pervasiveness and sophistication of HRM techniques. Also, many members and particular sections of the union felt the techniques actually constituted an improvement in industrial relations. Teamwork and employee involvement were popular, and in 1986 the Executive discussed the Ford Motor Company, where staff unions had put out posters indicating participation and support for Employee Involvement. The TGWU logo was on the posters and had created problems with the hourly-paid employees, who in line with the current policy, were resisting involvement in EI.[28] The response to this was to initiate a further consultation in 1987, and ask the Research Department to collate this into an updated version of the booklet on Quality Circles.[29] One of the most significant elements of this consultation was a document written in September 1987 by Tony Woodley, then a district officer but formerly the convenor of Vauxhall's Ellesmere Port factory, who later became the National Secretary of the Automotive Group and then General Secretary. This document provided a more sophisticated analysis of quality circles and teamworking – under the name of *Quality of Working Life* (QWL) – than had been seen in the union up to that point, and introduced the importance of an educational response to the problem:

> In its initial stages, at least, QWL is often popular with a portion of the rank-and-file. If the union seeks withdrawal it may force a rebellion from QWL enthusiasts who will then be drawn even more towards a company viewpoint. Local union leaders must educate members to the hidden traps and pitfalls of QWL. The second alternative is to make QWL work for the unions:
>
> 1. The union must develop its own goals and strategies before it enters 'joint' activities.
> 2. Union leadership at all levels must be united.
> 3. The union should do its own long-range planning.
> 4. The union should seek independent help and expert advice when determining the union's goals and training for QWL.
> 4. The union has to be prepared for hard bargaining to protect its interests in QWL.[30]

By underlining the sophistication of the HRM approach and the need to make education a central part of the union's response, Woodley opened up not only the way to a more complex and sophisticated approach to HRM, but also the central role of education in meeting the new challenge. At this stage, education was defined primarily as awareness raising, particularly with regard to the dangers inherent in the new techniques.

The union's Chemical, Oil and Rubber Trade Group were particularly alert to this, having suffered de-recognition during the 1980s in companies such as Norsk Hydro on Humberside, and in Shell. The co-operation between Region 10 with Northern College resulted in two booklets highlighting these experiences,[31] and in 1990 the group took the lead in producing a video about new management techniques called *Moving The Goalposts*, made with the involvement of Region 10. In September 1991, the National Committee of the trade group submitted a remit on new management techniques calling on the GEC to support the organisation of a series of national education courses on the subject of employee involvement, team briefings, total quality, core and periphery work organisation, and other matters.

As a result, an HRM working party was set up under the authority of DGS Jack Adams to examine the whole question of management techniques and de-recognition. From 1991 the approach of the union took on a more sophisticated and complex character, as the subtlety of the new techniques became better understood. The experience in the car industry, particularly in Vauxhall Motors, was crucial to this development. The early involvement of Ellesmere Port has already been noted, but it was in Luton that the integrated educational approach was developed. Luton had become a centre for the Region 1 education programme, and when HRM began to be proposed, the shop stewards readily accepted a leading role for education in developing their response. In March 1990, the region organised a special course on management methods for Vauxhall shop stewards at Wortley Hall, Sheffield. The tutors were Adrian Weir (researcher), Pete Batten, John Fisher and Tony Woodley. In 1991 a comprehensive programme of courses on new management techniques was held in the Luton plant and in IBC, a commercial vehicle plant nearby, including 30 courses in 1991 alone. This approach was then extended to other companies such as British Airways.

The evolving policy in responding to HRM, and how education played a central role in the union's response, was set out in 1992 by Pete Batten, Region 1 REO and the prime mover behind the education courses at Vauxhall's Luton, in a document *Union Training and the Management of Change*.[32] This document first made the point that trade unions had traditionally been suspicious of management involvement in union courses, and had resisted the idea of joint training. However, recent changes had meant that this approach was becoming of direct positive benefit to trade unions:

> If it is our general policy to involve ourselves in these developments, then this raises the question about whether trade union education and training as a whole should become involved under the same principle ... it is possible to argue that our involvement actually makes de-unionisation, or a reduction in union power through these techniques, more difficult. In practice, it is often junior management who are given the task of developing industrial relations changes on behalf of companies and senior management, in areas such as equal opportunities, training, health and safety, quality, job enlargement, team organisation, and so on. These people appreciate the expertise held by the union organisation and also understand that, in practice, there is an organic link between the company's employees and the union.[33]

Trade union education was identified not only as an awareness-raising exercise, but also as a key process in the evolution of industrial relations and changes in working practices, and also one which kept the union in a central position:

> Therefore, in practice, the position that we are in is that we are either involved in this way with a positive training policy or we become marginalized ... Many companies have realised that, so long as they do not wish simply to undermine the union, involvement of the union through training and education is a much better guarantee that progress can be made in industrial relations ... The whole purpose of our involvement in joint training is to make sure that management's requirements are not the only requirements on the agenda. Whilst we are involved, it is very difficult for management to walk away from the union without exposing itself as unilaterally anti-union. Our purpose is

> to maintain the strength and the trade union organisation through this joint training, not to abandon the union position by adopting a policy of pretending that the changes are not underway and thereby allowing management to take the lead in both actual industrial relations and training and education.[34]

This became the dominant element in the evolution of the union's policy of 'constructive engagement' through the 1990s, and underpinned the exponential growth in joint training courses with employers.

An important example of this new approach was a seminar 'Works Councils and the Management of Change' held at Eastbourne in December 1992, with over 120 delegates from automotive plants in France, Germany, Spain, Italy, Ireland and Belgium. The seminar was financed from the EU fund established to prepare the way for European Works Councils. Speakers included Dave Robertson from the Canadian Autoworkers' Union, Jack Adams, Tony Woodley, John Fisher, senior managers from Vauxhall and Rover, and Peter Wickens from Nissan, an arch-advocate of TQM. This seminar was followed by a series of similar events linked to the establishment of European Works Councils, but always including key issues of concern to the workers' representatives in the company, sometimes health and safety or globalisation, but always including HRM. In 1993-1994 seminars were organised for ICI, Fords, independent brewing companies, Hoesch (Herbert's) Paints, Cadbury's, Pepsico, Peugeot, Guinness and automotive components. The components conference was a major event held at the Birmingham NEC in November 1994, and primarily organised by Tony Woodley and Joe Irvin.

Another landmark in the union's educational response to HRM was the work carried out in the Rover company in 1992-1993. This project began with the negotiations surrounding the *Rover Tomorrow* agreement, which was concluded in 1992. This agreement represented the introduction of Total Quality Management into Rover Cars but, unlike some companies, Rover had taken its proposals through the negotiating channels of the Joint National Committee, which was chaired by Jack Adams. In these negotiations, the trade unions had managed to preserve certain aspects of mutuality and protection for employees under the intended new system, whilst at the same time having to concede the overall principles of the changes associated with TQM. Also, it was accepted that *Rover Tomorrow* would be an enabling agreement, the finer details of which would have to be developed at plant level between the company, shop stewards and district officers.

In these circumstances, it became necessary for an education programme to be developed, to raise the awareness of the principles of the agreement amongst the stewards, and look at the implications within each plant. The project consisted of a briefing for officers with membership in Rover, a one-day presentation on *Rover Tomorrow* for all TGWU stewards, followed by local seminars in each plant.

The officers' seminar was held in November 1992 in Coventry, and on the 23rd of that month, a *Rover Tomorrow* conference was held in the Exhibition Hall at Longbridge attended by 292 TGWU stewards from all the plants. Bill Morris gave the keynote address and underlined the importance of *Rover Tomorrow* and the TGWU within the company. This presentation was followed by one from John Towers, Managing Director of Rover Group, and Professor Dan Jones, co-author of *The Machine That Changed The World*, a seminal management text on 'Lean Production'. The conference was wound up with a presentation from Tony Woodley, who outlined the purpose of the seminars to follow in each plant. The local in-plant seminars were held in Longbridge, Solihull, Cowley and Swindon from November 1992 through to February 1993, usually led by Les Ford, REOs Bob Sissons and Gordon Pointer, and local district officers.

This was an unusual exercise for the union, using education after the conclusion of an agreement to explain the agreement and its implications. It is not normally the role of education to be directly involved in negotiations, either before or after the event. However, it was successful in that it established in the minds of the stewards that there was a role for TGWU education that had a direct bearing on their ability to organise successfully in the company, and in that sense it played a part in evolving a more sophisticated response to HRM.

One of the immediate results of these seminars was a resolution from the National VBA Trade Group Committee and a similar remit from the Region 5 Committee to the GEC in March 1993:

> The VBA National Committee requests the support of the GEC on the setting up of an Education and Awareness Programme as to the meaning and effects behind the new management techniques, known as lean production. This education programme should be instigated as soon as possible, bearing in mind that all Trade Groups and all regions are confronted with companies demanding major changes in working practices, all of which embrace a new ideology as companies attempt to win the hearts and minds of our members, in many cases resulting in the marginalisation of the destruction of the trade union organisation.
>
> Conference states that education and training about lean production and TQM cannot therefore maintain a simple oppositionist stance. We must seek to develop a strategy of positive engagement with the employers on the above whilst at the same time retaining the trust and support of the membership.[35]

In the year following the 1993 BDC, courses on HRM multiplied at national and regional level. In October 1994, a special advanced course was held on HRM in the tyre industry, and in March 1995 for the water industry. In January 1996, a seminar for Lucas on 'Change at Work' was held in Birmingham. Sixty delegates attended.

The HRM Working Group had also called for a booklet on HRM and in 1995 the union produced *Change at Work*, and a standardised set of education materials on HRM for use in the regions, backed by special tutor training in September 1994 and July 1996. Regular 'Change at Work' courses, tutored by Les Ford, were established for both general trade groups and for the FDT group. Brian Revell, National Secretary and Fred Higgs, Chemical National Secretary, regularly used these programmes in the 1990s on a company-by-company basis, for companies such as ICI, BOC, Cadbury and Unilever. In the public sector, courses on HRM in the Health Service and British Waterways were held in 1996 and 1997. In the regions, joint training with employers around change at work, health and safety, equalities, harassment and partnership became an ever-increasing part of the established education programme, reaching more than 50 per cent of the annual programme in Region 1 and being equally important in Region 8. Regions 5 and 6 also increased their participation in joint training in this period. In the later 1990s, particularly following the general election of 1997, new issues such as 'partnership', 'family-friendly' employment and annualised hours were introduced into the Change at Work modules.

Although many companies are now involved in partnership education with the union, early targets for this approach were the companies in the newly-privatised bus industry. At the very end of the public sector bus industry, in 1990, the Education Department had provided support for 'Worker-Directors', around the issue of ESOPs (Employee Share Option Schemes). A Worker/Director course was held in December 1990 at Eastbourne, and in March 1991 in Treesbank, Scotland. However, ESOPs faded away as privatisation established itself. In the early days of privatisation, in the 1980s, the private bus companies had acquired a reputation of being 'cowboys', but during the 1990s they had consolidated into conglomerates and were keen to establish the respectability that they associated with permanence. National Secretary Graham Stevenson and John Fisher offered joint courses to explore partnership in the industry, and the first of these was held at Eastbourne for MTHL in October 1996, followed by Stagecoach in 1998 and First Group in 2000. Other companies involved in joint partnership work at national level were Sainsburys, Argos, Birds Eye, BA, BAA, ICI, BOC and many others.

EUROPE AND INTERNATIONAL ISSUES

Throughout the period from the 1970s to the end of the century, TGWU education, increasingly, had to take account of the growing importance of Europe as a political and economic factor, and of the internationalisation of the economy. In the early stages, the programme had essentially looked on Europe as a source of funds, and had focused on how to deal with multinational companies, but by the end of the period the programme had broadened out to include training on European Works Councils, European social and economic policies, new legislation, and on international issues such as globalisation and world development. In June 1980, an 'Information Visit' to Brussels was undertaken by the REOs in order to investigate money and resources available for education and research projects. Despite financial inducements, little came of this initiative, perhaps because of the complexity of accessing European funding. Basil Bye continued to produce information on multinational companies, and the Eastbourne course on this subject, tutored by Les Ford, ran regularly. In December 1983, the union received a letter from Alan Leather of TUIREG at Ruskin College, which had begun an annual summer school in 1983 on the subject of international issues facing the Labour Movement, and the role of the trade unions. TUIREG was given the support of the union, and in 1986 the GEC voted £7,000 to the Commonwealth Trade Union Council training programme for African trade unionists in the UK.[36]

As European and international issues grew in importance, the Education Department began to look at a more systematic approach. In May 1984, a delegation of lay and full-time officials again visited Brussels as the guests of the EEC Trade Union Information Division. In May 1988, the Education Committee discussed a paper *Europe 1992*, prepared by Regan Scott, and in September 1988 a version of this report on the Single European Act was submitted and endorsed by the Council. Scott also suggested that it would be beneficial to the union to develop a completely new course possibly entitled *Europe 1992 – Forward with the T&G*, supplemented by programmes for key personnel, officers, joint courses with employers and tutors' briefings.[37]

At the GEC in December 1988, the implications of the single European market were again discussed, and the Council approved a membership awareness programme. However, once again, little came of this except the inclusion of references to '1992' in education materials and the inviting of speakers on the subject to events like the summer school and national political school.

In the wider international field the strategy of taking education beyond the general 'Multinationals' course, was led by Fred Higgs, later General Secretary of International Chemical Frederation. Higgs had an excellent understanding of how educational methods could be used to strengthen trade union organisation, and as he took over from John Miller as COR National Secretary, began to apply this approach, initially organising a national seminar in January 1987 for oil refining representatives in the UK. John Fisher and Fred Higgs tutored the seminar and other speakers were Rita McNulty (later Rita Higgs), Les Ford, Harry Moore and John Miller.[38] Higgs then organised an international oil industry seminar at Eastbourne in October 1989. The aim of this seminar was to develop contacts between shop stewards at European level in order to build on the successful establishment of the UK National Oil Refining Combine. The seminar was attended by 17 delegates from the UK, 6 from Spain, 6 from France, and 3 from West Germany. Speakers were Serge Christian (EC Commissioner), Alex Falconer and Alex Smith, (MEPs), Franco Bisegna (Secretary-General of the European Mine, Chemical and Energy Workers' Federation,) and Ron Todd, General Secretary. The programme looked at the '1992 Challenge', European trade union structure, developments in the European oil refining industry, the single market and 'how to jointly safeguard the interests of oil workers'. At the end, the delegates issued a declaration dated 6 October 1989:

> We, European delegates from the oil refining Industry recognise
>
> 1. That with the approach of the Single European Market in 1992 the need for co-operation between unions at European level is greater than ever.
> 2. That union co-operation is continually necessary in order to counteract the transnational organisation and activities of the oil companies.
> 3. That trade union co-operation is a vital ingredient in developing a process of harmonisation of wages and working conditions throughout Europe.

The European Works Council Directive became mandatory in September 1996, and by that time the union had already been involved in the establishment of Works' Councils in General Motors, Unilever, United Biscuits, ICI, Coates Viyella, BP Oil and other companies. Employers were required to pay for EWC training and John Fisher proposed that the union provide regular training for EWC members.

Again, Fred Higgs was quick to move, and in September 1995 a company-specific EWC training course was held for ICI shop stewards at Stoke Rochford with Les Ford and Gary Herman from the Labour Telematics Centre, who provided training in the use of e-mail for international communications.[39] This was followed with a course for the ICI European Works Council held in December 1996 with delegates from France, Germany, Ireland, Netherlands, Spain and the UK. In March 1996, a European Works Council Support Group was established through the Research and Education Department in order to provide information to TGWU EWC delegates. EWC training, however, became established as a core part of the national programme, supplemented by courses for specific company EWCs such as Coats Viyella, Calsonic Radiators, BOC, Autobar, Cargill, Gallaghers and Zeneca.

Another specific development was the piloting of the IFWEA International Study circles (ISC) project by the union. This project was being promoted by Dave Spooner, a TGWU member, International Officer of the WEA, and later IFWEA General Secretary. The basic concept was to use the Internet to support discussion groups of trade unionists working in multinational companies in a number of different sites around the world. They would hold regular discussion groups then feed their views into the Internet, after which they could read the views of all the other participants and make contact. The countries participating were the UK, Sweden, Peru, Bulgaria, Belgium, Taiwan, France, Germany, Estonia, South Africa, Barbados, Kenya and Spain. The pilot discussion groups began in October 1997 in Region 1 and in the spring of 1998 in Regions 1 and 6.

The election of the Labour Government in 1997 presented the union with an opportunity to address the problems of globalisation and development on a wider scale than previously. Under the Tory government trade unions were excluded from the type of funding given to NGOs, and from the development agenda. When the Labour Government was elected, trade unions were again included and, on the strength of the union's involvement with the ISC project, John Fisher was invited to join the Department for International Development (DFID) Development Awareness Working Group, and DFID agreed to fund a pilot course on globalisation at Eastbourne in November 1998.

The Department for International Development also created a Development Awareness Fund, and in 1999 the union was awarded £200,000 to run sector courses on globalisation and development, produce material for the Internet, and run events at the 1999 and 2001 BDCs. A steering group was established, involving National Secretaries, Dave Spooner and representatives from international trade secretariats and unions in the developing world; and Sharon Wentworth (formerly a Region 1 tutor) was employed as Project Development Worker. An exhibition was organised for the 1999 BDC, and the first course, for the Food and Agriculture Sector, was held in November 1999, followed by a course for regional tutors in February 2000, and for textile workers in November 2000. Courses for the chemicals and transport membership were planned for 2001. This project put the TGWU in the forefront of this type of education work, and the Department was making plans to extend its work on the agenda of Core Labour Standards and the trade union perspective on globalisation.

WOMEN'S AND EQUALITIES EDUCATION 1992-2000

Women's education in the TGWU had an important year in 1992. In July Bill Morris requested that there should be a post of National Organiser. This was agreed by the Council, and in September, Margaret Prosser was appointed.[40] In June 1993, the GEC interviewed four candidates for her replacement: Carol Forfar, Region 7; Diana Holland and Pam Tatlow, Region 1; and Maureen Twomey, GEC member, from Region 6. Diana Holland was appointed from 26 July 1993. Thus someone with a background in TGWU education took up the position as the leading women's officer in the union. In September she submitted her first report to the GEC from the National Women's Advisory Committee and included specific references to the importance of education in building women's organisation.[41]

In 1992 Joe Irvin met Margaret Prosser and Bob Purkiss to review the spread of equalities education, and he also met the officers responsible for Regional Race Advisory Committees. It was noted that some regions were providing only minimal equal opportunities education or were not achieving a satisfactory participation of women and ethnic minority members, and monitoring was patchy. The emphasis was placed on Equality at Work courses and membership involvement courses as being part of the core provision, and therefore REOs were asked to provide them without asking for a special budget. In February 1994, as a contribution to this exercise, the Education Department had presented a statement to the Education Committee entitled *T&G Education and Equal Opportunities*. The document looked at course provision with the objective of gaining greater involvement of women and other under-represented groups, and included negotiating and representation courses on equal opportunities. It also proposed that equal opportunities principles be built into all courses, including shop stewards and health and safety reps' induction and more advanced training. There was also a commitment to target more black and women tutors and the monitoring of sex and ethnic origin of students attending courses, and that the timing, venue, advertising and content of course programmes be regularly examined to ensure they were relevant and attractive to all members.[42]

During the same period, the regions were implementing the decisions of the 1989 BDC and appointing regional women's organisers. Yvonne Strachan,[43] Avila Kilmurray, Muriel Mayor and Diana Holland were in place and Sylvia Greenwood was appointed in the new Region 8 in 1993 following the tragic death of Deborah Leon, RWO in 'old' Region 8. In May of that year, Carole Rowe was appointed RWO in the new Region 2, to be followed by Lindy Whiston in Region 5. Carol Rowe resigned in April 1994, to be replaced in January 1995 by Margaret Petts. In December 1993 Maureen Byrne was appointed in Region 1 to replace Diana Holland, and in March 1994 Mary Edwards was given the dual role of REO and

RWO in Region 4. In Region 3, Fiona Marshall was appointed as Avila Kilmurray's replacement in December 1994.

This impressive new structure had a major impact on the provision of education nationally and in the regions. The clear identification of equalities as one of the 'core' education subjects, and the requirement for REOs to develop women and black/ethnic tutors, led to a special tutor training course for women and black tutors in November 1992, in order to allow REOs to develop new tutors for work in the regions. An equalities course was also introduced as a part of the National Members' School, and a political school exclusively for women members was held at Stoke Rochford in October 1995, in order to prepare women members of the union to develop skills for greater political involvement. In February 1996 the Department organised a full-time officers' course in order to assist officers in the special problems associated in representing women members.

In 1997 women's courses were restructured as *Women at Work* and *Women Beyond the Workplace*, the former based on workplace issues, and the second geared to wider issues and encouraging women's involvement in the union; and a dedicated women's tutor, Sue Rubner, was appointed to the Education Department. A major project for education was supporting the sexual harassment network, a service for women members who had been sexually harassed and wished to speak to a woman, in circumstances where most TGWU shop stewards and officers were male. Sexual harassment support training took place for RWOs in December 1995, followed by training for 'facilitators' for the network (mainly regional tutors) and members of the network, ordinary women members.

In 1997 the Education Committee accepted the proposal that there should be a National Members' School exclusively for women. Bill Morris opened the first one in October 1997 and was willing to support an annual event. However, he and Diana Holland accepted John Fisher's proposal to hold the school every two years, running alternately with the union's Women's Conference. The creation of the industrial sectors provided another opportunity for development. A recruitment problem on women's courses had been the difficulty of linking them to women in the workplace through the union's industrial organisation. With 14 trade groups, it would have been too cumbersome to organise a course for each, but with only four sectors, this became a possibility, and in June 2000 the first women's sector course, for Manufacturing, was held in Eastbourne.

In the mid-1990s, the TGWU was a strong supporter of the TUC 'Unite Against Racism' and the Stephen Lawrence campaigns. In response to this, educational provision was patchy. A statement from the General Secretary condemning any racist or sexist harassment was included in all course materials, and some regions (such as Regions 1, 8 and 5) had regular courses for black and ethnic members. A national black and ethnic minority workers weekend was held in Eastbourne in December 1994 and repeated in November, 1996, and a course for black women TGWU members was held at Eastbourne in October 1998. In September 2000, Bob Purkiss resigned, and Diana Holland was beginning the new task of developing the new Women, Race and Equalities Sector with a policy of positive mainstreaming, whilst retaining the identity and the strength of the Women, Race and Equalities organisation within the union, and taking on board the growing diversity, including young members, lesbian and gay networks.

CONCLUSION

The 1990s began with the union's education service being brought up short by the financial crisis facing the union, a crisis which it had previously ignored while in the process of forging ahead with new developments and assuming that the union would support an ever-increasing provision. The initial shock of accepting the discipline of budgets and the cuts of 1992 was replaced with a determination to continue to expand and diversify the service, but to avoid placing an undue financial burden on the union. This involved seeking external funding for as much as possible of the provision, whilst retaining both control and the maintenance of the union objectives for the courses.

The main sources of external funding were employers and the state, both directly through grants and more importantly through accredited partnerships. In 1998, whilst education expenditure totalled over £1 million, less than £400,000 of this came from Central Office direct, although the union spent a great deal more supporting the education infrastructure.[44] So, by the end of the decade, with the union's membership being around 880,000, overall student numbers were still around 10,000, a remarkable achievement considering the fall in membership and the reduction in expenditure, although the financial basis of the programme had been fundamentally altered. The attitude of the active membership and GEC was completely supportive throughout the period. The union's education programme was last put to the membership at the 1997 BDC, where a comprehensive resolution re-affirmed the support of the membership:

> This Conference congratulates the GEC on its support for the T&G education programme, in spite of the Tory attack on public funding provisions, and calls on the GEC to maintain T&G education programmes at least at its current level for the forthcoming biennial period. Innovations such as accredited courses, lay organiser training, European Works Council delegates' training and education for the Sexual Harassment Network show that the T&G is in the forefront of trade union education ... Conference states that in remembering the

> aims and struggles our union has striven to bring to fruition in its 75 years history, and in order to prepare our membership for the socialist dream we aspire to in the next millennium, pledges that trade union education remains high on our agenda.[45]

The resolution went on to call for more paid educational leave, wider public funding support, accreditation, and employee development programmes.

Up to the time of writing, the union has not been called on to bear the full cost of the education programme, as employer funding and state support through accredited partnerships have remained in place. One of the biggest growth possibilities for the future will be the new sectors, and especially the link between industrial and equalities sectors. Courses such as 'Women in Manufacturing', and 'Young Workers in Services' will be necessary both as a way of developing the sectors, targeting the new groups in the union, and as a core part of the union's organising agenda. If the union is going to recover its membership, and if a new organising strategy is to be brought into the union, then education and training will have to play a central role in its development.

NOTES

1. F&GP, 10 October 1991, Minute No 608, p171.
2. GEC, 12 and 13 November 1992, Minute No 696.
3. National Education Department Report, 4th quarter 1986.
4. The overall cost of weekend schools was £212,373 from June 1986 to June 1987.
5. Education Committee, 23 February 1987.
6. In the event, this did not happen, as Joe Irvin sought and was allowed that there would be no absolute cash reduction in total annual budget for a region after year one. (Comments from Joe Irvin, October 2001).
7. Document dated 28 March 1980, 'Education and Training Policy Draft'.
8. Ibid., p3.
9. Ibid.
10. Ibid.
11. Interview with Joe Irvin, 3 October 2001.
12. Bob Rolfe died 3 July 1991. Bob Harrison had reached retirement and stated that he was leaving the job with regret. 'He expressed his concern over the direction the union is taking and the splits that are doing great harm to the organisation'. GEC 19 September 1991, Minute No 559.
13. GEC, 5 May 1993, Minute No 264.
14. GEC, 6 March 1995, Minute No 77.
15. Following the 2001 general election, Joe Irvin amicably parted company with John Prescott. He returned to the T&G as Head of Policy in 2004.
16. GEC, 6 April 1995, Minute No 208.
17. Education Committee Report, 21 November 1989, Minute No 2314.
18. Region 10 Education Report December 1989.
19. Minutes of the Education Committee, 9 February 1993, Minute No 2565.

20. Education Committee, 14 November 1995, Minute No 2742.
21. Education Committee, 21 May 1993, Minute No 2579.
22. Later London Metropolitan University.
23. See E. Capizzi, *Learning That Works; Accrediting the TUC Programme*, Niace/TUC, 1999.
24. *Review of Budgets and Educational Provision*, TGWU Internal Document written by John Fisher, 1999.
25. For the general experience of the union with HRM, see J. Fisher, 'The Trade Union Response to HRM in the UK: the Case of the TGWU', *Human Resource Management Journal,* Vol. 5, Number 3, Spring, 1995, pp7-23.
26. Region 3 Education Report, July/September 1984.
27. GEC, 5 December 1984, Minute No 987, p229.
28. GEC, 2 December 1986, Minute No 961, p244.
29. GEC, 16 June 1987, Minute No 513, p113.
30. Tony Woodley, *Quality of Working Life (QWL) – Quality Circles*, September 1987.
31. See I. Linn, *Single Union Deals*, TGWU Region 10/Northern College, 1986; N. Heaton, and I. Linn, *Fighting Back*, TGWU Region 10/Northern College, 1989.
32. Attached to Region 1 Education Report, October/December 1992.
33. Ibid.
34. Ibid.
35. BDC, 1993, Composite 5, New Management Techniques (Motions 11-26 and amendments).
36. F&GP, 9 January 1986, Minute No 13, p4.
37. Education Committee, November 1988, Appendix.
38. Report on National Oil Refining Course, Eastbourne, 19 to 23 January 1987.
39. Education Report, 21 November 1995.
40. GEC, 1 July 1992, Minute No 452.
41. GEC, 21 September 1993, Minute No 613.
42. Education Committee, February 1994, Minute No 2629.
43. In 1999 Yvonne Strachan resigned to take up a position with the Scottish Parliament, and in 2000 Joyce Maginnes, from Dundee, was appointed RWO.
44. John Fisher, *Review of Budget and Educational Provision*, internal TGWU paper, 1999.
45. BDC 1997: motions 374 to 384 and amendments to 374; 375; 376; 377; 378; 379; 380; 381; 382; 383; and 384.

Chapter 9

Regional Education 1980–2000

This chapter looks at the progress of education in the regions up to the year 2000. Each region has a different story to tell, reflecting the overall regional diversity within the TGWU as a whole. There was more diversity in the 1980s, in part due to the absence of any real financial control, whereas in the 1990s the system of budgetary supervision and the core principles laid down by the '1992 Guidelines' resulted in a relatively standardised provision at the basic level, with innovations and regional initiatives as add-ons. However, it has never been the case that a TGWU member has been offered or received exactly the same educational opportunities, regardless of their regional membership; the factors governing the provision of union education are too complex, and too political, for that ever to be the case. The chapter looks in detail at this process within each of the regions, and brings the story in the twentieth century to a close.

From the appointment of the REOs at the end of the 1970s, the main volume of TGWU education passed from the national level to the regions, where it has remained. Each region developed at its own pace and with a particular character to its education programme. In quantitative terms, this meant that in any one quarter or year there would be a significant difference in the number of courses offered and/or carried out, and also, of course, in the number of students. At the mid-point of the 1980s, in the winter of 1985, the union provided a total number of 284 courses with 4,623 students, of whom an average of 22.4 per cent were women.

Throughout the 1980s and 1990s, various attempts were made to 'standardise' both the administration and one or more of the courses taught in the programme. Although the former attempt was successful, in the latter case there was very little standardisation. By the mid-1990s, all regions were carrying out the same core programme of courses, but the scope and character of these and the materials varied, and beyond the 'core', regional programmes were quite different. This was not necessarily a concern, as an amount of regional autonomy is essential to the character of the union as a whole, and the education programme was reflecting this. Also, the diversity encouraged innovations and spread

Courses and students 1985

Region	Courses	Students
1	42	484
2	29	256
3	36	619
4	21	225
5	14	229
6	46	1,531
7	31	429
8	14	183
9	18	230
10	11	184

(Source: Regional Education Reports, 1985)

best practice. It did mean, however, that TGWU members in some regions had access to a much wider and more varied programme of education than those who happened to live in another region.

In general, regional education provision flourished during the 1990s. The changes introduced in 1992, particularly the budgetary mechanism, led to a cut in Central Office funding, but the stability of the budgetary process and the expansion into accredited partnerships and joint work with employers more than made up for the shortfall in funding, and also led to an improvement in the quality, standardisation and relevance of most regional programmes. The team of REOs also remained relatively stable, with six out of eight regions beginning and ending the decade with the same REO as they began it, and only Region 6 having a major reorganisation, and then one which benefited the education programme in the region.

Overall student numbers throughout the period remained at around 10,000,[1] and expenditure on education also remained relatively static, with a high-point in the early 1990s. In 1982 it totalled £554,954; in 1985, £396,000; and in 1998-1999, £545,000. The new budgetary system of 1992 introduced a reduction in regional education expenditure of £103,000 from £443,000 (net expenditure after public fund return) to £340,000 – a cut of 30 per cent. National expenditure was reduced from £443,000 to £340,000, a cut of 149 per cent.

Regional expenditure through to 1998-99 was as follows:

Central Office Education Budget (£000s)

Region	1995-96	1996-97	1997-98	1998-99
1	150	143	146	150
2	57	60	62	64
3	24	29	30	31
4	28	28	29	30
5	48	63	65	67
6	68	70	72	74
7	27	28	29	29
8*	94 (73)	94 (73)	96 (72)	99 (est. 75)

Central Office Education Budgets
* As this region returned £21-24,000 to CO, this could be deducted from the above figure; i.e. £21k for 1995-6 and 1996-7 and £24k for 1997-8.[2]

As has been seen throughout this narrative, regional diversity is a complex process made up of a wide range of factors linked to the overall character of each region and its key personalities. Much regional activity in the 1990s was dominated by the development of accredited partnerships, and meeting the new requirements of equalities education and joint training with employers. I will take a detailed look at the other main events in education in each region.

THE SOUTHERN REGIONS 1, 2 AND 3

In the early 1980s, there were more than 400,000 members in Region 1, which included such TGWU strongholds as the ports of London and Felixstowe, London Transport, Heathrow and Gatwick airports, Ford of Dagenham and Vauxhall of Luton. There were also substantial bodies of membership in local authorities, the voluntary sector, oil and chemicals, construction and agriculture, all linked with an enormous membership in distribution and food and drink.

Barry Camfield was appointed REO in November 1978 with the support of the Regional Secretary, Sid Staden, who himself was appointed only in May of the same year. Staden was a lifelong Communist[3] who came from the Lightermens' Union. Although he had no experience of the type of education then being developed in the TGWU, he understood its progressive nature and was prepared to support it in principle and without suspicion. He also recognised the potential in Barry Camfield, and they developed a very close relationship which gave a supportive core to developments in the regional education programme. Initially Barry Camfield had taught courses himself, beginning with a week-long course at Freeman's Catalogues in Clapham. Having spent a week with 15 shop stewards, he realised that one person would never be able to provide a programme necessary to cover the hundreds or even thousands of potential students in Region 1, and that his job would have to be administrative and supportive of a team of tutors.[4] It was fortunate, therefore, that he was able to call on John Fisher and Pete Batten at Surrey University. As a result, an ideal situation of trust and innovation developed, which led to solidity and regularity in the basic programmes and creative thinking to meet new challenges.

The early schemes of 1980 were over-ambitious, and many courses had to be cancelled. The groundwork had to be done to convince district officers that a relevant quality programme could be delivered, but by 1982 the region was providing about 30 courses for 300 students per quarter. However, by the summer quarter of 1984, this had grown to 84 courses with 445 students. A number of district offices around the region were equipped with whiteboards and overhead projectors, and later with flipcharts and video equipment, and the clerical staff were prepared for their regular use at course venues. Apart from the regional office, the main centres were Stratford, Gower Street (Central London), Southall, Clapham, Chatham, Ipswich, Cambridge, Brighton, Eastbourne, Norwich and Luton, concentrating on shop stewards' and safety reps' courses, usually of two or three days' duration.

The innovations of the 'distance-learning' course and the regional political weekends have already been noted, but another important development was in the in-plant courses that were vital for such an important and far-flung industrial region. Courses were provided on-site, and in the early 1980s regular courses were held in companies such as Felixstowe Docks, Lyons/Tetley in Southall, Aviation Traders in Stanstead, Chivers/Hartley and May & Baker in London, and Wall's Meat in the Home Counties. Other regular venues were Bernard Matthews, Greene King, Berger Paints, the Wellcome Foundation, and International Distillers.

The mid-1980s brought a change in the leadership of education and of the region as a whole. In July 1986 Sid Staden made an application to the GEC for the upgrading of Barry Camfield, making reference to the growth of the Education Department and the additional responsibility this placed on the REO. This was agreed by the GEC, thus establishing an REO as a senior officer.[5] A month later Paul Bonython, Regional Organiser, announced his resignation from the union from March 1987. Consequently, with Staden's support, Barry Camfield was appointed Regional Organiser from 20 October 1986. Staden himself was on the brink of retirement, and in September 1987 Ken Reid, then National Officer in Power and Engineering, was appointed Regional Secretary.

This left a vacancy for the position of Education Officer, and with the support of Barry Camfield, Pete Batten was appointed from 5 January1987. Pete Batten had been a district officer in Southall since

1985, but before that had been a convenor, national and regional committee member (in Region 2) and then a full-time tutor at the University of Surrey. He had been one of the key tutors in developing the Region 1 education programme under Barry Camfield, and in the expansion of the national courses at Eastbourne and Cirencester. Ken Reid, although originally from Region 1, was politically out of sympathy with the progressive left-of-centre regional committee, but was canny enough to realise that officers of the calibre of Camfield and Batten were quite capable of taking a national lead in their fields, which would reflect well on the region and thus on himself.

Pete Batten set about firming up the relationship with Surrey University, and in the later 1980s he and John Fisher had a strong tutor team. The full-time tutors, though formally self-employed, were organised and paid through the university on a regular basis. This gave the region tremendous flexibility, as the REO could call on a number of qualified and experienced tutors at any time and for any location and have professional development support from the university. Adrian Weir, a former AUEW steward from Southampton, who then qualified at postgraduate level at the LSE, joined the region in 1983 as research assistant to the regional secretary, and remained as a key person in the organisation and support base for the education programme, teaching law and assisting in the administration of a very large programme. Also essential to this success was Petrine Picard, who was the staff administrator under both Barry Camfield and Pete Batten, managing a hugely complicated system of educational finance. The result was an expansion in both quantity and scope.

Innovations included Labour History courses and the systematic approach to employers to allow an on-going and comprehensive education programme for their stewards, safety reps and sometimes ordinary employees, on a long-term basis. In the later 1980s, such employers were Polygram, Bernard Matthews, Vauxhall Motors, London, Eastern Counties, East Kent and Southdown Buses, Unigate, Suffolk Sovereign Chickens, Cereal Partners (Nabisco), Courage, Guinness, Shanks McEwan, (waste management), Kodak and Eternit Building Products. Such provision rose from 10 per cent in 1984 to 40 per cent by 1990. In December 1989 a British Airways course was held at the Eastbourne Centre, one of the first joint courses involving senior management. An initial contribution of £10,000 from London Transport established the principle of employers funding long-term and systematic joint work with the region, and this formula was to be applied on a grand scale in the 1990s.

Region 1 courses and students

Year	Courses	Students
1983	112	1,256
1987	165	1,856
1990	223	2,341
1991	242	2,797

(Source: Regional Education Quarterly Reports)

Region 1 continued to provide a comprehensive education programme under Pete Batten throughout the 1990s. In the early part of the decade the region taught between 2,500 and 3,000 students per year on about 250 courses. By the early 1990s its in-plant programme was already comprehensive, with companies such as Vauxhall Motors, Sovereign Chicken, British Airways, Heinz, Servisair, Romford Brewery, Glaxo, Cape Boards, IBC, Mercedes-Benz and many others as regular partners in joint courses. Some companies such as Fords, Wellcome and Brittania Refined Metals opted for comprehensive training on health and safety, including not only representatives but also management and ordinary shop-floor workers. In the public and voluntary sector at this time the region provided regular courses for English Church Housing and the Boroughs of Greenwich and Waltham Forest, London Luton Airport and many divisions of London Transport.

The region's education department continued to provide political schools, and equal opportunities courses were beginning to be provided for specific companies such as Selkent Buses. There was also a basic skills day school in March 1992 for 19 students, looking at adult literacy with the targeting of workplaces where some of these skills formed part of the union's collective bargaining agenda. The region also provided speakers to secondary schools at this time. In the final quarter of 1991, for example, there were 43 school visits reaching 3,396 students, and in the first quarter of 1992 there were 75 visits to 2,817 students. School tutors included Gary Hosgood (later a full-time tutor) and Stan Nattrass in the Littlehampton Area, along with Richard Nicholas, Sharon Wentworth and Sue Gwillim.

The region engaged in a number of major international initiatives in the early 1990s; for example in March 1992 it joined with the French CFDT on an EU-funded project, and the first meeting, in Lille, was attended by Pete Batten and Pepe Garcia from Vauxhall Motors. This work was given a boost in 1994 when Les Ford, then a Region 1 tutor, was asked by SERTUC to become the UK EURES Advisor, a role funded by the EU and concerned with the trade union aspects of the cross-border European zone involving Kent, Nord-Pas de Calais, France, West Flanders, Belgium and Hainault, Holland. In 1996 Les Ford was to bring this role with him into the National Education

Department, but still assisted Region 1 in developing links with its near-neighbours. Linked courses with the CGT and CFDT continued into the new century.

Another important development in the early 1990s was the building of a specific link between education and recruitment and organisation. Whilst this had always been implicit in the objectives of the programme, these new developments made it explicit. In his role as Regional Organiser, Barry Camfield had begun to build an 'organising strategy' for the region, his concern was that education should play central role in two main ways, 'branch regeneration' and the training of 'lay organisers'. This approach was extended into a basic workplace organisation course called 'Union Work at Local Level', which concentrated on recovering local branch and workplace activity. Lay Organisers are activists who are trained in recruiting and organising techniques, and a special programme of training, called 'Organise for Strength', started in December 1993, followed by a second course in June 1994.

As part of the course, students were sent out into Eastbourne with surveys and found that basically people were not anti-union, and some were even recruited. Following the appointment of Barry Camfield as Regional Secretary and Ken Fuller as Regional Organiser in January 1995, the programme of organiser training was stepped up. In 1995 the region set up a Membership Support Unit, and secured agreement for two women recruiter-organisers to be employed; and a series of one-day branch regeneration courses were held round the region, beginning at regional office in June 1996. In 1999, Barry Camfield's appointment as Assistant General Secretary responsible for organisation provided an opportunity to extend these ideas at national level.

The two pillars on which the region built its programme were the in-plant courses and the UNL partnership. The partnership with UNL gave employment stability to the tutor core, and students had the option to progress into the Certificate of Professional Development and the higher levels of education provided through UNL. Students were able to follow three pathways: Industrial Relations, Health and Safety and Trade Union Studies, leading into a University Foundation Award.

In Region 2, the education programme in the early 1980s revolved around the relationship between the REO, Bob Purkiss, and the group of tutors led by Basil Bye. Purkiss had established a regular programme of shop stewards' and safety reps' inductions in the major centres of Southampton, Portsmouth, Reading and Bournemouth, and occasionally on the Isle of Wight and in the Channel Islands. This was supplemented with special courses for major groups such as Ministry of Defence workers and *ad hoc* follow-on courses linked to Basil Bye's particular interest in issues such as European trade unions, industrial democracy and defence conversion, a continuation of his work in the 1970s around the Southern Region Trade Union Information Unit.

In 1982, Region 2 was providing around 30 courses and 300 students per quarter. However, these figures need to be treated with caution, as, along with some other regions at the time, they included TUC courses in which TGWU students participated. Apart from the district induction courses, company courses in this period included Metal Box, Dreamland Appliances, Cyanamid, Basingstoke, and Lord Mayor Treloa Hospitals. A total of exclusively TGWU courses would have been much smaller. The two tutors were Gordon Pointer, a former Royal Marine, then senior steward at the Sainsbury's depot at Basingstoke, and Jim Brown, senior steward at Pirelli in Southampton.

With a wider team to call on, Bob Purkiss was able to expand the range of the programme, and notable courses at this time were a negotiating skills for dockers course in Guernsey in the summer of 1987 and a residential course on multinational companies and international trade unions in September 1987 at the Avenue Hotel, Southampton. Regular MOD work continued at centres such as Aldermaston, Salisbury, Portsmouth and Aldershot. In 1987 Gordon Pointer was appointed District Secretary for Salisbury, and Jim Brown's stint as a tutor also lasted only a short time, and he was appointed a District Officer for Basingstoke in June 1988. Their place was taken by Carole Rowe, one of the first regular women tutors in the programme.

With the appointment of Bob Purkiss as national officer at the end of 1989, responsibility for education moved temporarily to Frank Dixon, a Bournemouth district officer, who had been seriously ill and who was given this responsibility as 'light duties'. Under this arrangement, the programme almost ground to a halt, as Dixon was unable to devote any real effort to it. This arrangement was ended when Gordon Pointer was appointed to the position of REO from 1 July 1991. Pointer brought a systematic approach to the programme, and divided the education venues into northern and southern areas. The northern part was based around Reading, having a catchment area which also included Abingdon, Aldershot and Basingstoke and the southern part based on Southampton covering Bournemouth, Portsmouth and Salisbury. He also pursued new companies in the later 1980s, especially Wyeths (Pharmaceuticals) and Dunham Bush, of Portsmouth, Courage of Reading, BDH Chemicals, Poole, Bordon Chemicals and the Ford Motor Company, Southampton. By this time, an average quarter provided courses for about 90 students. Thus the scene was set for the merger with Region 3, which gave a much wider base for the programme.

In Region 3, the South-West, the 1980s began without an REO of officer status, as education was handled by a staff member, Tom Carlyle. The problem with that arrangement was that in the structure of the union, the only persons with 'clout' were officers, and it was very difficult for a non-officer staff member to persuade them to support the education programme. The region also had a Regional

Education Sub-Committee, who directly influenced the provision on the basis of their own views and those who had elected them. As a result, rather than develop a comprehensive TGWU education programme, Tom Carlyle relied on the TUC, especially Pete Kirby, particularly in Bristol and Gloucester, and also WEA tutors such as Mike Nix, Dave Parker, John Sullivan and Bill Murray. The use of these tutors continued into the 1990s.

In 1982, following the merger with the Dyers' and Bleachers' Union, one of their officials, Harry Lees, was reallocated to take over educational duties from Tom Carlisle. Lees had been a senior steward in the printing industry and in engineering before becoming a full-time official in the Dyers' and Bleachers'. The pattern established by Harry Lees was to use the TUC for the basic 10-day shop steward and health and safety training. The region provided TGWU-tutored 3-day shop steward and health and safety day-release induction courses which had to be completed before regional authorisation was given to stewards to attend TUC follow-on 10-day courses. There was some in-plant work with companies such as ICI, Birds Eye, Lloyd Maunders, Cadbury, Heathcoats, Bendix, Exel Logistics, Whitbreads and St Ivel, and with public sector bodies such as the MOD and Bristol University. As Lees was at that time unable to use regional lay tutors – because there were none – he enlisted support from Barry Camfield's team in Region 1, supplemented by tutors from the WEA and TUC. After some time he was able to field a TGWU-trained team of regional tutors.

All 3-day courses were held in district offices and the appropriate FTO always took a session. A common venue for residential courses at this time was the Manor House Hotel, Okehampton, on the edge of Dartmoor, which usually hosted weekend schools. Examples in the early 1980s included 'The T&G and the Labour Party' in April 1984 which included MPs Jean Corston, Dawn Primarolo, Margaret Beckett, and Stan Thorne, or a course in 1983 'Has the Textile Trade Cleaned Up?' using Pete Kirby, a specialist on asbestos hazards. In November 1987, the hotel was also the venue for an International Trade Unionism residential weekend school, which included General Secretary Ron Todd, GEC Chair Walter Greendale, and Sylvia Greenwood as speakers. Other regular subjects were pensions, the law, and trade group issues such as taxicab organisation, 'cabotage' and the role of multinationals.

There were also some educational innovations in the early 1980s. A Home Study course study circle was established at ICI Fibres in Gloucester at the end of January 1987 for one-and-a-half hours per evening for five weeks. In Barnstaple, a monthly evening course 'Your Union at Work' ran for 12 meetings from January to December 1987, at the Holywell Centre, Barnstaple.[6] In Bristol, Unigate milkmen[7] came together at the end of their daily deliveries to study for 10 weeks from 12 noon until 2 pm. The Department also produced monthly health & safety bulletins which were widely acclaimed throughout the union. The region was also the first to convene an Annual Youth Forum, and five-day youth courses were held on university campuses during their summer shutdown.

In 1986 Ron Nethercott, the Regional Secretary, announced his retirement, and the GEC appointed John Joynson, originally from Birmingham but who was, at that time, a Region 2 officer in Salisbury. Whilst Nethercott had had an indulgent if quaint attitude to education, Joynson sought to dominate the programme, using the Education Sub-Committee as his vehicle, and began to clash with Harry Lees. From the appointment of John Joynson, the heart went out of the regional programme, and as morale declined, so did student numbers. The report for the final quarter of 1990 was the first one with no residential schools included, and reports show that whilst in 1985 the region provided 157 courses for 2,124 students, by 1987 the figure had declined to 108 courses for 1,326 students; 1988, 78 courses for 823 students; 1989, 55 courses for 639 students, and by 1990, only 49 courses for 501 students.[8]

The boil was lanced in 1992 with the merger of Regions 2 and 3, which created redundancy for John Joynson as John Ashman, Region 2 Regional Secretary, was appointed RS for the new region. In July 1992, Harry Lees was appointed to the position of Regional Organiser, and Gordon Pointer became REO.

In the newly-amalgamated region, Gordon Pointer struggled to overcome the different educational cultures carried over from the two previous regions. Since the days of Basil Bye and Bob Purkiss, 'old' Region 2 had been a centre for the provision of education by the union using TGWU tutors, whereas Region 3 under Harry Lees mainly used tutors from TUC-linked colleges, especially in Gloucester and Bristol. To import the Region 2 model, which Gordon Pointer wished to do, meant breaking old relationships and also left the region with a financial problem, as 'old' Region 3's budget was significantly lower than that in 'old' Region 2. This was due to TUC's provision and a generally low level of demand towards the end of the Joynson era.

'Old' Region 2 and 3 Education Departments formally came together on 1 April 1993. Gordon Pointer divided the region into eight education zones. In a sense this exacerbated the financial problems as it led to a requirement to offer courses in each zone on an even-handed basis and limited flexibility and the ability to merge recruitment areas.

A continuing problem for the region was the legacy of the previous relationship with the TUC colleges, and in 1995 Gordon Pointer gave notice to the TUC that the region would move away from the reliance on TUC tutors and use its own lay tutors, in line with the union's policy. These problems were only to be overcome in 1999 with the partnership with Southampton College and later with City College,

Bristol.[9] The region achieved some success in the area of recruitment and organisation courses where Harry Lees (Regional Organiser) and Gordon Pointer put on some successful events in Plymouth, Taunton, Reading, Bristol and Portsmouth. The first Lay Organisers' course was run in the spring of 1995 in Plymouth and brought together key local activists and lay recruitment teams to expand their organising skills. Region 1 undertook much of the work. This model was then applied in other districts, for example in Portsmouth in April 1996. International work, mainly through Basil Bye, continued on an *ad hoc* basis, with European Works Council and Arms Diversification courses and an EU-funded project based around Pirelli in partnership with Southampton College of HE in 1993.

The new region started its programme in a confused state. In 1992, in the January to March quarter, only one course from the programme actually ran, and only 6 courses ran in the next quarter. Gordon Pointer's target had been to try to run 100 courses with 1,000 students a year and by 1998, at the end of the third quarter, the region had run 108 courses with 1,034 students. The final quarter of 1998 provided 52 courses, the largest quarter since the formation of the new region.[10] This, however, led to new problems as the inherent financial difficulties of the region led to a budget overspend, with the new region running a continuous deficit budget from 1994-1995. Following a complaint to the GEC from the regional committee about lack of resources, Bill Morris set up an inquiry in January 1999. This found that there was no mismanagement of the programme or the education budget; it was simply that the education demands of the amalgamated region were far greater than first predicted when the old education departments were joined together.

THE CENTRAL REGIONS 4, 5 AND 6

In the Welsh region no systematic or structured programme was developed, mainly because the REO, Keith Jones, did not have the same freedom to organise as other REOs. Jones, son of a previous RS, Tom Jones, had started work with the union in 1968 as a member of staff in North Wales and did a variety of jobs, in particular in the legal department, dealing with injury claims and social security tribunals. He had started organising shop stewards' courses in Wales in 1973, as part of his administrative officer's duties for the Wales TUC. He was appointed Education Officer in 1977 but was based in the Cardiff district with membership responsibility. In fact, Jones was used as much as an assistant to the Regional Secretary as an REO. No regular TGWU tutor team was established, but at different times during the decade the region used Geoff Beattie (formerly with Basil Bye in Region 2), Terry Dillon from the University of North Wales (a former TGWU researcher) and Coleg Harlech's tutors, particularly Joe England, the warden, and later Sean Holford (also from Region 2) and a younger generation of officers and senior committee members with an interest in education, notably Mike Jeffries, Brian Apsley and Ann McCall, all from North Wales.

The *ad hoc* programme had a reasonably strong base in health and safety, and in November 1987 a course on new technology and payment systems was tutored by Dennis Gregory of TURU (Ruskin College). A course on 'Japanisation' with 17 students was held in March 1991 in Builth Wells with Nick Oliver (University of Cambridge) as tutor. In-plant courses were few and far between, in a region that was run very strictly on a district rather than trade group basis, making the bulk of courses geographically-based.

In the early part of the 1990s, Region 4's small education programme was essentially delivered by the TUC. A provision of about 25 courses per year mainly consisted of basic induction courses for shop stewards and safety reps. The union recruited for courses, met the cost of fares and nominal subsistence, and the TUC Education Department paid for the tutors. There was therefore resistance in this region to providing the range of courses developing in most other regions, particularly equalities. In the early part of the decade, Keith Jones had responsibility for the Women's Committee, as well as being general assistant to the regional secretary, while the RS resisted the appointment of a regional women's organiser. This arrangement lasted until March 1994, after which the TUC was not able to provide funding, and in anticipation of this the region then looked to appoint another REO/RWO. Mary Edwards was appointed to the position of Regional Education/Women's Organiser from 28 February 1994. Prior to this appointment Mary Edwards worked as a staff member of the union in North Wales and before that was a shop steward in industry. She was also given responsibility for ethnic minorities, youth and disabilities.[11]

Mary Edwards did an excellent job in involving women and young people. The percentage of women students in Region 4 went up from 6.6 per cent in 1996 to 25.5 per cent in 1999.[12] The number of courses and students in all subjects also rose steadily, from an average of five courses and 50 students per quarter in 1994 to 15 courses and 180 students by the end of the decade. She built up a small team of lay tutors, including Steph Greedy and Paul Lloyd (who later became TUC tutors); and she introduced Roger Pickering, a health and safety specialist, and Sean Holford, who later moved to Southampton College. Officers carried out other teaching. Two computer-training centres were established in the region in 1998 and 1999, one in Cardiff and one in Flint.

The equalities agenda progressed steadily, with regular young members' and women's weekend schools, and special events to raise awareness. An equalities course took place in Newport in July 1993, and a course entitled Equality in the Workplace was held in Llandudno in July 1995 attended by members of the Regional Race

Advisory Committee, Regional Women's Advisory Committee and the region's representative on the National Disabilities Committee. A young members' summer school was held in Coleg Harlech in the same month, and another in November. A seminar for employers on the subject of employment and good practice in race awareness was held in Cardiff, on 15 March 1996, the first time a seminar involving the unions, employers and CBI had been run on this subject. Speakers included Bob Purkiss, Anne Robertson CBI (Wales) and Glenys Kinnock, MEP. Representatives from the police, the Welsh Office and other government departments also attended.[13]

In-plant courses were provided on a small-scale but regular basis. The main companies were Calsonic Radiators, TRW Steering Systems, Express Foods Oswestry, Lucas Girling, Otford Specialised Moulding, South Wales Transport, various parts of the steel industry, and the RAC. Courses were also provided for South Wales Transport and other bus companies such as Cardiff Bus, and also in and the public sector, particularly RAF Brawdy and RND Trecwn, and local authorities such as Wrexham. At one stage the region became involved directly in European Works Council training when in 1992 a school was run at Coleg Harlech, which included Margaret Prosser and delegates from Ireland. This course was financed by money from Europe organised by Mike Jeffries, full-time officer from Wrexham. In 1993, a European course was held in Milford Haven for representatives of the oil industry, and in 1994, two one-day conferences on the European Union were held, one in Cardiff and one in Swansea.

REGION 5

The Midlands region is the union's second largest, and in the early 1980s had established a comprehensive and systematic education programme in which staff members Alan Tuckwood in Nottingham and Tom Cook in Birmingham were supplemented by occasional lay tutors such as GEC member Bill Donald from Alvis in Coventry (later an officer in Region 2) and Peter Whitehouse from Stoke, overseen by the then Regional Organiser, Ron Marston. The TUC also had a strong presence in the Midlands, and shop stewards from many of the large automotive and engineering plants traditionally used these courses. In the early 1980s, the region provided around 80 courses with 800 students each year. However, these numbers included TUC courses attended by TGWU members. Courses for shop stewards and safety reps were held in the districts and in-plant courses were a feature in such a heavily industrialised region. Typical in-plant courses in the early 1980s were for Jaguar Cars in Coventry, Reckitt and Coleman in Nottingham, British Leyland Longbridge and West Midlands Ambulance Service.[14] Later, companies such as Northern Foods, Pork Farms, Marston's Brewery, Carlsberg, Trent Motor Traction, Midland Red Buses, and Pilkington Safety Glass also agreed to in-plant training.

In the latter part of the decade a wide range of in-plant courses were provided, including Austin-Rover, Ford Distribution, Daventry, Walker's and Smith's Crisps, Leicester, Schlegels and Plessey, Nottingham, Nestles and Golden Wonder, Corby, and many others.

Although this was a reasonably wide-ranging programme, the region was weak in the equalities, political and longer course areas, and there was also a fundamental structural problem in the way the region ran its education programme. In the late 1970s, the GEC had indicated that each region should have an REO, but the Regional Secretary, Brian Mathers, backed by his regional committee, refused to have one on the grounds that the Region 5 system was an adequate way of delivering education in the region.

Ron Todd agreed to meet with Brian Mathers and the Committee gave him their support. Little came of these discussions, as the region simply refused to agree. However, the Centre kept up the pressure on the grounds that course administration was not being handled as effectively as it would be if there had been a dedicated REO.

Another concern was that whilst other regions with REOs were introducing innovations and seeking out new ways of reaching the membership through education, the system in Region 5 was a passive, demand-led system, and numbers began to decline after the initial 'rush' of the early 1980s. In the spring quarter of 1987 the region provided only 7 courses with 65 students, and a year later only 6 courses, again with 65 students. At this time the slightly larger, but comparable, Region 1 was providing 40 courses with 400 students each quarter. Brian Mathers retired in 1986 and Jim Hunt became Regional Secretary in September of that year, and in the winter of 1989 the region finally accepted the GEC position. In March 1990 Bob Sissons was appointed REO. Bob Sissons was a long-distance lorry driver from Nottingham and a regional committee member with no formal qualifications but a strong interest in and good understanding of trade union education. He was thorough and systematic, and began to construct a regular pattern of provision on a region-wide basis.

In the 1990s, the accredited partnership with South Birmingham College gave a solid base from which Bob Sissons gradually developed a successful regional programme. Two principal tutors, Nick Price (ex-Lucas) and Jerry Vernon (ex-Rover) were able to work full time on the courses, and both took the opportunity to gain postgraduate qualifications. These tutors were supplemented by a part-time team including Diane Douglas, Julia Long and Pete Malbasa (later officers), Simon Powell also became officer, Bill Rackham, Mick Thorpe, Chris Kearney, Steve Peacock, Mick Evans, Zaf Saleem and Monica Taylor (the first black woman GEC member). In the early 1990s the region was providing an average of 15 courses and 150 students per quarter, whilst by the end this had risen to more than 30 courses with 300 students, and in some quarters exceeded 40 courses.

In-plant courses were conducted with a wide range of companies, necessary in such a large industrial region. Some of the principal ones were Rover, Peugeot-Talbot, Midland Red, Carlsberg, Kays, Kraft-Suchard, HP Sauce, Courtaulds, Bass Breweries, Triplex, Sun Valley Poultry, Premier Brands, Nestle, Goodyear and Bridgetown Industries. In the public sector the region regularly provided courses for Coventry and Birmingham City Councils, British Waterways, Birmingham Airport, MOD Castle Donnington, RAF Stafford and the National Exhibition Centre.

Women's courses were also held regularly, supported by Lindy Whiston, the RWO, and tutored by Julia Long, Caroline Crolley (later, both officers), Sonia McDermott (later a GEC member) and Diane Douglas. In early 1992 a successful regional women's course was held at Stoke Rochford with 13 women attending. This exercise was regularly repeated, and in the winter of 1995-1996 a women's weekend dealing with sexual harassment was held in Birmingham along with an Action on Disability course.

A major project for the region was the special certificate course provided in partnership with the University of Warwick. This was introduced from October 1996 and offered 30 credits at level 1, and 30 CATS points. The target was 12 students a year, and assessment included the completion of a written project normally of 4,000 to 5,000 words, and a presentation. Students met monthly on seven occasions between October and May, and each student also carried out a personal project. The course started well, with a group that included several future tutors and officers. The 1996-1997 and 1997-1998 courses were completed with 14 and 10 students respectively. After two years, however, the 1998-1999 course had to be cancelled because of the small number recruited.

By the end of the decade Region 5 was regularly exceeding its largest quarterly total of courses and students, and the education programme had covered new areas such as branch regeneration, lay organiser training and IT training in a new centre in the regional office. The region's programme was threatened by the decline in manufacturing industry, but generally Region 5 had become a model of a mainstream union education programme responding to the needs of the members in the districts, not dependent on the TUC and with a firm link to an FE accredited partner. The main problem for the programme was that it was unable to find a secure link to an HE establishment to pursue 'lifelong learning'.

REGION 6

In the North-West, Region 6, because of the complexity of the situation in the region, a large number of officers and lay tutors took part in the programme in the 1980s; Jim Mowatt was virtually full-time on education, Martin Howard was part-time and Brian Dawson did very little education work. It was felt that Mowatt was the most appropriate person to cover the whole region, especially as he was experienced in terms of presentation of materials, syllabuses and the development of lay tutors.[15]

The approach was to run basic courses periodically in the main locations in the region, and then supplement these with a wide range of courses on subjects for which it was felt there was a demand, supplemented again by in-plant courses. So, for example, the first quarter of 1983 included an unemployed activists' course in the Liverpool office, district courses and in-plants at Manchester Airport, Shell Stanlow, Shell Chemicals Carrington, and Bass Brewery Runcorn, sick pay courses at Schweppes Aintree and Bird's Eye Kirby, and a shop stewards' course at BNFL.

The education programme also included a range of courses around political and community issues, some of which were in effect thinly-disguised campaign briefings. The official size of the regional programme in the mid-1980s was around 100 courses and 1,200 students per annum, but numbers were inflated by these events. An example was a one-day 'course' called Employment Legislation, held on 21 January 1985 at the Britannia Hotel, Manchester, with 200 students in attendance and Ron Todd as speaker.

A retired members' course with 46 participants was held at Stoke Rochford in October 1986 with the regional secretary in attendance, and a women's education event was held in the Merseyside divisional office, Liverpool, in October 1986 with 71 students and Margaret Prosser in attendance. Although these were important meetings for the development of the union, they gave an inflated picture of educational activity in the region.

On the other hand, there was some specifically-targeted education provision, such as work on arms conversion and nuclear power. Sometimes the target was recruitment, such as in courses provided for contract cleaners and bar staffs. In August 1987, a four-day school was carried out in Liverpool for contract cleaners with 14 in attendance. Other targeted courses were for Tetley Walker, Warrington, Vauxhall, Ellesmere Port, and Crosville Buses.

In June 1988 Mowatt was appointed to the position of National Officer of the Power and Engineering Trade Group, and in January 1989 Tom Hart was appointed REO. Tom Hart worked for AKZO Nobel as a chemical operator and works convenor and was dismissed for trade union activities. He was very much involved in the Labour Party and Trades Council in Rochdale, and sat on the COR Trade Group National Committee and the GEC as a trade group representative. He had a small part in the education programme from 1985 onwards as a lay tutor, and he increased the amount of political and community-based elements in the programme, by involving Les Huckfield, MEP for Merseyside, John McIlroy, and GEC member

Alan Quinn. New courses included one in June 1989 on the Single European Market, with Les Huckfield, and a 'course' on the Poll Tax in Walkden Labour Club in May. Hart also introduced Spanish language classes in Liverpool in April, May and June, and a German language course in April at the Mechanics' Institute in Manchester.

Other innovations included a Lancaster and Morecambe study circle run in January and February 1990, run by Dave Smith, a lay tutor from the Public Service Group, and a COSHH course in Liverpool in the same month run by Ann McCall. The most significant new course, however, was the Regional Residential Weekend School, first held from 7 to 9 September 1990 in Northern College with 71 students in attendance. Tutors included Bob Fryer, Principal of Northern College, John McKilroy, and Keith Bradshaw and Ian Lynn from the Northern College staff. It was repeated in 1991, when 73 students participated. Tutors included Marjorie Thompson, Chairperson of CND; Eddie Roberts, a Regional Officer; Maria Fyffe, MP; Bobby Owens, and a speaker from the Campaign for Press and Broadcasting Freedom.

Within a year, Hart had built up a large group of lay tutors. It was alleged that many of the courses were in reality 'tutors' meetings' and political campaign meetings, paid for through the education budget. In the early part of the 1990s the region was registering a very large education programme, for example in the last quarter of 1991 it provided 51 courses and 473 students, followed by 40 courses and 427 students in the first quarter of 1992.

The region also provided a wide range of activities on new management techniques, equalities and the political issues of the day. Hart continued with the Distance Learning Course, and in 1993, 13 students successfully completed the course and attended a week-long residential summer school held at Holly Royde College in July.

The programme also included work on European issues. Apart from European Works Councils, there was a course in 1992 examining the social dimension of the European Community and European directives. Another course, 'Europe and the Single Market', was run by John McIlroy from the University of Manchester and concentrated on the European Parliament.

In August 1994, Hart was summoned to a disciplinary hearing and confronted with a number of charges linked to: financial administration, the use of his position to support particular candidates for elections to the GEC, and giving his name to published articles advocating actions against the union's policy. After a long session, Hart offered his resignation, which was accepted by the General Secretary. He subsequently claimed unfair (constructive) dismissal, but in 1997 his claim was rejected by a tribunal in Birmingham. An industrial officer, Brian Dawson, temporarily took over the duties of REO. A dramatic confrontation over the issue took place at the Regional Residential School at Northern College on the weekend of 16 to 18 September 1994 when 44 out of 78 participants left the college at mid-day on the Saturday following a demonstration at a plenary session in support of Tom Hart, who had been barred from attending the weekend.[16]

Ann McCall was appointed to the position of REO from 13 February 1995. Ann had been a TGWU activist in Region 4, working mainly in the textile industry, and lately a TUC tutor at Liverpool Community College. She set about developing a completely new departmental plan. When Ann McCall, took over in 1995 the tutors' list consisted of 105 names, including 12 women and 4 black tutors.[17]

She established criteria which involved reviewing the huge list of tutors and as a result a new list of 32 tutors was drawn up which included 10 women and 5 black and Asian tutors. A regional lay tutors' course was provided for tutors who had attended the national course, but had never been used, and tutors who had tutored, but had never attended the national course. This course took place from 27 to 29 March 1995 in the regional office, with John Fisher. Those who had not attended the national course were required to do so.[18] A new team of tutors was built, beginning with Maria Smyth and Pat Connolly, and extending to Lorraine Taylor (Health and Safety specialist), Clive Grimshaw, Anita Jones, Jane Kinnimonth, Clive Rimmer and IT specialist Phil Kirshner. Tutors were offered D32 and D33 assessor courses run by the TUC on behalf of Wirral Metropolitan College, and were encouraged to take qualifications such as IOSH and computer skills certificates.

In August 1995 the Regional Secretary Bobby Owens died suddenly, and his replacement, Dave McCall,[19] extended the support for education in the region. Joint tutor development courses were instituted with Region 8, the first one being held at Higham Hall in Cumbria in March 1996. A meeting of REOs held in the summer of 1995 in Ripon had a major impact on the region, and encouraged Ann McCall to finalise the accreditation agreement with Manchester City College. In the autumn of 1997, Ann McCall introduced a new one-year advanced training course for senior representatives, which began with 17 participants and was designed to prepare those who wished to develop as full-time officers.

In-plant courses had not been a particularly strong tradition in the region, with both Tom Hart and Ann McCall preferring to develop community-based education initiatives with colleges and other partners. However, both REOs maintained a regular flow of a small number of company-based courses. The Sainsbury's courses were organised with full-time officer Paul Davies, who concentrated on recruiting in that company. From 1994, briefings were held for representatives from Sainsbury's not just from the North-West, but also from the Midlands and Yorkshire. In 1996 a residential course for 40 reps from the company was held in Liverpool including Regions 1, 4, 5 and 8. This campaign was later adopted at national level, and shop stewards' courses were provided at Eastbourne, supported by the company.

Region 6 maintained a regular involvement in the equalities agenda throughout the 1990s. In 1992 the region held a one-day seminar for Liverpool City Council shop stewards on race discrimination. One of the tutors was Eudora Okoro, one of the first black female TGWU tutors.[20] The region also held an annual women's residential conference beginning in 1989. In 1994 the event had 37 students and took place at the GMB College, Manchester, and the 1995 school had 65 in attendance. The conference continued as an annual event until 1997 when it became biennial, held in the year when there is no BDC. The tutors' team also maintained a high proportion of women even after Maria Smyth became an officer.

The region also moved into the accreditation of IT training, initially at RSA CLAIT level, in partnership with Manchester City College. Later, this was extended to IOSH, GCSE in Law, City and Guilds Computer Studies and the Integrated Business Technology IBT2 courses following on from the CLAIT courses. By 1999 a GCSE course on information technology via distance learning had 176 participants. The region also established a library in 1996, and in 1997 a second IT centre opened in the Isle of Man, followed by one in Preston in 1998 and Liverpool in 1999. The region also secured the support of the Stagecoach bus company and in 1999 introduced a mobile IT learning centre, using a converted bus.

Region 6 was the most successful region in accessing the Union Learning Fund. In 1998 it managed a project supported by money from the EU, with the objective of 're-skilling' former Liverpool dockers in IT and in D32 and D33 NVQ Assessors' Certificates. In the first round of ULF funding, in 1998, the region secured £50,000 to develop a project looking at the training needs of road transport drivers, a notoriously difficult group to involve in education. The results were both surprising and encouraging, as many drivers revealed a previously-hidden thirst for learning, particularly in IT and languages. As a result, the region was given strong support from road haulage companies, and also became a recognised centre for a road haulage NVQ. In 1999 the ULF agreed to an extension of the project for a further year with another £50,000, and in 2000 approved a national bid involving Regions 1, 2, 5 and 8 to extend the principle of this project throughout the English regions.

In the last quarter of 1994 the programme delivered only 9 courses with 134 students, but by December 1996, Ann McCall had built the programme up to 38 courses with 403 participants, the highest since 1993, and throughout 1997 the region ran 154 courses with 1,352 students. By mid-1998 the region was achieving the highest number of courses and course participants since the resignation of Tom Hart, with 55 courses and 508 participants, and on a much firmer educational basis. A deepening of the relationship with Manchester City College meant that some tutors were given appointments in the college. The four who were appointed were Pat Connolly, Lorraine Taylor, Phil Kirshner, and Jane Kinnimonth. The college also agreed to pay the wages of (a further 20) part-time lay tutors when they taught on accredited courses. Ann McCall developed one of the most innovative and diverse programmes of all the regions, exploiting to the full the possibilities of her links with the TUC, Manchester City College and the community.

THE NORTHERN REGIONS 8, 9 AND 10

Region 8, based at Newcastle, was a small region with a traditional right-wing regime, firmly controlled by Joe Mills, the Regional Secretary. The REO, Tom Nesbit, was innovative and progressive, and had a link with young academic tutors, mainly John Stirling and Doug Miller, based at Newcastle Polytechnic. Nesbit had qualified with the Open University, and had also built a local base in the WEA. Mills had been happy to have members of staff organising education under his control, and was always suspicious of Nesbit. This led to Nesbit's resignation, forced by Mills, in 1988, but in the meantime the REO enthusiastically set about developing an innovative education programme. He was elected chair of the Regional TUC Education Committee, and built his tutor team with a lay tutors' course in April and May 1984 in the regional office.

In the early 1980s, the region ran an annual residential school at Hatfield College, Durham. This offered a choice of courses, including shop stewards, health and safety, education methods, negotiating skills, and pensions, and usually around 100 students attended. In 1983, for example, the residential week was held during the run-up to a by-election in Darlington, and course members travelled to the constituency to help with the campaign and to boost Labour support.[21] In 1984 the school included a visit to Tyne Tees TV and a meeting with local mineworkers who spoke on the miners' strike, then at its height.[22] Nesbit continued the standard pattern of basic inductions in TGWU district offices supplemented by in-plant and regional advanced courses. In the early 1980s in-plant courses were held for Mono Containers, Stirling Organics, Catterick Garrison government workers, Winthrops, Steetley Brick, and Pirelli in Carlisle. There were also courses linked to campaign issues, such as a bus industry privatisation course held for Darlington district branches, and a management techniques course also held in Darlington in February 1985 with Doug Miller as the main tutor, and another course held in Chester-le-Street.[23]

In 1987 John Stirling was seconded to the region for a year to work on a review of the distance learning course and on developing trade union education material for use in schools. Mills was determined to remove Nesbit, and challenged him on the basis of an allegedly false declaration in support of a union mortgage. By that time Nesbit had become involved with an American academic from Berkeley, California, and it may be that he was not averse to leaving. He resigned in May 1988, went to the USA, where he enrolled at Berkeley, married his American partner, and became a professor in Victoria, BC, Canada.[24]

Mill's initial reaction was to move slowly in requesting a replacement REO, but in March 1989 Alan McGuckin was appointed REO to replace Nesbit.[25] McGuckin was a chemical analyst in the pharmaceutical company Sterling Organics, and a member of the ACTS National Committee and a Labour Councillor on the Militant wing. McGuckin was able to recover the situation somewhat by 1991, with the support of a new crop of officers and tutors, notably Mick Brider, Deborah Leon, Stella Guy and lay tutor Nick Portues.

In Region 9, the Yorkshire Region, the Regional Secretary, Mike Davey, was a supporter of trade union education, defined approximately on the WEA model of personal improvement. He therefore encouraged his REO, Phil Scott, but did not demand a systematic or comprehensive approach with clear industrial and political objectives. Scott, for his part, had very little previous experience in TGWU education, and was rather eccentric.[26] In the early years, he would train individual shop stewards on a one-to-one basis, resisted the use of written course materials, and had to be reprimanded by the Education Committee for sending in hand-written quarterly reports.[27] The focus on schoolchildren and trainees has already been noted, and this left the TUC and district officers to organise shop stewards' training, the latter on an *ad hoc* basis. This was supplemented by frequent and expensive weekend schools, usually at hotels in Bridlington or Scarborough. In a typical quarter in 1983, for example, there were only 3 courses: one trade group, one on SSP (sick pay regulations), and one on health and safety at work.

In-plants were mainly organised by local officers and included Tetley in Otley, John Smith's in Tadcaster, Hayworth Glass at Mexborough, ICI at Huddersfield and at KP Nuts at Rotherham, and Hickson and Welch, Castleford, which became a mainstay of the merged Region 8 programme in the 1990s.

The residential weekends were an important feature of the Region 9 programme. Typical events were those in 1987 beginning with an 'Organisation and Recruitment' weekend in April at the St Nicholas Hotel, Scarborough, with 45 in attendance, focusing on agriculture and bus workers. This was repeated for 87 students from the textile industry in May, with speakers including MPs Kevin McNamara and Max Madden, Bill Morris and Eddie Haigh.[28] This pattern continued to the end of the decade; many more residential courses were held at the St Nicholas Hotel, Scarborough, or the Monarch Hotel,

Bridlington. By the time the region was ready to be merged with Regions 8 and 10, the education programme had run into a blind alley. The new financial stringency had forbidden the extensive use of residential courses, expecting the programme to be delivered locally and on a day basis. The REO's concentration on schools and youth, whilst laudable, diverted his time and energy from the establishment and administration of a firmly-based and credible shop stewards' and safety reps' programme throughout the districts. With the merger, the much more experienced and strategic Region 10 REO, Chris Russell, who was supported by the Left majority on the GEC, became the merged REO and Phil Scott became an industrial district officer. Alan McGuckin also became an industrial officer in Carlisle.

In Region 10, Humberside and East Coast, Chris Russell had begun his period as REO in a time of turmoil. After only 18 months, the Regional Secretary, Dave Cairns, resigned following a period of bitter conflict with officers and members of the regional committee, and became a manager with Manpower. Initially, Russell was supported by the previous unofficial 'education officer', Peter Grant, until his retirement, and also consulted Barry Camfield on the pattern of the Region 1 programme. At the end of 1980, in the interim period between Cairns's resignation and the appointment of Mal Snow as the new RS, the region was run by Ron Todd, then National Organiser, who was extremely supportive of Chris Russell and assisted in the development of an effective education programme.[29]

Much of the membership in the region was in large industrial companies, and in the early part of the decade Russell himself taught the shop stewards' committees, particularly BP, Reckitt and Coleman, Findus, and British Sugar Corporation. Union offices were also used for basic induction courses. Russell's approach at this time was to work in partnership with the TUC, who were well established in the region, to give the basic shop steward and health and safety training. In November 1982 the two institutions which had previously catered for Trade Union Studies, the Industrial Studies Unit at Hull University and the Trade Union Studies Centre at Humberside College of Higher Education, were brought under one umbrella. The TUC, having been convinced by arguments submitted by some major unions, including the TGWU, jointly designated both institutions as the Hull Trade Union Studies Centre.

A further resource for the region was Northern College, where courses began in 1983 on a residential five-day programme including economics and management strategies. A regional shop stewards' advanced school was held at Northern College from 21 to 26 October 1984 and a special school for agricultural and allied workers from 4 to 9 November 1984.[30] The partnership relationship with the TUC, WEA and Hull colleges worked well through the early and mid-1980s, with the region providing around 10 courses each quarter for about 150 students, with Northern College, and occasionally Stoke Rochford, being used for special courses on topical issues such as media studies, politics, change at work and 'compulsory competitive tendering'.

In the later part of the decade, however, the situation changed, and Russell himself identified a growing pressure on the programme from three sources. First there was the growing trend amongst employers only to grant paid release for basic induction and introductory courses for shop stewards and safety reps; second, the lack of adequate facilities throughout the region in different districts; and third, the availability of TUC tutors had become much more restricted as TUC course numbers declined and colleges came under pressure from cuts.[31]

The TUC, through its Regional Education Officer, Malcolm Ball, began to resent the exclusive use of Charlie Ferguson by the TGWU, and sought to force the TGWU back into the TUC programme. In response to this, Russell had to emulate the Region 1 experience and set out with an almost exclusive TGWU programme, using his own tutors. In 1987 Ferguson left Hull for a job at Coleraine University, and John Morrison of the WEA, also transferring to other work, recommended Mick Bond as a dedicated TGWU tutor. Bond was then an NUR branch secretary and Labour councillor in York who had earlier left the Army, joined NUPE as a hospital worker and attended Northern College, Warwick University, and Huddersfield Teacher Training College. He began teaching shop stewards' and safety reps' induction courses in the early summer of 1987 and soon became the principal tutor in the region. By 1988 Bond was the only tutor on most regional courses and had developed new education materials on COSHH and other health and safety issues.

The region was also a leader in making links with the rest of Europe. A course 'Multinationals and the Single European Market' was held in November 1989 in Hull with 15 students. In 1990 Russell was approached by the Waterways District Committee to undertake health and safety training in relation to the specific requirements of waterways workers. It was agreed to set up a Waterways Working Party to examine the particular problems in the industry. Dan Vulliamy of Hull University, who had already produced a health and safety programme for the National Union of Seamen, agreed to be involved, and a special report was produced. The Waterways Report included a discussion with local MPs Kevin McNamara and John Prescott, and 1,000 copies were printed jointly by the University of Hull and the union.[32]

In 1991 an application was made to the EC under the aegis of the European Year of Safety, Hygiene and Health Protection at Work. The application was successful and secured 14,000 ECUs (£10,000). Chris Russell and Dan Vulliamy made an explanatory visit to Duisberg,

Dusseldorf and Osnabruck in Germany, where they met with trade union officials, and to the European Trade Union College in Brussels. The grant funded two national waterways safety courses, the first held at Wortley Hall in Sheffield in September 1992 and the next in February 1993.

In November 1992, a further funding application was submitted to Europe for trans-national meetings between employees' representatives and 79,850 ECUs (£63,000) was awarded. In August and September 1993 Chris Russell visited the Dutch, German and Belgian transport workers' unions. As a result of their co-operation, two conferences were held in Europort from 13 to 15 October and 24 to 26 November 1993. The main items on the agenda were the framework of health and safety legislation in the member states and the Commission, consultation procedures, industrial agreements and the application and impact of European Directives on working conditions. In particular, the Working Time Directive and the draft directive on health and safety provisions in transport were discussed.[33]

As the merger approached, the region reviewed its advanced course at Northern College, which had fallen foul of the new financial restrictions on residential courses, and looked to develop a locally-based advanced course, which was piloted in 1990. It also increased its in-plant work with companies such as BP and Courtaulds Fibres.

THE 'NEW' REGION 8

In the newly-amalgamated Region 8, almost the entire decade was supervised by Russell, who only moved to the position of Regional Organiser in 1999, to be followed as REO by Mick Bond in April 2000. The new region came together in the early part of 1993, and it was difficult at first to provide a satisfactory programme. Out of the 37 courses offered in the first quarter, only 16 ran. There was a significant inequality between the number of courses and students in 'old' Region 10 and Regions 8 and 9; the last two being much smaller. Chris Russell at this point was defending tutors and his education system from criticism from the new regional committee, dominated by representatives from 'old' Region 9. Criticism was also being made about the extensive employment of Mick Bond as regional tutor, reflecting criticism made at the GEC Education Committee. However, this soon died down and the Regional Secretary, Mike Davey, became very supportive of Russell's programme. Shortly after the establishment of the new region, Ian Wood and Alan Middleton (later a TUC tutor) were added to the tutor team. Ian Wood in particular was to become a senior tutor in the 1990s, before becoming an officer.

Other steps to be taken were the standardisation of the programme throughout the region, the removal of inappropriate reliance on the TUC, and the progression towards accreditation. After almost a year, there were still difficulties. At the end of 1993 the region provided 20 courses with 215 students. However, 48 per cent of courses offered were cancelled because of lack of support. All six equality courses and half of the basic induction courses were cancelled.[34]

Russell established a systematic approach to training for stewards and safety reps. The four units of the basic shop stewards' training were 'Induction', 'Effective Communication', 'Workplace Bargaining' and 'Labour Law Update'. The safety modules were 'Safety Reps' Briefing', 'COSHH Update', 'Safety Audits and Risk Assessment' and 'Kinetics, Ergonomics and DSE', 'going under the more popular label of aches, pains and strains'. Other new courses covered 'European Issues' and 'New Management Techniques'.

By 1996 Russell and Bond were firming up the approach into a major joint training initiative with employers throughout the region. The final quarter of 1996 showed a 26 per cent increase on the same quarter in 1995, because of the growth in in-company training provision. Chris Russell argued that this, in turn, depended on the quality of courses and tutors:

> One of the first issues raised by companies who are examining the possibility of using the T&G's training facilities, is the standard/qualifications of the tutors. All of our tutors are recruited from the broad group of T&G activists through a clearly-defined development route which can result in them qualifying in certain specialist subject areas such as Health and Safety, Personal Safety and obtaining recognised teaching qualifications. Not only does this enable the T&G to be seen as a professional training organisation, but also provides a visible example of how we can establish a meaningful partnership with employers and provide the workplace organisation with a positive profile.[35]

By the end of 1997 the region was organising a conference – 'New Partnerships for Training and Development' – held at the East Durham Community College, Peterlee, on 26 February 1998. The conference was attended by 250 participants, including 217 delegates from 57 private sector employers. This was timely, as the day before the event the government published its Green Paper on Lifelong Learning, *The Learning Age*. Speakers at the conference included Bill Morris, Tessa Blackstone (Higher Education Minister) over a videolink, John Fisher, the Chair of the local TEC and Stephen Hughes, MEP. Although this conference was a climactic event, the standard of involvement with employers and joint training did not fall off, and was maintained into the new century, where companies like Terra Nitrogen (formerly ICI) Billingham, Superlife Dairies, A.H. Marks, Bradford, and Federal Mogul (Ferrodo) at Chapel-en-le-Frith, Derbyshire, signed up for major partnership projects. Region 8 was also a regular contributor to education programmes supporting the equalities agenda.

In the spring of 1994, the new region organised a weekend school for the Regional Race Advisory Committee which included Bob Purkiss and Jack Thornley, solicitor on the case of Haggas, a current example of race discrimination in employment. Following these early developments, race equality became a regular feature of the regional programme, also with in-plant courses linked to the wider anti-harassment agenda. A boost to this aspect of equalities education was the appointment of Tas Sangha, a Sikh and former busworker, to the tutors' team. Tas Sangha contributed effectively to all aspects of the region's programme up to his appointment as an officer in Sheffield in October 2000.

The women's courses established in the 1980s continued and were integrated into the new region's provision. Region 8 regularly used women tutors, mainly Jane Blakeman and Maggie Hazlehurst, supplemented for short periods by Gill Hughes and Cyndi Beaver-Hughes.

The latter part of the decade saw the region become highly sophisticated in joint training. By mid-1997 in-company training represented 43 per cent of the total training provision, which by 1998 was averaging around 28 courses and 300 students per quarter. In 1998 the total number of courses held in the year reached 164 with 1,856 students. In the three-year period from 1996 there was an increase of 55.5 per cent in student numbers and 39 per cent in the number of courses held.[36] The region was also a leader (with Region 6) in developing education materials using computer technology. Chris Russell had been one of the first officers to regularly use a computer and Region 10, then Region 8, materials were smartly produced under this system. In 1998 computer training commenced in Leeds and Sheffield and in the same year £28,990 was secured from the Union Learning Fund for a project called 'Transferable Skills for Work-based Learning by Telematic Delivery'. Hull University also secured £50,000 from the European Social Fund for the same project. The project was used as a further link to supportive employers, connecting to their workplace learning centres.

SCOTLAND AND IRELAND REGIONS 7 AND 11

Although Scotland has had a trade union and political tradition in the Labour Movement second to none, in terms of TGWU education Region 7 has never taken the lead, and this situation was to be maintained through the 1980s and 1990s. There were a number of reasons for this; the very political progressiveness created a situation in which it was possible to be complacent and to feel that the traditional ways were sufficient. In Region 1 or 2, for example, the home of Thatcherism, something – anything – was better than the *status quo*. Scotland also had both the TUC and the Scottish TUC (STUC) providing courses, leaving less room for individual union initiatives, especially when the STUC had such a strong political tradition and its own education centre – Treesbank, near Kilmarnock – as a facility. In the early 1980s, the region provided about 14 courses with about 150 students in a quarter. During the first part of the 1980s, TGWU education in Scotland was dominated by Jimmy McIntyre, who combined his commitment to education with a responsibility for the Public Service membership and also with a leading political role in the region. He also expected full-time officers to teach union courses, regardless of their background or ability to teach, and the concept of lay tutors was never fully established in Scotland. McIntyre was suspicious of this concept, and felt that as education was an official business of the union, then officers (referred to as District Education Officers, although they were normal district officers) should lead it, with lay tutors in a subsidiary role.

The focus on the districts inhibited a region-wide approach, as each district was able to develop its own idea of an education programme. This was the system being operated by Jim McIntyre when he died of employment-related cancer on 12 October 1986. He was replaced by Lesley Sutherland, who had an entirely different background (in the voluntary sector), and who found it difficult to build credibility in this Left, but traditional, environment. Having requested an REO in the spring of 1987, the GEC failed to appoint a candidate in the summer. It was not until December 1987 that Lesley Sutherland was appointed, and she took up her duties in January 1988, the first woman to hold the position of REO. She was supported by the broad left on the GEC, and by its representatives in the region such as Willie Queen (later Regional Secretary). She was academically qualified and a trained teacher, with extensive language skills. She had been Research Officer for the National Union of Students in Scotland, and on appointment was Education Officer for the Scottish Vocational Education Council.

In the late 1970s Treesbank was used as a 'Scottish Cirencester', and during August a summer school was held there over 4 weeks. There were 112 students, including members drawn from Regions 8 and 9. The courses were directed by Jimmy McIntyre and full-time officers from Region 7. The region even asked for follow-on provision, but in the mid-1980s applications began to dry up, as employers became more confident in refusing release for week-long residential courses.

A more fertile seam was the work based on the two tutors at FE colleges providing TUC courses Tony Kinder of Falkirk College of Technology and Mike Morris of Lauder Technical College, Dunfermline. The link with the TUC was facilitated by a special agreement from 1984, which used the TUC for exclusively TGWU in-plant courses, something which in England the TUC was reluctant to provide at this time.

Morris was an innovative and energetic tutor who used modern methods and was able to respond to specialist demands from the region. Kinder, though less bankable, was also in a position to provide courses. There were also other TUC tutors at centres such as Stevenson College in Edinburgh. Apart from the normal day-release courses, these tutors also provided weekend schools on issues such as pensions, company accounts, disclosure of information and change at work. They also had access to EU funding, and in 1984, for example, ran courses funded from this source on collective bargaining and the role of multi-national companies, comparing British and other EU experiences.[37] However, because of the reliance on the college-based TUC, in-plant courses were rare in the region. In January 1984, a health and safety course was run at Rosyth Dockyard, and sometimes courses were organised in the districts for particular groups such as chemical workers in Grangemouth or dockers in Glasgow.

Lesley Sutherland had a difficult task. The TUC courses continued, and there was no strong team of lay tutors on the Region 1 model to help her. Short of completely overhauling the system, which she did not have the seniority or the credibility to do, she had to find space in other areas, such as progressing the under-developed equalities agenda, along with the RWO, Yvonne Strachan. Issues such as childcare were introduced, and equalities course materials were issued as part of regional education, and a 'Women at Work' course was introduced from 1989 with EU funding. However, this activity ran the risk of stereotyping the REO as primarily concerned with equalities rather than industrial issues, which was a prejudice already held by some officers.

Without active support from the officers in the districts, such a systematic approach was bound to fail, and the region struggled to provide a comprehensive programme outside of the TUC. In the first quarter of 1990, for example, only two courses were run, and a number of courses planned for the quarter had to be cancelled due to insufficient registration. These included a health and safety induction course, bursting at the seams in most other regions, a COSHH course, and a shop stewards' course for the voluntary sector branches in the Glasgow district.[38] The range of in-plant courses was expanded; for example in 1989 at Patons & Baldwins, Alloa and Coates-Viyella and William Grant & Sons, Paisley. A four-day in-plant course tutored by Jimmy Livingstone, Aberdeen District Officer, was held at Sullom Voe, the Shetland oil terminal, and in 1990 there was a health and safety course at RAF Kinloss. In 1991, a study circle was set up at Michelin Dundee, and an in-plant at GE Plastics at Grangemouth. In 1991 it was announced that Treesbank was about to close. The TGWU tried its best to assist, at one point in 1990 organising joint district residential courses for the Aberdeen/Dundee districts and for Galashiels and Dunfermline at the centre, clearly not a genuine economic prospect. In circumstances where the TGWU was cutting down its own residential provision, it was difficult to sustain such initiatives.

Lesley Sutherland stayed on as REO throughout the new decade up to the autumn of 2000, when she took up an appointment in the devolved Scottish Education Administration. Some of the frustrations of the 1980s remained, and Region 7 continued to be the only region not to have secured an accredited partnership, mainly because of external difficulties with educational attitudes and administration in Scottish HE and FE colleges. The tradition of industrial officers teaching courses also continued, and whilst this may have led to some excellent local courses, it mitigated against a standardised programme for the whole region, and prevented the appointment of full-time dedicated tutors who would have been in a better position to develop new initiatives, as happened in other regions.

At this time the region was providing about 9 courses each quarter with about 100 students. A typical scenario for the time was the third quarter of 1993; 12 courses were organised but 7 had to be cancelled due to the shortage of students. The regular tutors in the programme remained in their normal employment and some became industrial officers; the most regular were John Cowden, Jackson Cullinane, (appointed REO in 2000) Ian McDonald (later an officer), Joyce Magennis (later RWO), Patricia Stuart (GEC member), and Jimmy Carmichael. Although the region was the base for Lesley Sutherland, Yvonne Strachan, Carol Forfar, Jane Mackay and other important women activists, it struggled to organise a significant equal opportunities programme.

At the end of 1999 the region was still providing around 10 courses for 100 students each quarter. The regional programme remained essentially shop stewards' and safety reps' inductions, with the occasional addition of an in-plant course. The reason for this state of affairs was the same as that in the 1980s; the tradition of local district control by industrial officers which included the running of education for the shop stewards in their allocation, and the unwillingness to give the REO a credibility sufficient to break this down. In the period immediately before Lesley Sutherland's resignation, efforts were being made to broaden the programme and in particular to secure an accredited partnership for the region. The new REO, Jackson Cullinane, is committed to bringing the region up to par with the others in this respect and the prospects look much better.

The Irish region, Region 11, was divided between North and South, and therefore had a complicated arrangement which sometimes involved the WEA, and at other times the Irish Congress of Trade Unions, ICTU. This complexity spilled over into the organisation and funding of ATGWU education. Therefore, although Sean Morrissey was the REO, he was based in the regional office in Belfast and concentrated on Northern Ireland. In 1981 the ICTU engaged an education officer, Mick Murray, an adult educator from the university sector, who was then seconded to the ATGWU and took up his position from the beginning of 1982. Murray wanted to develop a lay tutor team in the Republic, and in January 1983 a course for lay tutors with 12 students was held in Dublin with John Fisher as the tutor. Women members were put through an ICTU women tutors' course in February that year.

In the early 1980s Region 11 (North) provided 38 courses for 478 students each year and Region 11 (South) 10 courses for 180 students. However, many of these were provided through other agencies. Unusually in the TGWU, at this time the bulk of courses involved one day per week, day-release rather than block-release. Tutors were a mixture of officers and lay activists, including Mick O'Reilly, then Dundalk district officer, who became Regional Secretary, Liam McBrinn, who was to follow Morrissey as REO, Brendan Hodgers (also appointed Regional Secretary), and the late Malachy Gray, a long-term activist within the Irish region, whose name is now given to a seminar room in Transport House in Belfast. The region made use of sympathetic academic tutors such as lawyer Richard Steele and economists Mike and Hazel Morrissey.

In the Republic, the 1984 programme under Mick Murray provided 10 courses, attracting 142 stewards and leading activists. Mick Murray completed the year's programme by organising five courses in Dundalk, Donegal, Dunmore East, Clonmel, and Waterford with an aggregate attendance of 71 shop stewards. The union then discontinued its arrangements with Mick Murray, who left to take up an appointment for two years at Limerick University from September 1984, returning to ICTU as a core tutor. Joe Foley was seconded in his place, but he resigned from the position in 1988 after agreeing to become owner-director of Tipperary Crystal.

In July 1986 Sean Morrissey retired from employment with the union and the region applied to the GEC for the re-designation of Liam McBrinn as REO.[39] Liam McBrinn had been appointed a district officer in Belfast at the end of April 1984, covering breweries, hotel, catering and bar staff, but had already been involved as a lay tutor in the education programme. He was very much the choice of Sean Morrissey as his successor; he was bright and enthusiastic, on the young side of 40, and with an Irish CP background, politically acceptable to Morrissey and the Regional Secretary, John Freeman. McBrinn came from a Belfast docks background and had extensive industrial experience as an activist, holding nearly all the appropriate lay-member positions in the union, including representation for the RTC Trade Group on the GEC. The region argued that the legal, economic and political situation in Northern Ireland, and even more in the Republic, were different from the UK; also, it was difficult and expensive for large numbers of Region 11 students to travel over to Stoke

Rochford or Eastbourne. For these reasons, it was agreed that the region hold its own advanced residential course, and the first of these was held in June 1987 in Dun Laoghaire. The course attracted 26 members from Northern and Southern Ireland. McBrinn organised a second part of this school in September, with 30 students. The tradition of this school was maintained into the 1990s with invited guests such as Kevin McNamara MP, and representatives from mainstream left-of-centre political parties.

As McBrinn began to re-shape the programme, he increased the focus on equalities, particularly after the appointment of Avila Kilmurray. The women's courses have already been covered, but there were other aspects of equalities, such as one-day course on AIDS at the Royal Group of Hospitals in June 1989, with ICTU tutor Ann Hope and in the same year the region supported the ICTU anti-sectarian campaign called 'Hands Off My Mate'.[40] In-plant courses included health and safety for Plessey's in January 1986, a pensions seminar at Lambeg Mill in 1988, and in 1989 courses for Moy Park Chickens, Craigavon, and Du Pont, Derry, both in May. Much of the work on health and safety and industrial relations in the Londonderry district from the early 1990s was carried out by Ciaran Brolly, tutor at North-West College, Derry, who was to play an increasingly important role in the 1990s.

In 1989, under pressure from McBrinn and Freeman, the ICTU indicated its willingness to continue to support an education organiser in the Republic, and after the departure of Joe Foley and with the support of the region, Tom Moore was appointed to undertake and tutor TGWU courses in the Republic of Ireland, under the authority of the REO. Tom Moore came from a very active industrial and political background and was a full-time trade union studies tutor with WEA in NI. He also was active in 3/71 branch and a former shop steward in the meat industry, a member of the regional committee and the regional F&GP. He continued to deliver the regional education programme in the Republic, and also introduced some innovations, such as a pre-retirement course, held in 1989 at ICA College Termonfeckin, Co. Louth, with himself and ROI District Secretary Charlie Douglas as tutors. In 1989, McBrinn gained approval for the introduction of language courses in French, German and Irish on a region-wide basis. These ended in 1991 in the north, as due to civil unrest, people were unwilling to come into Belfast town centre in the evenings. However, the programme continued in the Republic until 1993 when ICTU provided its own pathway on a range of similar courses.

Tom Moore was a successful and professional organiser, but in 1992 he was appointed to a permanent position as the ICTU Education Officer in the North of Ireland. Tom Moore continued to work closely with McBrinn in his new capacity as NIC/ICTU education officer, and in 1995 the region engaged Pat Neill, from Clonmel, as a full-time tutor, mainly in the Republic.

Liam McBrinn remained REO throughout the 1990s and steadily expanded the programme, raising the provision from 4 courses in 1988 with 44 students to 74 in 1991 with 1,138 students.[41] The programme was taught by officers and a number of part-time lay tutors, notably Harry Taylor, Peter Black, Jimmy Kelly (later a GEC member) and Greg Sachno, originally from Region 1.

The region also maintained a systematic approach to joint training with employers and education on HRM and new management techniques. In 1992 a programme of training for Ulster Bus/City Bus was provided for five consecutive weeks, which included some membership education, beyond shop stewards, to the membership. Similar work was provided for Du Pont in Derry and Waterford Glass. A special Waterford Glass HRM course was held in December 1993 in the Clonmel Arms with Steve Turner (Region 1) and Pat Neill. John Fisher, and later Les Ford, came over from Central Office to work with the stewards from this company on Change at Work. Tony Woodley and John Fisher attended an HRM residential course held in Dublin in May 1995 which was also attended by senior stewards from all parts of the region. In 1996, the region established a senior shop stewards HRM forum, the first meeting of which took place on 16 February with an attendance of 15 representing the membership in Northern Ireland. In the Irish Republic, the idea of 'partnership' sponsored by the state was much stronger than in the UK, and the union participated in this, but sought to develop a trade union perspective on it – critical, if necessary, of the ICTU.

The regional programme was also strong on equalities, and the biennial youth school and annual regional women's school continued. In December 1994 the GEC appointed Fiona Marshall (later Fiona Cummins), previously a staff member in the region, to succeed Avila Kilmurray. In the middle years of the decade, following these developments, the region fell behind its own standard for women's involvement, and in 1996 the regional committee discussed a document from Liam McBrinn, called *Education and Women's Development in Region 3*. This paper noted that Region 3 had been the first to establish a regional women's committee ten years before, but that there needed to be a new boost for women's education in the region to increase the amount of specific educational development programmes targeted at women and setting clear targets for women's participation and development within the union up to the year 2001.[42]

In 1998 this aspect of the region's work was improved with the establishment of a European-funded Diversity Project. The object of this project was the delivery of a political perspective and future developments on the changing social/economic and political opportunities that were emerging as a result of the Good Friday agreement. The

ATGWU was the only trade union or organisation in Ireland to venture into this area of progressive, cross-cultural work that involved the participation of union reps, officers, staff, general membership and local communities. The project worker was a union activist and lay tutor, Theresa Kelly, from Derry.

Ireland is a country with a younger age profile than the UK, and the Irish Region continued to develop an active youth provision, with an annual youth school. The region also made a special provision for health and safety. In the early part of the decade Tom Moore translated the *Health and Safety Representatives' Handbook* from the British law into the 1989 Republic of Ireland legislation. In 1989 Liam McBrinn was appointed as the Chair of the NIC-ICTU Advisory Health and Safety Committee that expanded in the following years to become one of ICTU's most effective and successful committees. Having been one of the NIC/ICTU nominees to the Health and Safety Agency (NI), McBrinn was later nominated and appointed in 1999 as the first Chairperson (and Trade Union Officer) of the newly structured Health & Safety Executive for Northern Ireland. This was recognition of the good work of the region in this field.

CONCLUSION

Even from these brief summaries of education provision in the regions, it is clear that in the 1980s and 1990s regional TGWU education represented an enormous undertaking, with each region carrying out far more courses for a larger number of students, and with a much greater range of provision, than the union as a whole had carried out in its earlier years. This reflects the greater formality of education – defined in its widest sense – in the latter part of the century, as former 'educational' processes around workshop organisation, community and political party were weakened and replaced with union education based around day-release. There is no way of measuring or comparing the 'effectiveness' of these processes over time, and in order to maintain its organisation and meet new challenges, the union had no choice but to replace the previous processes with new ones.

The great diversity of the provision, highlighted in this chapter, reflected the various balance of political forces and traditions within each region, and the varying strength of the various lobbies requiring educational support in achieving their objectives. It also reflects the particular formulation of the REO's role as set out in the '1992 Guidelines'. These make it clear that the regional secretary, not the director of education, is the immediate supervisor of the REO, and the quarterly report presented to the GEC Education Committee is only a copy of the REO's report to the regional committee. The GEC members themselves, of course, are also firmly rooted in their regions and depend on them for their political base. In these circumstances it will be inevitable that the REO will be far more influenced by pressures in his or her region than by those originating at the national level.

The decision to allow accreditation to be organised on a regional basis and with regionally-based colleges, which increased diversity in the 1990s, was a reflection of this regional pre-eminence in the union. It may be thought that the accreditation of courses would have increased the standardisation of provision, and in some cases this has been the case, especially where a specific qualification such as the European Computer Driving Licence or D32 NVQ Assessor's Certificate has been offered. However, apart from some accreditation through the National Open College Network, most accreditation has not reduced regional diversity. The principal reason for this is that the accrediting colleges themselves have resisted the standardisation of accreditation, so that awards from one college or university are not necessarily accepted as having the same value, and the procedures and standards to achieve formal acceptance of courses by colleges vary.

By the end of the century, the union had established a sustainable pattern whereby the bulk of union education was provided at the local level in a non-residential setting using lay tutors; arguably the cheapest way in which a union could meet its educational needs and still retain full control of its own programme. In the short term, the TUC might offer free courses to the union, but this would be the TUC programme, and any attempt to develop education provision completely tailored to the needs of the TGWU would have involved costs, especially the cost of customised course materials and tutoring fees. The other part of the union's programme is a relatively small number of national advanced courses provided in the residential setting of the Eastbourne Centre. These courses are normally taught by the staff members of the Education Department, and are relatively expensive. However, the payment to Eastbourne is an in-house financial transfer from one part of the union to another, and represents a subsidy for the Centre, which is an important institution that the union needs and wants for reasons wider that the education programme.

This programme appears to be sustainable and manageable in the long term, but it would be threatened if the government changed the rules on financial support for lifelong learning and adult students from 'non-traditional' backgrounds, of which trade unions provide a significant number. If the accredited partnerships are removed, this would represent a threat to the financial basis of the programme which the union, with static or even falling membership, would probably find difficult to meet. The removal of this support is unlikely under a Labour Government, and the other principal external source of funding, from joint work with employers, also looks to be sustainable, particularly as 'partnership' has replaced Human Resource Management as a desirable approach to industrial relations.

Even if the current external funding sources are removed, the history of the union's education programme shows that even with reduced resources, education in the union will continue in one form or another, and possibly in new forms. The need for people to learn about their union roles, to network, and to debate the issues of the day, has shown itself to be stronger than any financial or organisational restraint. These last factors strongly influence the scope and quantity of provision, but not whether it will be carried out at all. This history of TGWU education shows that so long as the union itself survives, then activity of whatever form, which can reasonably be defined as education, will be carried out.

NOTES

1. This includes counting each attendance as a separate student, so it is inflated.
2. Source; Internal Paper written by John Fisher, 1999.
3. Sid Staden used to say that he was 'on secondment' to the Labour Party when carrying out his necessary duties as TGWU Regional Secretary with the London Labour Party.
4. Interview with Barry Camfield, 10 July 2000.
5. F&GP, 3 July 1986, Minute No 530, p137.
6. Region 3 Report, 1987.
7. They were all men.
8. Region 3 Education Officer's Report, January/March 1991.
9. Region 2 Education Report, June 1997.
10. Region 2 Education Report, December 1998.
11. In 2001 Mary Edwards was appointed Regional Organiser.
12. Region 4 Education Report, July/September 1999.
13. Region 4 Education Report, January/March 1996.
14. Regional Education Report, Region 5, last quarter 1983.
15. Interview with Jim Mowatt, 1June 2000.
16. Region 6 Education Report, January/March 1995.
17. GEC, 9 March 1995, Minute No 150.
18. Region 6 Education Report, January/March 1995.
11. Husband of Ann McCall.
20. Others being Carol Forfar in Region 7, Dion Baugh (née Easy), Anooshah Farrakish and later Chantelle Brown in Region 1.
21. Region 8 Education Report, June 1983.
22. Region 8 Education Report, June 1984 quarter.
23. Region 8 Education Report, 1st quarter 1985.
24. Interview with Chris Russell, 29 May 2000.
25. Interview with Chris Russell, op. cit.
26. Frank Cosgrove had actually supported another candidate, John Elliott, a regular Cirencester tutor, but he did not come through at interview. There was no appointment on the first round, and Scott came through on the second.
27. Education Committee Report, 25 February 1986.
28. Region 9 Report, June 1987.

29. Interview with Chris Russell, op. cit.
30. Education Officer's Report from Region 10, April/June 1984.
31. Region 10 Education Officer's Report, October/December 1986.
32. Region 10 Education Report, 1st quarter 1990. Region 10 Quarterly Report, 1st quarter 1991.
33. Region 8 Education Report, October/December 1993.
34. Region 8 Education Report, October/December, 1993.
35. Region 8 Education Report, December 1996.
36. Region 8 Education Report, December 1998.
37. Region 7 Education Report, December 1983.
38. Region 7 Education Report, March 1990.
39. F&GP, 8 May 1986, Minute No 347, p87.
40. Region 11 Report, June 1989.
41. Region 11 Education Report, final quarter 1991.
42. Region 3 Education Report, December 1996.

Conclusion

The turn of the century brought to an end the first 80 years of the TGWU, and the first 60 years of a specific TGWU education programme. The history of the programme is an enormously rich story, full of activity and commitment, as is the union's wider history. It is worth recalling that this is only the story of the *formal* education system in the union, based around education courses, whereas thousands of activists and local leaders in the union received their education through less formal, but no less effective encounters with their peers in family, workplace, community, and political party.

Some individuals stand out, as do some particular regions and educational innovations. For different reasons many people and events have not found their way into this story, and because of the course reporting system, a silence often surrounds the students themselves; they were the *raison d'être* for the programme, and also the life of the courses and what motivated the tutors and organisers to go back again and again. The students in this union's education programme, as in that of all the other unions, were motivated not by career progression or paper qualifications, but by a realisation that their involvement in the union's education programme could make up for their lack of initial education; provide them with the knowledge and skills to serve their fellow men and women; and sometimes land a blow for working people against injustice or corporate power.

Beyond these statements, how can we judge the success or otherwise of the union's education programme? In the introductory chapter it became clear that it is impossible to quantify the success or otherwise of an unaccredited programme (and even of an accredited one only superficially), and that measurements based on the rise or fall of the union's membership bear no obvious relationship to the provision of the education programme. In that sense, Arthur Deakin's comment that funding TGWU education was 'throwing bread on the waters' would seem to be apt. It is evident that the programme must have had some impact, or even a great impact on the development of the union; but is difficult to quantify it. Rather than make a quantitative judgement, therefore, it may be better to evaluate the education programme as a contributor to the union's development. Of course, there is no proof that the union would not have developed in the way that it did if no education programme had existed, and this must be conceded. On the other hand, it is surely reasonable to assume that the sum total of all the activity discussed here, and the continuing support of the union's officers and its active members, over the generations, shows that on a daily basis they were experiencing the positive effects of involvement in the programme. In circumstances where there was no compulsion to attend, an irrelevant programme would surely have withered away over the years.

In the first phase, under Bevin and John Price, the primary aim of the programme was to build and consolidate the very concept of a general union, and in particular the constitution and objectives of the TGWU. The correspondence course and its associated day-schools were heavily oriented towards providing an understanding of how the union worked – or should work. Bevin (and Deakin) were convinced that oppositional militancy within the organisation sprung from an ignorance which made people vulnerable to outside political forces intent on turning the union in what they saw as an undesirable direction, and that the union could counter this through its education provision. Bevin also took the view that the informal transfer of knowledge, which existed in industry in his younger days, had died away with the decline of 'heavy industry', and needed to be replaced by a more formal system of education. Thus he embarked on the project around the correspondence course which, although interrupted by the war and the subsequent departure of John Price, remained a fundamental part of the union's induction for its activists. Although there have been extensive changes to the union's constitution, particularly in the Jones period and at various times under Bill Morris, it is widely recognised that with its democratic core and balance between regions and industrial trade groups and sectors, the fundamental basis of the constitution is sound and relevant and sufficiently flexible to survive well into the twenty-first century. The massive effort on the part of TGWU education in developing and disseminating, promoting and defending this complex constitution surely deserves some recognition.

A second key phase in the union's development was initiated by the leaders of the next generation, notably Frank Cousins and Jack Jones. Their approach was to build on the reality of workplace organisation, particularly the shop steward – increasingly important, yet for so long unacknowledged in the TGWU rulebook. They recognised that the interaction between the worker and his or her union representative was the true heart of the union, and the key to organisation, recruitment and power. With little encouragement, and active discouragement in some quarters, the shop stewards kept coming forward and making themselves the personification of the union to thousands of members. It was clear to them that in order to be effective, lay officers would have to undergo training, and Jack Jones was the first recorded official to use his local office in this way, as a mini 'workplace university' on weekends in Coventry in the war years. In the immediate post-war years, this approach was adopted by other forward-thinking officers, and formalised by a new generation of educators. The institution of the Beatrice Webb and Cirencester summer schools was a direct consequence of the growth of plant bargaining and the extension of the role of the shop steward, and also a significant contributor to this extension. It would be difficult to defend the idea that the thousands of TGWU stewards who passed through this system from the early 1950s up to the present day have made no impact on collective bargaining or trade union organisation; rather, these schools must have played a major part in its development.

The third phase was more complex, and covers the period from the end of the 1970s to the present day. The key to understanding this phase is the word *diversity*. The appointment of REOs at the end of the Jones era released yet another generation into TGWU education; it was also a time when the Labour Movement came under attack such that the 'prospect of hanging' focused minds on union organisation and purpose. In the 1980s generation, many of the REOs and influential figures in TGWU education had experience beyond the union's traditional industrial base; they had often been through Higher Education, or had a political background on the left of the Labour Party, as Communists or in the ultra-left. Many of them were also familiar with gender and race politics. Bob Purkiss (and his key influence Basil Bye), Barry Camfield, Chris Russell, Tom Hart, Lesley Sutherland, Liam McBrinn, Tom Nesbit, Regan Scott, Jim Mowatt, Pete Batten, Joe Irvin, John Fisher, Harry Lees, Les Ford and Diana Holland all fit into one or more of these categories. They were therefore setting an agenda for TGWU education which went far beyond the training or 'role education' of shop stewards and safety reps. In this sense, 'diversity' did not just refer to opening up the union to more women or ethnic groups and wider industrial and employment sectors, but also to a broader debate about what the TGWU and the trade union movement were about. The new TGWU education focused just as much on workplace organisation, but it saw this as a base to debate and develop wider perspectives.

This approach coincided with the union's own soul-searching during the Thatcher period and beyond. Bill Morris in particular associated himself with not only adjusting the union to a harsher financial and membership reality, but also to the promotion of women and black/ethnic representation and campaigns such as 'Link-up' to extend the union into new or hitherto not represented groups of workers. The education programme was seen as one of the keys to changing the face of the union, and it is surely significant that the *1992 Guidelines*, drawn up by Joe Irvin but supervised by Morris, included as the union's core educational objectives not only shop steward and safety rep education, but also equalities, something that would have been unheard of a generation before.

How did the education programme contribute to the political character of the TGWU? Once again, this is a complex question with no quantitative answer. What, indeed, was or is the political character of the union? It is a cliché to assert that in Bevin's day the TGWU was part of the 'Right' in the TUC, and then, following the untimely death of Jock Tiffin, Frank Cousins was able to lead it into the arms of the 'Left', where it has remained. This is surely one-dimensional and gives far too much importance to statements made by general secretaries at TUC and Labour Party conferences. The TGWU, like all great organisations, has always been multi-layered and fractured into hundreds of different elements, depending on region, district, industry and even company or type of employment. It also contained the many contradictions typical of trade unions in capitalist societies, and faced both ways on many issues, where different elements in the organisation took different positions on particular questions.

Beyond the particular stance of general secretaries, it is possible to identify some elements which have been continuous throughout the union's history, and which have provided a set of core values for the union. It may then be possible to evaluate the education programme's influence on these. The first is the democratic structure of the union. It is still true that in the TGWU profound disagreements are settled by reference to the decisions of the Biennial Delegate Conference. General secretaries have often been overturned by the BDC, even on important issues, and the GEC will not follow an executive officer if it can be shown that a proposal violates a decision of the conference. This is not a pretence; it really happens in the union. Also, on a day-to-day basis, all officers of the union are accountable to elected committees and the tradition has long been established that these lay committees are treated with the respect which real power gives. Of course, the full-time staff meet behind the scenes and submit documents to the committees and frequently get their way – the general secretary more than anyone else. It should be realised, however, that in the TGWU elected committees are not 'paper tigers' and elected members have real power. Where there has been a conservative general secretary, such as Bevin or Deakin, they have been constantly challenged by 'unofficials' with a strong base in the union; those like Jack Jones brought the 'unofficials' and particularly the shop stewards into official recognition in the organisation. Any general secretary must walk a tight-rope between the demands of the union's bureaucracy, the government of the day (particularly if it is Labour), his own inclinations and the voice of the active membership, but in the TGWU the last group cannot be placed bottom of the pecking-order.

How then has the education programme contributed to this state of affairs? If the above principle is that democracy is a real force in the TGWU, then it is evident that the union's education programme has encouraged this development over the years. From the earliest days of the programme, with *Your Union, its Work and Problems*, through the summer schools and into the core induction programmes, the paper democracy of the union's constitution has been worked over and explained, and students have been encouraged to take part in it and make it work. In the fifty years since the development of plant bargaining and the growth of the influence of shop stewards, those stewards have been trained by the union's tutors on how to bargain and how to represent people and in most circumstances it has been taken as the norm that the full-time officer is there as the last resort. If it is not necessary to call him/her in, so much the better. Thus at the level of much industrial bargaining and within the union's constitution, the full-time official, whilst commanding respect as an expert, has never been able to dictate, and this message has continually been promoted by the education programme.

Over the years, the education programme has attempted to harmonise with the union's industrial activities rather than work against them or operate in a separate world. The union's leading educators have often been an unusual mix of people: academically educated but at the same time disdainful of the opinions of academics and concerned to keep them under strict control. John Price, Ellen McCullough, Tony Corfield, Regan Scott, Joe Irvin and John Fisher all conform to this type. Tony Corfield's insistence on military-style 'training' methods and standardisation did not sit well with academics used to giving a 'balanced view' or playing the 'devil's advocate' with students, but they gained the support of McCullough and of students and officers, who were convinced that the education programme was directly useful and relevant to their role in the union.

The tradition established at this time was carried on in later years by the next generation and by the REOs. In this way the industrial character of the union was reinforced by the education programme, and both evolved dialectically, the one feeding off and encouraging the other. This is one of the key reasons for the continuing support of the education programme amongst the union's activists, and also the maintenance of an active shop steward culture in the union, even in the most difficult times.

The education programme also played its part in locating the union as part of the Labour Movement, historically, nationally and internationally. Whilst it is true that the principal focus of the programme was on the structure and policies of the union, and on role education for the union's activists and representatives, there was always a 'sub-plot' of wider political education attached to the mainstream programme. At times this was concerned with the struggle against Fascism and support for the idea of a progressive 'people's war', and later with internationalism and raising awareness of Europe or concerns about the activities of multinational companies and globalisation. Still later the programme concerned itself with the promotion of equalities and the fight against sexism and racism, and with environmental issues. The practicalities of the education programme were such that members who often began their involvement in an instrumental manner looking for training in a particular defined role came back time and again to learn about wider issues because they had found the education programme stimulating and relevant. The organisers of the programme themselves recognised this, and realised that if they wanted to involve members in education on these wider issues, then they had first of all to 'deliver the goods' on the basic induction work for stewards and safety reps. In my view, this balance was achieved, and the only concern is that it was not possible over the years to expose a greater number of the union's membership to this process, as of necessity only the active minority put themselves forward for lay office.

The programme was always limited by the almost insuperable difficulty of reaching beyond the activists into the mass of the membership. The union often claimed that courses such as the Home Study or the National Members' School were targeted at the membership itself and not just the activists or representatives, but in practice membership education has been insignificant. This is not as serious a deficiency as it may first appear, given that most of the ordinary membership of any union will never be active, and in circumstances where there is always a need for representatives, anyone who has the inclination to be active can easily become a shop steward or safety rep, thus often gaining access to time off for training and involvement in the union's education programme. The demand for a *separate* membership education programme has never been significant in the union, and would be confusing in circumstances where active members quickly become shop stewards. Nevertheless, it must be conceded that the TGWU education programme has been centred on the activists rather than the membership as a whole, and any evaluation of its impact must be primarily concerned with this layer of members. In theory, a programme which reached down to the lowest levels of membership would have been more likely to have had a greater impact on the union, but practicalities prevented the possibility of this.

How did the TGWU programme sit in the wider trade union movement and in comparison with other trade unions? The reports from the early years contain some disappointment at the reluctance of the union to support its members in their involvement with WETUC or NCLC courses, especially financially, and there are many reports of students in these classes comparing the meagre TGWU grants with the more generous levels of support from other unions. Bevin's conviction was that employment in heavy industry was being replaced by types of employment in which union tradition did not serve to educate workers through informal and community methods, and that formal and deliberate education methods were necessary to fill this gap. This gave the impetus for the correspondence course which vaulted over the demand for more resources for WETUC and NCLC schools into something new in trade union education which put the union ahead of its contemporaries.

That there was a need for this was demonstrated by Jack Jones in Coventry. He used the union office as an education centre to build the TGWU primarily because the AEU was the dominant union in the district, and that union still felt it could rely on the craft tradition to educate its active members. The TGWU, on the other hand, primarily represented the unskilled, including almost all its women workers; they had no craft tradition, indeed often no trade union tradition at all. They had to be trained to understand their agreements, and the process of collective bargaining and representation. Exactly the same approach was then adopted by the other innovators like Fred Horne for the workers in the new light industries around London, which also employed large numbers of women workers. Once the summer schools were established, the former workplace traditions were instilled into these schools, and thousands of TGWU members were guided and sometimes enthused by their attendance into a realisation of the objectives of the union and their role as representative, which they may not have received had they only remained in their workplace.

Of course, this type of education was not exclusive to the TGWU, and in the post-war period unions such as the GMWU (GMB), USDAW, NALGO, NUR and AEU all introduced residential schools and education programmes on issues such as work study and industrial management. Between 1948 and 1952, unions' expenditure on education doubled to £100,000.[1] The NUM developed an education programme in some of its Federations far in advance of the TGWU in terms of longer periods of study, political content and involvement of ordinary union members beyond the level of representative. Compared with the NUM, the TGWU suffered from the great diversity of its membership, with an involvement with thousands of different employers in almost every sector of employment and in every part of the country. The NUM had only one nationalised employer to deal with, and employment was much more concentrated in particular communities. NALGO (now part of UNISON) also developed comprehensive education programmes for its members, which included professional vocational training. It had the benefit (at least up to Mrs Thatcher's day) of having often supportive employers in local authorities and other public institutions, and large resources.

The particular value of the TGWU programme was welding a strong union identity despite the diversity, and helping to replace craft and single-industry identity with a confidence in the union primarily based on the activities of the shop steward in industrial bargaining, and in his or her dual role on the district, regional and national committees of the union. Although there has been and still is political division in the union, it has only rarely poisoned relations and crippled the development of the organisation.

The TGWU education programme also compares well with other unions in its sponsorship of active learning methods, and for this we should thank Tony Corfield, Jack Lucas and their descendants like Frank Cosgrove and the first generation of REOs. Discovery learning and role-play were being used in the TGWU long before their institutionalisation in the TUC scheme and whilst some other unions were still organising weekend schools mainly consisting almost entirely of traditional lectures from MPs and similar worthies, the TGWU was insisting on participative methods and experimenting with filmstrips and other audio-visual aids.[2] Once the TUC scheme was established, the union fully participated in it, and up to the creation of UNISON in the 1980s, provided the largest number of TUC students. At the same time, the union also developed its own regional programmes exclusively for TGWU members, using the TUC courses as the filler in a 'sandwich' of induction courses as the lower end and follow-on courses after the TUC stage.

It is difficult to say whether the union's own courses were superior or otherwise in comparison with those provided by the TUC. In some TGWU regions, such as Region 1 and Region 10, a comprehensive and high-quality programme was developed in the 1980s, which outstripped the TUC courses in its scope, relevance and quality. In Regions 9, 5 and 7, a more limited programme was developed which did not necessarily provide more than TUC centres such as Lauder Tech, Leeds or Solihull and sometimes ran in parallel with them. In other parts of the union such as Region 4 or 'old' Region 3, TGWU courses were effectively provided by the TUC through centres such as GLOSCAT. It should also be recalled that up to the mid-1980s, the majority of tutors on the union's summer schools were provided by the WEA, and most of these were tutors who throughout the rest of the year provided TUC courses or even management studies. In the later 1980s and 1990s a growing confidence in the union's own tutors meant that Frank Cosgrove agreed that only tutors who taught TGWU courses could teach on the summer schools, and, with their accredited partnerships, Regions 6, 8, 1 and 5 began offering a comprehensive programme which went well beyond that offered by the TUC in terms of scope, and was equal to the TUC courses accredited through the Open College Network. This process was encouraged by the *1992 Guidelines*, which prevented financial support being given from the union for students to attend TUC courses. In comparison with most other individual unions, the TGWU programme in the 1980s and 1990s had much greater range, given that it offered both a basic programme in each region and also a programme of advanced residential courses at Eastbourne. Most other unions offered one or the other; those like the GMB, CWU or MSF concentrating on residential courses, while those like NUPE or NALGO focused on local provision. It is significant that through the 1980s and 1990s, when student numbers on TUC courses were declining rapidly, the TGWU programme continued to expand.

External providers played a key role throughout the history of TGWU education. The WEA played a key role, particularly in the early years. The Beatrice Webb and Cirencester schools, and much else besides, were formally WEA schools, and at least into the 1980s WEA tutors and the Association itself supported the union with its tutors and through course development. In the later years co-operation tended to be linked to specific projects, such as the work on globalisation in the 1990s. Although formally 'even-handed' towards WETUC and the NCLC, it is clear that in both volume and inclination the TGWU programme was much closer to the WEA. The NCLC played an important part within particular localities, and through its correspondence courses, whilst the WEA had both a local and a national input into the courses, and key union figures such as Arthur Creech-Jones, Harold Clay, Ellen McCullough and Tony Corfield had a close, organic relationship with the Association. It was only after the appointment of the REOs, the access to public funds through the TUC, and the development of lay tutors that the reliance of the union on the WEA diminished. The union's relationship with other external providers such as university extra-mural departments and colleges of technology tended to be built around productive individual relationships between union officials and tutors. In the early years Ruskin College, and London and Oxford universities, were important, then later Leeds, Hull, Southampton, Strathclyde, Surrey, Newcastle Polytechnic, Manchester, Liverpool, Queens Belfast, Northern College and North London. Further Education colleges such as Birmingham and Coventry were important at first; they were then supplemented by TUC-supported colleges such as GLOSCAT, Filton, Slough, and South Birmingham, and later still by Manchester City College, Southampton City College and North-West Institute Derry. The development of accredited partnerships with both FE and HE colleges in the 1990s has moved the relationship beyond particular supportive individual tutor-organisers into a much more structured and integrated partnership, involving close financial as well as academic interaction. The long-term effect on the balance of the union's programme has yet to be seen.

How can we evaluate the education programme's significance and its effect on the development of women's and other groups in the equalities agenda? It is true to say that Mary Carlin and the other women's organisers received very little support from Bevin and the other leaders, with the Women's Guild actually representing a step backwards, in that it made the implicit assumption that full members would be male. In the early education programmes, including the day-schools linked to *Your Union, Its Work and Problems*, women were viewed simply as an invisible part of the membership. The war and the growth of the new industries, and the fight for equal pay and acceptance in the buses and other services, made the union take notice of a new constituency. The brief post-war flurry involving Muriel Rayment and Vi Taylor quickly went away, and apart from the Scottish Region under Jessie Murray, little dedicated education work was carried out. Ellen McCullough mainly concerned herself with encouraging promising female individuals to rise through the ranks as she had done.

The generation of Jack Jones and Jack Lucas instituted a new approach, and also by that time racism had become an important political issue. Jack Lucas particularly tried to encourage the organisation of women through education, and Jack Jones led on the principled condemnation of racism. By the late 1970s yet another generation of women were emerging with a much broader agenda, and the first of these to reach prominence was Margaret Prosser. Along with others, she had benefited from involvement in the expanding education programme, and was instrumental in encouraging dedicated women's courses in the regions and at Eastbourne. She also promoted the idea of 'Women's Week' at Stoke Rochford, and women's events around the regions, helping to build a cadre of leading women in the union. Although only 20 per cent of TGWU membership are women, in a union of 2 million (as in 1979), this is still 400,000 – bigger than the total membership of most trade unions; and on the 2000 membership of 850,000 it still amounts to 170,000. With the encouragement of Bill Morris, these women established equalities as a 'core' education provision in 1992, and a mandatory system of women's representation and women's sector and National Members School courses by 2000.

Some of the earliest women's courses in the union were linked to encouraging women's organisation and membership. However, the more common approach was to try to persuade more female students to attend the general courses at the summer schools, by declaring a special women's course, or later a 'women's week', with better childcare provision. Essentially, however, the courses these women were expected to follow would be the same as the men's, and the likelihood would be that they would have a male tutor. It was not until the 1980s that a regular programme of women's courses with a dedicated syllabus, materials and tutors was introduced with the dual objective of building a cadre of active women, and also building confidence to encourage women to play a greater part in the union both in the workplace and within the organisation itself. These courses laid the basis for much more comprehensive programmes in the 1990s which have led, if not to a significantly higher percentage of women's membership, at least to a much higher percentage of women attending courses and a much higher profile in the union.

In the area of race equality, the union was fortunate that the leading official, Bob Purkiss, had also been an REO and fully understood the importance of education. The TGWU had always taken a casually progressive approach to race, linked to a vague Socialist and internationalist position (we would now call it 'mildly politically correct') and none of the general secretaries before Jack Jones gave any significant time to the issue beyond this benevolent overview. The union received a great shock in the early 1960s when it was known that the Powellite dockers were TGWU members and when the extent of racism in TGWU strongholds such as Wolverhampton and Dagenham became obvious.

Jack Jones led a principled campaign against racism and some regions began to hold weekend schools on the issue. However, actual courses for black and ethnic members were late in coming, and a few regions such as 1, 5 and 8 began these courses in the mid-1980s. The process was given an enormous boost with the rise of Bill Morris, the first black general secretary of any union, who won in 1991 in the teeth of a campaign which included using the 'race card' against him.

These programmes, and the constitutional changes brought in under Morris, have helped to create a cadre of activists and some black and ethnic tutors, but only moderate progress has been made. It cannot be denied that the education programme played a significant role in the promotion of equalities in the union, particularly the main areas of women and race, and the union was fortunate to have a generally progressive leadership over the years preventing overt racism and sexism. That greater progress has not been made is a reflection of wider issues in society, but at least the union can never go back to an all white, male GEC, and the training given to the Executive in the 1990s has increased the element of equality in appointments, even though some regions were behind others.

What of the attitude of the leadership of the union to the education programme? Bevin's attitude has been examined in the first chapter, and without his support, or that of other general secretaries, there would have been no official programme, or a much more limited one. One of the surprises of this story has been the support for the programme exhibited by Arthur Deakin. Another surprise is the apparent lack of active involvement of Frank Cousins with the programme. Cousins seems to have been entirely a product of the industrial wing of the union, without any real experience of its formal education programme. This may be linked to his background in road haulage, traditionally the trade group with one of the lowest levels of involvement in the programme, because of the nature of their work. Cousins gave political support to the programme, without ever showing that he was comfortable in a classroom situation, or making statements which called for new approaches to education. His attitude appeared to be one of indulgence rather than 'hands-on' involvement.

In this he was joined by both Moss Evans and Ron Todd; both general secretaries with equally strong industrial backgrounds, they presided over periods of rapid growth in the education programme and gave it their support, without becoming greatly involved in the detail of what was being provided.

Jack Jones did get involved in the details of T&G education. Jones was a genuine innovator for whom education, industrial organisation and political development were inseparable. When Jones reached the position of executive officer, he attempted to extend the education programme into the ranks of the union's paid officials – a long-standing and still unresolved gap in the provision – and also supported the use of educational methods to bring workers together from different parts of the world and from within global companies. When he became General Secretary he presided over three of the most important steps taken by the programme in the post-war period – the introduction of health and safety at work as a core element of the programme, the building of the Eastbourne Centre, and the appointment of the REOs. All three of these are still fundamental to the union's education programme, and the concept of using education as an organising tool is still accepted as a thoroughly modern approach.

Bill Morris was different again. Financial adjustment in an economic crisis and the promotion of the equalities and diversity agenda in the union will probably be seen as Morris's legacy, and, in terms of the education agenda, these were to some extent contradictory. Morris was not opposed to education, and in general favoured it and felt he himself owed his rise in part to it. He also understood that education had an important part to play in the promotion of diversity within the union, and that courses for women and black and ethnic members and against racism had to be part of the core provision. To this end, he maintained a 'hands-on' approach to education throughout his period as Deputy General Secretary, and for almost the whole of his time as General Secretary, hardly ever missed a meeting of the Education Committee and personally approved the Department's report and the Committee's minutes.

On the other hand, education was a spender and it was Morris who in 1992 brought to an end the period of encouragement for expansion of the programme, cut the financial allocation of both national and regional courses, and introduced strict budgets. That this potentially involved the loss of some control to accrediting universities and colleges was no doubt a source of concern, but so long as this was watched, he presided over both the recovery of the programme and its expansion into new areas of joint provision with employers and accreditation.

Overall, the educators in the TGWU have been blessed with general secretaries and an Executive Council who at times pushed them or even initiated innovations; at other times they showed less interest in education, but their gut feeling was that it was a good thing for the membership and for the political development of the union and the society as a whole. In all the years of the union's existence, during alternative periods of Right or Left-wing ascendancy, the union has never had a general secretary who was fundamentally opposed to the education service or simply thought it was a waste of money. This may be luck, it may be related to the process of the election of the leadership in the union, or even may be a reflection of the good work and the reputation of the education service itself. Most likely it is a combination of all three.

The question whether the education provision in the union gradually improved over the years is also not easy to answer. The assumption would be that it started off in an uncertain manner and learned by its mistakes over time in a developmental, linear manner. To some extent this is true, most particularly in the areas of the breadth and scope of provision, especially when we take into account advances in materials and educational technology. It is also true that in some of the regions, the modern provision is far superior to that of fifty years ago. On the other hand, for many of the other regions, the programmes offered by Tom Wylie in Region 5 or Jack Lucas in Region 1, and the courses offered by the NCLC and WETUC, were a match for some of today's provision, and would certainly have satisfied the needs of their students. The greatest advantage in the modern programme was the establishment of a dedicated REO in each region, able to devote all or most of his or her time to organising and administering the programme, and also the establishment in 1992 of clearly-defined core requirements and standardisation of provision across all regions.

On the wider question of the development of the programme as a whole, it is not true that a minimal programme gradually expanded and improved in an unbroken continuum. Rather, the record shows that the programme went through 'heroic' periods followed by relatively quiet times, and then entered a new period of rapid development. How and why this happened was determined by a complex mix of changing external circumstances, particular individuals and to some extent the waxing and waning of generations within the union.

The war was one such period, where a general burst of energy in the population as a whole was mirrored in the establishment of union-only day-schools using the new correspondence course and the war itself as a focus. It is ironic that this was not particularly carried out by John Price and Bevin, both of whom, having set the pattern for the new education programme, quickly moved on to other work, never to return. Rather, implementation was much more in the hands of Deakin and Ellen McCullough. Following a post-war lull, a second heroic period began with the Beatrice Webb and Cirencester summer schools in the early 1950s. These were a product of new thinking around Training Within Industry and the focus on workplace issues. It also allowed a new generation of tutors an opportunity to promote their mixture of Left politics and a practical industrial orientation through new learning methods.

Another period of regeneration came in the 1960s with the growth of day-release and in-plant courses, and the rise of yet another generation, this time often people who had begun as trade union activists and taken advantage of adult education to qualify as tutors. In the TGWU this new approach laid the basis for perhaps the most fertile period of all, the 1970s, with its enormous investment and expansion. Yet another generation of tutors and REOs, often well-educated politically and in teaching methods, carried this through into the more difficult days of the 1980s and 1990s. In between these spurts were the quieter times of the early 1930s, late 1940s, late 1950s and early 1990s when the union was changing its leadership or preparing itself for new challenges. However, in these periods it very rarely went backwards in its education provision. When resources were cut, or events conspired to make provision more difficult, ways were found to maintain an education service for the members whatever the difficulties. This was true for Harold Clay's and Arthur Creech-Jones' championship of education after the General Strike, when the war broke out in the very weeks when the new home study course was launched, and when financial stringency and Tory government policies threatened to decimate the programme in the early 1990s.

It is not true that today's REOs and tutors are 'better' than their predecessors. Course materials may look more attractive, but who is to deny the effectiveness of Tony Corfield's six-foot long demonstrator slide-rule or the union's filmstrips on the audiences of their day? Who can deny that the all-night debates at Beatrice Webb House or in the 'Tithe Barn' at Cirencester in the 1950s or 1960s would have been just as effective and inspirational as anything in the 1990s? Those who built their officer and steward teams through education, and those like Harry White and J.S. Brandie who set up regular programmes in their districts, must have had an impact as great as any tutors forty years later.

In this new century the union has new challenges; first, of survival and refocusing itself away from declining industries and into the employment growth areas, and rebuilding the natural link with workers so effectively broken by the two decades of Thatcherism. Education has an important role to play in that process; training existing representatives in the skills needed to organise in the new environment and in the knowledge to be effective and service the membership. It will also have a role in developing the 'organising strategy' which oversees this rebuilding process. There are also opportunities linked to the new technology, in particular the use of the Internet as a vehicle for learning and in new ways of reaching members and the public as a whole. If Lifelong Learning is to take root in the working population of the country, then the new creature, the 'union learning representative', will have to be trained in the same way as the new safety reps were in the 1970s and 1980s. If the education service is true to the events in the wonderful story of the union's education programme in the twentieth century, there is no doubt in my mind that it will rise up to and above the challenge.

NOTES

1. See Halford, op. cit., pp57-85.
2. I personally attended schools run by the Sheet Metalworkers (now part of MSF) and the AEU in the 1970s and 1980s consisting entirely of lectures, mainly from outside speakers.

Bibliography

P. Addison, *The Road to 1945*, London: Quartet Books 1977.

V.L. Allen, *Trade Union Leadership*, London: Longman 1957.

J. Atkins, *Neither Crumbs Nor Condescension: The Central Labour College 1909-1915*, Aberdeen: Aberdeen People's Press/WEA 1981.

M. Barratt-Brown, 'What has Really Changed in the Educational Needs of Workers?', *The Industrial Tutor* Vol. 4, No 5, Spring 1987, pp7-14.

A. Bullock, *The Life and Times of Ernest Bevin: Volume 1 Trade Union Leader 1881 to 1940*, London: Heinemann 1960.

J. Burrows, *University Adult Education in London: A Century of Achievement*, University of London 1976.

A. Calder, *The People's War*, London: Pimlico 1969.

P. Caldwell, 'State Funding of Trade Union Education', *Trade Union Studies Journal*, No 3, 1981.

E. Capizzi, *Learning That Works*, Niace/TUC 1999.

H.A. Clegg and Rex Adams, *Trade Union Education* London: WEA 1959.

K. Coates and T. Topham, *The Making of the Transport and General Workers Union Vol 1 Part 11*, London: Blackwell 1991.

K. Coates and T. Topham, *Workers' Control*, London: Panther 1970.

M. Cohen, 'The Labour College Movement between the Wars', in B. Simon, *The Search for Enlightenment*, London: NIACE 1992, pp137-152.

A.J. Corfield and E McCullough, *Trade Union Branch Officers' Manual*, London: Chapman and Hall 1964.

A.J. Corfield, *Epoch in Workers' Education*, London, WEA 1969.

W.W. Craik, *Central Labour College*, London: Lawrence and Wishart 1964.

W.W. Daniel and N. Millward, *Workplace Industrial Relations in Britain*, various dates from 1980 onwards; 1984, 1990 and 1998, London: Policy Studies Institute.

Department of Education and Science, *Adult Education: a Plan for Development*. London: HMSO 1973.

C. Edwards et al, 'Student-Centred Learning and Trade Union Education: a Preliminary Examination', *The Industrial Tutor*, Vol. 3, No 8 1983.

J. Field, 'Learning for Work', in R. Fieldhouse, *A History of Modern British Adult Education*, London: NIACE, 1996, pp333-353.

R. Fieldhouse and Associates, *A History of Modern British Adult Education*, London: NIACE 1996.

J. Fisher, 'The Trade Union Response to HRM in the UK: the Case of the TGWU', *Human Resource Management Journal,* Vol. 5, No 3, Spring 1995, pp7-23.

J. Fisher, 'Competition or Collectivism?', *Adults Learning,* Vol. 8 No 9, May 1997, pp236-237.

J. Fisher and B. Camfield; 'Missing Link in Trade Union Education', *The Industrial Tutor*, Autumn 1986, Vol. 4 No 4, pp30-36.

J. Fisher and D. Holland, *Training for Full-Time Officials of Trade Unions*, University of Surrey 1988.

P. Flynn and D. Miller, 'Racism Awareness Training for Trade Unionists – Report from the North East', *The Industrial Tutor,* Vol. 4, No 1, Spring 1985, pp23-29.

K. Forrester et al, 'Industrial Studies in a University Adult Education Department', *The Industrial Tutor*, Vol. 4, No 8, Autumn 1988, pp57-65.

K. Fuller, *Radical Aristocrats: London Busworkers from the 1880s to the 1980s*, London: Lawrence and Wishart 1985.

J. Fyrth, 'Industrial Studies in an Industrial Society', in E. Coker and G. Stuttard (eds) *Industrial Studies 3,* London: Arrow, 1980, p162.

G. Goldman, *Dons and Workers: Oxford and Adult Education Since 1850*, Oxford: Clarendon 1995.

J. Goldstein, *The Government of British Trade Unions*, London: G. Allen & Unwin 1952.

G Goodman, *The Awkward Warrior: Frank Cousins: His Life and Times*, London: Spokesman 1979.

D. Gowan, 'Student-Centred Approaches Revisited', *Trade Union Studies Journal,* No 7, 1983.

A. Grant, 'Trade Union Education, a TUC Perspective', *The Industrial Tutor,* Vol. 5, No 1, Spring 1980, p12.

C. Gravell, 'Trade Union Education; Will State Funding lead to State Control?', *Trade Union Studies Journal*, No 8, 1984.

G.C. Griggs, *The TUC and the Struggle for Education 1868-1925*, Brighton, Falmer 1983.

J. Halford, *Union Education in Great Britain,* University of Nottingham 1994.

T.H. Hawkins and L.J.F. Brimble, *Adult Education: The Record of the British Army,* London: Macmillan 1947.

N. Heaton, and I. Linn, *Fighting Back*, Hull: TGWU Region 10/Northern College 1989.

D. Holly, 'Politics of Learning', *Radical Education 7,* Winter 1976, p6.

P.G.H. Hopkins, *Workers' Education: an International Perspective*, Milton Keynes: Oxford University Press 1985.

B. Houlton (ed), *Residential Adult Education – Values, Policies and Problems*, Society of Industrial Tutors 1977.

Interim Report of the Committee on Adult Education: Industrial and Social Conditions in Relation to Adult Education, London: HMSO 1918.

J. Jones, 'A Liverpool Socialist Education', *History Workshop Journal,* Issue 18, Autumn 1984.

J. Jones, *Union Man*, London: Collins 1986.

J. Jones, *Equal Pay and Equal Opportunities*, TGWU 1975.

R. Kisch, *The Days of the Good Soldiers*, London: Journeyman 1985.

J.L. Kornbluh and M. Frederickson (eds), *Sisterhood and Solidarity: Workers Education for Women, 1940 to 1984*, Philadelphia: Temple University Press 1984.

I. Linn, *Single Union Deals*, TGWU Region 10/Northern College 1986.

W.E.J. McCarthy, *The Role of Shop Stewards in British Industrial Relations*, Research Paper No 1, Royal Commission on Trade Unions and Employers Associations, HMSO 1967.

J. McIlroy, 'The Triumph of Technical Training?', in B. Simon, *The Search for Enlightenment,* London: NIACE 1992, pp208-243.

J. McIlroy, 'Adult Education and the Role of Client: TUC Education Scheme 1929-1980', *Studies in the Education of Adults,* No 2, 1985.

J. McIlroy, 'Education for the Labour Movement: UK Experience Past and Present', *Labor Studies Journal,* Vol. 4, No 3, Winter 1980.

J. McIlroy, 'Goodbye Mr Chips?', *The Industrial Tutor,* Vol. 4, No 2, 1986, pp3-23.

J. McIlroy, 'Independent Working-Class Education', in R. Fieldhouse et al, *A History of Modern British Adult Education,* Leicester: NIACE 1996, pp264-289.

J. McIlroy and B. Spencer, 'Methods and Policies in Trade Union Education; a Rejoinder', *The Industrial Tutor,* Vol. 3, No 10, 1985, pp49-58.

M. Merrigan, *Eagle or Cuckoo?*, Dublin: Matmer Publications 1989.

A. Miles, 'Workers' Education: The Communist Party and the Plebs League', *History Workshop Journal,* Issue 18, Autumn 1984, pp102-114.

J.P.M. Millar, *The Labour College Movement*, London: NCLC 1979.

D. Miller and J. Stirling, 'Evaluating Trade Union Education', *The Industrial Tutor*, Vol. 5, No 5, Spring 1992, pp15-26.

D. Miller, 'Student-Centred Learning in Trade Union Education; Some Further Considerations', *Trade Union Studies Journal*, No 8, 1983.

T. Nesbit, 'Labor Education', *Adult Learning*, 2(6), 1991.

T. Nesbit and S. Henderson, 'Methods and Politics in Trade Union Education', *Trade Union Studies Journal,* No 8, 1983.

M. Newman, *The Third Contract*, Darlinghurst, NSW, 1993.

J. Price, *Labour in the War*, Penguin Books 1940.

Report of a Committee of Inquiry into the problems of Fircroft College under the chairmanship of Andrew Leggatt, QC, House of Commons, April 1976.

D. Robertson and T. Schuller, *Stewards, Members and Trade Union Training,* University of Glasgow, April 1982.

Royal Commission on Trade Unions and Employers Associations, HMSO 1967, Cmnd. 3623.

T. Schuller and D. Robertson, 'The Impact of Trade Union Education: a Framework for Evaluation', *Labour Studies Journal,* Spring 1984.

B. Simon, *The Search For Enlightenment*, London: NIACE 1992.

E. Taplin, *The Dockers' Union*, New York: St Martin's Press 1985.

T. Topham, 'Education Policy in the Transport and General Workers Union, 1922 to 1944: A Tribute to John Price', *The Industrial Tutor*, Volume 5 No 5, Spring, 1992.

T. Topham, 'Women in the Union's History', in *One Big Union,* University of Nottingham 1991.

D. Vulliamy, 'The Politics of Trade Union Education', in J.A. Jowitt and R.K.S. Taylor (eds), *The Politics of Adult Education*, The Bradford Centre 1985.

F. Williams, *Ernest Bevin*, Hutchinson 1952.

T. Wintringham, *New Ways of War*, Penguin 1940.

Postscript: 2000 to 2005

The TGWU entered the new century at a time when two different issues were at the forefront of the trade union education agenda. On one hand, the New Labour Government's promotion of the skills and lifelong learning agenda had grown significantly, and this type of activity was becoming ever more important. On the other hand, the same government had been reluctant to restore more than a minimum of trade union rights at work; although it had moved a firmly tilted playing-field some way back towards the level, it had not created the conditions for a surge in either trade union membership or influence.

In the Lifelong Learning field, the government was delighted with the success of the Union Learning Fund, and steered more resources into it, through the mechanism of the Learning and Skills Councils. The government also endorsed the TUC's idea of the Union Learning Representative, and in the spring of 2003 ULRs were granted statutory rights to paid leave to pursue their activities, with unpaid time granted to their clients, the employees.

This support inevitably led to trade union education departments at the TUC and in the individual affiliates giving more time to lifelong learning activities, as reasonably plentiful government resources were made available to support them. Projects, project workers, basic skills, company learning centres, e-learning, Learndirect access points and other manifestations of this agenda all became familiar parts of trade union education activities, to the extent that the TUC and some unions began to make it their single-most resourced activity.

In the TGWU, some regions embraced this agenda more than others. Region 6 (North West) and Region 8 (Northern) were heavily involved, with a great deal of activity around basic skills and company learning centres; there were also initiatives such as the North West Logistics College, driven by REO Ann McCall – a consortium within the haulage industry of unions, TUC, employers, colleges and providers. This was strongly backed by the government, who eagerly promoted skills and training developments in the road haulage sector: the launch in 2002 was personally endorsed by Chancellor Gordon Brown. In 2003-4 the Northern Region involved itself in a replica project.

Other regions were less involved, but all had some projects running continuously from 2000 onwards, usually based around company learning centres, basic skills projects, and computer-based learning. The Irish and the Welsh regions used lifelong learning to promote their equalities and diversity agendas, using devices like English as a Second Language to contact immigrant workers.

The lifelong learning agenda was particularly effectively promoted in East Anglia, developed by Kenny Barron, a Region 1 tutor who had previously been TGWU Convenor at Birds Eye Walls Lowestoft, a subsidiary of Unilever. Kenny Barron set up all sorts of partnerships with learning providers, colleges and unions, for the training and development of Union Learning Representatives and the involvement of union members as learners. In 2004, funded by the Union Learning Fund, he took up a position at Central Office, with a brief to promote and evaluate the lifelong learning agenda throughout the union.

At national level there were a number of projects designed to promote lifelong learning. These involved companies like First Group and some in road haulage. Such projects also involved making officers and senior representatives aware of the opportunities provided by lifelong learning for building the union. In 2003, a Union Learning Representatives' Handbook was produced and distributed throughout the union, and at that time there were about 1000 ULRs in the TGWU.

Despite all this positive activity, there were those who saw lifelong learning as a diversion from the 'real' task of trade union education, of strengthening the cadres, building organisation and recruiting members. It had been argued that by involving people in learning and development opportunities which were clearly a result of union activities, this would raise morale, bring new people into the union and convince the unconvinced that trade unions were 'part of the solution and not part of the problem'. However, this view tended to be based on optimism, or at best anecdotal evidence. There was little real evidence of union growth, or a consolidation of union strength.

Among the critics of the lifelong learning agenda was Tony Woodley, the new General Secretary, elected in May 2003. Tony Woodley had campaigned on a left 'back to basics' platform, critical both of Bill Morris's 'partnership' approach, and of Tony Blair and New Labour. He rode the tide of frustration that many officers and representatives felt, and won the election with a handsome margin against Jack Dromey (who won the election for Deputy), Barry Camfield (also a left candidate) and Jimmy Elsby.

Tony Woodley took the view that as many of the union's resources as possible should be focused on a 'Strategy for Growth', based on the twin objectives of growing the union and winning in the workplace, or 'fighting back'. This approach was very popular amongst members, representatives and officers, but it did throw into question whether lifelong learning could be part of this agenda, and what changes to the education programme would be necessitated by the Strategy for Growth.

After a short period when the idea of the Union Learning Representative and the commitment to lifelong learning in general was thrown into question, matters settled down and it became accepted by Tony Woodley that lifelong learning had an important, but not a central, part to play.

One of the consequences of the election of Tony Woodley was the early retirement of AGS Jimmy Elsby, and his replacement by Barry Camfield as Executive Officer responsible for Education. As Barry Camfield was an ex-REO, and he and John Fisher had worked together for many years, this gave a boost to the management of the education programme. It also removed the artificial distinction made by Bill Morris and Jimmy Elsby that the Education Department should not have a role to play in officer and staff training. A Staff Training Co-ordinator, Carol White, had been appointed in 2003, but was not able to work through the Education Department. This divide was now removed, and new programmes for Officer and Staff training began to be developed.

Barry Camfield and John Fisher also set about revising the *1992 Guidelines*, essentially retaining the main structure of the programme, but refocusing the education programme to meet the requirements of the Strategy for Growth, and including references to Union Learning Representatives, externally-funded bids, accredited partnerships and other elements missing from the original guidelines.

The national programme continued much the same as in the 1990s, but in 2004 the National Members School was discontinued. It was felt that the school had become something of an anomaly, as basic courses were being provided in the regions, and the requirements of the Strategy for Growth were that resources should be focused elsewhere. However, the Women's National Members' School was retained, as this played a key role in building and focusing women's involvement in the union.

The national programme also introduced a new course on understanding company information, linked to the EU Information and Consultation Directive, and taught by Les Ford and Rita Higgs, formerly Deputy Head of the Research Department. Tutor training was retained as before, but the government's requirement that all tutors teaching in the public sector – including those through accredited partnerships – reach a minimum standard of City and Guilds 7407 meant that the union is now looking at establishing a formal qualification for its tutors.

During 2004, the TGWU took part in discussions at the TUC on the establishment of a new 'Union Academy', for which the government had indicated its support, and AGS Barry Camfield represented the union on the Task Group. The union was very keen for the Academy to begin from the broadest vision, and to take trade union education and lifelong learning forward into the new century.

In the regions, the first few years of the new century brought a number of changes. In Region 1, Pete Batten retired in 2004 and was replaced by John Perry, formerly a District Officer. He began to re-shape the programme, but maintained the link with London Metropolitan University. A link with the past was broken in August 2004 with the tragic death from illness of Patrick Hayes, who had liaised between the University and the Union, and who contributed to the whole development of Region 1's programme over the years.

In Region 2, Gordon Pointer took early retirement in 2003 and was replaced by Lydia Gascoigne. At the same time, the region acquired a new Regional Secretary, Andy Frampton, and a new Regional Organiser, Alan Beynon, replacing Harry Lees. This complete new team had to take over and revitalise a programme which had suffered through the long-term sickness absence of the REO. Another major change was the ending of the accredited partnership with Southampton City College, and its replacement, first by the WEA and then, in 2003, by City College Bristol.

In 2004, some new ideas began to be tried, such as the developments, on a district basis, of 'learning groups', which could keep together from one course to the next; and the withdrawal of a brochured course programme, encouraging and requiring district officers to take responsibility for recruitment to courses and the management of the 'learning groups'. At the time of writing, the jury is still out on the success or otherwise of this experiment.

In Region 3, Liam McBrinn's retirement in 2002 became the subject of a political conflict between different elements within the union. Following events at the 2001 BDC, and other alleged developments within the Region, Bill Morris ordered an investigation into the activities of the Regional Secretary and Regional Organiser, culminating in their removal from their positions of seniority, a decision reversed in 2004, after a replacement RS and RO had already been appointed. Part of the fall-out from this was the refusal of the GEC to appoint a replacement for the REO until the matter was settled, and during 2003 and 2004 the Regional Women's Organiser, Fiona Cummins (née Marshall) stood in as REO.

In Region 4, the partnership with Llandrillo College was replaced with a working relationship with Deeside College in the north, and Bridgend College and the WEA in the south, with the Welsh TUC and WEA/Coleg Harlech also working with the region. A new venture for the region was work with migrant workers, particularly Portuguese, who were coming into parts of Wales to fill a labour shortage, particularly in the food processing industries.

Region 5 continued with Bob Sissons as before, as did Region 6 with Ann McCall. As noted above, a particularly successful initiative was the Region 6 initiative in the road haulage industry, the North West Logistics College.

In Region 7, the new REO, Jackson Cullinane, was unable to establish an accredited partnership with a college, because of the differences in attitudes and administrative systems under the devolved Scottish Executive. Such a partnership is still being sought. Problems of a similar nature to those in Region 3 also hampered the education provision in the region during 2004.

Region 8 continued its work under Mick Bond, and in 2002 became the first to link into Learndirect via a ICT-based 'hub', the T&G Leeds Learning Exchange. This development was then repeated in Regions 5 and 6.

THE FUTURE

At the time of writing, new General Secretary Tony Woodley is in his first two years of office, and the new drive to make the TGWU an 'organising union' is in its early stages. Certainly, there has been no attempt to marginalise or undermine TGWU education, rather to make it re-focus itself to meet the requirements of the organising strategy. To change to meet the requirements of the union's policy and to adjust to new developments in the world outside has always been a central part of the approach of TGWU education, and these changes will be a continuation of the tradition established in the early years, particularly in the post-war period.

During 2004, a consultation exercise was conducted by Assistant General Secretary Barry Camfield and John Fisher, who visited every region and met with the REO and Regional Secretary, asking them to refocus their education provision to meet the needs of the Strategy for Growth. A report was prepared by each region, and by the National Department, describing the changes which would be implemented from January 2005. The basic principles were to place organising at the top of the agenda, and to make the programme 'shot through' with the Strategy.

Each REO presented his or her plan at a seminar in early October, at Eastbourne; and regional tutors were trained in organising techniques by Sharon Graham (National Development Secretary), John Fisher and Mel Dando (Organiser, Region 2) in two groups, also at Eastbourne, later in the month. In November, the GEC Education Committee approved a new Education Policy document to replace the *1992 Guidelines*, and this policy was adopted by the full GEC on 7 December 2004.

This policy indicated that: 'The overriding objective of T&G Education is to deliver the union's Strategy For Growth. This requires building the collective strength of our members and of the union in the workplace first and foremost, then at the regional, national and international levels.'[1]

The role of the National Department in providing advanced courses was confirmed, and the Home Study Course was removed from being mandatory into being something which all members and course students were encouraged to take part in:

> All members are encouraged to enrol in the *Your Union At Work* home study course, and all students applying for courses should be sent a registration form and encouraged to complete the course. Those seeking bursaries must have first completed the current home study course as a minimum.[2]

The role of the regions was confirmed as being required to provide basic courses, defined as follows:

- Organising the Workplace (shop stewards)
- Organising for Health and Safety (safety reps)
- Organising for Equality
- Organising the Branch
- Organising for Lifelong Learning

This meant that Union Learning Rep training now entered the core provision for the first time. Each region's education was also required to offer flexible education support for workplace organising.

The REOs were renamed 'Regional Education and Development Organisers', and their duties set out, as in the *1992 Guidelines.* These included the management of the budget and of their tutors, as before. The existing tutor training and apprenticeship system was confirmed, but the paper proposed a formal scheme, whereby tutors will be able to reach the minimum standard of City & Guilds 7407 via a programme established by the union in partnership with an outside college. The union's commitment to its accredited partnerships was also confirmed in the paper.

The budgetary system was pulled back from the entirely mechanical system established by Bill Morris in 2000, and although the formula remained linked to a certain figure per member, the new policy also required each REDO to submit an Annual Education and Development Plan each year, setting out each region's estimate of courses and expenditure for the coming calendar year.

The new policy also agreed that future aspects of TGWU education provision would be covered by separate policy papers, including accreditation, lifelong learning, externally funded projects, and officer and staff training.

This new policy will re-establish the basic structure of TGWU education on its existing foundations, whilst encouraging its refocusing to meet the requirements of the new leadership in the union, and the new priorities as set out in the 'Strategy for Growth'. The test of the policy will be whether the education service continues to gain the support of the membership, maintains its standards and its student and course numbers, and contributes to a revival in the growth and influence of the union.

As this book goes to print, steps are being taken which could possibly lead to the creation of yet another new trade union, a merger of the T&G with AMICUS and the GMB, creating a new 'super-union' of more than two million members. Clearly, if this happens, it will inevitably launch a new chapter in what was TGWU education, and this will be the education programme of a new union.

There will always be a need for an education programme to breathe life into the formal structures of the union, and to give the members no less than they deserve. So long as the union has an organisation on the shop-floor, made up of ordinary men and women without a great deal of formal schooling, who need to develop new and important roles, and to begin a process of liberation and development through their involvement in the union, then education through their union will be essential, and vital to their future.

1. *T&G Education Policy 2004-5*, December 2004, p1.
2. *Ibid*, p2.

Index